The New Guide to Sea & Sea

By Joe Liburdi and Cara Sherman

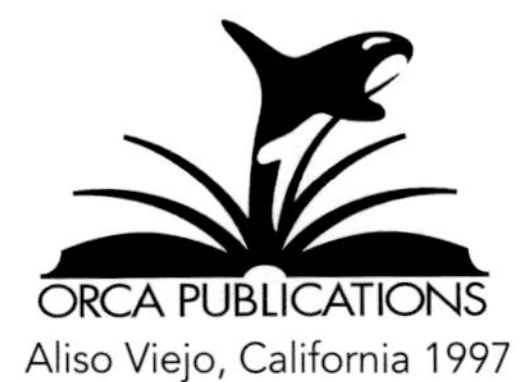

ORCA PUBLICATIONS
Aliso Viejo, California 1997

Other books by Joe Liburdi and Cara Sherman:
How to Use Sea & Sea
The Underwater Photo Log Book
How to Use the Motor Marine II
The Complete Guide to Sea & Sea

Photographs by Joe Liburdi and Cara Sherman
Cover design by Bradley Girard
Illustrations courtesy of Sea & Sea Products Ltd and Bird Design
Cartoons by Bob Brown and Evan Sherman

Printed in Korea
ISBN 0-9621111-3-9
Library of Congress Catalog Card Number: 98-065719

Contents

Preface

"No army can withstand the strength of an idea whose time has come."
Victor Hugo

The first camera was a box the size of a room. In fact, it was a room. The *camera obscura* was a pitch-dark room with a small hole in one wall. Light rays from outside were directed through the hole to form an image on the opposite wall.

It was 500 years before anyone came up with anything better. An Italian scientist named Giovanni Battista della Porta discovered that by inserting an optically-ground piece of glass into the opening in the wall, the image became brighter and sharper. When he demonstrated his discovery, his audience was greeted to the sight of a group of actors cavorting outside. All well and good except for the fact that they were projected upside down. Pandemonium ensued. Poor Della Porter barely escaped being burned at the cross for sorcery.

The missing element, film, was discovered in 1826 by a French engineer, Joseph-Nicephore Niepce. He coated a pewter plate with an asphalt solution, inserted it into a small version of the camera obscura, and placed it on his windowsill. Eight hours later he had the world's first photograph: a dim, fuzzy image of his farmyard.

In 1839 Daguerre discovered how to create a direct positive image on a metal plate. At the same time William Henry Fox Talbot discovered a negative-positive process that enabled duplicate prints to be made from the same negative. Daguerre sold his process to the French government and became immortalized, his name forever synonymous with photography: daguerrotype. Talbot guarded his patents and became obscure.

By the end of the 19th century, photography was on a roll. In 1888 George Eastman introduced the No. 1 Kodak Camera with celluloid-base roll film, thus launching the sport of amateur photography. In 1893 Dr. Louis Boutan, a French biologist, sealed a fixed-focus camera in a huge watertight copper box and managed to obtain photographs in 30 feet of water. In 1925 Leica inaugurated the era of the 35mm camera with interchangeable lenses and a rangefinder viewfinder. Kodachrome was introduced in 1935. Kodacolor negative film was introduced in 1942. Kodak dominated the market till the '80s when the invention of the microprocessor made autoexposure an inexpensive reality. 35mm point and shoot became the rage.

The first successful underwater camera was Cousteau's Calypso, and for three decades that basic system underwent a score of design changes, culminating in the Nikonos V.

Then came the Motor Marine, a radical concept in underwater photography, a quality instrument that was easy to use, had built-in lenses with an exterior mount that let users change lenses underwater, and was affordably priced. Underwater photography was revolutionized. Now it was for everyone.

When English astronomer Sir John Herschel first saw a daguerrotype, he called it a "miracle." But photography, we now know, is neither heaven nor satan sent. It is a science. In this technological age of electronic wizardry, we have cameras that produce an image in milliseconds. We have the APS camera that lets you crop, enlarge and alter exposures. There are digital cameras that create images in bits instead of on film. And photographers, we know, are neither witches nor saints. Some are artists, most are just plain folk. And just as the basic principles of photography are essentially the same as they were over a century ago, so is man's drive to preserve a precious moment in time.

Technology has given us the tools to capture the beauty and mystique of the underwater world on film, a world of colors and patterns beyond the artist's imagination. Cameras have enabled us to bring this wondrous world to the surface for all to see.

Well, maybe photography is a kind of miracle after all . . .

Acknowledgements

The year was 1972. Masateru and Masaoki Yamaguchi were university students with a Nikonos I and a flash that used bare flashbulbs. Each bulb cost $1 US, very expensive for the young scholars. They used them sparingly, shooting mostly ambient light photos and silhouettes. Then they saw a picture of a battery-powered waterproof flash unit in *Skin Diver* magazine and, necessity being the mother of invention, decided to build one. Masaoki, an amateur ham radio operator, assembled the electronics. Masateru, a model airplane enthusiast, sculpted the housing of fiberglass. They worked evenings at the family's kitchen table, listening all the while to the radio. The top pop hit of the day was "Yellow Submarine." They loved that song. So they colored their strobe yellow and dubbed it the Yellow Sub. Thus, a global corporation was born.

To Masaoki and Masateru, our reverence for their vision and genius, our gratitude for their friendship and trust.

To Tak Sakimoto and Jeff Mondle, whose dynamic management and dedication have so appreciably impacted the market in the Americas.

To Matthew and Evan, who share the passion.

To Bradley Girard, Danny Evans, and Niccole Chicca, for the finishing flourishes.

And to all the divers who want to capture the beauty of our undersea world with Sea & Sea. You have made this book necessary.

Thank you.

How to Use this Book

The challenge for every underwater photographer is to create ever more beautiful and technically perfect photographs. The purpose of this book is to help you meet that challenge, to help you master your equipment and become an accomplished and happy photographer.

The best way to use this book is with product in hand. Do it as you read about it. No film, please! When you come across something that is unclear, mark it with a highlighter and continue on. Go back to it later after you have read more. It will probably make sense to you then.

While the book is obviously divided into chapters of specific interest, the content of each chapter is not exclusively about that particular piece of equipment, nor is it exclusively for owners of that equipment. Each chapter contains information, techniques, tips that are of value to all photographers.

For example, the chapter on the MX-10 contains a page called Oops!, depicting common mistakes. The Motor Marine II-EX chapter has a section on how to take pictures of fish. Everyone, regardless of which camera you own, can benefit from reading these pages. To take full advantage of this book, do not confine your reading to the chapter on your equipment. Leaf through the entire book, page by page, paying particular attention to the illustrations and sidebars.

Start by reading Chapter 1: *The Basics of Underwater Photography.* For those with advanced skills, consider it a refresher course. For novices, it's a prerequisite.

A Word on Digital Imaging

This is a book on underwater photography. This is a book on how to use Sea & Sea photographic equipment. It is about how to combine technical skill with imagination to create compelling images.

Digital imaging is the use of computer technology to create images. Digital imaging is a skill and an art.

Photography and digital imaging are not the same thing.

There is a place for digitized images. But not here, not in a book that has been written to teach you how to use your equipment skillfully. The challenge is to create great pictures underwater.

None of the images in this book were digitized. All images were recorded by the lens on film. What you see printed here is what we shot. We did it. You can, too.

A Request

"To see like a fish, you must swim like a fish."
Jacques Yves Cousteau

And so he and Gagnan gave us the Aqua Lung, the apparatus land-locked man needed to venture freely amongst the creatures of the sea. The sea has intrigued man for centuries, been an endless source of mystery and myth. Not till this century has man been privileged to venture into this alien world.

What began as a daring sport for macho men is today gender equal. Scuba crosses all boundaries and barriers: age, gender, size, strength, even physical handicaps are no longer obstacles to diving. Everyone can be trained and engage in the discovery of our underwater world.

It is a natural progression then, from swimming amongst the fishes to taking pictures. The sea is a source of life and information, inspiration and joy. We who respect it, protect it.

Please keep it clean and healthy.

Leave it as you find it.

Let it endure.

CHAPTER ONE

Underwater Photography: the Basics

Underwater Photography: The Basics

To Begin With, What is a Camera?

A camera is basically a lightproof box with a hole in one side that allows light to enter. Every camera has five fundamental components: a lens, shutter, aperture, film transport, and viewfinder.

A lens is fitted into the hole of the camera to concentrate and focus light onto the opposite side of the camera, where it is captured by a chemically-treated light-sensitive material called film.

Light is a form of energy. Light can be transformed into other forms of energy. Heat energy is one. Chemical energy is another. The science of photography is based upon the ability of silver halide crystals to absorb light energy in the form of a chemical transformation.

Light exhibits other properties. Light travels in straight lines unless otherwise directed. If it hits an opaque object, some of it bounces off, or *reflects*. When light passes through transparent objects of different densities, such as glass or air, it is bent, or *refracted*. When light passes through water, it is *absorbed*. When light is simultaneously refracted in many directions, it is *diffused*.

All of these properties of light come into play when you take a photograph. The lens *refracts* the light that is *reflected* off the subject; the film *absorbs* light energy and transforms it into chemical energy.

What is a Lens?

The lens is the most important part of the camera. It is a transparent piece of material, usually glass or high-tech plastic. The main function of a lens is to project a sharp image onto the film. It does that by gathering and bending the light rays so that they converge at a specific point: on the film. Just how much it bends depends upon the composition and degree of curvature of the lens, the angle at which the light ray hits the lens, and the wavelength of the ray of light.

Essentially, there are two types of lenses: *simple* and *compound*. A simple lens is made of a single piece of glass and is found in older cameras. Because these early lenses had many optical aberrations that prevented them from forming a truly sharp and accurate image, they've been replaced by the compound lens. The modern compound lens eliminates the defects by combining multiple pieces of glass of various shapes, thicknesses, and composition, called *elements*.

Lens elements come in many shapes. Today, when computer-aided optical engineers design a lens, they use different shaped elements of various compositions in various combinations to make the light do precisely what they want it to do. By turning the focus control on the lens or camera, the elements are moved back and forth inside the lens to sharpen the image at various distances from the film plane.

A lens inverts and reverses an image. Thus, when the image of a diver in an upright position strikes the film, the diver's head will be on the bottom and his right arm will be on the left side of the frame. The human eye functions the same way.

The "Camera as a Room" Analogy

Picture a room in total darkness. On one wall is a door. On the opposite wall is a giant piece of film. When the door opens, light comes in. Since the film is extremely sensitive to light, when light touches it, the film changes. The change is in the form of an image.

On a camera, the door is a **shutter.** When closed, all light is kept out. When opened, light comes in. A **lens** fitted into the door controls the way the light filters in. Without the lens, the image would be indistinct. Once light has changed the film, it must be moved out of the way. The **film transport** is like moving men, taking the film off the wall and bringing in a fresh piece so the process can begin again.

A Lens is Characterized by its Focal Length

One of the most important attributes of a lens is its *focal length*. Focal length is the distance from the optical center of the lens to the film plane (the film). Focal length is set when the lens is designed. The focal length is always measured when the lens is focused on infinity, designated by the infinity symbol (∞) on the lens barrel or focus dial or knob. This number is expressed in millimeters (mm), such as 15mm, 20mm, 35mm.

Focal length affects the image formed on the film in two ways: the amount of the scene shown and the size of the image. Focal length and picture area are inversely proportionate: the shorter the focal length, the wider the picture area. Likewise, the longer the focal length, the narrower the picture area.

A lens's *physical* length is shortest when it is focused at infinity. When the lens is focused on closer subjects, it extends. There is a limit to how close a lens can focus and retain the subject in sharp focus. That limit is called *minimum focusing distance*. It is determined by the design of the lens.

Lenses vary in design, with different types made to perform some tasks better than others. Each lens has its own particular characteristics: angle of acceptance, depth of field, advantages and limitations. Each lens will record the subject in a different way.

Lenses are referred to as normal, wide angle, telephoto, or close-up. The normal lens creates realistic, life-like images; it encompasses the same angle of view as the human eye with the same relative sizes of objects. The normal lens for a 35mm land camera is 50mm. The normal lens for an underwater camera is generally 35mm. Wide angle lenses have a shorter-than-normal focal length and are characterized by a wider-than-normal angle of acceptance; they provide a wider view and smaller images than the eye sees. Telephoto lenses have a longer-than-normal angle of acceptance; they have a narrower angle of view, magnifying subjects and compressing space.

Fixed Focus and Focusable Lenses

There are two types of lenses in use today: *fixed focus* and *focusable*. With fixed focus (also called focus free) lenses, the focus is irrevocably set at one distance, depending on depth of field to deliver subjects from several feet away to infinity in acceptably sharp focus. The MX-10 has a fixed focus lens.

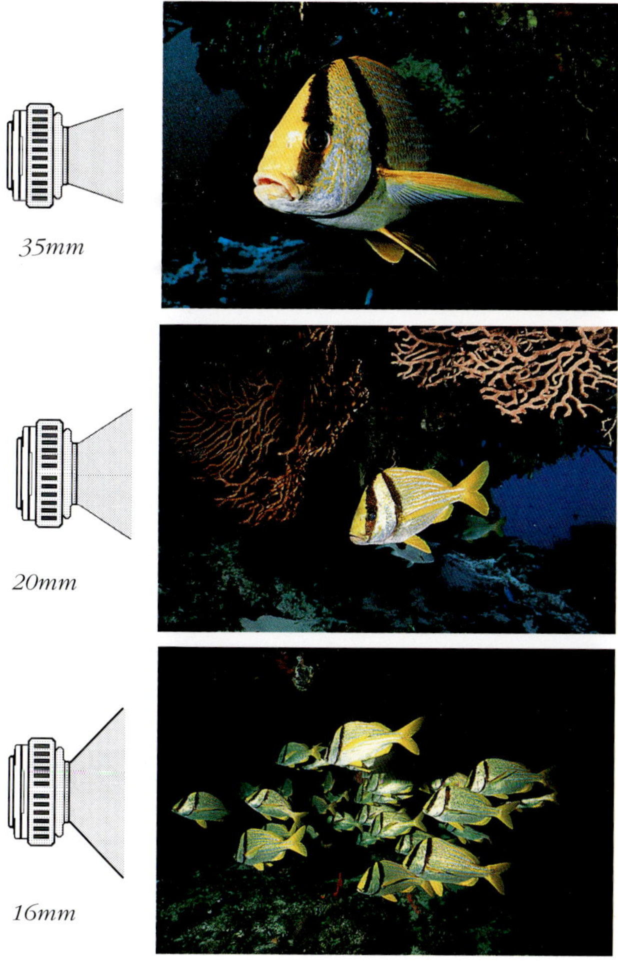

Focal length controls field of view and magnification of the subject. All three of these photographs were taken from the same camera-to-subject distance.

Focusable lenses can be manual focus or autofocus. With manual focus lenses, you turn the focus control to focus the lens. The focus control may be a focusing ring on the barrel of the lens, typical of SLR cameras, or a dial on the camera body, as on the Motor Marine II-EX.

Autofocus lenses are automatic. You center the subject in the viewfinder and lightly depress the shutter. The lens will automatically focus on the subject. The Nikon N90 camera accepts autofocus lenses.

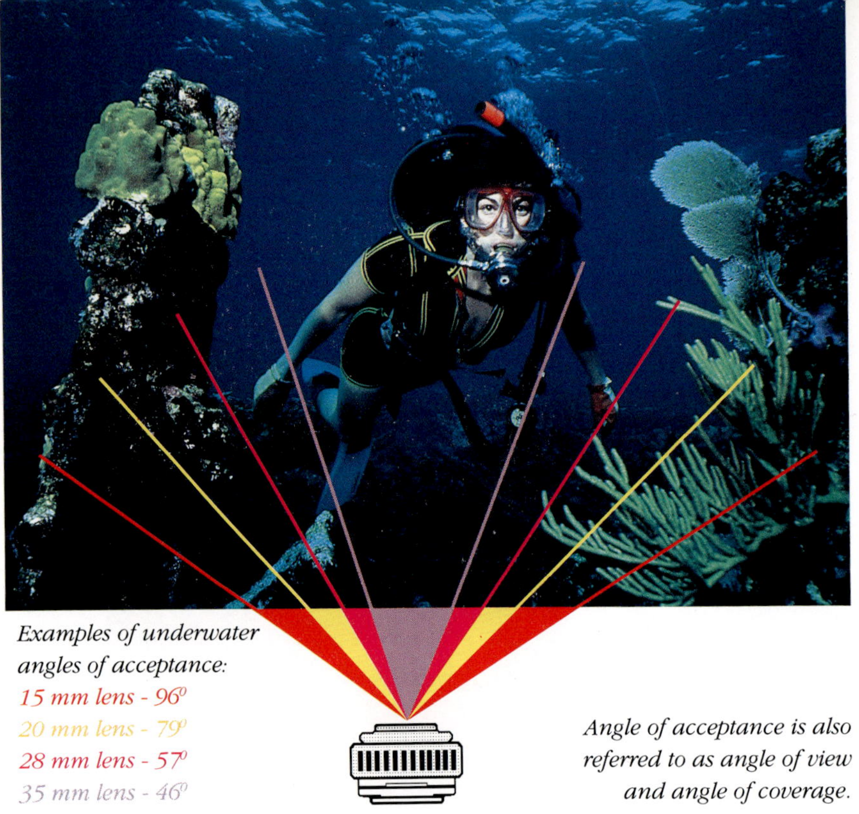

Angle of acceptance is also referred to as angle of view and angle of coverage.

What Do We Mean by Angle of Acceptance?

The angle of acceptance of a particular lens is the angle at which it will accept light. It is similar to a beam of light, except that light is reflected into the camera instead of away from it. Normal lenses accept light at an angle of approximately 50°. Wide angle lenses accept light at a wider angle than normal lenses and can take in more of a scene or subject than the normal lens at the same camera-to-subject distance.

Perspective and Apparent Distance

Different focal length lenses translate the subject in different ways. A normal lens will recreate the image as the human eye sees it. A wide angle lens will make objects appear farther away and smaller. A close-up lens will make them appear larger and closer. The key word is *appear;* the subject need not change position. It is all in how the lens interprets the size and distance.

What is a Shutter?

The shutter is a mechanical device that lets light into the camera and keeps light out. It is like a movable protective shield that opens and closes. Its function is to control the duration of time light is allowed to strike the film.

When you are not taking pictures, the film sits in the camera in total darkness. When you depress the shutter release, the shutter flicks open, light passes through the lens, strikes the film, and creates an exposure. An *acceptable exposure* is when the film has received the correct amount of light for the proper amount of time.

One way to control the amount of light that enters the camera is with *shutter speed.* Shutter speed is the length of time the film is exposed to light. The faster the shutter speed, the less time light strikes the film. The slower the shutter speed, the longer light strikes the film. Shutter speeds are expressed in fractions of a second, such as 1/15, 1/30, 1/60,1/125. Each consecutive shutter speed is twice as fast as the one preceding. Thus, a shutter speed of 1/30 of a second will allow light to enter for twice as long as 1/60 of a second.

Aperture and F-stops

Another mechanism used to control the light coming into the camera is the aperture. The aperture (also known as diaphragm or iris) is an adjustable opening in the lens which controls the precise amount of light striking the film when the shutter is open. It is like a circular door that doesn't quite close all the way. The important thing to remember here is that shutter speed controls the *length of time* light passes through the lens and aperture controls the *amount* of light.

Primitive cameras did not have adjustable openings. Instead, metal plates with a hole in the center were placed in front of the film. These were removable,

Each consecutive f-stop lets in half as much light as the preceding f-stop.

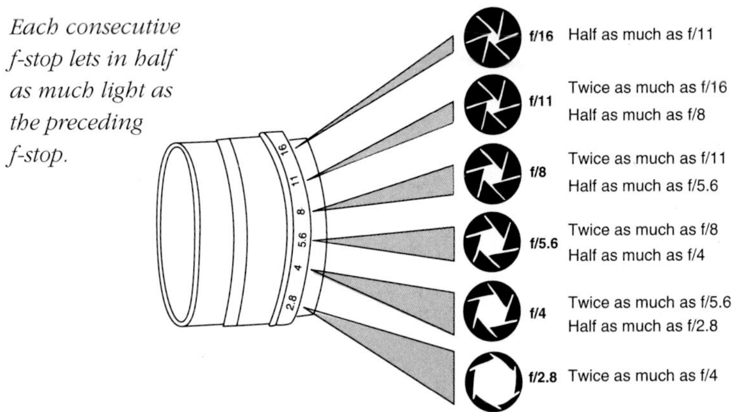

and the photographer had an assortment to choose from, all with different size holes. The principle behind this was that the metal plate *stopped* all light except for that which came through the hole. Changing the plate to let more or less light strike the film was called *changing stops*. The word *stop* stuck.

The size of the opening of the lens through which light can enter can be increased or decreased by turning the aperture control to numerical positions called *f-stops*. They might read f/4, f/8, f/16, and so on. Think of them as fractions: f over 4, f over 8, f over 16. Then it's easy to remember that the largest openings have the smallest numbers, and vice versa: the smallest openings have the highest numbers. The numbers below may also help you remember which f-stops are large lens openings and which are small lens openings:

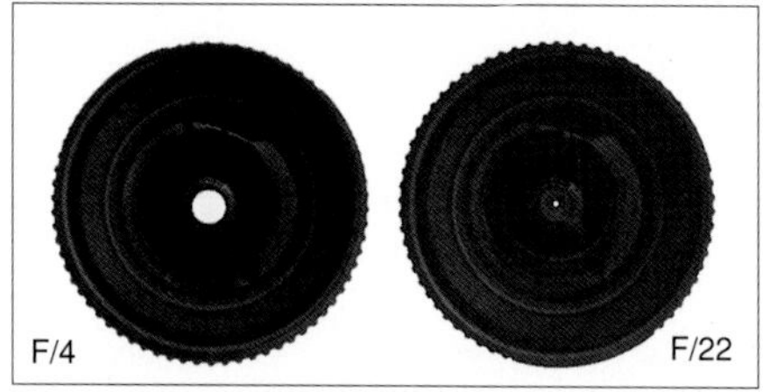

2.8 4 5.6 8 11 16 22

Depth of Field

When you focus on a particular subject, there is an area in front of and behind the subject that is also in focus. This is depth of field. It is a range of distance, expressed in feet or in inches. Think of it as the *zone of sharp focus*.

Three things affect depth of field: aperture setting, lens focal length, and subject-to-camera distance.

No matter what type lens you are using, it is important to remember the following incontrovertible principles:

- The smaller the lens opening, the greater the depth of field.
- The larger the lens opening, the less depth of field
- The longer the focal length of a lens, the shallower its depth of field.
- The shorter the focal length of a lens, the greater its depth of field.
- Depth of field increases as the subject-to-camera distance increases.
- Depth of field decreases as subject-to-camera distance decreases.
- Depth of field is greater behind the subject than in front of it.

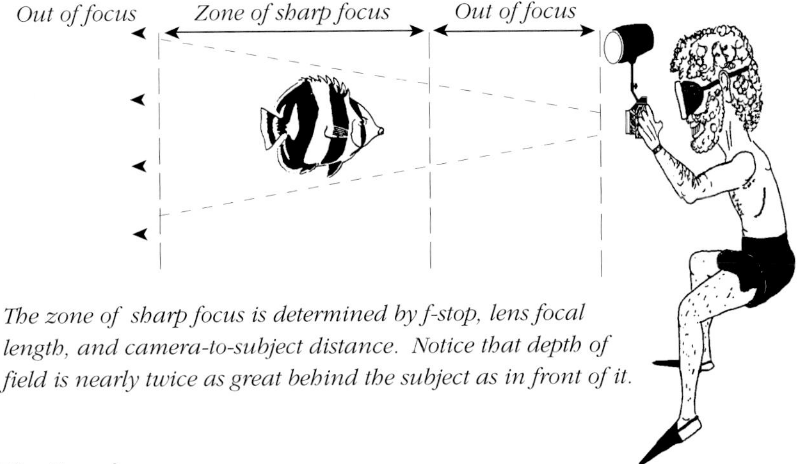

The zone of sharp focus is determined by f-stop, lens focal length, and camera-to-subject distance. Notice that depth of field is nearly twice as great behind the subject as in front of it.

Film Speed

Film speed is a measure of the sensitivity of film to light as compared to other films. It is, quite simply, the amount of exposure a film *needs.* The more sensitive a particular film, the less exposure it will require.

ASA, ISO, and DIN are number rating systems that indicate the speed of a film. ASA is an abbreviation for American Standards Association. ISO stands for International Standards Organization. DIN is a rating system used in Europe and stands for Deutsche Industrie Norm. ISO is presently the accepted industry designation.

The ISO number is printed on the box the film comes in, the film instruction sheet, and on the film cassette. The higher the number, the more sensitive or *faster* the film. Conversely, the lower the number, the less sensitive or *slower* the film. The amount of light required for a correct exposure is predetermined for each type of film. Slower film will require a greater amount of light over a longer period of time to achieve a correct exposure.

The numbers are designated in multiples. For example, ISO 50 is twice as sensitive as ISO 25, and ISO 200 is twice as sensitive as ISO 100. This translates into aperture settings as follows: ISO 50 is one f-stop faster than ISO 25; ISO 100 is one f-stop faster than ISO 50; ISO 200 is one f-stop faster than ISO 100.

Shutter speed, f-stop, and film speed are synchronized to control the amount of light that reaches the film.

How to Select a Film Speed

If you were to enlarge a photograph many times, you would notice that it is composed entirely of tiny dots. The smaller the dots, which are actually silver halide grains in the emulsion, the sharper the photograph. The larger the dots, the grainier the photograph. The ISO rating of a film is an indication of the size of the dots.

Slow films have ISO speeds of 50 or less. Slow films typically provide extremely fine grain, excellent clarity and tonal contrasts, and produce a very sharp picture with vivid colors. These are best for macro photography where detail and color saturation are critical.

Medium speed films have ISO speeds between 64 and 200. ISO 100 is the one most often used for underwater photography. It is a good all-purpose film. ISO 100 and 200 combined comprise 70 percent of the photofinishing market because they are so versatile. They perform well for macro, close-up, and wide angle.

Fast films have ISO speeds of 400 or more and are selected for fast action and low-light conditions: deep diving, wreck diving, dark, overcast days. Ultrafast films are seldom used in underwater photography today. They were popular years ago but with the advent of powerful strobes, ultrasensitive films are no longer necessary. Ultrafast films are very grainy and when enlarged, lack the sharpness, contrast, and clarity of medium speed film.

Select your film speed to suit the type of photography you will be doing.

Types of Film

The camera is the means of projecting and focusing light; the only other thing needed to take a picture is a light-sensitive material that records the light patterns in the form of an image: *film.*

The ancient Greeks discovered that certain salts turned dark when exposed to the sun. An enterprising merchant by the name of Pornographus attempted to merge chemistry with commerce when he posed several young nude nymphs on plates of silver compounds and created the first erotic silhouettes. Alas, his dreams of fortune faded as quickly as the images did, but he left an indelible impression just the same.

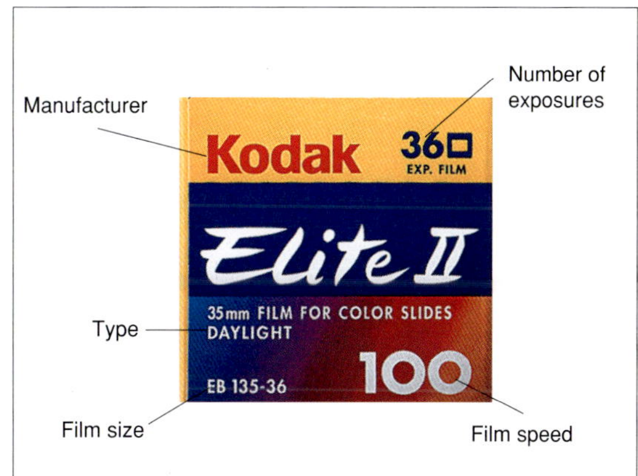

The flap on the film carton identifies it as slide or print film, tells you the size and type, film speed, and the number of exposures.

Film today is essentially the same as it was then: a chemically-sensitive emulsion, only today this emulsion is coated on a flexible transparent polyester film base. When exposed to light, the the silver halide compounds darken.

There are basically two types of films: *color negative film* and *color reversal film*. Color negative film produces a negative in which the colors and tones are the opposite of those in the original scene. Light tones look dark and dark tones look light. The negative is then printed on paper to make a print. The manufacturer designates this film with the suffix "color," as in Kodacolor and Fujicolor. The lower speed films make the highest quality prints.

Color reversal film is given a special reversal processing to produce a positive transparency, better known as a slide. Slides are mounted in small plastic or cardboard frames and are used for projecting onto a screen. These films are designated with the suffix "chrome."

Color slide film may be daylight-balanced, which is manufactured to record images correctly in daylight illumination, or tungsten-balanced, which is manufactured to record images properly in tungsten illumination. In underwater photography, since your source of illumination will be the sun and/or an electronic strobe, which emits light similar in color to daylight, daylight-balanced film is used.

The Film Transport

The film transport system consists of the film advance, the take-up spool, and the film pressure plate. The *film advance* is the device that moves the exposed film out of the way and replaces it with an unexposed piece. It enables the film to slide smoothly from the cartridge to the take-up spool without sticking or scratching.

The film *take-up spool* measures the amount of film pulled across the film transport so that there is even spacing between all frames. The take-up spool also turns the gears that count the number of frames that have been exposed.

A spring-loaded support called a *film pressure plate* keeps the film flat and unwrinkled, prevents it from bulging, sticking or scratching as it moves from cartridge to take-up spool. This may be built into the back cover or it may be on the inside of a separate door that closes over the film transport.

Film manufacturers cut the film into appropriate sizes for use with different cameras. For 35mm cameras, it is cut into strips 35mm wide and packaged in 12, 24, and 36 exposure cartridges. The film leader, also called a film tongue, sticking out of the cartridge is dark because it has been completely exposed to light. The rest of the film is stored safely in total darkness inside the cartridge.

The Motor Marine II-EX, the MX-10, and Nikonos cameras are all 35mm cameras. They use 35mm film. This film measures 35mm wide; hence, the name for the type of camera. 35mm film typically looks like this:

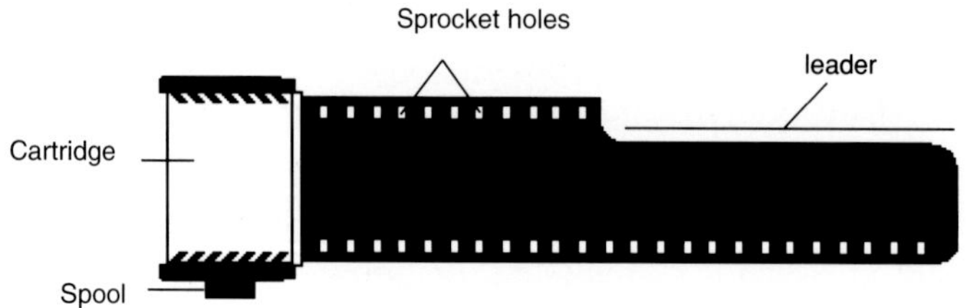

All 35mm film cartridges are packaged in light-tight canisters in rolls of 12, 24, or 36 exposures.

Viewfinder

A viewfinder is simply a sighting device. It enables you to see what you are photographing so that you can aim your camera and compose your photo accurately.

There are three types of viewfinders: the auxiliary viewfinder that mounts to the accessory shoe on top of the camera, the single-lens reflex, often called SLR, built into the camera, which allows you to view your subject through the camera lens, and the rangefinder type, also built into the camera, with etched markings which allows you to view your subject through a window on the back of the camera.

Sea & Sea and Nikonos cameras all have the rangefinder configuration. The single-lens reflex (SLR) configuration is typical of land cameras. Nikon's N90 is an SLR camera.

What is the Difference Between Land Photography and Underwater Photography?

The difference is the medium you shoot through. Water is 800 times denser than air. Air is essentially a transparent environment; light travels through it relatively unhindered. Water is dense. Light travels through water slower; it scatters, losses color and intensity. The properties and behavior of light underwater create special problems for the photographer and consequently necessitate a modification of certain photographic principles.

Reflection

For sunlight to be utilized in taking pictures underwater, it must first penetrate the water surface. However, the water surface acts like a barrier to light rays, causing them to bounce back into the atmosphere. How much light is reflected is dependent upon the position of the sun and the condition of the seas. When the sun is directly overhead at midday, reflection is minimal. Early morning and late afternoon, when the sun is nearest the horizon, light must penetrate the water surface at an extreme angle, and reflection is greatest. Rough seas reflect more light than calm waters.

The best time and conditions for the best light for underwater photography is from 10 a.m. to 2 p.m. on a bright, windless, cloudless day.

Refraction

As light rays travel underwater, they undergo a change of direction. Because of the difference in density between air and water, light rays are refracted, or bent. Refraction creates optical illusions:

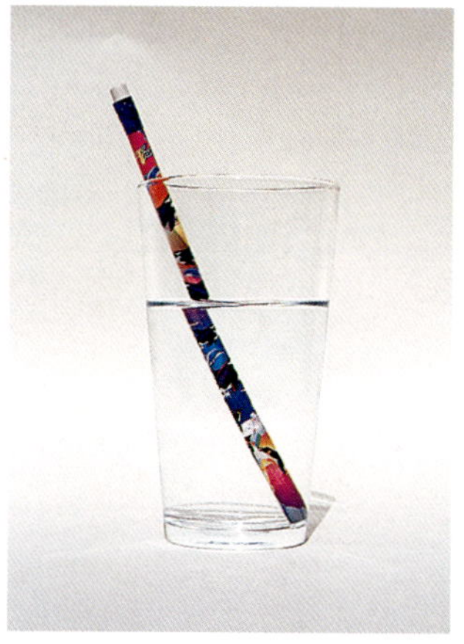

- Objects appear about 25 percent closer than they actually are. This *apparent distance* is what we and the lens see, as opposed to the actual, or measured, distance. For example, if your subject appears to be three feet away from you (apparent distance), it is actually four feet away (measured distance).

  A lens sees apparent distance. To achieve a sharp, clear picture, you must set your focus for the apparent distance.

- Objects appear larger than they actually are. An image underwater is magnified by about one-third, so a fish that appears to be three inches long is actually two inches long.

  The pencil in a glass of water is an often used demonstration of the visual effects of water. Note how the portion of the pencil in the water seems (appears) larger and closer than the portion in air.

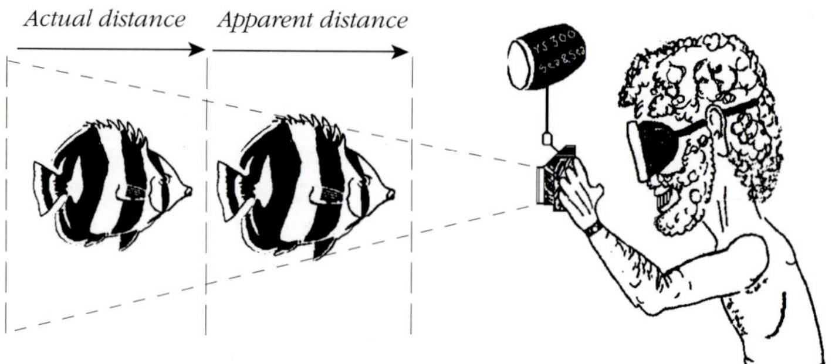

Subjects underwater appear 25 percent closer and one-third larger than they actually are.

Selective Color Absorption

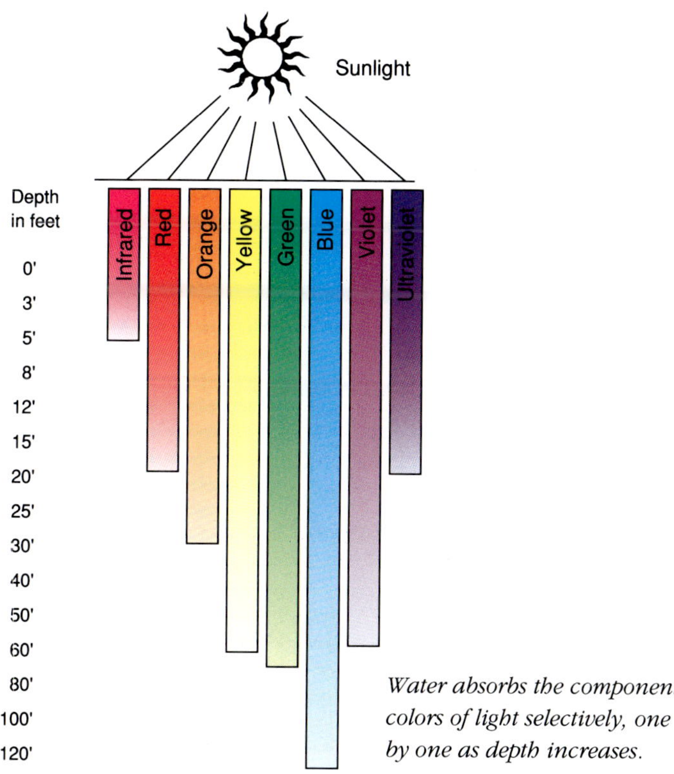

Water absorbs the component colors of light selectively, one by one as depth increases.

Absorption

Direct light from the sun is called white light. Though it appears to have no color, it is actually composed of all the colors in the visible spectrum. If you were to project it through a prism, you would see it break up into bands of color. Each color is a wavelength of light.

Water absorbs the wavelengths of light selectively, one by one as depth increases. Though exact absorption rates will vary depending upon water conditions, you can assume that red will disappear at a depth of 15-20 feet, orange at 25-30 feet, yellow at 45-60 feet, green at 70 feet, and at 100 feet, everything will appear blue or grayish green. At extreme depths all light is absorbed and everything will appear black.

The loss of color is deceiving. The human brain compensates for much of this color loss, and even at depths below 30 feet, you will still see red. The film in your camera will not. To overcome this problem, artificial light sources are used.

Horizontal Color Loss

Progressive color loss is not a function of depth but is dependent on the distance light travels through water in any direction. The greater the distance light has to travel through water, the more color will be absorbed. For ambient light to strike your film, it first travels vertically through the water column to your subject. It then reflects off the subject and travels horizontally to the camera and through your lens to the film. Let's just say you're shooting at a depth of 10 feet and the fish you're aiming at is four feet away. That means the light must travel a total of 14 feet. As a result, most of the warm colors will be filtered out. A vivid orange fish will look a dull brown. Your buddy with the sunburn will look ghostly.

The best way to obtain bright natural colors underwater is to get close to your subject and to use an artificial light source: a *strobe.*

Strobes

A strobe is an electronic flash. It has been engineered to emit light that is equivalent in color to daylight. It can be used to supplement available light or it can function alone when no ambient light exists. It restores the color to photographs that would otherwise be a monochromatic blue. A strobe "paints" your photograph with color, enabling you to record the colors even the human eye cannot see in the underwater environment.

When a strobe is used in combination with ambient light, it is called *fill lighting* or *balanced lighting.* In close-up or macrophotography, the strobe is used as the primary light source. We discuss strobes, their purpose and proper usage, in Chapter 7.

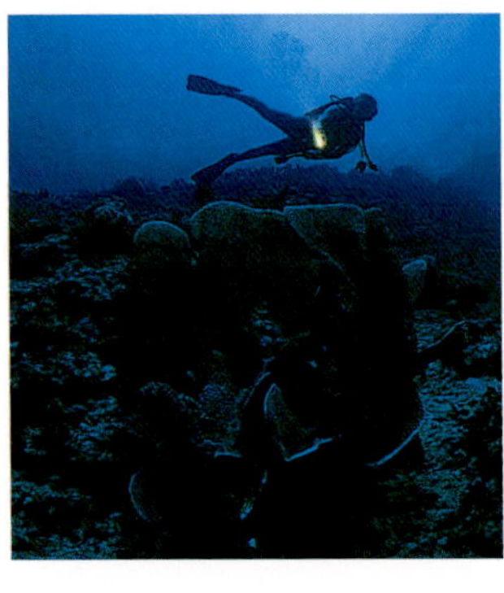

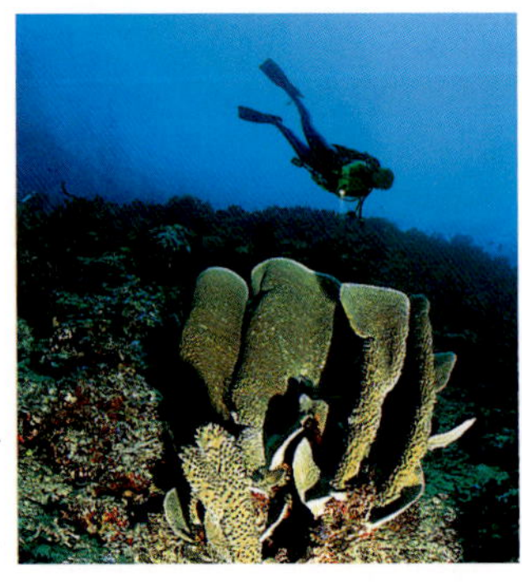

◄ *Without strobe*

With strobe ►

◄ *Without color*

With color ►

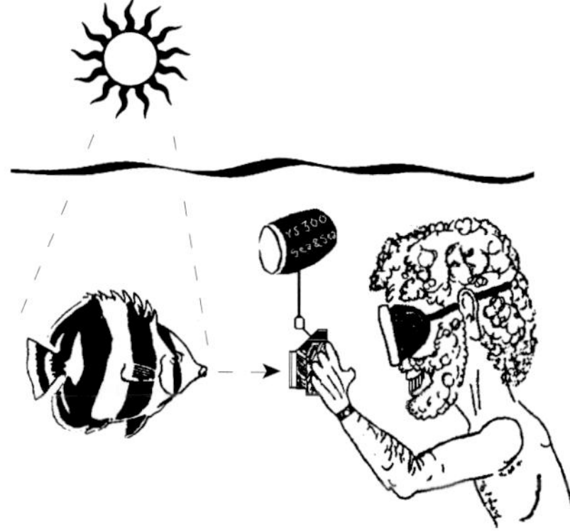

In ambient light photography, light first descends the water column and strikes the subject. The reflected light must then travel horizontally to the lens.

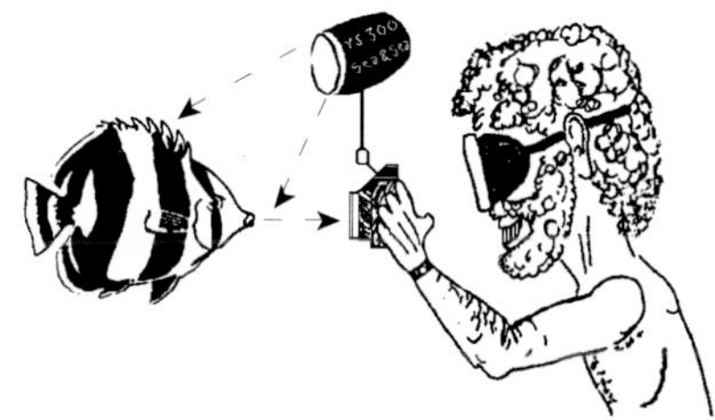

Horizontal color absorption affects strobe light as well. Light must travel from the strobe to the subject, and then to the lens.

Backscatter

While strobe light solves one problem, that of color filtration, it creates another problem: *backscatter.* Backscatter looks like snow or dust in your photograph. Sometimes it looks like blurry hexagons. It is actually neutrally buoyant particles of sand, plankton, algae, and other organic matter suspended in the water. When your strobe is fired, the particles act like thousands of tiny mirrors reflecting the light back to the lens. The resultant exposure is not only marred by grayish specks but is lacking in finite detail and richness of color.

Backscatter can be reduced by better diving techniques (extreme caution not to stir up the bottom with fins or dangling scuba equipment) and proper placement of your strobe.

Reread and Review

We have just covered the fundamental principles of underwater photography. In the following chapters we explain how particular pieces of equipment function and present some advanced shooting techniques. Don't proceed unless you thoroughly understand all the precepts and terms in this chapter. Go back. Reread and review.

If you think you understand all the preceding information, good, now turn the page and test yourself.

A QUICK QUIZ

BEFORE YOU GO ON

	TRUE	FALSE
1. The five basic components of every camera are: lens, shutter, aperture, film transport, and viewfinder.	❑	❑
2. The primary function of a lens is to gather light rays and project a sharp image on film.	❑	❑
3. The focal length of a lens determines the amount of a scene shown on film and the size of the image.	❑	❑
4. Angle of acceptance of a particular lens is the angle, measured in degrees, at which the lens will accept light.	❑	❑
5. A shutter speed of 1/125 of a second is slower than 1/60 of a second.	❑	❑
6. Aperture controls the amount of light that passes through the lens.	❑	❑
7. An aperture setting of f/5.6 allows twice as much light to strike the film as f/8.	❑	❑
8. Depth of field is the area between the lens and the subject that is in acceptably sharp focus.	❑	❑
9. The smaller the lens opening, the greater the depth of field.	❑	❑
10. Film speed refers to how fast you can take pictures.	❑	❑

	TRUE	FALSE
11. Fast films like ISO 400 have a fine grain and are best for close-up photography.	❑	❑
12. The film transport is the chamber that holds the film.	❑	❑
13. You compose your picture by looking over the top of the viewfinder.	❑	❑
14. Underwater photography is different from photography on land because light behaves differently underwater.	❑	❑
15. Due to refraction, objects underwater appear farther away than they actually are.	❑	❑
16. There is a progressive loss of perceptible color as sunlight descends the water column.	❑	❑
17. The loss of color underwater occurs as light travels horizontally through water.	❑	❑
18. A reflected light meter reads light reflected from the subject.	❑	❑
19. Underwater photographers compensate for the loss of light and color by using the largest aperture possible.	❑	❑
20. Backscatter is what happens when you kick up sand with your fins.	❑	❑

Answers on next page . . . . ➤

Answers to the Quick Quiz

1. True	11. False
2. True	12. False
3. True	13. False
4. True	14. True
5. False	15. False
6. True	16. True
7. True	17. True
8. False	18. True
9. True	19. False
10. False	20. True *and* False

Your Score

0-2 wrong:	*Excellent*
3-4 wrong:	*Good*
More than 4 wrong:	*Not so good.*

Those of you who scored *Good* and *Not so good* should go back to the beginning and read this chapter again. The information in this chapter is the foundation on which you will build all your underwater photographic skills. When you know the basics, *really* know the basics, you can proceed.

CHAPTER TWO

The MX-10

The MX-10

The Motor Marine 35 MX-10 is an uncomplicated camera that makes underwater photography fun. Underwater photography is *supposed* to be fun. Yet one of the most surprising things we've found over the years is that many divers think underwater photography is work. They hesitate to buy a camera because they've seen other divers with elaborate and obviously expensive systems and wonder, what if that thing flooded? They watch the owners of those systems spending hours cleaning and nurturing the system and wonder, why are they doing that when they could be relaxing in the sun? And then they hear those divers whining about the fish shot they missed, and think, underwater photography is too hard. All I want is to get some nice snapshots of pretty fish.

With the MX-10 you can.

Taking a cue from divers with underwater photo cold feet, Sea & Sea has designed a rugged and reliable camera that is remarkably easy to operate. It is hassle-free and practically foolproof, with a full complement of built-in functions that simplify the picture-taking process: automatic film load, advance and rewind, fixed shutter, and a built-in metering system for accurate exposure control. It incorporates an optical-grade focus-free lens with exterior mount that enables you to add on and take off accessory lenses underwater. The MX-10 also features a revolutionary infrared signaling system that synchronizes the accessory strobe with the camera shutter without the use of cords or cables, so you never have to worry about leakage at the flash connection.

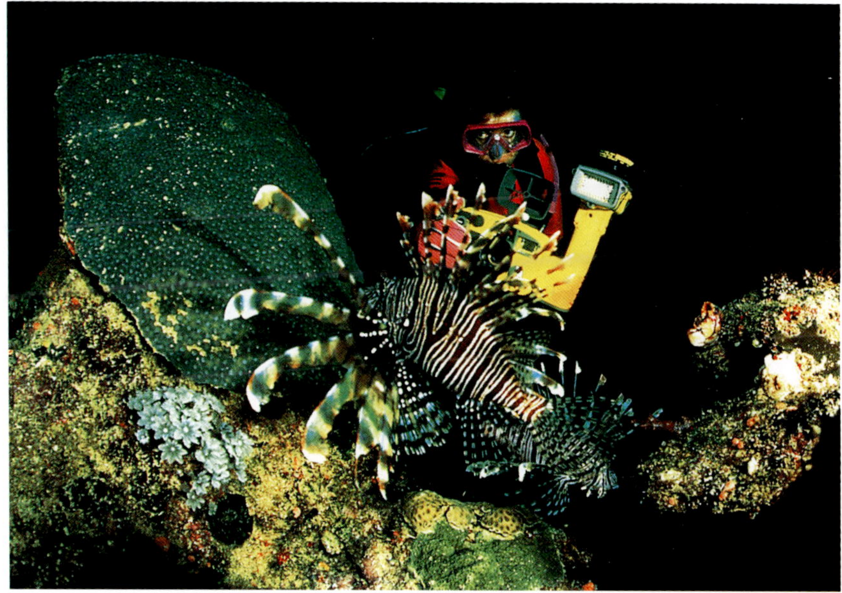

Here is a compact camera that takes pictures anywhere. Hermetically sealed against water, dust, sand, the MX-10 is hardy and distinctive in its solar yellow Sea & Sea case. Cast of rust and impact-resistant molded polymers for long life and minimal maintenance, it's ideal for all outdoor activities where you dare not take a land camera: surfing, river rafting, boating, hiking, fishing, water or snow skiing. Wherever your adventurous spirit takes you, you can take the MX-10. It's built to withstand the rigors of outdoor life.

But don't confuse the MX-10 with *weatherproof* cameras. A weatherproof camera is sealed against the elements, but it is not designed to be submerged. It is a shallow water system with limited depth range, designed primarily for snorkeling or skin diving, not scuba diving. The MX-10, on the other hand, is a self-contained amphibious camera that performs equally well at 150 feet as it does on and at the surface.

The MX-10 is just right for the neophyte who wants to capture the true beauty of the undersea world with all the ease of a point and shoot.

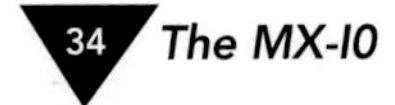

Identification of Parts

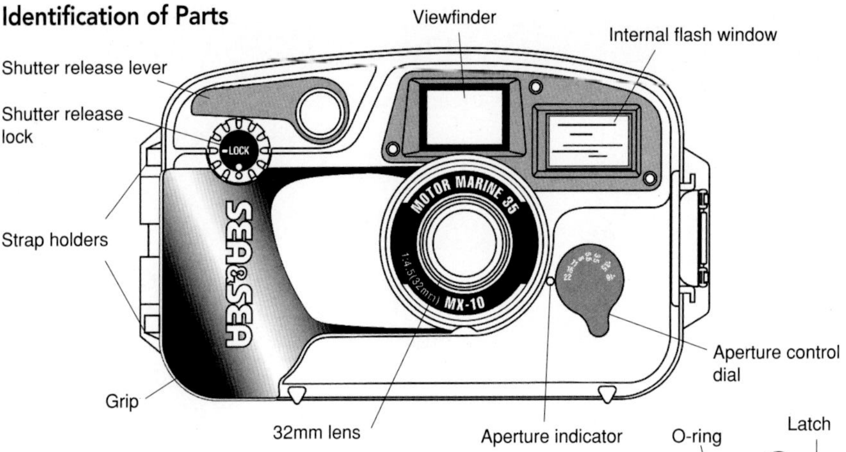

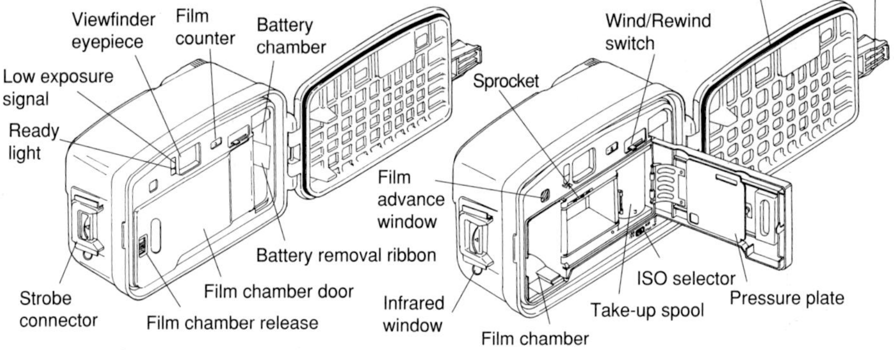

Viewfinder
Internal flash window
Shutter release lever
Shutter release lock
Strap holders
Grip
32mm lens
Aperture indicator
Aperture control dial
O-ring
Latch
Viewfinder eyepiece
Film counter
Battery chamber
Low exposure signal
Ready light
Film advance window
Battery removal ribbon
Film chamber door
Strobe connector
Film chamber release
Infrared window
Wind/Rewind switch
Sprocket
ISO selector
Take-up spool
Pressure plate
Film chamber

Specifications

Type of camera:	35mm amphibious camera
Construction:	ABS molded polycarbonate
Maximum depth:	150 feet (45 meters)
Film format:	36mm x 24mm
Type film:	Standard 35mm cartridge
Film speed:	ISO 100 or ISO 400
Lens:	32mm f/4.5 (4 elements in 4 groups)
Angle of coverage:	68° land, 51° u/w
Shutter:	Fixed
Shutter speed:	1/100 second
Exposure control:	Manual
Exposure meter:	Built in with LED display
Aperture range:	F/4.5 ~ f/22
Focal distance	
land:	8.25 feet ~ ∞ (2.5m ~ ∞)
underwater:	4 feet ~ ∞ (1.2m ~ ∞)
Film load:	Automatic

Film advance:	Power drive
Film counter:	Automatic
Film rewind:	Automatic
Viewfinder:	80% frame coverage; 0.45 magnification
LED display:	Low exposure warning; flash ready light
Electronic flash:	Built in
GN (ISO 100):	33 (feet); 10 (m) land
Synchronization:	1/100 second
Flash ready light:	Built in
Power source:	2 1.5-volt AA batteries
Dimensions:	6.3 x 3.7 x 2.8" (W x H x D) (159 x 94 x 71mm)
Weight:	21 oz. (595g) on land (batteries not incl)
Accessories included:	Strap, O-ring set, silicone grease

The Main Components

Shutter

The MX-10 has been designed with a mechanical leaf shutter fixed to operate at 1/100 second. The fixed shutter speed simplifies the picture-taking process and is the ideal shutter speed for freezing motion on land and underwater.

Lens

The MX-10 has a built in wide angle 32mm f/4.5 fixed-focus lens. It can take pictures both on land and underwater. It provides 68° coverage on land and 51° underwater. The lens is sealed and protected by a circular glass window and is equipped with an exterior bayonet mount to accept auxiliary lenses.

Aperture

The aperture control dial has eight settings. Six are ▶ f-stop positions, ranging from f/4.5 to f/22. To select an f-stop, you simply rotate the aperture control dial from one click-stop to another. The two additional settings, set off in the orange area, are f/4.5 ⚡and f/11⚡; these settings activate the internal flash. The face of the aperture control has icons for sunny and cloudy conditions; these indicate approximate exposure settings for topside photography using ISO 100 film.

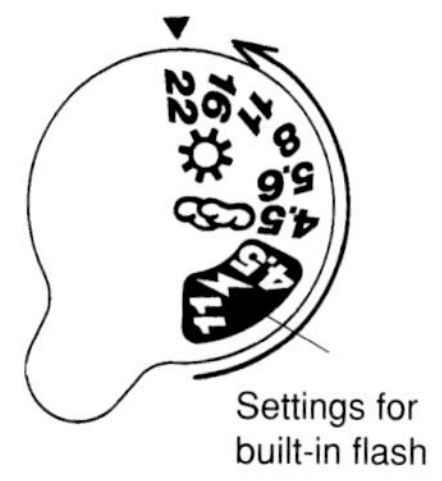

Settings for built-in flash

Film Transport

The film transport advances the film from the cassette to the take-up spool. Each time an exposure is made, the built-in motor drive advances the film to the next frame. The exposed film moves in precise increments. The film pressure plate on the inside of the film chamber door, keeps the film flat and unwrinkled.

Viewfinder

The viewfinder is used to compose your photograph, but unlike your SLR land camera, it doesn't show *exactly* what the lens sees and what image will be recorded. This a rangefinder viewfinder. It provides 80 percent frame coverage; its field of view is slightly less than that of the lens. Thus, more of the scene will be recorded than what you see through the viewfinder. In addition, when you look through the viewfinder, the subject will always appear to be in perfect focus. That is not the case. The recorded image will be in focus *only* if you have the correct camera-to-subject focusing distance.

Opening the Camera

To anyone who owns a land camera, opening the back cover may seem pretty basic and step-by-step instructions unnecessary. But, as you will learn, an amphibious camera is quite different from a land camera. An amphibious camera is encased in a waterproof housing. All ports and controls are watertight. All external components are impervious to water damage. *Internal components are not.*

To protect the delicate internal electronic mechanism from water damage, special care is required. The first step in providing this special care is to open the back cover in such a way that water will not penetrate.

1. Before opening the camera, inspect it thoroughly. Make sure the camera is clean and dry. Check for sand, dust, lint, hair, as well as water. If necessary, rinse it with fresh water and dry thoroughly with a soft, dry cloth.

2. Hold the camera with the the back ▶ cover facing down and the lens facing up. *Always* open the camera in this position. It's a prudent precautionary measure. After a dive, water or sand may be trapped between the camera body and the back cover O-ring. If you are holding the camera with the back cover facing up, as you would a land camera, water will be sucked into the interior.

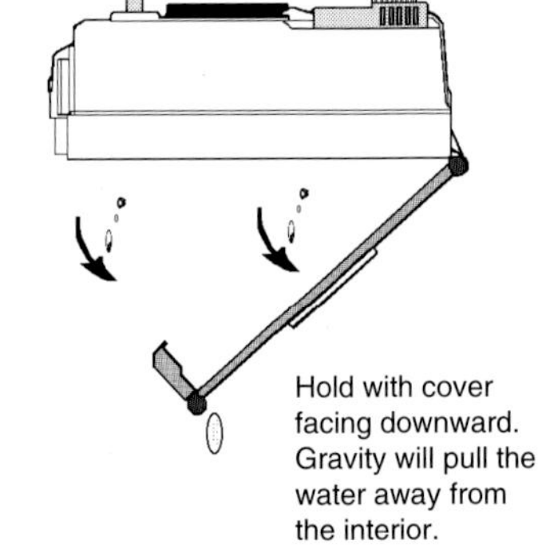
Hold with cover facing downward. Gravity will pull the water away from the interior.

3. To unlock the back cover, push ▶ the lock release in the direction of the arrow. The latch will release, and the cover will open.

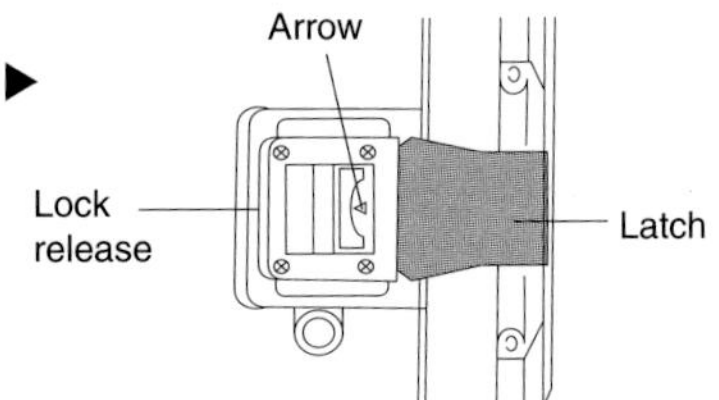

Note: Never pull on the latch. The latch is ▶ not a handle to use to open the back cover. Excessive force will break it. If the door will not open when the latch is released, there is a build up of pressure inside the camera. Place two fingers on the solid part of the latch hinge and firmly pull the door open.

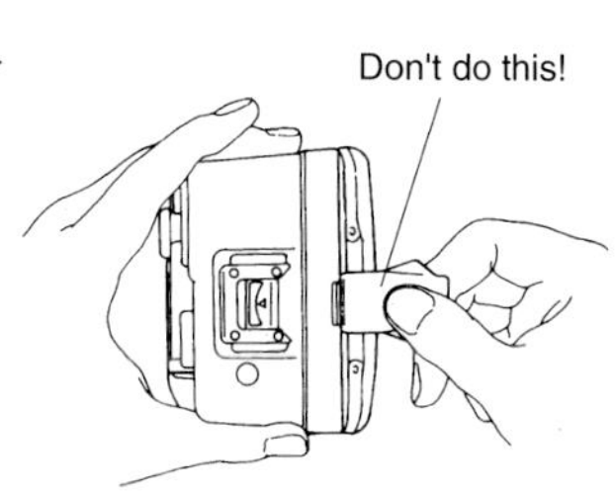

Never use a screwdriver or any other tool to pry open the door. You risk damaging the housing and the O-ring.

The Back Cover O-ring

Unlike your land camera, your MX-10 has an O-ring seated in a channel around the back cover. An O-ring is a rubber gasket. When subjected to pressure underwater, it flattens in the channel and forms a watertight seal. But it will only form a watertight seal if it is in perfect sealing condition. It can't be "almost" clean or have "just one little nick." If the O-ring isn't flawless, the camera will flood. Special attention and meticulous care must be given the O-ring to ensure its sealing capability.

1. To remove the O-ring from its ▶ channel, press down with thumb and forefinger to create a bulge, then lift gently from its groove.

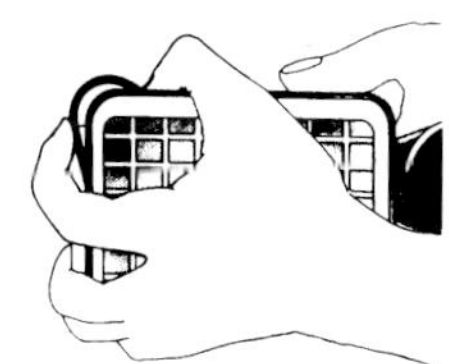

   Because it is so important for the O-ring to be flawless, Sea & Sea has made a special little plastic O-ring remover for safe and easy removal. It is available at your Sea & Sea dealer. You can use the rounded corner of your C-card, too. Carefully tuck it under the O-ring and lift it from its groove.

   Warning: Never use a sharp or pointed object to remove this or any other O-ring.

2. Examine the O-ring carefully for scratches, debris, deformity, etc. If it is caked with silicone grease or if sand, salt crystals, lint or dust are stuck to it, wash with soapy water. Then rinse it with fresh water, pat dry with a dry lint-free cloth, and lightly coat with silicone grease.

3. To grease an O-ring, squeeze a dab of grease (about the size of a grain of rice) on your forefinger. Rub forefinger and thumb together, then gently pull the O-ring through your fingers. You want to lightly and evenly coat the O-ring.

Important: With the blue O-ring, you must use the tube of silicone grease with the blue cap and blue lettering. This O-ring is chemically incompatible with the grease in the tube with the black lettering. Please see page 279 for details.

4. Flatten a cotton swab with fingers or pliers and swab all around the O-ring channel. After cleaning, check that there is no residual lint from the cotton swab on the channel. If you don't mind the added expense, you can clean the channel with a few bursts of canned air sold in photographic equipment stores.

5. To reseat the O-ring, insert one side into the channel and, while holding it in position, roll the other side into place.

See Chapter 9, *Care and Maintenance*, for more detailed instructions on how to care for O-rings.

Installing the Batteries

The MX-10 is powered by two 1.5-volt AA alkaline batteries. *Warning*: Do not use ni-cad batteries in this unit.

Insert the batteries with the positive (+) and negative (-) ends as indicated by the polarity decal inside the battery chamber. ▶

Polarity markings

Battery removal ribbon

▾ Be careful not to reverse polarity; if polarity is reversed, your camera will not function.

▾ Reversed polarity can cause acid leakage.

▾ Be sure the battery removal ribbon is under the batteries so that they can be easily removed by just pulling the ribbon up.

▾ Be sure the end of the ribbon is tucked in and does not interfere with the O-ring seal when you close the back cover. If the ribbon interferes with the seal, the camera will flood.

Selecting Film

The MX-10 takes a standard 35mm film cassette. It accepts ISO 100 and ISO 400. Both are available in print film or slide film. Novices should start with print film which has the advantage of extended exposure and color latitude. Exposure latitude means exposure "forgiveness." With print films in the ISO 100 to 400 range, you can err on selecting your aperture by as many as five f-stops: three f-stops over and two f-stops under the correct f-stop before you get a discernible deficiency in a print. The photofinisher can correct the exposure error and provide you with a good color print. On the down side, the prints are only as good as the technician operating the printing machine.

Prints cost more than slides, about 20 to 30 percent more for film and processing, but prints are easy to view, display, carry, show and share.

ISO 100 film is a good general purpose film with a fine grain structure that produces sharp and colorful images with an acceptable depth of field. It is suitable for most recreational diving situations.

ISO 100 film is a good choice for neophytes because the exposure information provided by Sea & Sea is based on ISO 100. Rule-of-thumb exposures and depth of field tables presented in this book are based on ISO 100.

But there is also an advantage to using ISO 400 film. It is twice as fast as ISO 100, so you can stop down two f-stops from the recommended f-stop provided in the tables, and thereby extend depth of field. ISO 400 doubles the maximum range of a flash over ISO 100; this, too allows for smaller f-stops and extended depth of field. This is an important benefit for beginners who have difficulty estimating apparent distance. With the extended depth of field, you increase the zone of sharp focus enough to compensate for the misjudged distance.

Setting Film Speed

The MX-10's internal light meter ▶ is programmed to provide ambient exposure information on two film speeds: ISO 100 and ISO 400. It is necessary to set the ISO selector switch to the film speed being used.

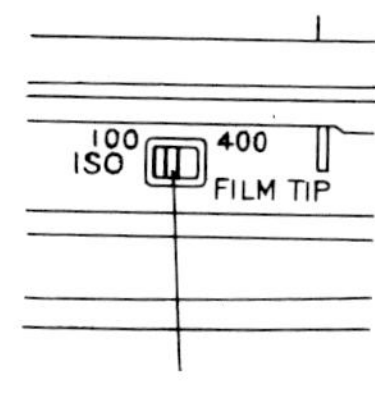

ISO film speed selector

Loading the Film

The camera is equipped with an autoload mechanism that simplifies the procedure so that it's practically mistake-proof.

1. Set the Wind/Rewind switch to "W." If the switch is in the "R" position, the film will automatically rewind when the film chamber door is closed. Switch to "W" before loading the film. ▶

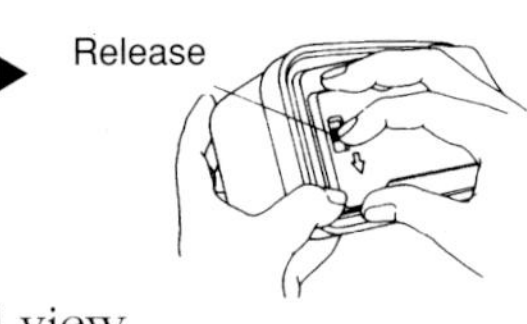

Wind/Rewind switch

2. To open the film chamber door, press downward on the release. The door will open. ▶

Note: To provide you with an unobstructed view of the film chamber, we've omitted the film chamber door from the following illustrations.

3. Insert the flat end of the cassette into the film chamber. Be sure the rewind cog is fully engaged or the film may jam. Lower the other end of the cassette into place. ▶

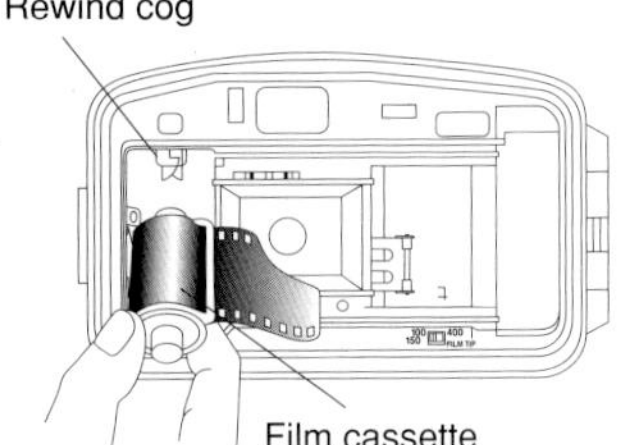

4. Pull out the film leader from the cassette. Lay the film flat across the film transport. Be sure the edges of the film are positioned between the film guide rails. ▶

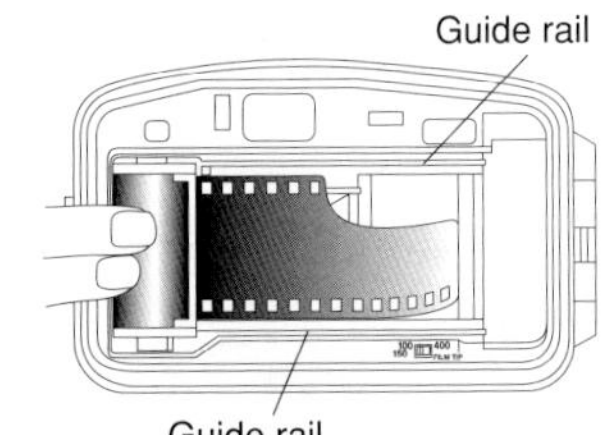

5. Align the tip of the film leader with the film tip mark. Make sure the film sprocket holes are securely fitted over the sprocket teeth. Be sure there is no slack. ▶

6. Close the film chamber door.

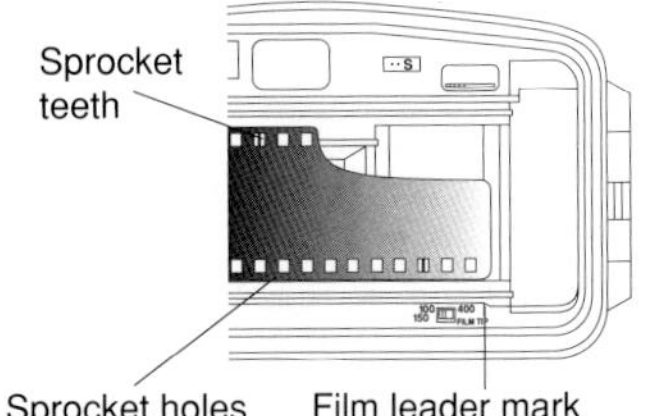

Warning: Never open the film chamber door until all the frames have been exposed and rewound into the cartridge. Doing so will expose your film.

Tip: Avoid loading film in brightly-lit areas. If changing film outdoors, shield the camera from direct sunlight with your body.

Closing the Back Cover

Before closing the back cover, take another look at the O-ring. Is it clean, seated properly in its channel, lubricated? Is the back cover clean and dry? Is the Wind/Rewind switch set to "W"? If the answer is *yes* to all these questions, you can close the back cover.

Hold the camera in both hands. ▶ Make sure that the back cover latch is facing forward and is not in a 90° (upright) position. Press the cover firmly against the camera body. Engage the latch with your thumb. You will hear a click. The back cover is locked.

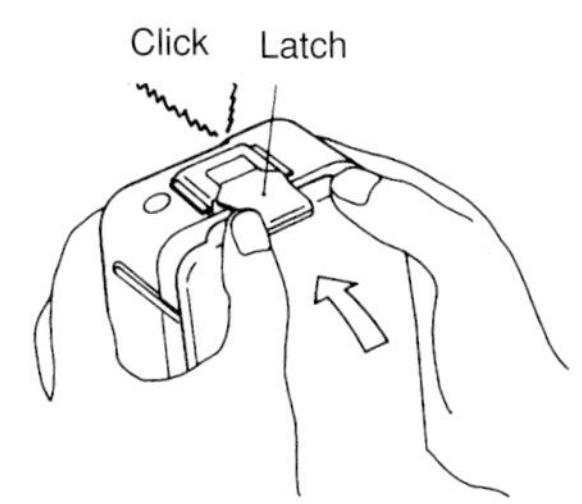

Advancing the Film

Turn the shutter release lock to ▶ the "Open" position. Depress the shutter release lever a few times until the number "1" appears in the film counter window.

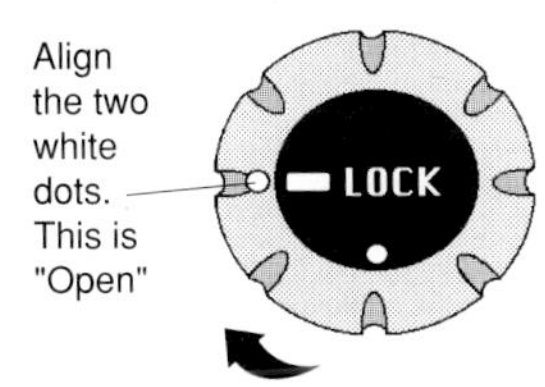

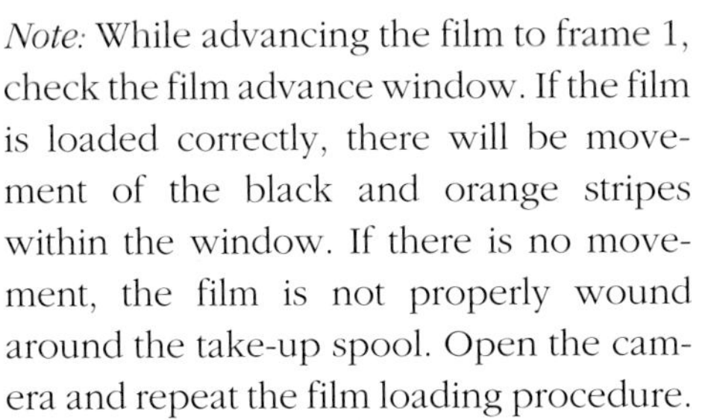

Note: While advancing the film to frame 1, ▶ check the film advance window. If the film is loaded correctly, there will be movement of the black and orange stripes within the window. If there is no movement, the film is not properly wound around the take-up spool. Open the camera and repeat the film loading procedure.

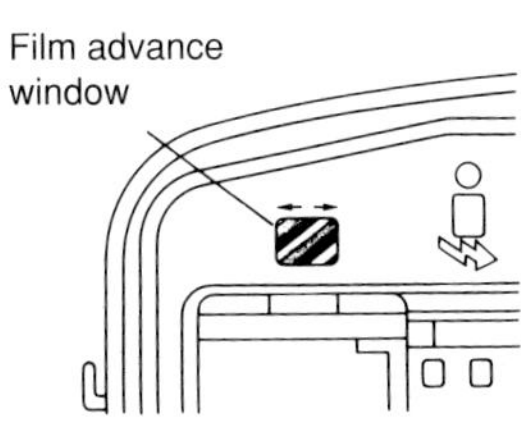

You are now ready to take pictures!

USING THE MX-10 TOPSIDE

Although you bought it to take photographs underwater, it's a good idea to use it on land first. You should get comfortable with the handling and operation of the camera, get accustomed to the controls, and practice estimating distance and selecting f-stops.

The MX-10 has a built-in 32mm lens. It is usually referred to as a *standard* lens. It is also referred to as the *primary* lens for auxiliary lenses. In this way, the built-in lens is a building block for expanding your system. The built-in lens is dual-purpose; it takes pictures on land as well as underwater. It is *prefocused;* you need not worry about setting camera-to-subject distance. The shutter is preset at 1/100 second, so you need not concern yourself with shutter speed either. The only determination you must make is which f-stop to use for a correct exposure. To do that, you use the built-in exposure meter.

Using the Built-in Exposure Meter

The MX-10 is equipped with a built-in reflective type exposure meter (also called a *light meter*); this measures the brightness of light available to help you determine the correct f-stop for a proper exposure.

1. Select the proper f-stop according to the conditions of the available light. The rule-of-thumb f-stops for topside photography are:

Conditions	ISO 100	ISO 400
Indoors	f/4.5 ⚡	f/11 ⚡
Outdoors, Cloudy	f/4.5 ~ 5.6	f/16
Outdoors, Partly Sunny	f/8 ~ 11	f/22
Bright Snow	f/16 ~ 22	NA
Bright Sun	f/16 ~ 22	NA

2. To confirm that the f-stop you selected will yield a proper exposure, use the exposure meter. Assuming you're outdoors on a partly sunny day. The above rule-of-thumb exposure chart suggests f/8 or f/11. Set the aperture at f/11. While looking through the viewfinder at your subject, depress the shutter release lever *halfway.* If the red low exposure warning light comes on, you don't have enough light for a proper exposure. You need to "open up."

3. Set the aperture at f/8. Looking through the viewfinder, depress the shutter release lever halfway. If the red light does *not* come on, you have the correct f-stop; you can take the picture. But if the red light does come on, you still don't have enough light for a proper exposure. Open up once more.

4. Set the aperture at f/5.6 and repeat the above procedure. The objective is to find an f-stop where the low exposure warning signal *does not* come on. If it still comes on at f/4.5, use the internal flash.

Camera-to-Subject Distance for Ambient Light

With a fixed focus lens, sharp focus is dependent upon depth of field. So after you have selected your f-stop, you must determine the proper camera-to-subject distance for that f-stop. Remember from Chapter 1, depth of field is the *zone of sharp focus.* Any object outside that range will be out of focus. The following calculations are based on ISO 100.

F-stop	**4.5**	**5.6**	**8**	**11**	**16**	**22**
Feet	4.5 ~ 45.6	4.1 ~ ∞	3.4 ~ ∞	2.8 ~ ∞	2.2 ~ ∞	1.8 ~ ∞
Meters	1.4 ~ 14.0	1.3 ~ ∞	1.0 ~ ∞	0.9 ~ ∞	0.7 ~ ∞	0.5 ~ ∞

Using the Built-in Flash

The built-in flash may be used indoors or outdoors when ambient light is insufficient for a proper exposure. To activate the flash, turn the aperture control knob to f/4.5⚡or f/11⚡. The orange ready light will illuminate in the viewfinder window. This signals that the flash is charged and ready to fire. You choose the flash position based on camera-to-subject distance for the speed of the film you are using. The chart below shows the effective range for each flash position. Choose the flash position that best suits the subject.

	F/4.5⚡		**F/11⚡**	
ISO	**Feet**	**Meters**	**Feet**	**Meters**
100	4.6 ~ 7.5	1.4 ~ 2.3	3.0 ~ 4.3	0.9 ~ 1.3
400	8.2 ~ 14.4	2.5 ~ 4.4	3.3 ~ 5.9	1.0 ~ 1.8

Note: Do not leave the aperture control setting at either f/4.5⚡ or f/11⚡ when not using the internal flash, as this will drain the batteries.

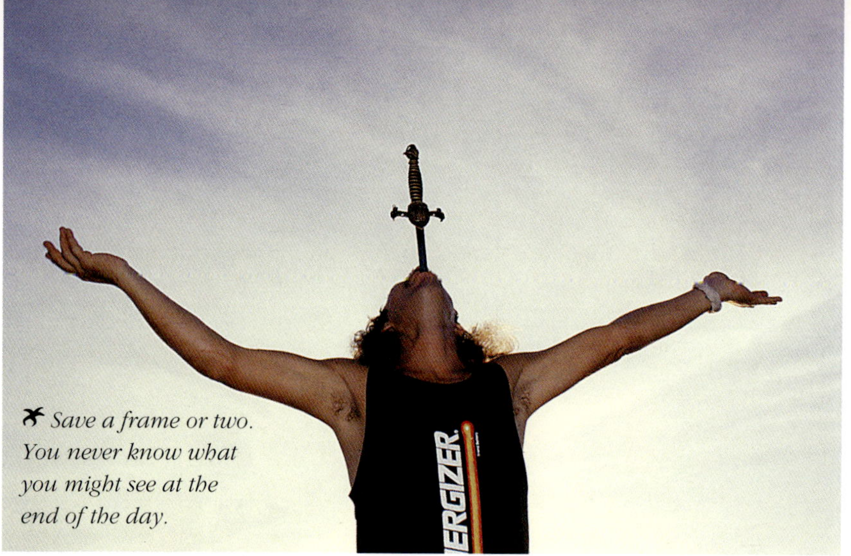

Save a frame or two. You never know what you might see at the end of the day.

Taking the Picture

Once you have determined the correct f-stop and camera-to-subject distance, you are ready to take the picture. Hold the camera in your right hand, with your index finger resting lightly on the shutter release lever. Your left hand will support the opposite side of the camera. Tuck elbows close to your body for maximum steadiness. Compose your photograph looking through the viewfinder, not above it. Press down on the shutter release lever. The MX-10 has an electronic motor drive that automatically advances the film each time the shutter is triggered. You do not have to advance the film mechanically.

Tips for Taking Good Topside Pix

While the best time of day for taking pictures underwater is midday when the sun is overhead, it's the worst time of day for topside photos. The light is too intense, harsh and colorless. The best time of day for taking pictures on land is after sunrise and the hours before sunset. With the sun nearing the horizon at those times and the rays striking the subject at an oblique angle, the light is soft, warmer, flattering people subjects and scenics.

- ▼ Hold the camera steady. Even the slightest movement will create a fuzzy photo.
- ▼ Keep the sun behind you so the sun shines onto your subject and not into your lens.
- ▼ Use the built-in flash on overcast days. The flash adds color and sharper detail.
- ▼ Keep it simple and uncluttered. One strong visual makes a better picture than several competing ones.

More tips in Chapter 8, Composition.

UNDERWATER PHOTOGRAPHY

Basic Pre-dive System Check

	Yes	No
1. Are there fresh batteries in the camera?	❑	❑
2. Did you clean and lubricate the back cover O-ring?	❑	❑
3. Is the back cover securely closed and locked?	❑	❑
4. Look through the lens and slowly rotate the aperture dial from f/22 to f/4.5. Does the opening in the lens open and close? Does the dial move smoothly and easily?	❑	❑
5. Set the aperture control dial to f/4.5 ⚡. Look into the viewfinder window. Did the flash ready light for the internal strobe come on?	❑	❑
6. Turn the shutter release lock to the "Open" position. Set the aperture at f/22. Look through the viewfinder and depress the lever halfway. Is the red low-light lamp on?	❑	❑
7. Are there fresh batteries in the strobe?	❑	❑
8. Did you clean and lubricate the strobe's battery cap O-ring?	❑	❑
9. Mount strobe to camera. Turn the strobe to the "On" position. Did the strobe ready light come on?	❑	❑
10. Trigger the shutter. Did the strobe fire? Did the ready light come on within five seconds?	❑	❑

What to do if you answer *No.*

1. Install fresh batteries.
2. Open the back cover and remove the O-ring. Inspect it for debris and deformity. If necessary, replace it with a new one. Clean and lubricate the O-ring as described on page 37.
3. Open the back cover, then close and lock it again.
4. If the dial rotates normally but the opening inside the lens does not open and close, then the aperture is malfunctioning. Send the camera to a Sea & Sea repair facility.
5. If the flash ready light does not come on, the batteries are probably exhausted. Install fresh batteries.
6. If the red lamp does not come on, your exposure meter is not functioning. Change the camera batteries and perform the test again.
7. Install new alkaline batteries or recharge your ni-cads.
8. Open the battery compartment, remove and inspect the O-ring. Clean or replace as necessary.
9. If the strobe ready light does not come on, either your batteries are dead or installed incorrectly. Open the battery chamber and check that you have not reversed polarity. If they are installed properly, then you probably need fresh batteries.
10. The optimum recycle time for the YS-40/YS-40A is five seconds with alkaline batteries, three seconds with ni-cads. If it takes longer than 10 seconds with alkalines or six seconds with ni-cads, your batteries are weak and need to be replaced or charged.

If your camera and strobe have passed the above checks, then all systems are *go* and you are ready to take underwater pictures.

Setting the Exposure for Ambient Light Photography

In ambient light photography the exposure is created using available light: *light from the sun.* In shallow water you will have more available light than at depth. On a bright, sunny day you will have more ambient light than on an overcast day. You will have more light at noon when the sun is directly overhead than at four in the afternoon when the sun is low on the horizon. You will also have more light when the water is clear than when the water is murky. All of these factors and conditions come into play when determining how to create a proper exposure, meaning, quite simply, which f-stop to use.

To determine the proper f-stop for ambient light photography, you use the built-in exposure meter. This is the same procedure as described on page 42.

1. Set ISO selector for film speed.
2. Turn the shutter release lock to the "Open" position.
3. Set aperture control dial at f/22.
4. Looking through the viewfinder, position your subject in the frame.
5. Depress the shutter release lever halfway. If the low exposure warning signal comes on, reset to f/16.
6. Depress the shutter release halfway.
7. If the red lamp is illuminated at f/16, then you still need more light. Reset to f/11.
8. Repeat the procedure until the red light *does not* come on.
9. If at f/4.5 you still get a low exposure warning, you cannot take the picture with available light. You must use the accessory strobe.

Rule-of-Thumb Exposures*

Depth	F-stop
Surface	f/16
10'	f/11
20'	f/8
40'	f/5.6
60'	f/4.5

Note: One f-stop every 10 feet.
* Based on ISO 100 in clear tropical waters. Coastal or turbid waters, open up one f-stop.

Note: Do not refer to the icons on the aperture control dial. They apply to topside photography only.

Why start with f/22? Because the LED display does not warn you of an *overexposure.* There's an underexposure warning light but none to indicate too much light. Best to start at an obvious underexposure.

Camera-to-Subject Distance

Now that you know which f-stop to use, you need to determine the correct camera-to-subject distance for that f-stop. The *depth of field chart* below provides that information.

F-stop	**4.5**	**5.6**	**8**	**11**	**16**	**22**
Feet	3.0 ~ 5.5	2.9 ~ 5.9	2.6 ~ 7.9	2.3 ~ 13.0	2.0 ~ ∞	1.6 ~ ∞
Meters	0.9 ~ 1.7	0.9 ~ 1.8	0.8 ~ 2.4	0.7 ~ 4.0	0.6 ~ ∞	0.5 ~ ∞

Note: The above camera-to-subject distance is *apparent* distance underwater, *not* measured distance.

Since the f-stop has the most profound effect upon depth of field, you always want to use the smallest aperture possible. That's not to suggest you shoot at f/22 all the time. If you did, your pictures would be grossly underexposed (dark). How then to increase depth of field and still get a good exposure?

Tip: Shoot in shallow water where ambient light is brightest. Shooting in shallow water will allow optimum f-stop settings, provide greater depth of field, brighter backgrounds, and better colors.

Estimating Distance

The major drawback of every standard lens is its not-very-close focusing ability. For the 32mm lens, the closest you can get to your subject underwater and have it in sharp focus is three feet apparent. If you get closer than that, your images will be out of focus. The challenge is to know exactly where three feet is underwater. Mastering apparent distance for this lens will be the most difficult thing you ever do with your MX-10.

You can't "eyeball" distance underwater. Due to the refraction of light underwater, everything seems 25 percent closer than it actually is. You can learn to judge distance using the "arm's length" method.

Extend your arm. From bicep to fingertips on an average-sized adult is approximately 24 inches measured distance. That is 18 inches apparent underwater. Two arms lengths would be four feet measured distance, which is equivalent to three feet apparent. The lens of your camera sees *apparent distance* underwater. ▶

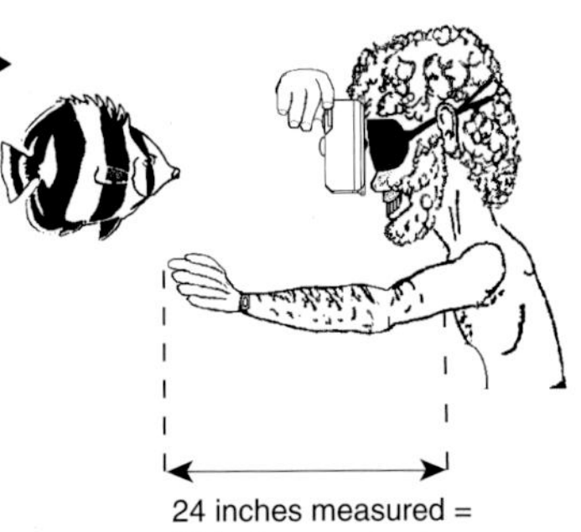

Camera Angles for Ambient Light Photography

The horizontal camera angle is the one you'll want to master. Don't shoot down at a subject; the image will be two-dimensional. Shoot at eye level or slightly upward. These are the most natural angles and enable you to achieve good color separation of subject and background. Always keep the sun behind you and facing the subject. Shooting into the sun results in washed-out, overexposed pictures.

There is an exception to this rule: *silhouettes*. This is one of the easiest types of available light photograph, and the images are striking. Position your subject in front of the sun and aim at an extreme upward angle toward the water surface. Try to get the subject to block the sun. The resulting picture will have a bright blue or green background, depending upon the waters you're in, and a dark, flat subject in the foreground, haloed by streaks of light. The recommended f-stop with ISO 100 is f/22. Recommended depth: 15-35 feet.

Using the Built-in Flash Underwater

The built-in flash has been designed primarily for land photography. It can be used successfully underwater only under optimum conditions; it should be used only in very clear water. Because the flash is in such close proximity to the lens, the illuminated particles in the water will be recorded as backscatter on the film. To minimize backscatter, always shoot as close as possible:

- at f/4.5⚡ minimum camera-to-subject distance is 3 apparent feet
- at f/11⚡ minimum camera-to-subject distance is 2.3 feet.

Do not use in depths shallower than 10 feet. The available light/flash combination will create an overexposure. You can use the built-in flash at depths below 10 feet. Use it on cloudy, overcast days. Use it on night dives.

The best way to achieve bright colorful pictures with this camera is to use an external electronic strobe. The YS-40 and its successor the YS-40A have been designed exclusively for use with the MX-10 camera. For details on how to use the YS-40 series strobes, turn to page 226.

Tips on Taking Good Underwater Pictures

Learning to take good underwater pictures is more than just knowing the fundamental principles of underwater photography. To a large degree, it is a trial-and-error process. A few general rules will help you get started:

- Be careful not to stir up the sea bed with your fins or gauges; carelessness causes backscatter.
- Hold the camera steady. If the current has you moving about, steady yourself by planting your feet firmly on the sea bottom or kneeling on the sand (not on the reef). Please do not grab any part of a reef to steady yourself. Better to lose the shot than kill the coral.
- Look for contrast between your subject and its background.

▼ To minimize vertical color absorption, confine your picture taking to depths of 10 to 15 feet when shooting with available light.

▼ To minimize horizontal color loss, shoot as close to your subject as the f-stop allows. The less water you shoot through, the sharper the image.

▼ Practice on stationary subjects.You must get proficient at estimating apparent distance, composition, and using the built-in light meter.

▼ To minimize backscatter in your photos when shooting on a stirred up sandy seabed, frame your subject against the sandy bottom and shoot at a slight downward angle. Backscatter will blend with the sand.

▼ In turbid conditions, shoot with the reef as your background.The particles in the water will blend with the clutter of colors and shapes of the reef.

▼ Don't throw away the bad shots. Study them. Try to figure out what you did wrong. Is the picture fuzzy because you were too close? Is the subject too tiny and too blue because you were too far? Is the image overexposed or underexposed? Do you know why?

The Most Important Tip

Know the range of capabilities of your camera. Don't expect your system to create images beyond its design limitations.

The MX-10 built-in lens will take excellent head-and-shoulder diver portraits, photos of medium-size fish, silhouettes, and reef scenics in clear water. It will not take a full-frame picture of a candy-banded shrimp. That type of image requires a macro lens. A photo of a shipwreck requires a super wide angle lens.

Don't attempt to create the kind of photo that requires a different lens from the one you're using. Many novices make this mistake and set themselves up for disappointment. Experienced underwater photographers know to select their subjects based on the system in hand.

The right size subjects for your 32mm lens

Medium-sized fish, buddy head shots, crinoids, featherstars, soft and hard corals, tube sponges, vase sponges, lobster, spider crabs, sea cucumber, anemones, starfish. Notice, except for fish and dive buddies, most of these subjects do not move very much. They are easy to photograph.

Oops!

Mistakes you may make. Here's what they'll look like.

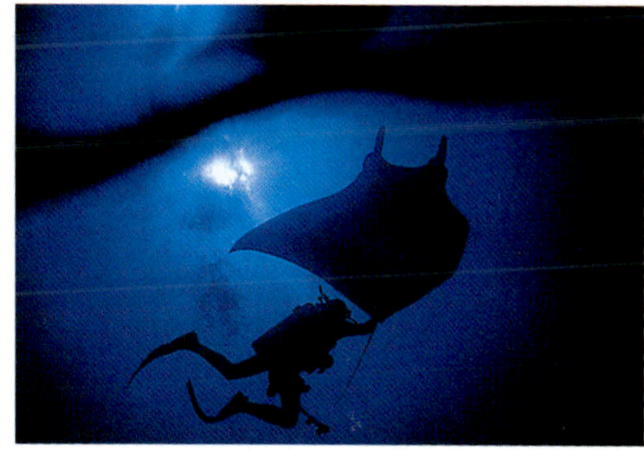

Stray Hand Strap

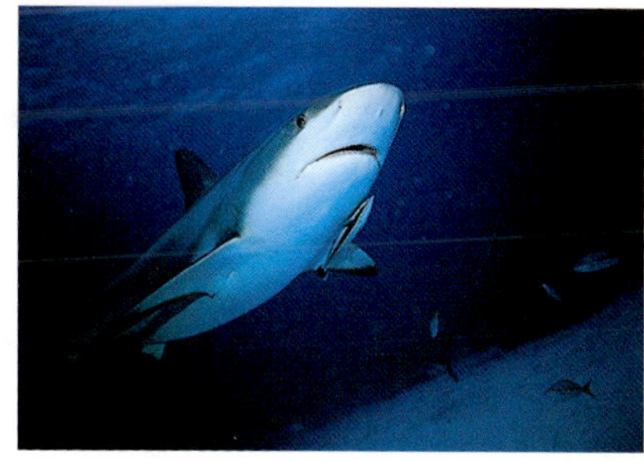

Backscatter

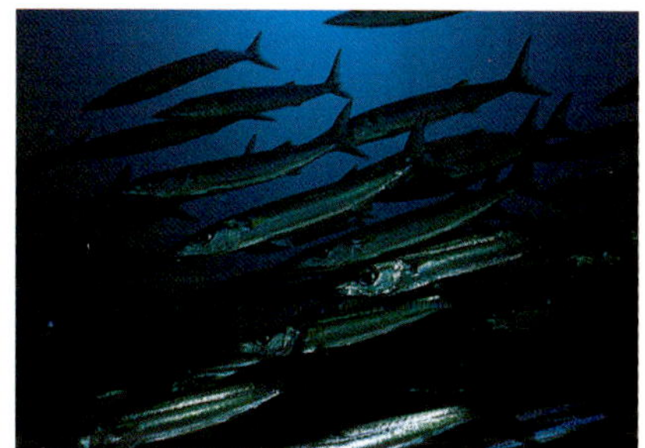

Underexposed

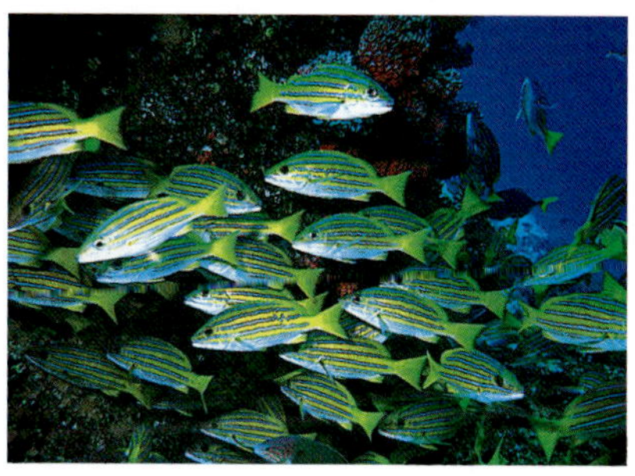

Overexposed

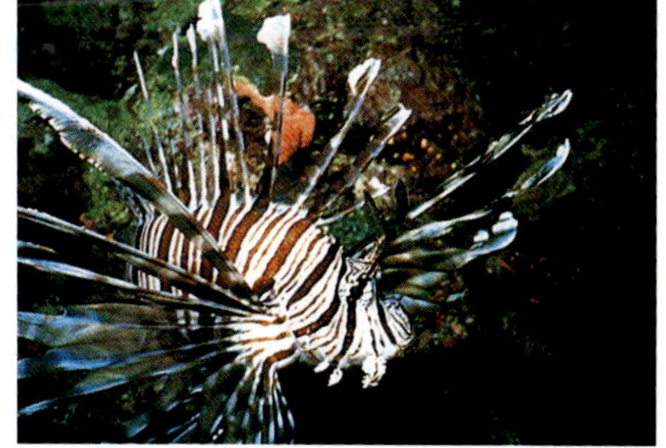

Too close

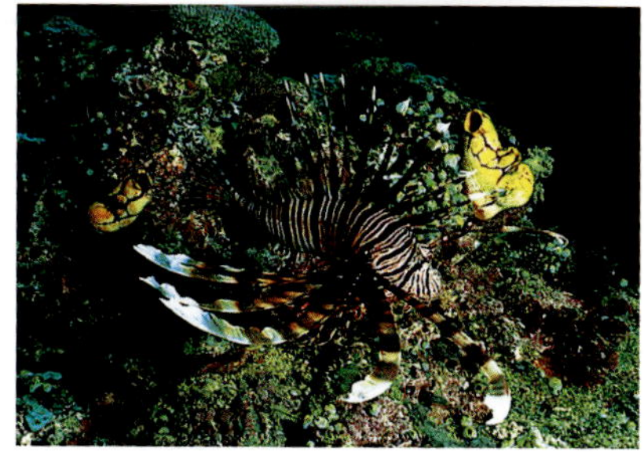

Just right

MX-10 Accessories You Should Know

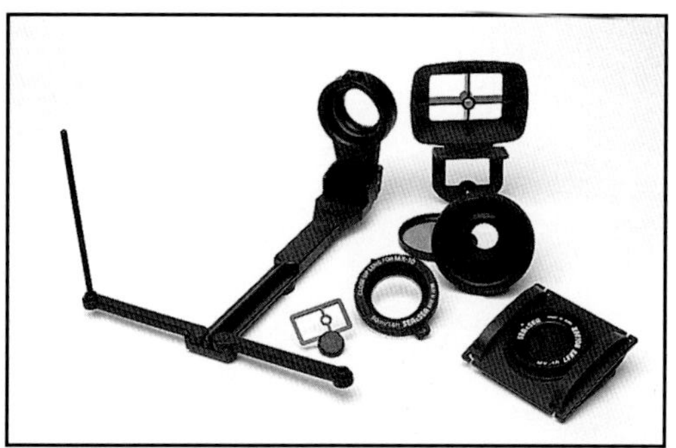

The MX-10 is an expandable system. When you've mastered the 32mm lens and feel ready to expand your range of images, you may purchase accessory equipment designed specifically for the MX-10. As of this writing, Sea & Sea offers three interchangeable lenses, each designed to produce a particular type of image that the 32mm lens cannot.

▼ The MX-10 20mm Wide Conversion Lens extends the angle of view of the built-in lens from 51° to 74.4° and reduces minimum focusing distance to 16 inches (at f/22). It is ideal for taking photographs of large fish, schools of fish, reef scenes, and fellow divers. It is paired with a Sportsfinder, a viewing aid that corrects for parallax and ensures accurate framing. See page 98.

▼ Companion 20mm U/W Color Correction Filter. You cannot restore actual color lost to absorption but a filter can enhance the warm hues for more natural-looking images. It mounts to the 20mm lens and can be attached and detached underwater.

▼ The MX-10 Macro Lens is designed for capturing big bold images of the sea's smaller subjects. It mounts to the built-in lens and reduces minimum focusing distance to nine inches from the focal plane. See page 148.

▼ The MX-10 Close-up Lens reduces minimum focusing distance to 18" at f/4.5, 12 inches at f/22. This is the lens of choice for bright, detailed images of subjects too small for the 32mm lens and too big for the macro lens. It comes with a snap-in parallax correcting viewing mask for accurate framing and composition. See page 140.

▼ All three lenses are equipped with a bayonet fitting that mounts to the front of the built-in lens as well as to the MX-10 Lens Caddy.

The MX-10 Lens Caddy is a convenient little holder with a bayonet mount that enables you to safely tote an extra lens. It attaches securely to the top of the strobe by two heavy-duty elasticized bands.

Unloading the Film

After all the frames have been exposed, the film rewind system is automatically activated, the film rewind switch automatically moves to the "R" (rewind) position, and the exposed film is rewound back into the film cassette. The motor drive is audible during operation. When the motor stops, you can safely open the film chamber door to remove the film. ▶

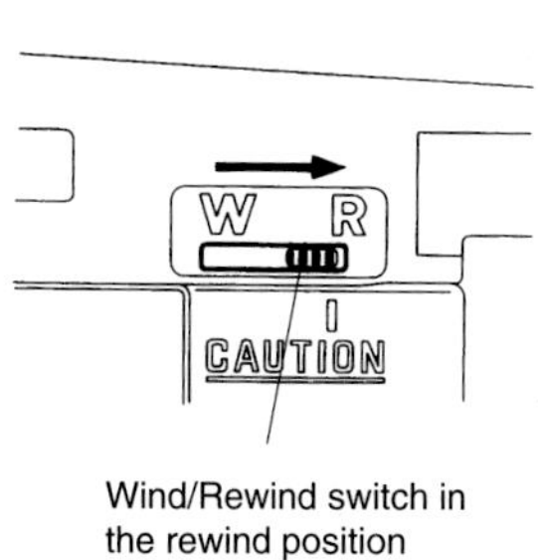

Wind/Rewind switch in the rewind position

Warning: If your batteries are drained, the rewind mechanism will not operate.

Tip: After removing the cassette from the camera, manually rewind the film tip all the way back into the cassette to avoid accidentally reloading the roll and shooting it again.

Care and Maintenance

To protect your camera from the corrosive effects of saltwater and to keep it functioning at its maximum efficiency, you must adhere to a program of meticulous care and maintenance. Chapter 9 provides detailed instructions. Please read it carefully. Neglect and/or improper care will not only result in poor pictures but will ruin your equipment and cause you unnecessary expense for repair.

One more tip . . . . ➤

Give Yourself a Break

There is no doubt, the images you see in diving magazines are awesome. They can also be somewhat intimidating. The authors of those images are professionals who have spent years perfecting their skills to attain such a lofty level of expertise and artistry.

Don't use those images as your standard. Don't think that because you have an underwater camera, that's what you must do with it. *Lighten up*. Take pictures to record your diving experiences and preserve the timeless memories. Make the good times last forever. Enjoy yourself.

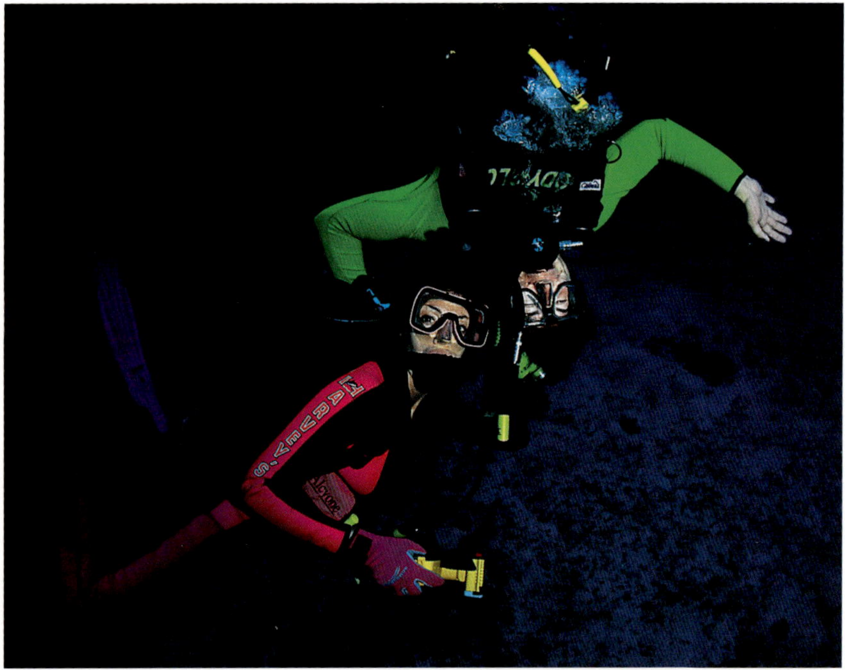

Cara, so happy, on her first dive with her son. Evan, newly certified and literally flipping with joy. Joe, behind the camera preserving the memory.

CHAPTER THREE

The Motor Marine II-EX

The Motor Marine II-EX

In the summer of 1989 Sea & Sea introduced the Motor Marine II and transformed the sport of underwater photography. Constructed of bright yellow polycarbonate, it became known as "the little yellow camera" that was unquestionably rugged and user friendly. Designed for complete ease of operation, it incorporated automatic film loading and film advance, power driven film rewind, automatic ISO indexing, an in-viewfinder LED with low exposure warning, flash readiness and TTL confirmation, and a built-in flash for topside photography. It had a built-in optical-quality 35mm lens and a revolutionary built-in close-up lens that reduced minimum focusing distance from three feet to 18 inches at the turn of a dial. It sported an exterior bayonet mount to accommodate macro and wide angle lenses that could be assembled and detached underwater, providing six focal length possibilities on any single dive. No other underwater camera could!

"But," skeptics asked, "can it take really good pictures?"

Yes, it could. The proof was in the pictures.

The little yellow camera challenged the supremacy of the Nikonos V. Demand for the camera grew wildly. *But...*

Underwater photographers wanted more. Some wanted a camera that just looked a little less cute and little more professional. So in late 1993 Sea & Sea released the Seamaster Pro, a steel-gray and yellow model.

But serious underwater photographers wanted a camera that not only looked "pro" but performed like one. Responding to the call for greater creative flexibility, Sea & Sea expanded the capabilities of the benchmark Motor Marine II and developed a more electronically sophisticated model: the Motor Marine II-EX.

The Motor Marine II-EX is lightweight and compact, like its predecessor, has the same body design and the same automatic features, only this model has the features photographers need for limitless creative control. For one, the MMII-EX offers variable shutter speeds; it is the world's first and only popularly-priced 35mm amphibious camera to synchronize for TTL flash photography at speeds of 1/15, 1/30, 1/60 and 1/125. It has automatic film indexing of three film speeds, a redesigned built-in flash that allows shutter-flash synchronization at 1/125 at any f-stop, and includes both film advance confirmation and low battery signals in the LED in-viewfinder panel.

The MMII-EX has been designed as a state-of-the-art system for underwater photographers of all skill levels. The novice can appreciate its ease of operation, the amateur its range of accessories and versatility, and the professional its superior performance.

The Motor Marine II-EX is a precision instrument, and for it to perform at its optimal efficiency, you must know how to use it. We will lead you through it step-by-step. Go slowly. Practice and allow your skills to build one upon another. Take lots of pictures and, most of all, have a good time!

Identification of Parts

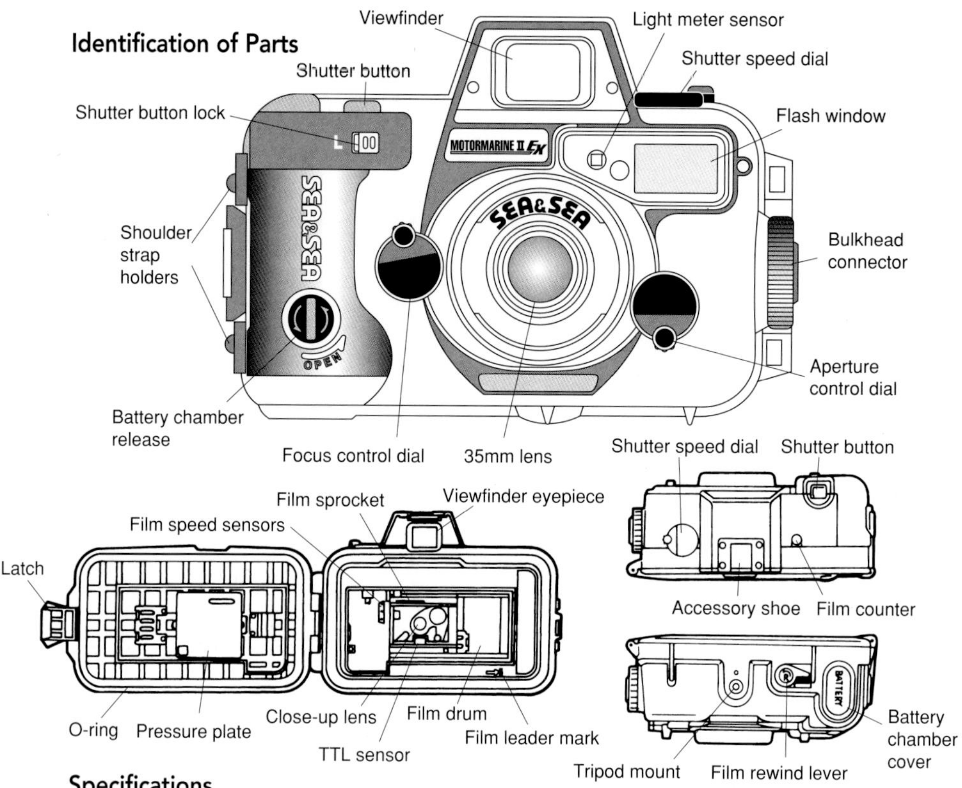

Specifications

Type of camera: 35mm amphibious camera
Construction: ABS molded polycarbonate
Maximum depth: 150 feet (45 meters)
Film format: 36mm x 24mm
Type film: Standard 35mm cartridge
Film speed: Automatically set at ISO 50, 100, 400 with DX coded film
Lens: 35mm f/3.5 (4 elements in 3 groups)
Angle of coverage: 62° land; 46° u/w
Shutter: Electronic shutter
Shutter speed: 1/15, 1/30, 1/60, 1/125 sec.
Exposure control: TTL or manual
Exposure meter: Built in with LED display
Aperture range: F/3.5 ~ f/22
Focal distance
- **35mm lens:** 3.3 feet ~ ∞ (1 m ~ ∞)
- **CU lens:** 18 inches (0.5m)

Film advance: Automatic
Film counter: Automatic
Film rewind: Motor driven
Viewfinder: 85% frame coverage
0.5 magnification
LED display:
- Low exposure warning
- TTL confirmation
- Internal or external flash ready light
- Film advance
- Battery check

Electronic flash: Built in; manual
GN (ISO 100): 10 (m); 32 (ft.) land
Synchronization: 1/125 second
Flash ready light: Built in
Power source: 2 1.5-volt AA batteries
Dimensions: 2.8 x 4.4 x 6.3" (L x W x H) (70 x 112 x 160 mm)
Weight: 1.4 lbs/22.6 oz. (640g) (incl. batteries)
Accessories included: Shoulder strap, back cover & battery cap O-rings, silicone grease, batteries, exposure decal

The Main Components

Despite its sophisticated electronic devices, the Motor Marine II-EX is essentially a box with five basic components:

Shutter

The Motor Marine II-EX has a electronic focal plane ▶ shutter. The top mounted shutter speed dial offers a selection of four shutter speeds: 1/15, 1/30, 1/60 and 1/125 second. All synchronize with an external strobe in both TTL and manual modes.

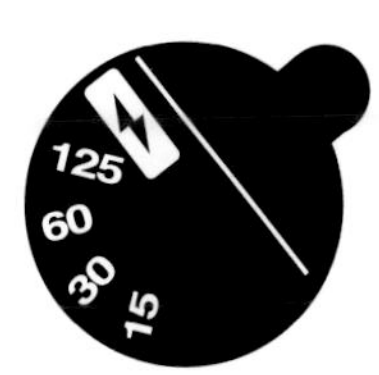

An additional setting marked by a thunderbolt (⚡) activates the built-in flash at 1/125 of a second for manual flash only. It operates at all f-stops.

Lens

The Motor Marine II-EX is an amphibious camera with a built-in amphibious lens. The term is derived from the Greek word "amphibious" which means "to lead a double life." And it does. The built-in 35mm lens can take pictures both on land and underwater. It provides 62° coverage on land and 46° underwater. The lens is protected and sealed by a circular glass window and is equipped with an exterior bayonet fitting to accommodate auxiliary lenses.

The dial on the front of the camera sets the focusing ▶ range of an image at various distances from the film plane. Two concentric half-circles of numerals in feet and in meters calibrate distance.

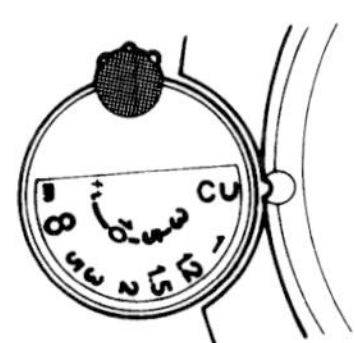

The camera also incorporates a built-in close-up lens which can focus to 18 inches. Turning the focus control dial to the "CU" position moves the close-up lens into the image path over the rear element of the 35mm lens.

Aperture

The aperture dial on the face of the camera has six pre-set f-stop positions, ranging from f/3.5 to f/22. To set the f-stop, simply rotate the aperture control dial from one click-stop to another. Icons for sunny, partially sunny, and cloudy conditions indicate approximate settings for topside photography.

Film Transport

Some 35mm cameras have a separate door that closes over the film compartment. The door on this camera is actually a *film pressure plate*, the purpose of which is to keep the film flat and unwrinkled as it moves from cartridge to take-up spool. The pressure plate of the MMII-EX is located on the inside of the back cover. When the back cover is closed, this support keeps the film flat on the film plane to ensure the sharpest possible image.

Viewfinder

The built-in viewfinder is multi-purpose. Interior etched frame lines delineate the area of coverage for the 35mm lens at a distance of 3 feet to infinity and parallax correction when shooting at minimum distance. There are separate guide marks for shooting with the close-up lens at a distance of 18 to 36 inches. An LED display panel indicates low light exposure, TTL confirmation, flash readiness, battery voltage, and film advance.

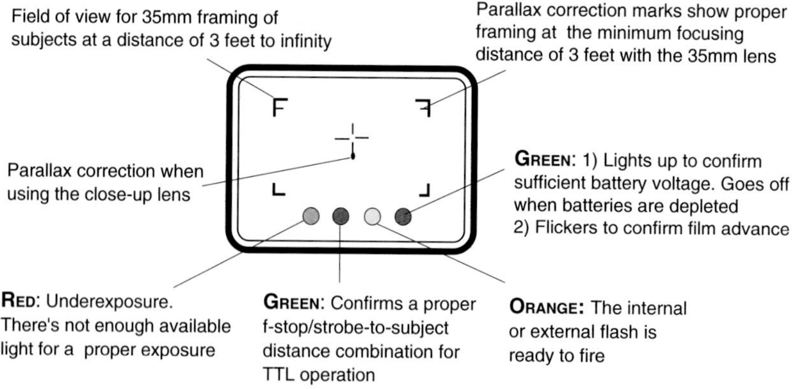

Important:

- The frame lines show only 85 percent of the true image area. Your photograph will reveal more of the scene than you expected and subjects will appear larger in the viewfinder than they will be on film. Compensate when composing your picture: disregard the frame lines and use the entire window to frame your subject.
- When you look through the viewfinder, the scene is always in focus. Don't let that mislead you. Your subject will be in focus only if it is within the focusing range of the lens.

Opening the Camera

1. Before you open the camera, inspect it thoroughly. Be sure the camera is completely dry and clean. If necessary, rinse it with fresh water and dry thoroughly with a soft, dry cloth.

2. Hold the camera with the back ▶ cover facing downward. *Always* open it in this position. This is a precautionary measure. If water or debris is trapped between the cover and the camera body, gravity will pull it out and away from the internal mechanism.

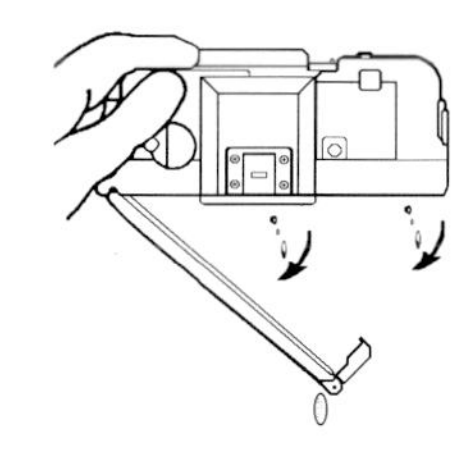

3. Push the back cover lock forward ▶ in the direction of the arrow. The latch will release; the back cover will open.

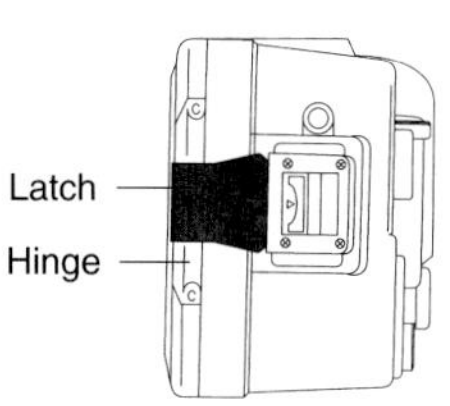

Caution: If the back cover doesn't pop open and appears to be "stuck," you have either a vacuum created by pressure or a dry O-ring. *Do not use the latch as a lever to open the back cover.* Undue pressure on the latch may cause it to break. Grasp the solid parts of the latch hinge with your forefinger and middle finger and firmly pull the door open. Never use a sharp object to pry it open.

The Essential O-ring

O-rings are the most important components of your camera system. They seal it and make it watertight. If an O-ring is damaged, deformed, or improperly seated in its channel, water can penetrate and flood the internal mechanism.

There are three serviceable O-rings on the Motor Marine II-EX: on the back cover, the battery chamber cover, the bulkhead connector cap.

Always examine all three of the O-rings before using the camera. Check for cuts, scratches, sand, etc. If any foreign matter is evident on any O-ring, remove the O-ring and clean it. If any damage or deformity is found, you will need to replace the O-ring with a new one.

How to remove the O-ring:

1. Press forward on the O-ring with ▶ thumb and forefinger. The O-ring will bulge out. Grasp it with your other hand and gently lift it from the groove. Do not yank it out or pull it. It can tear.

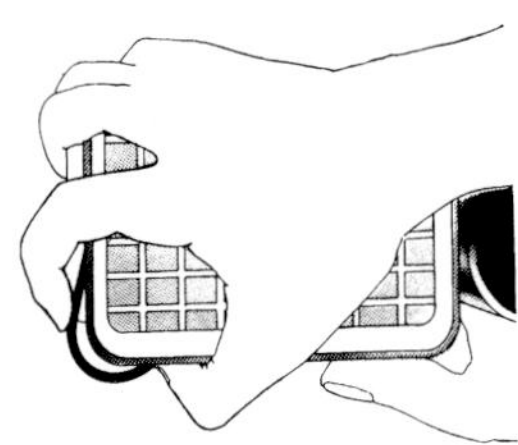

2. Use Sea & Sea's specially-made O-ring remover. Or use a plastic credit card with a rounded corner; slip the corner under the O-ring and gently lift the O-ring from its groove.

Warning! Never use a knife, screwdriver, or any sharp object to remove the O-ring. This can damage both the O-ring and the O-ring channel.

Gently wipe the O-ring with a soft, lint-free cloth. Sometimes it will be necessary to soak it in soapy water to dissolve salt deposits or accumulated lubricant. Dry it thoroughly. Lightly coat the O-ring with the recommended silicone grease. Use sparingly, as excessive grease will attract debris, which can cause flooding. Clean the O-ring channel with a cotton swab before replacing the O-ring. See Chapter 9 for step-by-step instructions.

Installing the Batteries

The Motor Marine II-EX is powered by two AA 1.5-volt alkaline batteries. *Do not use ni-cad batteries in this unit.*

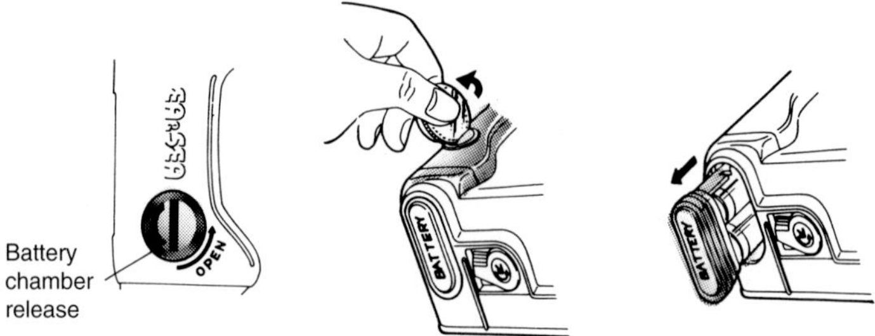

1. Hold the camera with the battery chamber facing downward. Use a coin to turn the battery chamber release counterclockwise 90°. The battery holder will slide out. If it doesn't, press the letter "B" on the battery cover while turning the release counterclockwise.

2. Pull out the battery pack. Insert batteries according to the illustration inside the compartment. Do not reverse polarity. The camera will not function if the batteries are installed incorrectly.

3. Inspect and service the O-ring on the battery pack cover.

4. Insert the battery holder into the battery chamber. Press down. You will hear a click. The chamber is now automatically locked.

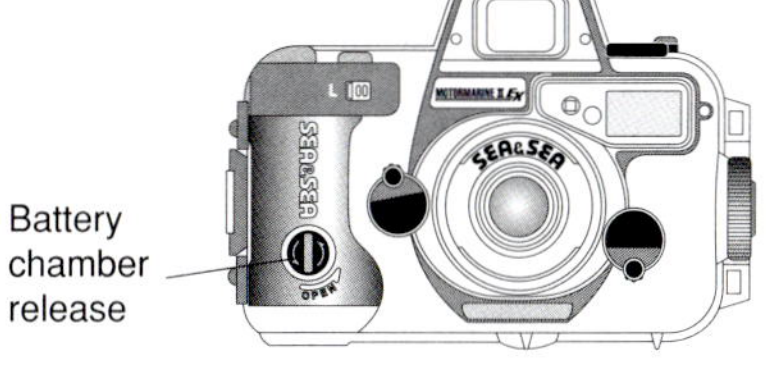

Warning: The battery chamber release is only for opening the battery cover. Once the battery holder snaps into place, the chamber is locked. Never turn it clockwise; you will damage the locking mechanism.

Recommended Battery Usage

- ▼ Always use batteries from the same manufacturer.
- ▼ Always use batteries with the same expiration date.
- ▼ Never mix old and new batteries.
- ▼ Never use batteries with different model numbers.
- ▼ Zinc carbon batteries may be used, but they yield fewer exposures than alkaline batteries.
- ▼ Store batteries in a cool, dry environment, such as the refrigerator.
- ▼ Allow batteries to warm to room temperature before inserting in your camera.

Loading the Film

The Motor Marine II-EX uses a standard 35mm film cartridge. The camera is equipped with an autoload device that simplifies film loading and makes it almost impossible for you to load incorrectly.

1. Inspect the back cover O-ring and O-ring channel for moisture, damage, debris. If necessary, clean or replace it.

2. Check for dust and film chips in the film transport area. Such material must be removed because it will scratch the film. Use a rubber syringe to blow the particles away.

3. Insert the flat end of the film cartridge into the film chamber cradle on the left, then lower the other end. Make sure the cartridge is seated in the chamber. ▶

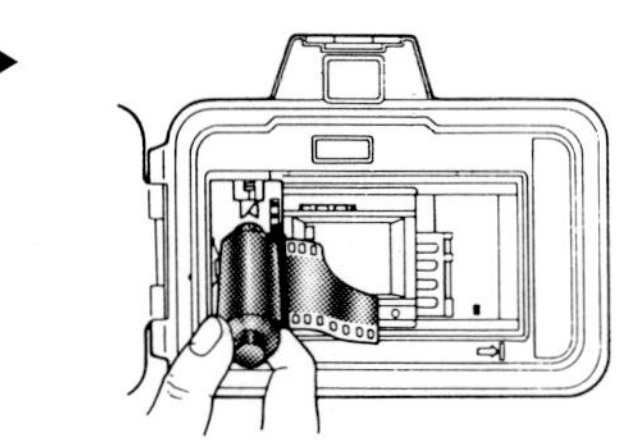

4. Pull out the leader from the cartridge and pull it straight across the back to the take-up spool on the right. ▶

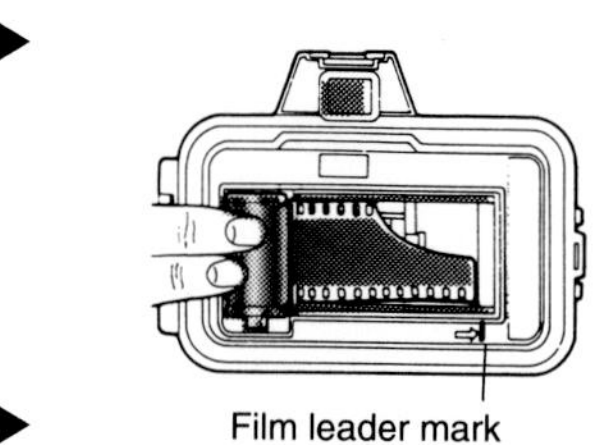

5. Be sure the edges of the film are positioned between the film guide rails. The sprocket holes must be securely fitted over the sprocket teeth. See that there is no slack. If the film has been properly seated, you will be able to read the exposure numbers printed along the edge of the film. ▶

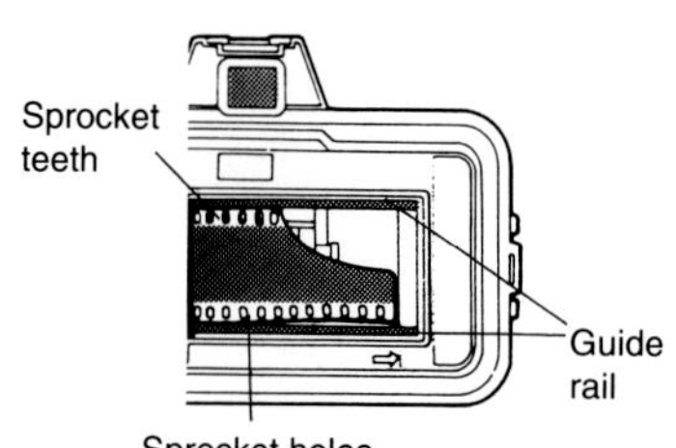

Note: Never load in direct sunlight. Stray light can leak into the cartridge and cause streaks of unwanted exposure. Load in subdued light or shield the film with a draped towel or your body.

Closing the Back Cover

The back cover is fitted with an O-ring that securely seals the internal mechanism against water. It locks by means of a sturdy plastic latch. Before closing the cover, check the O-ring one last time. Be sure it is clean and properly seated in its channel.

Hold the camera vertically in both hands. The latch must be forward and not up or the cover will not close. Push down on the cover. When the O-ring has seated against the camera body, snap the cover closed and secure the latch. ▶

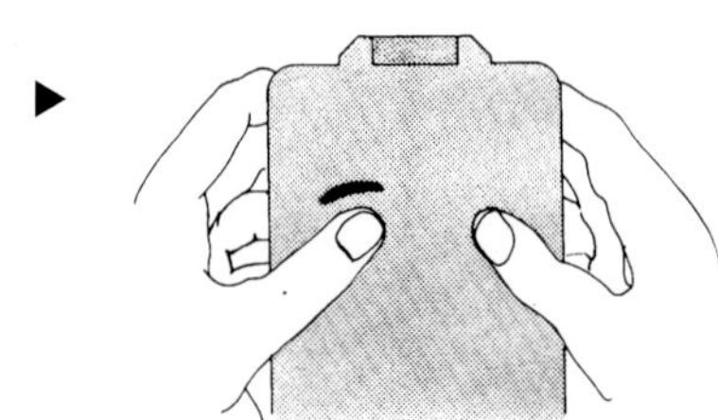

Automatic Film Advance

1. Unlock the shutter release by sliding the shutter button lock in the direction *opposite to* "L".
2. Depress the shutter button a few times.
3. While the film is advancing, check the LED inside the viewfinder. A green blinking light confirms that the film is advancing. If the light does not blink, the film is incorrectly loaded. Rewind the film, then open the back and repeat the above procedure. *(Note:* This indicator functions only when there is film in the camera.)
4. You are now ready to take pictures.

Film Speed

There is no need to set film speed. The camera does it for you. The MMII-EX is equipped with an electronic system called DX coding. DX coded films have a bar code imprinted on the cassette; this is actually a metal strip containing film speed information. When using DX coded film, the camera is programmed to read the magnetic data on the cassette and automatically adjust its internal metering circuitry for that film speed.

The MMII-EX metering system can read three film speeds when using DX coded film cassettes: ISO 50, ISO 100 and ISO 400. If the film cassette is DX coded and rated at a speed *other* than these, the meter will:

a) operate at ISO 50 with films rated lower than ISO 50
b) operate at ISO 100 with films rated lower than 400
b) operate at ISO 400 with films rated higher than 400.

If the cassette is not DX coded, the system will default to a setting of ISO 100.

Note: Any film speed can be used. However, you will not be able to use the internal light meter to select your f-stop because the metering system is programmed to function only with ISO 50, 100 and 400. So what can you do if you want to use a film other than 50, 100 or 400? You can use an external light meter. Or you can use the built-in meter and determine f-stop as follows:

▾ With ISO 25, the meter will convey exposure information as if the film were ISO 50. Compensate by opening up one f-stop.

▾ With ISO 200, the meter will convey exposure information as if it were ISO100. Compensate by stopping down one f-stop.

USING THE MOTOR MARINE II-EX TOPSIDE

We're going to start with topside photography for two reasons. One, the Motor Marine takes excellent pictures on land. It's the ideal camera for traveling. It's compact, rugged, and you don't have to worry about taking it to the beach or out on a boat; it's built to withstand the elements. So you'll want to use it topside.

The second reason we start with topside photography is to help you become familiar with the feel of the camera, the controls, and the sequence of steps involved in taking pictures in an environment you can control. It is more difficult to take pictures underwater than on land because everything is in constant motion—the water, your subjects, and you, too. If you practice using the camera on land, the picture-taking process will become almost second nature, so that later, when underwater, you can concentrate more on creativity and less on working knobs and levers.

Start by moving the shutter release button from the lock position (L) to the unlock position.

How to Hold the Camera

The Motor Marine II-EX is ergonomically designed for maximum comfort, balance, and ease of handling. Hold the camera cradled in your right hand with your right thumb nestled in the indentation in the back cover. Your elbow should be kept close to your body for maximum steadiness. Rest your index finger lightly on the shutter release button. When using an external strobe, your left hand will be supporting the strobe arm. When not using an external strobe, place your left thumb in the indentation on the back cover.

When taking pictures underwater, rest the camera lightly against your face mask.

Setting the Focus

The built-in 35mm lens has two controls fixed on the front of the camera: a focus control to the left of the lens and an aperture control dial to the right of the lens. You use the focus indicator to set for the correct lens-to-subject distance. Meters are designated in yellow numerals, feet in white. The correct setting for close-up photography is marked by "CU" in orange.

If you have a newer SLR land camera, you are probably accustomed to autofocusing and will have to get used to setting the Motor Marine II-EX for distance.When you look through the viewfinder, the subject will look sharp, perfectly focused, and you might assume that you've set for the correct distance. However, with underwater cameras the correct subject-to-camera distance is not automatic. You must estimate the distance and set the focus control for that distance every time.

- ▼ The 35mm lens can focus sharply on subjects from three feet (one meter) to infinity. If the subject is more than 16.5 feet (five meters) distant, set the focus at infinity.
- ▼ The built-in close-up lens can focus sharply on subjects at a distance of 18 inches (.5 meter) to 36 inches (one meter). Set the focus indicator at the "CU" position.

Setting the Shutter Speed

The Motor Marine II-EX has four shutter speeds: 1/15, 1/30, 1/60 and 1/125 second. Shutter speed is the length of time the shutter is open to allow light to expose the film. The longer the shutter is open, the more light enters. The shorter the shutter is open, the less light enters. Each consecutive shutter speed is approximately twice as fast as the one preceding. Therefore 1/30 allows twice the amount of light to enter as 1/15, 1/60 allows twice as much light as 1/30, and so on. The shutter speed dial sets the shutter so it remains open for the selected fraction of a second.

Shutter speed and aperture work together to control the light. Please turn to page 75 for more a more detailed explanation of the purpose of shutter speeds and their relationship with f-stops.

To set the shutter speed, simply rotate the shutter speed dial to align the selected shutter speed value with the indicator.

Note: You cannot set the shutter speed halfway between the given values. When set on the ⚡ position, the shutter speed is fixed at 1/125 for built-in flash operation.

Warning: Do not leave the shutter speed dial at the ⚡ position. This will drain the batteries.

Setting the Exposure

To select the proper f-stop for ambient light conditions, you adjust the exposure by means of the aperture control dial. A built-in light meter (also called an *exposure meter*) will measure the amount of available light and calculate the correct aperture for a proper exposure. The information will be relayed via the LED display in the viewfinder. We discuss exposure meters in greater detail on page 76.

1. Set the aperture control dial at f/22.

2. Depress the shutter button halfway while looking through the viewfinder eyepiece.

3. If the LED light *does not* come on, you have the correct f-stop for a correct exposure. You can take the picture. But if a red light comes on (the low exposure warning lamp), you do not have sufficient light for a proper exposure. You must change your f-stop for a larger aperture. Reset the f-stop to f/16 and repeat the procedure.

4. If the red lamp glows at this f-stop, you must reset to f/11. If necessary, reset again at f/8, again at f/5.6, and yet again at f/3.5.

5. If the red lamp appears at f/3.5, you cannot take the picture using available light. You need artificial light for a proper exposure.

Using the Built-in Flash On Land

The built-in electronic flash may be used indoors or outdoors when ambient light is insufficient for a proper exposure.

When using the built-in flash with the 35mm lens:

1. To activate the flash, rotate the shutter speed dial to the ⚡ position. Shutter speed is automatically fixed at 1/125 second.
2. An orange ready lamp will appear in the viewfinder, indicating the flash is ready to fire.
3. Set the camera focus control dial for the camera-to-subject distance.
4. Select desired f-stop. Determine by using the standard guide number formula. See page 209. The guide number for the flash is 33 (feet)/ 10 (meters). Or use the following rule-of-thumb chart:

Strobe-to-Subject Distance						
Feet	**3**	**4**	**5**	**6**	**8**	**10**
Meters	**1**	**1.2**	**1.5**	**1.8**	**2.4**	**3.3**
ISO 50	f/8	f/5.6	f/3.5	f/3.5	-	-
ISO 100	f/11	f/8	f/5.6	f/5.6	f/3.5	-
ISO 400	f/22	f/16	f/11	f/8	f/5.6	f/3/5

With the built-in close-up lens:

1. To activate the flash, rotate the shutter speed dial to the ⚡position. Shutter speed is automatically fixed at 1/125 second.
2. An orange ready lamp will appear in the viewfinder, indicating the flash is ready to fire.
3. Set the focus control dial at the "CU" position.
4. Select desired f-stop. Determine by using the standard guide number formula. Or use the following rule-of-thumb chart:

Strobe-to-Subject Distance			
Feet	**1.5**	**2**	**3**
Meters	**0.45**	**0.6**	**1**
ISO 50	f/16	f/11	f/8
ISO 100	f/ 22	f/16	f/11
ISO 400	-	-	f/22

Best results are achieved with ISO 100 at 18 to 25 inches.

Note: To conserve battery power, do not leave the shutter speed indicator at the ⚡ position.

Taking the Picture

Look through the viewfinder to correct for parallax. Compose your picture. Depress the shutter button firmly. The camera is equipped with a motor driven film advance. Every time you depress the shutter, the film will automatically advance by one frame and the shutter is cocked for the next frame.

Note: If there are no batteries in the camera or if the batteries are exhausted, the shutter button will depress but the shutter will not trigger and the film will not advance.

Tips on Topside Photography

▼ The lens records everything indiscriminately in its view. What you may not notice when viewing the scene through the viewfinder, the lens will. Pay attention to what surrounds your subject. Keep your subject matter simple.

▼ The best time of day to take topside pictures is early morning and late afternoon when the sun is near the horizon and the light is diffused.

▼ Overcast conditions are also favorable. They create softer shadows. If you are taking pictures of people, they are less likely to squint and you can get more natural facial expressions.

▼ Place the horizon high in the photo to emphasize the foreground and impart a sense of closeness. Place it low in the horizon to emphasize the background and provide a feeling of distance and space. Avoid placing the horizon dead center. That's boring.

▼ Don't cut off hands, feet, or tops of heads.

▼ Frame your subject with tree branches, arches, doorways, anything which will eliminate empty sky in the background and provide a near/far effect.

▼ Don't try to cram the whole scene into the shot. Keep the image simple. If it's a really interesting scene, take several shots, each with a separate and distinct point of view. Busy is not better.

And on Topside Flash Photography

When natural light is insufficient or when shooting indoors or when shooting at night, you will need to use a flash. You may use the built-in flash but beware of red-eye, which is caused by the flash being parallel to the lens. Better results will be achieved with an external strobe. Be sure to read Chapter 7, *Strobes.*

The Most Important Tip

Know the limitations of your equipment. The built-in 35mm lens has an angle of coverage of 62° on land. It is capable of taking a great picture of your baby blowing out the candles on her birthday cake but not of Dan Marino throwing a pass on a football field. For that type of picture you would need a telephoto lens. Remember, different lenses are designed to do different jobs. Don't expect your equipment to do more than it was designed to do and you won't be disappointed. Work within the limits of its capabilities. Learn to use the features creatively, and you will have wonderful pictures to show for it.

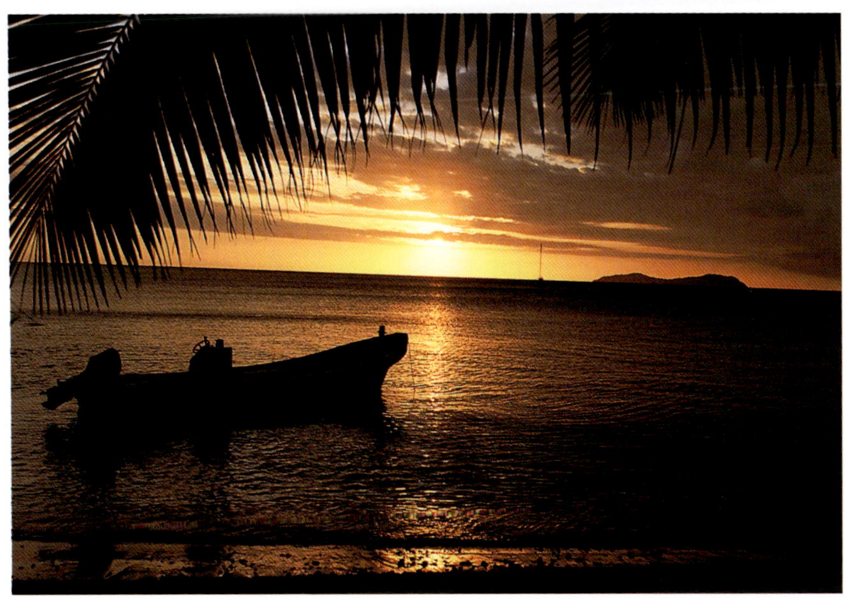

*With the 35mm lens,
you can capture
Fiji's teeming reefs
by day, its coppery
tranquility at dusk.*

UNDERWATER PHOTOGRAPHY

Okay, so you've mastered the camera on land and you're all set to get it wet. But wait! Not yet! We've work to do first. In underwater photography, it's a cardinal rule: *check your gear before you use it.* Check all ports, internal systems and controls on your camera and strobe before you dive. Conduct your check before loading the film; this way you won't waste a single frame.

Pre-dive Checklist

1. O-rings
2. batteries
3. shutter
4. motor drive
5. aperture control
6. focus lever
7. 35mm lens
8. close-up lens
9. back cover
10. film counter
11. internal flash
12. external strobe
13. TTL

1. Inspect the **O-rings**. Are they clean, in perfect sealing condition? Freshly lubricated? Are they properly seated in their channels?

2. Have you installed new **batteries** in your camera? Always check your batteries. They provide the power for operating the camera's electronic system. When in doubt, remove the battery and test with a battery tester.

3. Check the **shutter.** Open the back cover of the camera. Set the aperture at f/3.5 and depress the shutter button. Hold the camera up to the light and look inside. The shutter blades should open and close quickly, revealing an aperture diameter of about 1/4". Now rotate the aperture to f/22 and again depress the shutter button. This time the aperture diameter should close down to the size of a pinhead.

4. Notice that after depressing the shutter button, take-up spool and sprocket teeth rotate clockwise. This is evidence that the **motor drive** is working.

5. Test the **aperture control.** Even if the dial rotates normally, it doesn't mean that the aperture is changing. Look into the lens and slowly turn the aperture control the full range of the scale one way and then the other. The opening should open and close smoothly and easily.When turning the aperture control dial, you will feel distinct clicks as you change f-stops. The dial will not rotate smoothly but will move from click-stop to click-stop.

6. Test the **focus control**. Look into the lens while rotating the focus dial from minimum distance to infinity and back again. The lens will move approximately 1/16" up and down. If your camera fails either of these tests, don't attempt to use it. When a dial or knob or button does not move with the usual ease, something is wrong. *Do not force it.* Take the camera to a qualified repair facility.

7. Examine the front elements on your **35mm lens** for fingerprints, grease, salt deposits, etc. Inspect front and rear elements on your accessory lenses. Clean if necessary.

8. Look into the back of the camera and rotate the focus dial to the "CU" position. This should move the **close-up lens** into place over the rear of the primary lens. Now rotate the focus dial out of the "CU" position; the close-up lens should move entirely out of the area of the primary lens.

9. After loading the film, check that the **back cover** is securely closed.

10. Look at the **film counter** window to confirm that the camera is counting each frame as the film is advanced.

11. Check the **built-in electronic flash**. Turn the shutter speed dial to the flash position. The ready light will illuminate. If it doesn't, install fresh batteries.

12. Perform an **external strobe** check. Attach the sync cord to the bulkhead connector. Turn the strobe to the "On" position. When the ready light glows, trigger the shutter. The flash will fire. Time how long it takes to recycle. If it takes longer than double the manufacturer's recommended recycle time, your batteries are low and need to be changed or charged.

13. To test the **TTL**, set the lens at any f-stop. Point strobe into camera lens from about a foot away. Trigger the shutter. The green light in the viewfinder and the green light on the strobe will illuminate for about three seconds. If they do not come on, the TTL isn't working and the strobe is delivering a full power flash only.

Reviewing the Basics

▼ The difference between photography in air and underwater is the density of the medium you shoot through.

▼ As light travels through water, light rays are bent, making objects appear larger and closer than they really are.

▼ An exposure is created when light passes through the lens and strikes the film plane.

▼ Aperture controls the amount of light that strikes the film and shutter controls the duration.

▼ The size of the opening of the lens through which light can enter can be adjusted by changing the f-stop.

▼ When you focus on a particular subject, there is an area in front of and behind your subject that is in sharp focus. This is depth of field.

▼ To reduce absorption and minimize backscatter, the closer you get to your subject the better.

Focusing

The behavior of light underwater creates an optical illusion. Objects appear 25 percent closer than they actually are. This is called *apparent distance.* The lens on your camera also sees apparent distance. Therefore, you must always set your subject-to-camera focusing distance for apparent distance.

Estimating Distance

Judging apparent distance accurately takes practice. Some photographers carry a measured length of string with them. We prefer the "arms's length" method.

Extend your arm. From bicep to fingertips is approximately two feet *measured* distance. That is equivalent to one-and-a-half feet *apparent distance.* Two such lengths would be three apparent feet. Three lengths is equivalent to four-and-a-half apparent feet. With practice, you'll get the hang of it.

Parallax Error

The lens and the viewfinder are located at different positions on the camera. The viewfinder is situated approximately two inches above the lens. Therefore, the scene you see through the viewfinder is not the same as what the lens is seeing. What you see is not what you'll get. This is called *parallax error.*

The solution is to use the parallax correction marks etched inside the viewfinder. By framing your subject within these marks, you automatically tilt the lens enough to frame your subject correctly.

Setting the Shutter Speed

Shutter speed controls the duration of time the shutter will be open. It therefore determines how long the film will be exposed to light. It also affects how moving subjects will be recorded. Fast shutter speeds can freeze motion, recording moving subjects in sharp focus. Moving subjects with slow shutter speeds will blur because the subject was moving during the exposure. Slow shutter speeds are more effective with stationary subjects; they permit more light to strike the film and therefore provide brighter pictures.

Shutter speed selection is also determined by water conditions. For dark or murky water conditions, you would tend toward a slower shutter speed to get more light on your subject. You would also favor a slower shutter speed to extend depth of field with a smaller aperture.

There is a reciprocal relationship between shutter speed and aperture. Proper exposure isn't just one shutter speed/f-stop combination. It's a number of them. If you change the shutter speed one step, such as from 1/125 to 1/60, you can maintain the same exposure by changing the f-stop one step, such as from f/8 to f/11.

For example, if any one of the following is a correct exposure, then all of the following are correct exposures: 1/125 at f/8, 1/60 at f/11, 1/30 at f/16, 1/15 at f/22.

These pictures, taken on Joe's teaching reef, illustrate the effect of shutter speed on exposure. All were taken at f/8, but at different shutter speeds. Note the differences in brightness and color saturation.

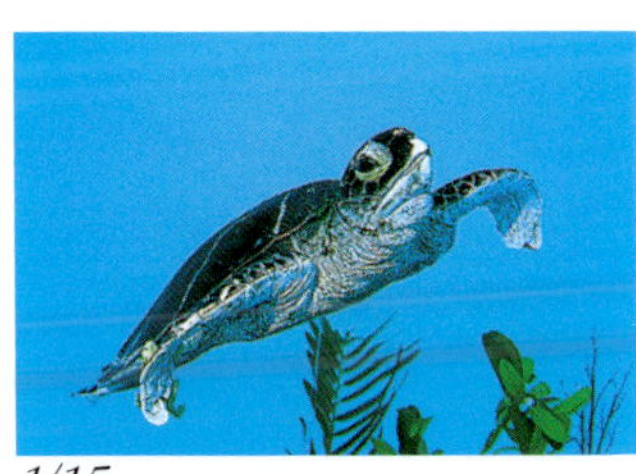

1/15

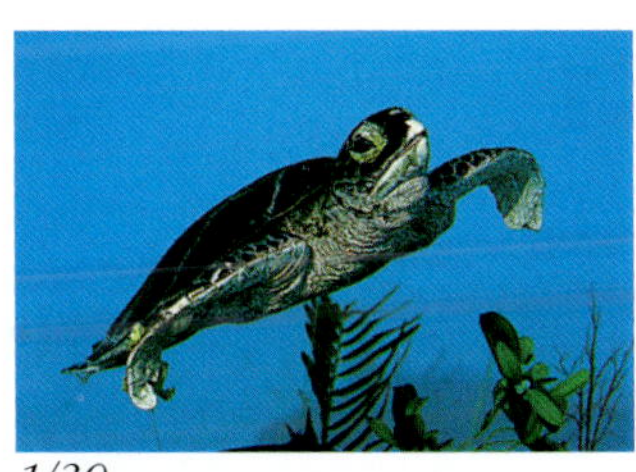

1/30

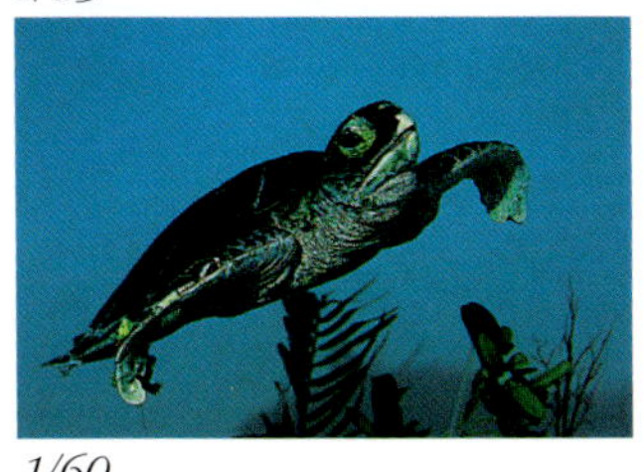

1/60

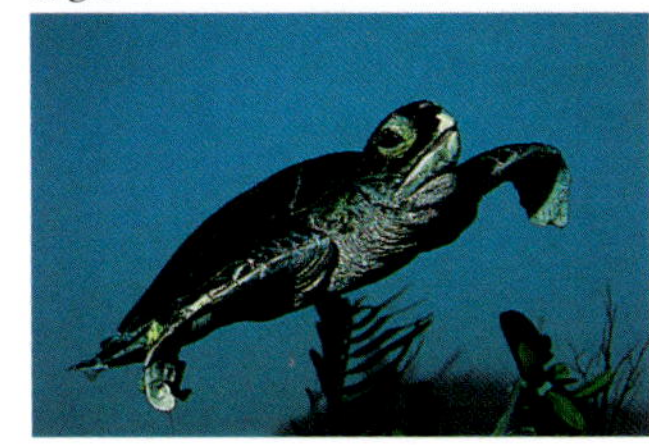

1/125

Setting the Exposure for Ambient Light Photography

After you've set the focus control for subject-to camera distance, you must determine which f-stop to use. For this you use the built-in light meter.

There are two types of light meters. An *incident light meter* reads the light striking the subject. A *reflected light meter* measures the amount of light reflected from your subject. The Motor Marine II-EX has a reflected light meter. It measures a wide area, not just the subject you're pointing at. It measures all the light, medium, and dark tones in its angle of view, adds them up, and then averages them to a medium gray. The exposure information in the viewfinder is based on the light the meter reads as medium gray.

The Motor Marine II-EX has a *center-weighted metering pattern*. This means the light sensors are designed to respond more to the light near the center of your viewfinder than to the outer edges. The light reflected from this area is what you want to measure. Therefore, this "center" area is given more "weight" or significance than the areas toward the outside of the frame.

To determine the f-stop for a correct exposure, select a shutter speed, then adjust the aperture control dial until the low exposure warning signal inside the viewfinder does *not* come, indicating sufficient light.

1. Set the shutter speed at 1/125.
2. Set the aperture control at f/16.
3. Look through the viewfinder and depress the shutter button halfway.
4. Exposure is correct unless the red lamp glows, indicating a low exposure. You need more light for a correct exposure. You may choose a larger aperture or a slower shutter speed.
5. Either open up to f/11 or set the shutter speed dial at 1/60.
6. Looking through the viewfinder, depress the shutter release button halfway. If there is no red low exposure warning, you have the correct combination of shutter speed and aperture for a proper exposure.
7. If the red lamp appears, you still do not have enough light for a proper exposure; reset to f/8 or the shutter speed to 1/30.

Warning: A shutter speed of 1/30 may create blurred images of moving subjects. This shutter speed is best-suited for shooting stationary subjects and when used with a very small aperture and a slow film speed such as ISO 50. Best results with ISO 100 film and the 35mm lens will be achieved at 1/60 or 1/125 second.

8. If necessary, reset the aperture, always checking the LED for the low exposure warning, until you are set at f/3.5.
9. If at f/3.5 the red lamp appears, you must use artificial illumination.

Rule-of-Thumb Exposures*

Depth	F-stop
10'	f/11
20'	f/8
40'	f/5.6
60'	f/3.5

Note: One f-stop for every 10'

* Based on ISO 100

Note: Because the meter averages all the tones in the scene, if you have a very light or very dark subject, the exposure recommendation can be wrong. Be sure to get close to your subject and exclude as much as possible of the background from the meter's angle of view.

Tip: Bracket! How to on page 82.

Don't Forget Depth of Field

The proper combination of shutter speed and aperture will produce a properly exposed image. But there is one more factor to consider: depth of field. Remember from Chapter 1, depth of field is the *zone of sharp focus*. The size of the aperture you select will affect the sharpness of the image. Every lens is designed with a range of sharpness at each f-stop. The following table shows the depth of field (range of sharpness) for your 35mm lens at each f-stop and each focus setting. *All figures are in feet.*

Focus Setting	f/3.5	f/5.6	f/8	f/11	f/16	f/22
10	7~17	6~29.6	5~∞	4.4~∞	3.5~∞	2.8~∞
5	4.2~6.3	3.8~7.4	3.4~9.4	3~14	2.6~∞	2.2~∞
3	2.7~3.4	2.5~3.7	2.4~4.1	2.2~4.8	1.9~6.7	1.7~12.4

Note: Best range of focus for any given f-stop with the 35mm lens is three feet to infinity. Objects closer than three feet will soften and be out of focus.

Tips for Ambient Light Photography

- The best time of day is when the sun is directly overhead, between 10 a.m. and 2 p.m.
- Weather and water surface conditions affect ambient light photographs. Bright sunny days and calm seas are best.
- Vertical color loss increases with depth. To retain the warm colors in your pictures, stay in shallow water.
- Keep the sun behind you and facing the subject.
- Shoot in clear water only.
- To minimize horizontal color loss, shoot as close to your subject as possible. Best shooting range is between three and five feet.
- Camera angle should be horizontal or slightly upward.
- Experiment with silhouettes.

See page 80: *Tips for Taking Good Pictures* and page 83: *More Tips.*

Using the Built-in Flash Underwater

The built-in flash is best used for taking pictures on land. Its effectiveness underwater is limited because the flash is in alignment with the lens and the angle of the reflected light will cause backscatter. The internal flash can be used in emergency situations when an external strobe is unavailable or is malfunctioning. Use only in very clear water.

Note: The following information on how to use the built-in flash underwater is not an endorsement for such use. We do recommend you purchase an external strobe. All Sea & Sea strobes with a four-pin connector are compatible with the Motor Marine II-EX. See Chapter 7 for details.

The internal flash is activated when the shutter speed dial is set at the flash (⚡) position. The shutter speed is automatically set at 1/125 second. The internal flash operates in manual mode only; it does not operate in TTL. Shutter and flash will sync at any f-stop.

With the 35mm lens:

1. Set the shutter speed dial at the ⚡ position. An orange ready lamp will appear in the viewfinder, indicating the flash is ready to fire.
2. Set the focus control for the camera-to-subject distance. Remember to set for apparent distance.

3. Set the aperture control at desired f-stop. The guide number for the flash is 33 feet/10 meters on land. The underwater GN is 1/2 the land value. Therefore, the GN is rounded off to 16.Use the standard guide number formula on page 209 or the following rule-of-thumb table.

Strobe-to-Subject Distance				
Feet	**3**	**4**	**5**	**6**
Meters	**1**	**1.2**	**1.5**	**1.8**
ISO 50	f/5.6	f/3.5	-	-
ISO 100	f/8	f/5.6	f/3.5	-
ISO 400	f/16	f/11	f/8	f/5.6

With the close-up lens:

1. To activate the flash, set the shutter speed dial at the ⚡position. An orange ready lamp will appear in the viewfinder, indicating the flash is ready to fire.
2. Set the focus control at the "CU" position.
3. Set f-stop. Use the standard guide number formula or the following rule-of-thumb table.

Strobe-to-Subject Distance			
Feet	**1.5**	**2**	**3**
Meters	**0.45**	**0.6**	**1**
ISO 50	f/5.6	f/5.6	f/3.5
ISO 100	f/16	f/11	f/8
ISO 400	-	f/22	f/16

Best results are achieved with ISO 100 at 18 to 25 inches.

Warning: Do not leave the shutter speed dial set at the ⚡ position. It will drain the batteries.

Tip: Before the dive, copy the f-stop/distance data for the ISO film you are using onto a strip of surgical adhesive tape. Tape to the back of your camera.

Tips on Taking Good Underwater Pictures

Learning to take good underwater pictures is more than just knowing the fundamental principles of underwater photography. To a large degree, it is a matter of trial and error. You will need to become proficient at judging apparent distance underwater. You will need to practice composition and lighting. You will need to get adept at matching your subject to your lens.

The most common mistake beginners make with the 35mm lens is to attempt to take in too much of the scene. To get the whole wreck or whole school of fish, you must back off so far from the subject that you will lose color, contrast and sharpness.

The second most common mistake is to photograph a subject that is too small for this lens. If you move in close enough to fill the frame, the subject will be out of focus. If you can reach out and touch the subject, you're too close.

BE AWARE DOWN THERE! Showing respect for the underwater environment is another good photographic technique.

- ▾ Don't touch or take
- ▾ Don't kneel or lean or sit or stand on any living thing
- ▾ Don't let your octopus or gauges drag or bump
- ▾ Don't stir up the bottom with your fins
- ▾ Weight yourself for neutral buoyancy

Showing respect will keep the water clear of disturbed silt, sand and debris that will end up as backscatter in your pictures and you'll be doing your part to keep our seas alive.

A few tips to help you get started:

- ▾ To avoid blur, hold your camera steady and your body still. Press the viewfinder eyepiece lightly against your face mask.
- ▾ Release the shutter by applying gentle pressure, not a "push" to the shutter release button. Release the shutter right after exhaling. That's when you're steadiest.
- ▾ Should you or another diver stir up the bottom, wait for the debris to settle or move on to a site that is clear.
- ▾ Practice on stationary subjects so you have plenty of time to adjust controls.
- ▾ Look for contrast between your subject and its background.
- ▾ Bracket.
- ▾ Don't throw out the bad pictures. Study them and learn from your mistakes.

More tips in Chapter 8: *Composition*.

Oops!

Mistakes you may make. Here's what they'll look like.

Wrong focus setting, backscatter

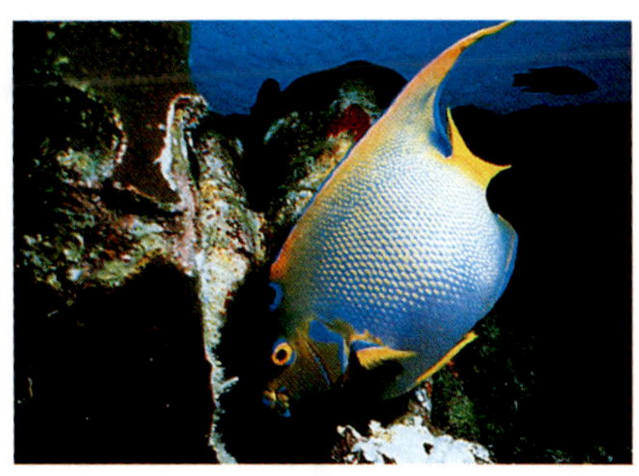

Too close, overexposed

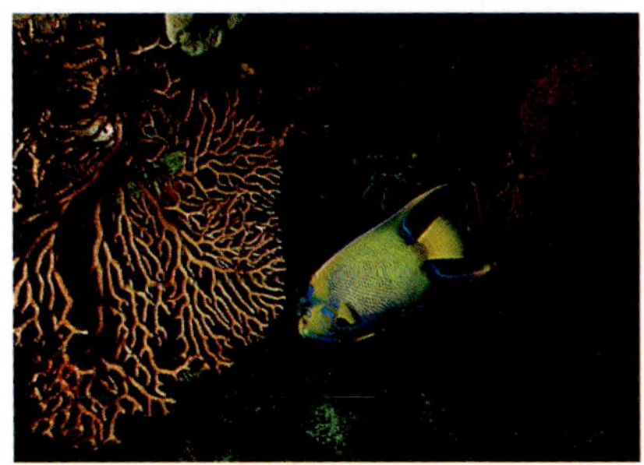

Too far, underexposed

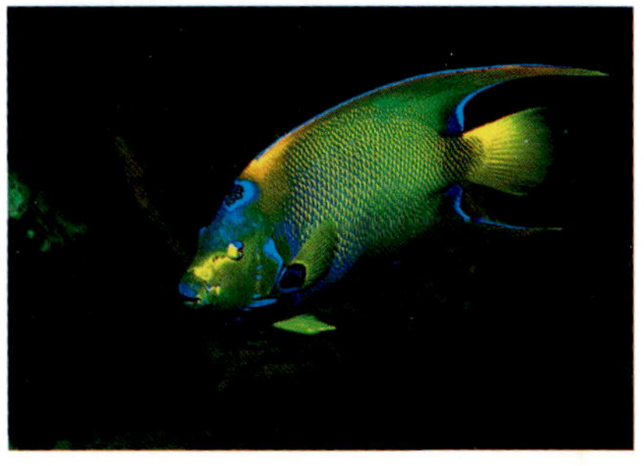

Too close, underexposed

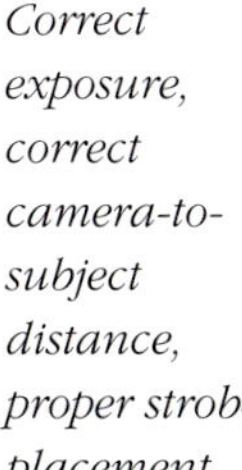

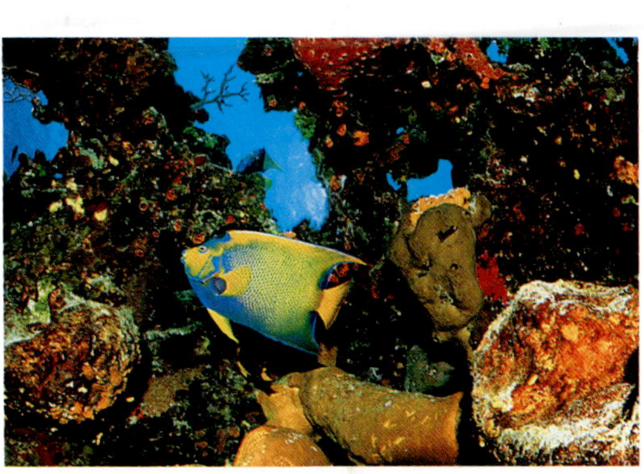

Correct exposure, correct camera-to-subject distance, proper strobe placement

How to Bracket

The term bracket means taking three pictures of the same subject at three different exposures. There are several ways to alter exposures.

Statistics Back up Bracketing
Results of a year-long survey by a large West Coast processing lab found that the number one cause of ruined or wasted film was due to underexposure. Don't take chances: bracket.

When shooting ambient light or with an external strobe in manual mode:

1. Change the f-stop. Take the picture using three different f-stops. For instance, if the light meter indicates that f/8 is the correct f-stop for a proper exposure, take two more to be on the safe side. Take one with more light at f/5.6 and one with less light at f/11. One should be just right.

2. Change the shutter speed. For example, if shutter speed is set at 1/60, change to 1/125 or 1/30. Do not change the f-stop.

When shooting with an external strobe in TTL mode:
When using your strobe in TTL mode, it is impossible to bracket in the same manner as when using it in manual mode. No matter which f-stop you select, the TTL sensor will automatically compensate for the measured light reflecting off the film plane. Therefore, we must intentionally over or underexpose to create different exposures.

1. Bracket by altering strobe-to-subject distance. Take your first picture at the recommended f-stop and strobe-to-subject distance. Then remove your strobe from the base plate and handhold it, or if using a Sea Arm V, adjust the arm so that you can move the strobe toward your subject or away from it. One foot forward or backward will effectively change your exposure by one f-stop.

2. Bracket by changing shutter speed. Change it one speed faster and one speed slower than the recommended exposure. Do not change f-stop.

More Tips: Camera Angles

There are three basic camera angles: *down, horizontal,* and *up.* Downward shots tend to be popular with novices. Unfortunately, they produce the least pleasing effect. When you shoot down at a fish, you get a two-dimensional picture. The subject blends with the sea bed. And since looking down isn't how we view the world, the image isn't natural.

Horizontal or slightly upward camera angles are the most natural and allow you to achieve attractive contrast, known as *separation.* Position your camera level with or just below your subject.

Silhouettes: Up and Easy

Silhouettes are one of the easiest photos to take, and the results are striking. Silhouettes are taken with the extreme upward angle. They are taken using only available light. Frame your subject in front of the sun, blocking the direct rays from the lens. Shoot upward toward the surface. To record a silhouette, the subject should appear black, distinctly contrasted against the open water background. Use f/22, ISO 100 film, and a shutter speed of 1/125 second.

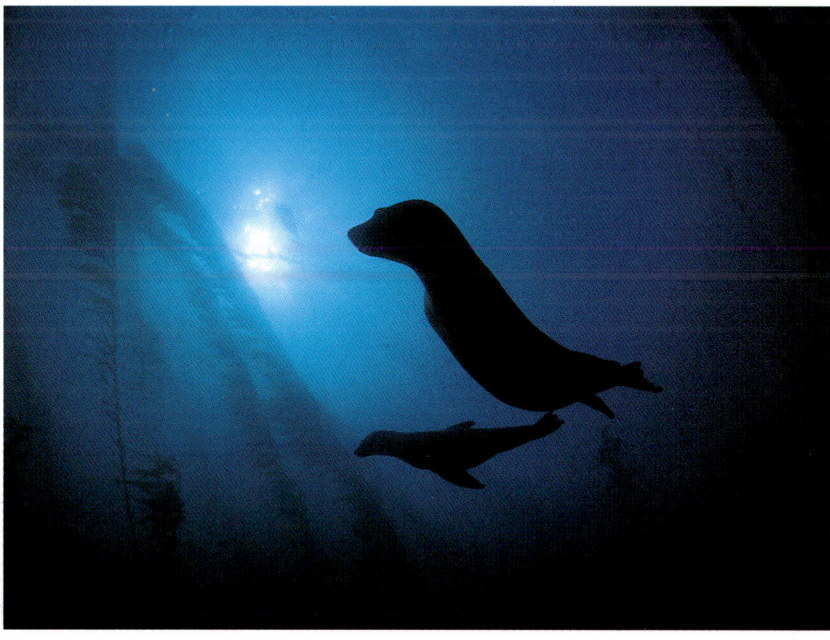

On Taking Pictures of Fish

The 35mm lens is well-suited for pictures of medium-sized fish. But, alas, there are more good fish stories than there are good fish pictures. And for good reason. Fish don't stop and pose. Taking fish photos would try the patience of Job. But we never met a diver with a camera who didn't continually try.

▼ Don't be a fish chaser! Chase a fish and you'll end up with shots of fish tails. Be patient. Settle down and just watch for a while. Wait for it to swim toward you or wait for it to stop and rest or feed.

▼ Instead of a lateral view, shoot head on. Tilt the camera slightly upward.

▼ Match your expectations with your equipment. You don't use a close-up lens to take pictures of seals. You don't use a 35mm lens to take pictures of clownfish. Select the right size fish for your 35mm lens. Fish 12 to 18 inches long are perfect.

▼ Control your exhaust bubbles. The noise frightens fish away. Learn to breathe slowly and evenly. Emit a small, steady, quiet stream of bubbles instead of a large sudden explosion.

▼ Small schooling fish, such as grunts, jacks, yellowtail and snappers, create interesting patterns and make excellent subjects.

▼ Identification shots inform; they show the viewer what the species looks like. The best way to do that is with the fish parallel to the film plane. Strive for good separation between the fish and the background. The entire fish should be in the frame, and all parts of the fish should be in sharp focus.

▼ Bait to get close but please don't feed. Place some fish food, such as anchovies, inside a container with small holes. The holes will allow the scent to get out but not the food. Keep the container outside of the angle of view of the lens. Wait. Don't wave the container around expecting a fish to come swimming by to grab it. Dogs may play that game, but not fish!

▼ Do not clutter. Make certain there is no distracting sea life in the foreground or background. Keep it simple so the focus is on the fish.

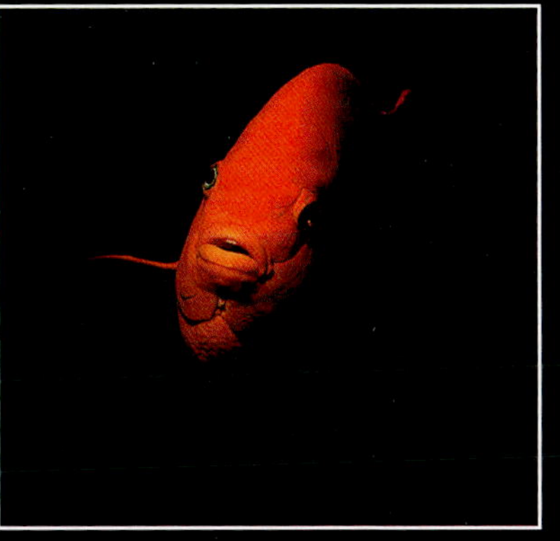

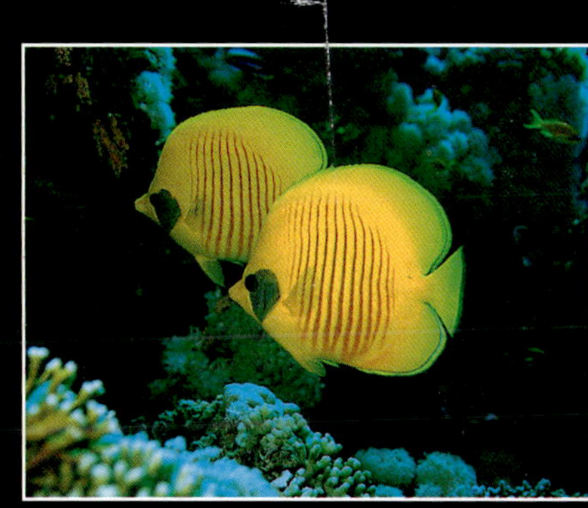

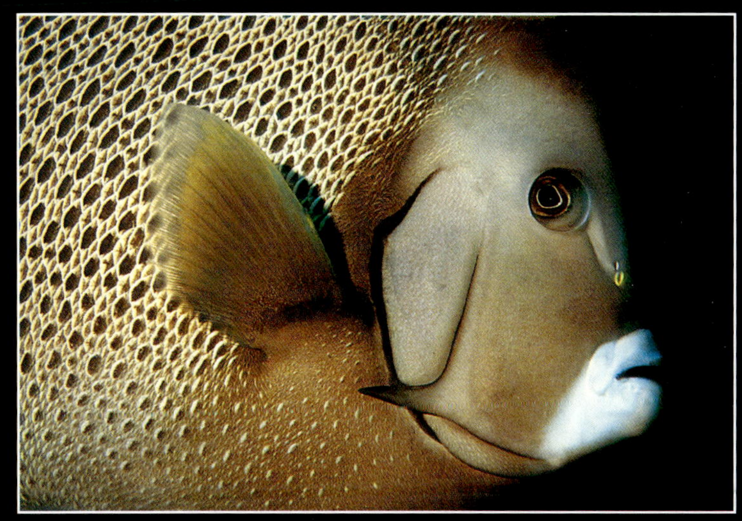

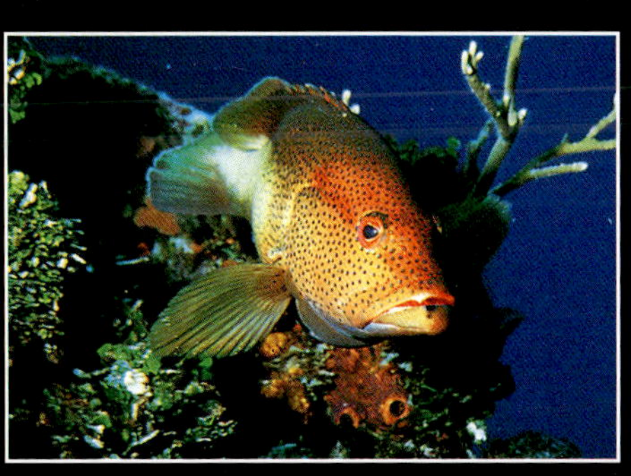

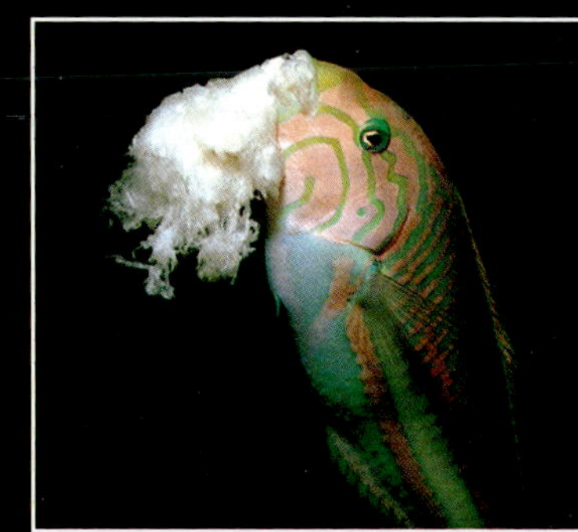

Fish photos taken with the Motor Marine II-EX built-in lenses. Clockwise from top left: Close-up, 35mm, Close-up, Close-up, 35mm

MOTOR MARINE II-EX CLOSE-UP LENS

A close-up lens is a supplementary lens placed in front of or to the rear of the camera's primary lens to reduce minimum focus distance. It is similar to the plus-diopter elements used in eyeglasses to correct for farsightedness. Just as the eyeglasses enable the human eye to focus on objects closer than it normally can, a close-up lens enables the camera lens to focus on objects closer than it normally can. Like corrective eyeglasses, a close-up lens magnifies objects for the lens to which it is attached. In essence, it is a magnifying glass.

The Motor Marine II-EX's built-in close-up lens flips down behind the camera's 35mm lens and reduces the minimum focusing distance from 40 inches to 18 inches.

Close-up photography is different from 35mm lens photography:

- the subjects are smaller
- you usually use strobe light to illuminate your pictures
- you always shoot at a distance of less than three feet.

The reduced lens-to-subject distance allows you to shoot smaller subjects at a closer range and enables you to fill the entire frame with a sharp detail of your subject. The closer you are to your subject, the larger its image on film. It also reduces the amount of water you must shoot through. At such close range, the image is unaffected by the filtering and scattering effects of water. Therefore, it enables you to achieve intricate, colorful photos in even turbid water. Good results can be realized in depths to 10 feet using ambient light but only on bright sunny days in very clear water. Best results are achieved with artificial light; colors are more brilliant and images more vibrant than possible with a 35mm lens.

Subjects

As a rule of thumb, the subject sizes in close-up photography range from a minimum of 3 x 5 inches to a maximum of 12 x 18 inches. Good close-up subjects are: anemones, sponges, sea stars, small coral formations, sea fans, medium-sized fish such as angelfish, triggerfish and damsel, and your diver buddy's head.

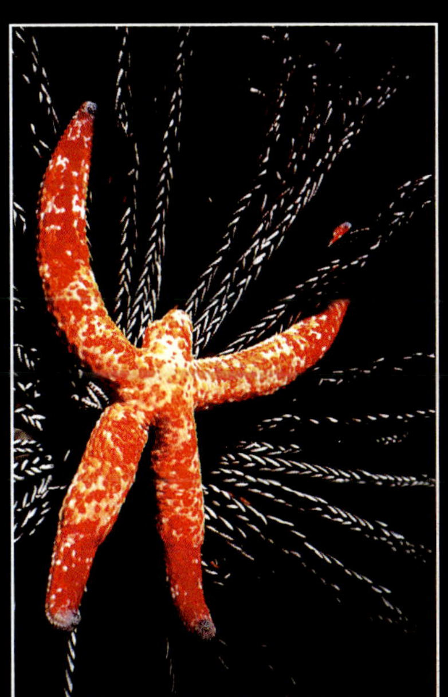

Starfish, stationary and so easy to shoot: f/22 from 18 to 25 inches.

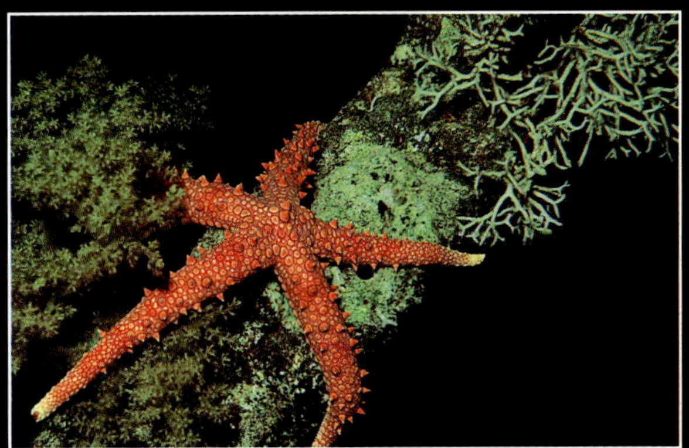

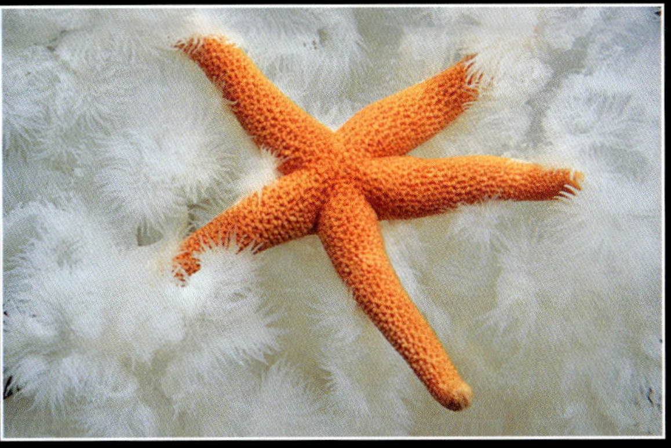

Depth of Field

By reducing camera-to-subject distance, you also decrease depth of field. Remember, to increase the zone of sharpness, you make the aperture smaller. The manufacturer's *depth of field guide* is as follows:

Preset focus to CU position	F-stop	3.5	5.6	8	11	16	22
	Feet	1.5~1.8	1.4~1.9	1.4~2.0	1.3~2.2	1.2~2.5	1.1~3.2
	Meters	0.5~0.5	0.4~0.6	0.4~0.6	0.4~0.7	0.4~0.8	0.3~1.0

Notice that the greatest depth of field is achieved at f/22, proving the axiom: *in close-up photography, you always use the smallest aperture possible.*

How to Use

Close-up photography with the Motor Marine II-EX's built-in close-up lens is easy. All your camera and flash controls can be preset. This is a technique called *zone focusing* and is used when photographers anticipate a particular subject and want to be prepared to just point and shoot.

1. To move the close-up lens down into the image path, rotate the shutter speed dial to the "CU" position.
2. Select your f-stop. To maximize depth of field, you want to use the smallest aperture possible: f/16 or f/22.
3. Your strobe should be held or mounted at a fixed predetermined distance from your subject. At f/16 the strobe-to-subject distance should be approximately 24 inches. At f/22 the strobe-to-subject distance should be approximately 18 inches. Position the strobe above the camera at a 45° angle. Aim at the top and slightly to the left of your subject.
4. Approximate camera-to-subject distance. Best results are achieved at 18 to 25 inches (fingertip to bicep is approximately 18 inches apparent distance).
5. Look into the viewfinder to compose your picture. Align the center of your subject with the dot below the "+" mark at the center of the frame.
6. Hold steady and shoot!
7. Bracket. If necessary, refer back to page 82 for instructions on how to bracket.

Unloading the Film

When all the frames have been exposed, the film advance automatically stops and the shutter button will not depress. Look in the film counter window. You will see a number, such as 24 or 36, whatever is the maximum number of exposures in the roll of film you are using.

1. The film rewind lever is recessed into the bottom of the camera body. Note the red "R" (for Rewind) and the red arrow.

   To activate the rewind system, ▶ push the lever in the direction of the arrow. Do not release until you hear the motor stop. It will stop when the film has been completely rewound.

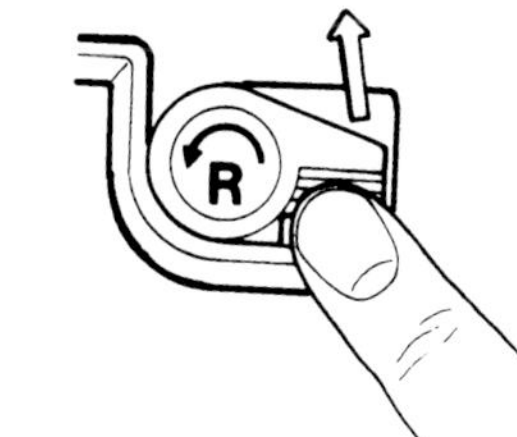

2. Before opening the back cover to remove the film, be sure the camera is clean and dry. Always open the camera with the back cover facing downward.

3. Remove the film cartridge. (Avoid removing film in direct sunlight.)

4. The film does not rewind entirely back into the cassette. The film leader will be exposed. Manually rewind the leader back into the cassette to avoid accidentally loading and shooting the roll again.

Note: If the rewind lever should be pushed unintentionally before all the frames have been exposed, the film will rewind. It will continue to rewind as long as pressure is exerted on the lever. Once the lever is released, the rewind mechanism will stop.

Camera Care and Maintenance

The Motor Marine II-EX is constructed of rugged molded polycarbonate. The absence of metals in the camera body and fittings reduces incidence of metal corrosion. But that doesn't mean you can neglect your system. All underwater photographic equipment requires diligent care and maintenance. Please see Chapter 9.

THE MOTOR MARINE II-EX SYSTEM

The Motor Marine II-EX is an expandable system. Sea & Sea manufactures a wide assortment of accessories. As your skills develop and your desire for more creative and diverse images grow, so will your need of ancillary equipment. The chart below shows the accessories compatible with the Motor Marine II-EX and how they are interrelated and interchangeable. The function and operation of these accessories are covered in subsequent chapters.

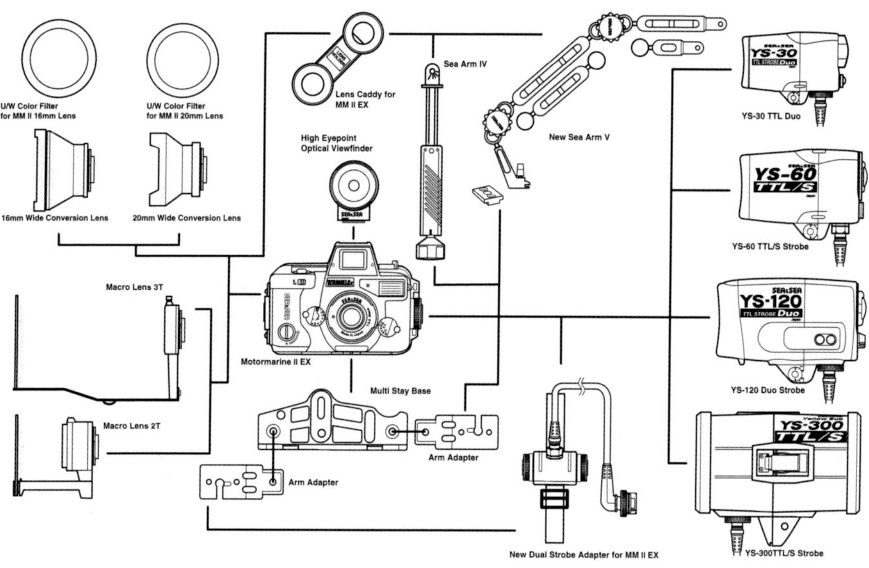

CHAPTER FOUR

Wide Angle Lenses

Wide Angle Lenses

After using your standard lens for a while, you've probably begun to feel a little inhibited by its limitations. Granted, you've been getting some excellent pictures and you fashion yourself a pretty good underwater photographer. But you can't manage to get the kind of images you see in the scuba magazines: those panoramic reef scenes and the big schools of fish. You aimed at a school of one-eyed jacks and ended up with three whole fish and a bunch of disembodied heads and headless tails. That magnificent Fijian reef of soft coral lost its pink and purple hues and ended up cast in blues. The Bahamian wreck looked shrouded in a haze, and the shark that seemed so huge and fearsome, well, it, too, ended up too small and too blue, more minnow than majesty.

Sound familiar?

It's not what you're doing. It's which lens you're using. To create sharp and colorful images of the subjects we've just described, you need a lens designed specifically to project such images.

You need a wide angle lens.

What is a Wide Angle Lens?

A lens is a series of polished glass elements that are precisely ground and set in groups. Its purpose is to sharply focus the light rays reflected from a subject onto the film inside the camera. The lens will determine the amount of light reaching the film. It will also determine the size of the image and how much of a scene will be recorded on film.

Not all lenses do the same job. Lenses are constructed and classified according to their *focal length*. Focal length affects the image formed on the film in two ways: the amount of the scene shown and the size of the image. The focal length number is expressed in millimeters (mm), such as 16mm, 20mm, 35mm.

In underwater photography there are three basic lenses: normal, wide angle, and macro. In underwater photography the 35mm lens is considered the normal, or standard, lens because its angle of view underwater approximates the perspective of the human eye. Any lens that has a wider angle of view than the normal lens is called a *wide angle lens*.

Two Types of Wide Angle Lenses

All Sea & Sea lenses are computer designed based on the latest optical technology. Sea & Sea offers two types of wide angle lenses for amphibious cameras: wide angle *primary* lenses and wide angle *conversion* lenses.

Characteristics of a Wide Angle Lens

- ▼ It has an angle of view greater than 46°.
- ▼ It has a wider angle of view than human vision does.
- ▼ More of the scene appears in the picture.
- ▼ It increases depth of field.
- ▼ It provides for enhanced close focusing ability. The wider the lens, the shorter the minimum focusing distance.
- ▼ It enables you to shoot larger subjects at shorter distances. Larger subjects can fill the frame.
- ▼ Decreasing subject-to-lens distance decreases the amount of water you must shoot through. You decrease the filtering effect of water and achieve better color saturation and greater image sharpness.
- ▼ It is the lens of choice for shooting in poor visibility because lens-to-subject distance is reduced.
- ▼ It exaggerates spatial relationships. It makes near objects seem larger than normal and far objects seem smaller than normal.

Sea & Sea Wide Angle Lenses

Compatible Camera	Focal Length	Type	Angle of Coverage	Focus Range
MX-10	20mm	Conversion	74.4°	1.3 ft. ~ ∞
Motor Marine II	16mm	Conversion	91°	1.0 ft. ~ ∞
Motor Marine II-EX	20mm	Conversion	80°	1.3 ft. ~ ∞
Nikonos	12mm	Primary	167°	0.4 ft. ~ ∞
	15mm	Primary	96°	1.0 ft. ~ ∞
	16mm	Conversion	91°	1.0 ft. ~ ∞
	20mm	Primary	80°	1.3 ft. ~ ∞

A primary lens mounts directly onto the camera body and has no other glass elements in the light path.

A conversion lens is an auxiliary lens that mounts onto a primary normal lens. Its name states its purpose: to convert the primary lens into a wide angle lens, thereby expanding its angle of coverage and increasing depth of field. Unlike primary lenses, conversion lenses can be attached and detached underwater.

For Underwater Use Only?

Due to the refraction of light underwater, the wider the picture angle of the lens, the more distorted the image becomes at the four corners of the photograph. To compensate for this distortion, the front portions of a wide angle lens are specially treated. Once treated, these lenses cannot focus on land.

The 32mm lens for the MX-10 and the 35mm lenses for the Motor Marine and Nikonos are amphibious; they can focus on land and underwater because their picture angle is narrow enough so that the need for underwater aberration compensation is eliminated.

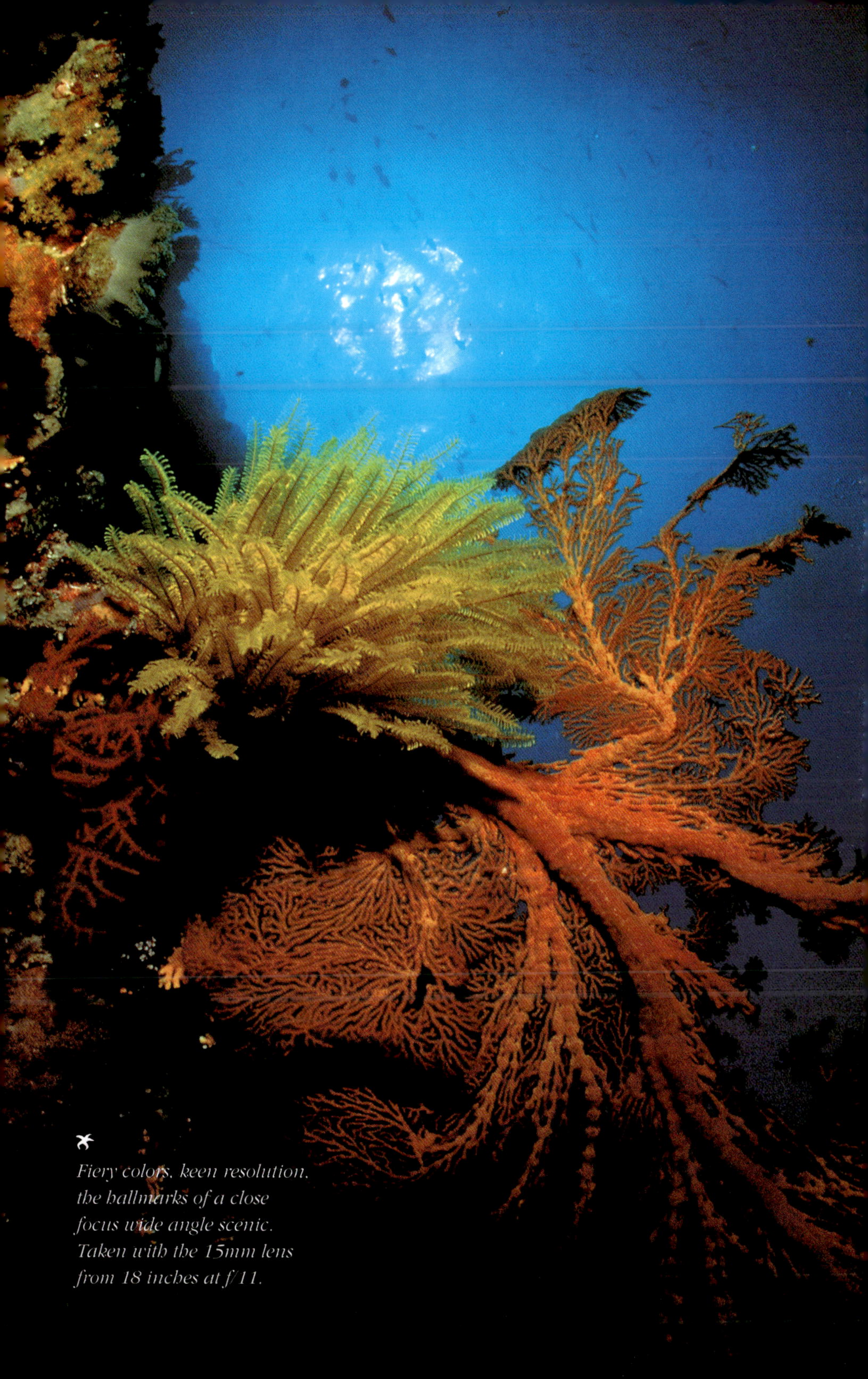

Fiery colors, keen resolution, the hallmarks of a close focus wide angle scenic. Taken with the 15mm lens from 18 inches at f/11.

WIDE CONVERSION LENSES

Sea & Sea has designed one wide conversion lens for the MX-10 and two wide angle conversion lenses exclusively for use with the Motor Marine II and Motor Marine II-EX. All three lenses are for underwater use only.

Preparation for Use

The lens is the key to any camera system. For optimal performance, the lens must be completely unblemished. A damaged lens surface produces a degraded image.

In Chapter 9 we detail how to care for your auxiliary lens before and after use. Please read it and heed it. Below is an abbreviated version of those instructions.

1. With lens caps in place, use a soft brush or a rubber syringe blower to clean dust from the lens barrel. Be careful to use this brush only on metal surfaces.

2. Remove the lens caps and check the front and rear elements for salt crystals, dust, etc. Use a rubber syringe blower to blow off dust and dirt from the lens.

3. Clean the lens only with photographic lens cleaner on a photographic lens tissue.

4. Hold the lens up to the light; look into the lens at an angle. Check for fingerprints, dirt, or smudges.

5. Inspect the lens mount for lint, dust, sand, or any other foreign matter. Rinse in clean water, if necessary. Dry lens body and mount with a clean, lint-free cloth.

6. Wipe down the lens body with a clean soft cloth. Recheck the elements and clean again if neccessary. Replace the lens caps.

20MM WIDE CONVERSION LENS FOR THE MX-10

Designed specifically for use with the MX-10 camera, this 20mm lens converts the built-in 32mm lens to a wide angle lens, expanding angle of view from 51° to more than 74° and reducing minimum focusing distance from four feet to less than two feet— just what you need to capture captivating images of large subjects like groupers, schools of fish, and full-body diver portraits. It can be attached or detached underwater so you have ready use of an additional focal length lens on any single dive. It is for underwater use only.

Identification of Parts

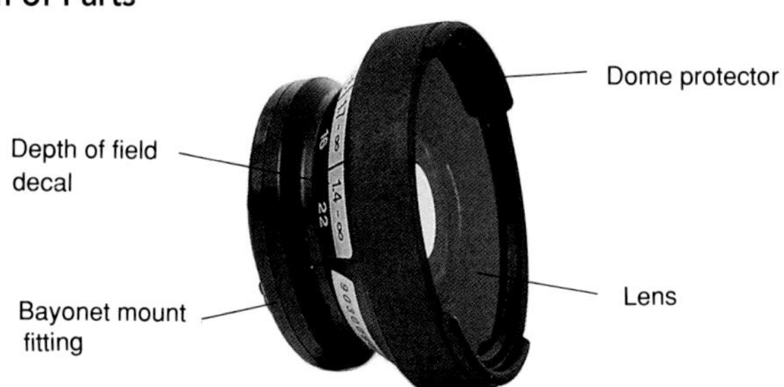

Specifications

Focal length:	20mm	**Dimensions:**	2.6 x 1.6" (D x L) (64 x 39mm)
Coverage:	74.4°		
Aperture range:	F/4.5 ~ f/22	**Weight:**	4.7 ounces (135g)
Max. aperture ratio:	1:4.5	**Body material:**	Hardened aluminum, anodized finish
Focusing range:	1.3 feet ~ ∞ (0.4m ~ ∞)		
Maximum depth:	150 feet (45 meters)	**Included:**	Front and rear lens caps; depth of field decals
Construction:	3 elements in 3 groups		

How to Mount

Place the lens upright so that the white dot on the back of the lens aligns with the white dot on the built-in lens. Push the lens into the camera's mount and turn clockwise until it clicks into place. ▶

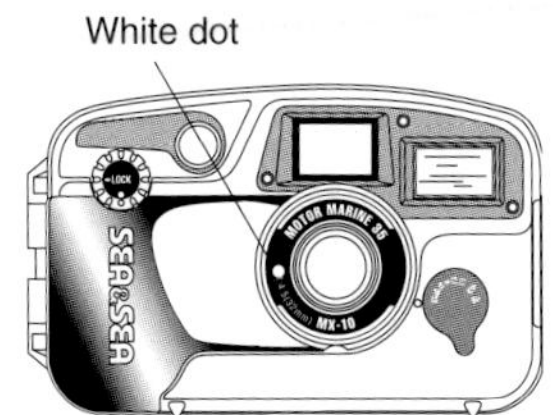

Depth of Field Decal

Two depth of field decals are included with the lens: one in meters and the other in feet. Select the decal you need and affix it to your lens as follows:

1. Clean dirt and oil from the barrel of the lens with a mild solution of soap and water. Dry the lens.
2. Mount the lens.
3. Apply the decal to the lens with f/8 and f/11 centered on the top.

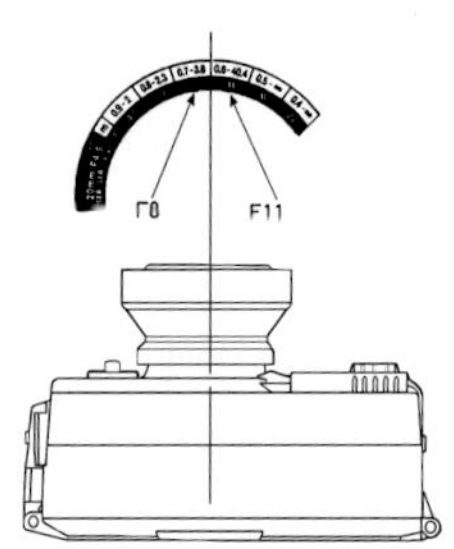

Depth of Field

The MX-10 is a fixed-focus camera. The focus is permanently set at one distance. With this type of lens, you are dependent upon depth of field to attain a sharp image. The smaller the aperture, the greater the range of sharp focus.

The following depth of field table shows range of sharp focus for the 20mm lens at varying f-stops. Remember, when you select an f-stop, your subject must be within this range.

F-stop	4.5	5.6	8	11	16	22
Feet	2.8 ~ 6.5	2.7 ~ 7.6	2.3 ~12.6	2.0 ~ 13.6	1.7 ~ ∞	1.4 ~ ∞
Meters	0.9 ~ 2.0	0.8 ~ 2.3	0.7 ~ 3.8	0.6 ~ 4.2	0.5 ~ ∞	0.4 ~ ∞

Note: All the above are apparent distance not measured distance. Remember, your lens sees apparent distance underwater, just as you do.

Sportsfinder

The companion Sportsfinder is a simple viewing device that corrects for parallax and enables you to frame your photos with accuracy.

To assemble, fit the finder onto the back cover of the camera and turn the fixing screw clockwise until tight.

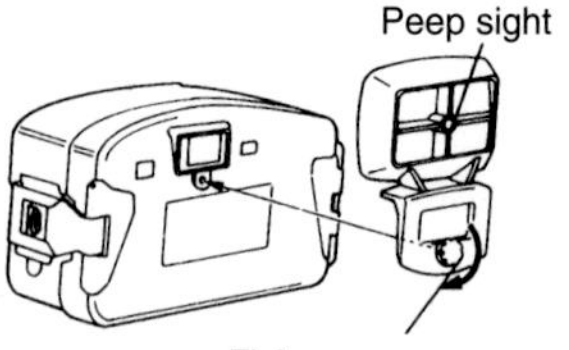

Note: The Sportsfinder is made of plastic. Do not apply backward pressure to the lower portion; it can break.

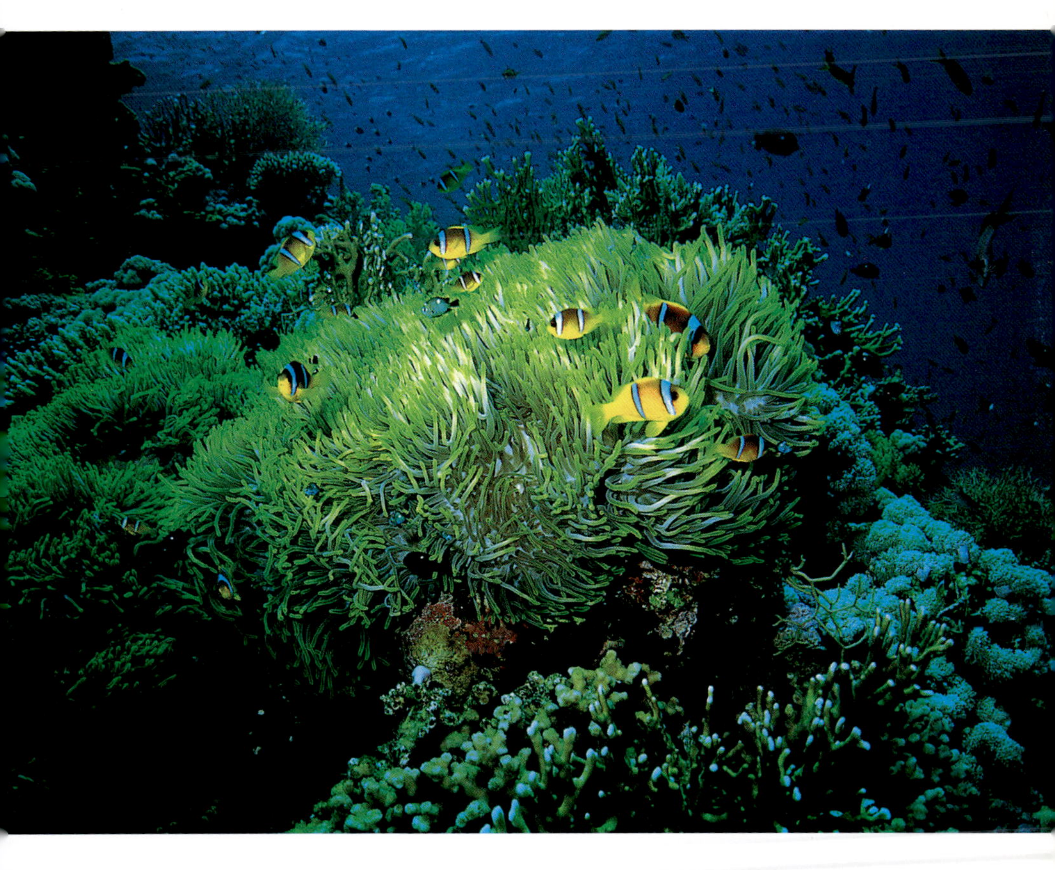

A popular image for all photographers: clownfish at home in an anemone. With the 20mm lens you can get two feet close at f/8 to capture the colors and fine details.

How to Use Lens and Sportsfinder

1. Loosen the lens underwater to vent trapped air and to allow water to flood the space between the built-in lens and the 20mm conversion lens. Water is an integral part of the optical formula. If you fail to do this, your images will be out of focus.
2. Click the lens back to the lock position.
3. Set your f-stop. The smaller the f-stop, the greater the depth of field. Always use the smallest aperture possible under existing lighting conditions.
4. Refer to the depth of field decal for the correct camera-to-subject distance.
5. The Sportsfinder is parallax-corrected to approximately three feet. Look through the peep sight to view your subject. When photographing subjects within the three-foot range, target your subject from a point about a 1/4 inch below the peep sight.
   Tip: Make a permanent white mark below the peep sight to remind you that parallax correction is necessary when shooting in close.
6. The Sportsfinder provides only 80 percent frame coverage, meaning your lens will record more of the scene than you see through the finder. Put another way, your photograph will show more of the scene that you expected. Compensate for this variable by looking over the finder at the whole scene before you shoot and note all the surrounding elements. If you notice anything you don't want in your picture, crop the unwanted elements by adjusting the camera angle or lens-to-subject distance while looking through the finder.
7. Hold the finder about an inch to three inches away from your facemask.
8. Take the picture.
9. Bracket. See page 82 for how to.

16MM WIDE CONVERSION LENS FOR THE MOTOR MARINE II-EX

The 16mm Wide Conversion Lens provides super wide angle coverage, expanding the angle of coverage of the 35mm lens from 46° to 91°. It allows for extreme close focusing, down to 12 inches, and yields distortion-free images with edge-to-edge sharpness. It has a high-quality metal barrel and a bayonet mount. It can be attached or detached underwater, so you have ready use of an additional focal length lens on any single dive. An accessory rubber lens hood mounts to the front of the lens, protecting the front lens element from flare and impact damage.

The 16mm offers several distinct advantages over the Motor Marine's built-in 35mm lens: it provides a wider angle of coverage, closer focusing, and increased depth of field. You can photograph larger subjects from a closer vantage point, thereby reducing the water column you shoot through. Images are crisper and more saturated with color. It is the lens of choice for photographing schools of fish, reef scenics, wrecks, and special encounters with friendly pelagics.

Identification of Parts

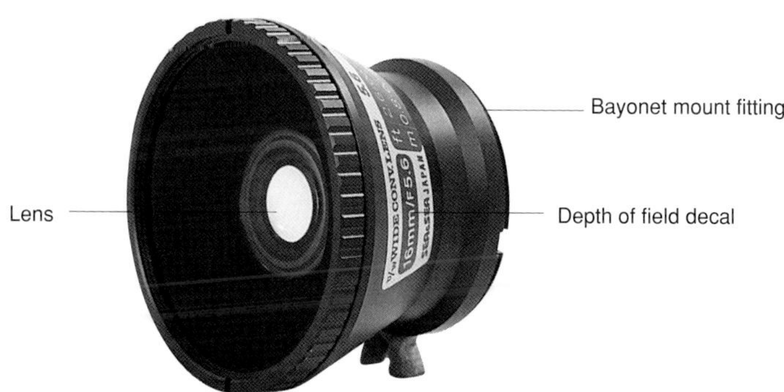

Specifications

Focal length:	16mm	**Dimensions:**	3 x 2.2" (D x L); (78 x 55mm)
Coverage:	91°	**Weight:**	13.6 ounces (388g)
Aperture range:	F/5.6 ~ f/22	**Body material:**	Hardened aluminum, anodized finish
Max. aperture ratio:	1:5.6	**Included:**	Lens caps, depth of field decal, lens hood
Focusing range:	1 foot ~ ∞ (0.3m ~ ∞)		
Maximum depth:	150 feet (45 meters)		
Construction:	4 elements in 4 groups		

How to Mount

The 16mm lens for the Motor Marine II-EX has a bayonet mount.

1. Align the yellow mark on the rear ▶ of the lens with the white dot on the camera's primary lens.

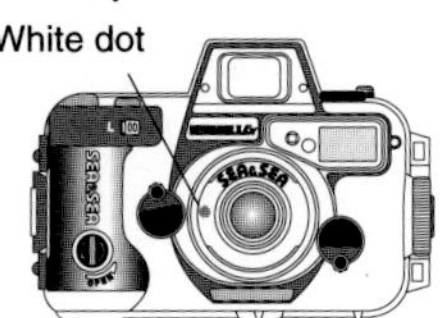

2. Push the lens into the primary lens and turn clockwise until secure. The lens will click and lock into place.

Note: A wide slot at the back of the lens allows water to flood the space between the lenses. Because the elements have been ground to incorporate the magnifying effect of water, water becomes part of the total optical design.

It is recommended that the lens be attached underwater. If the lens is attached on land, be sure to "burp" it by loosening it underwater to allow trapped air to escape from between the lenses and for water to flood the area. Air in this pocket will adversely affect resolution. Be sure you snap the lens back into the lock position.

To detach the lens, turn the lens counterclockwise and pull straight out.

How to Focus

When using the 16mm conversion lens, the focus dial on the camera must be set on infinity (∞). Depth of field is determined by f-stop.

Depth of Field

The following depth of field table demonstrates the superior focusing range of this lens.

Preset focus at infinity for all f-stops	**F-stop**	**5.6**	**8**	**11**	**16**	**22**
	Feet	2.6 ~ ∞	2.0 ~ ∞	1.6 ~ ∞	1.3 ~ ∞	1.0 ~ ∞
	Meters	0.8 ~ ∞	0.5 ~ ∞	0.4 ~ ∞	0.35 ~ ∞	0.27 ~ ∞

Notice how depth of field increases as you stop down to a smaller aperture.

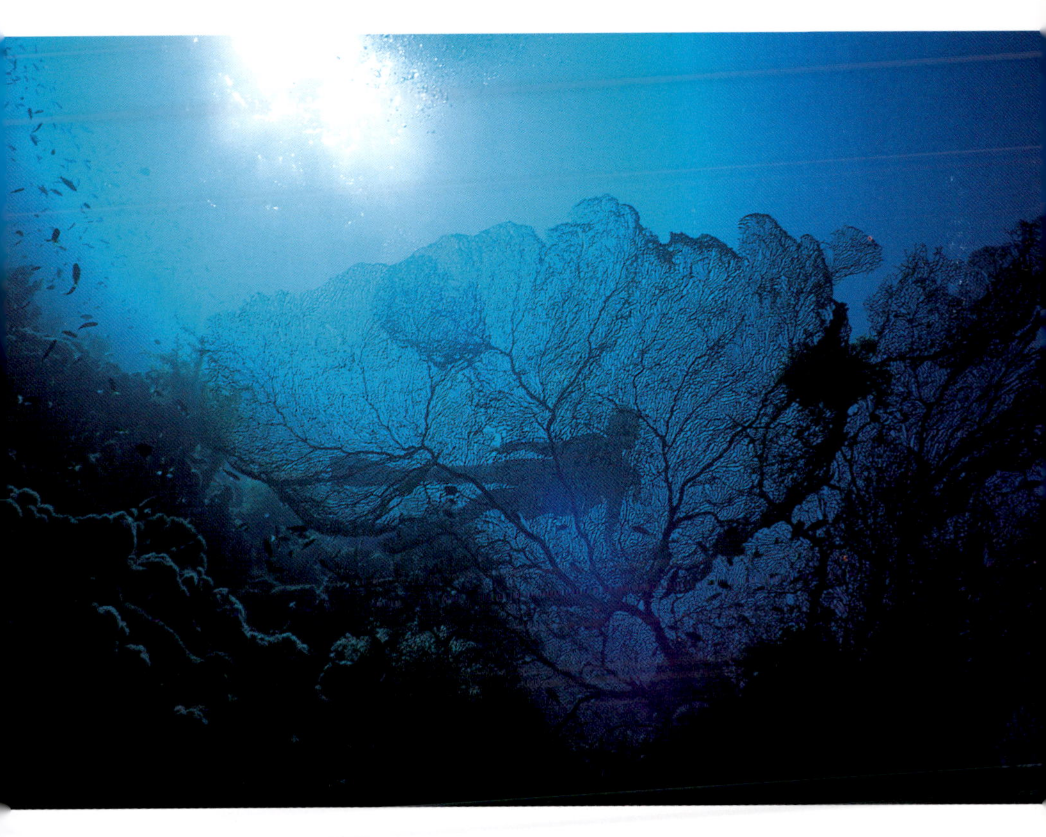

Simple, subtle and sensual, an ambient light silhouette of a diver and seafan as seen by the 16mm lens. Shot at f/16, 1/60 second.

How to Use

1. Set the focus dial on the camera at infinity (∞).
2. Set shutter speed.
3. Set the aperture control dial on your camera for the desired f-stop.
4. Compose. *Note:* You need an auxiliary viewfinder for accurate framing with this lens.
5. Take the picture.
6. Bracket.

How to select an f-stop for ambient light:

1. Activate the built-in light meter by aiming the camera at your subject and pressing the shutter release button halfway. (To review *light meter,* see page 68.)
2. Look into the camera's viewfinder for exposure information. If the LED underexposure lamp glows, open up to a larger aperture.
3. Repeat. Press the shutter release and look into the viewfinder. If the underexposure warning lamp is *not* illuminated, you have the proper f-stop for a correct exposure.
4. Refer to the depth of field chart on page 102 or to the decal on the 16mm lens. Shoot within the zone of focus for the f-stop selected.

How to select an f-stop for manual strobe operation:

1. See page 209, Manual Strobes, and Guide Numbers Made Easy. Or refer to the Rule-of-Thumb Exposure Chart on page 223.
2. Refer to the depth of field chart on page 102 or to the decal on the conversion lens. Shoot within the zone of focus for the f-stop selected.

How to select an f-stop for TTL photography:

1. See page 209, Guide Numbers Made Easy. Or refer to the Rule-of-Thumb Exposure Chart on page 223.
2. See Chapter 7, *Strobes,* for the TTL operating range of your strobe.
3. Once f-stop and operating range have been determined, refer to the depth of field chart on page 102 or to the decal on the 16mm conversion lens. Shoot within the zone of focus for the f-stop selected.

20MM WIDE CONVERSION LENS FOR THE MOTOR MARINE II-EX

The 20mm Wide Conversion Lens is manufactured specifically for use with Motor Marine II cameras. It mounts onto the camera's built-in lens and effectively expands your field of view from 46° to 80° and reduces minimum focusing distance from three feet to just 16 inches. With a wider angle of view and closer focusing, images are crisper, sharper, more saturated with color. The 20mm features superior water-corrected optics for distortion-free images, corner-to-corner sharpness, and pure color rendition.

With 80° of coverage, it may not be wide enough for that whale of a lifetime shot, but it is a highly versatile and practical portrait lens for imaging medium to large-sized fish, small schools of fish, and fellow divers.

Identification of Parts

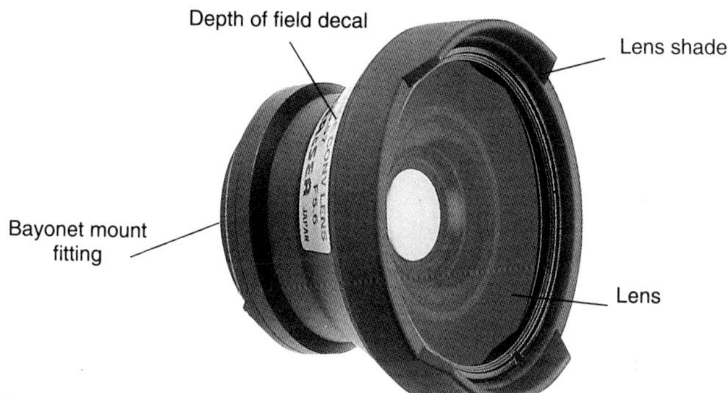

Specifications

Focal length:	20mm	**Dimensions:**	2.8 x 2.1" (D x L) (72 x 54mm)
Coverage:	80°		
Aperture range:	F/5.6 ~ f/22	**Weight:**	9.2 ounces (263g)
Max. aperture ratio:	1:5.6	**Body material:**	Hardened aluminum, anodized finish
Focusing range:	1.3 feet ~ ∞ (0.4m - ∞)		
Maximum depth:	150 feet (45 meters)	**Included:**	Front and rear lens caps; depth of field decal
Construction:	4 elements in 4 groups		

How to Mount

The 20mm lens for the Motor Marine II/EX has a bayonet mount.

1. Align the yellow mark on the rear ▶ of the lens with the white dot on the camera's primary lens.

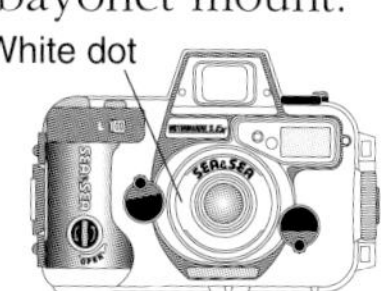

2. Push the lens into the primary lens and turn clockwise until secure. The lens will click and lock into place.

FILM TIP
A good all-purpose film for wide angle photography is ISO100. It has an ultra-fine grain and excellent color saturation.

Note: A wide slot at the back of the lens allows water to flood the space between the built-in lens and the conversion lens. Because the elements have been ground to incorporate the magnifying effect of water, water becomes part of the total optical design. Therefore, it is recommended that the lens be attached underwater. If the lens is attached on land, be sure to "burp" it by loosening it underwater to allow trapped air to escape from between the lenses and for water to flood the area. Air in this pocket will adversely affect resolution. Be sure you snap the lens back into the lock position.

To detach the lens, turn the lens counterclockwise and pull straight out.

Tip: Don't stuff it in your BC pocket. Carry it safely in the accessory lens caddy that mounts to your strobe arm. See page 90.

How to Focus

When using the 20mm conversion lens, the focus dial on the camera must be set on infinity (∞). Depth of field is determined by f-stop.

Depth of Field

The broad focusing range of this lens is evident in the chart below. Notice how depth of field increases as you stop down to a smaller aperture.

Preset focus at infinity for all f-stops	**F-stop**	**5.6**	**8**	**11**	**16**	**22**
	Feet	2.3 ~ 5.9	2.1 ~ 9.2	1.8 ~ ∞	1.5 ~ ∞	1.3 ~ ∞
	Meters	0.7 ~ 1.8	0.6 ~ 2.8	0.6 ~ ∞	0.5 ~ ∞	0.4 ~ ∞

You need an auxiliary viewfinder with this lens. See page 126.

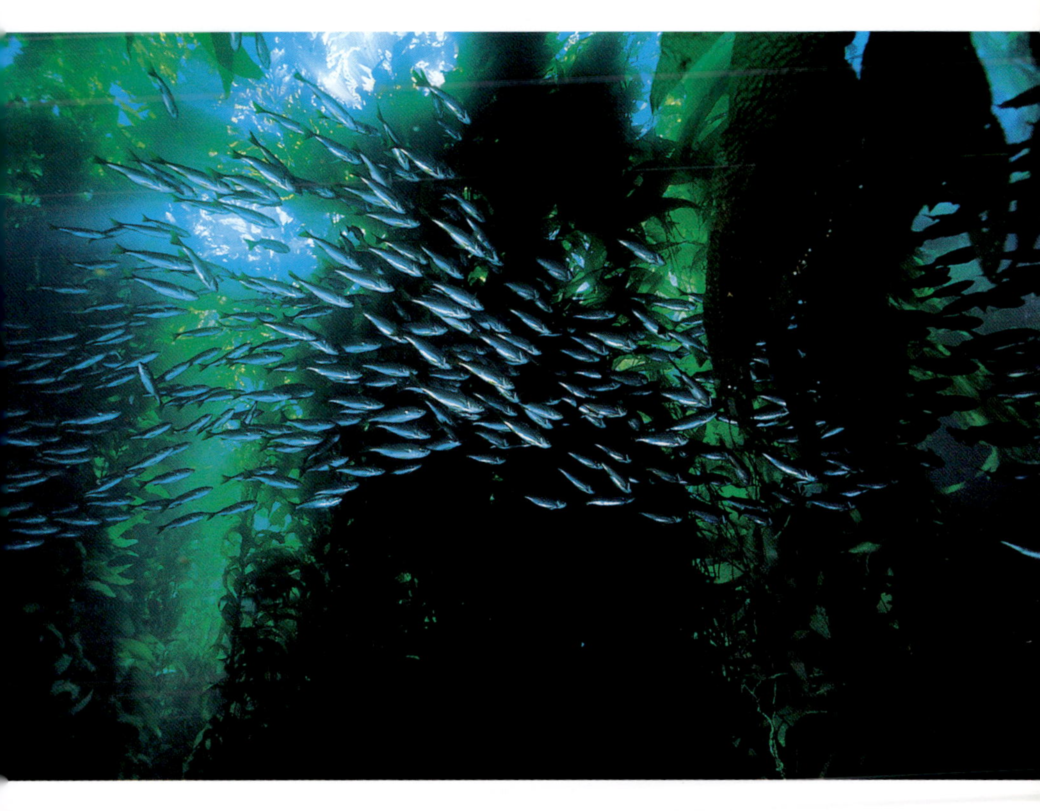

California kelp undulating in the gentle current. Schooling fish weaving through. More than a wide view, you can almost feel the motion.

How to Use

1. Set the focus dial on the camera at infinity (∞).
2. Set shutter speed.
3. Set the aperture control dial on your camera for the desired f-stop
4. Compose. *Note:* You need an auxiliary viewfinder for accurate framing with this lens.
5. Take the picture.
6. Bracket.

How to select an f-stop for ambient light:

1. Activate the built-in light meter by aiming the camera at your subject and pressing the shutter release button halfway. (To review *light meter,* see page 68.)
2. Look into the camera's viewfinder for exposure information. If the LED underexposure lamp glows, open up to a larger aperture.
3. Repeat. Press the shutter release and look into the viewfinder. If the underexposure warning lamp is *not* illuminated, you have the proper f-stop for a correct exposure.
4. Refer to the depth of field chart on page 106 or to the decal on the 20mm lens. Shoot within the zone of focus for the f-stop selected.

How to select an f-stop for manual strobe operation:

1. See page 209, Manual Strobes, and Guide Numbers Made Easy. Or refer to the Rule-of-Thumb Exposure Chart on page 223.
2. Refer to the depth of field chart on page 106 or to the decal on the conversion lens. Shoot within the zone of focus for the f-stop selected.

How to select an f-stop for TTL photography:

1. See page 209, Guide Numbers Made Easy. Or refer to the Rule of Thumb Exposure Chart on page 223.
2. See Chapter 7, *Strobes,* for the TTL operating range of your strobe.
3. Once f-stop and operating range have been determined, refer to the depth of field chart on page 106 or to the decal on the 20mm conversion lens. Shoot within the zone of focus for the f-stop selected.

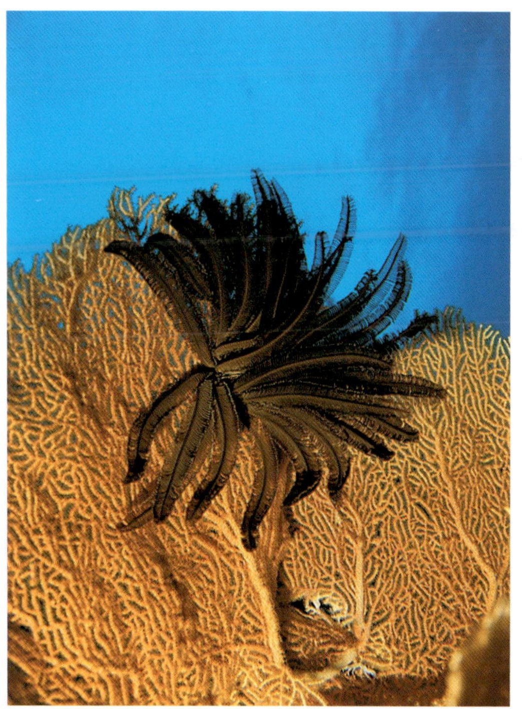

When to use the 16mm

The 16mm has a shorter focal length than the 20mm and should be used when you want to include more of a scene. The extreme wide angle coverage reduces shooting distance 50 to 80 percent and makes it possible to record full-frame images at close range. It's ideal for large schools of fish, panoramic reef scenes, wrecks, and large animals that will let you get close. Good choice for seals, sharks, and wrecks. Just as good a choice for a close focus portrait of a crinoid on a seafan.

When to use the 20mm

The 20mm lens has a much longer focal length than the 16mm. Subjects are magnified without exaggerating perspective at close range. Ideal for small reef scenes, schools of fish, divers with fish. You don't have to get as close to the subject to fill the frame, a benefit when trying to photograph fish that are wary of divers. Take to Cocos Island for the hammerheads. Take to Cozumel for the butterfly fish.

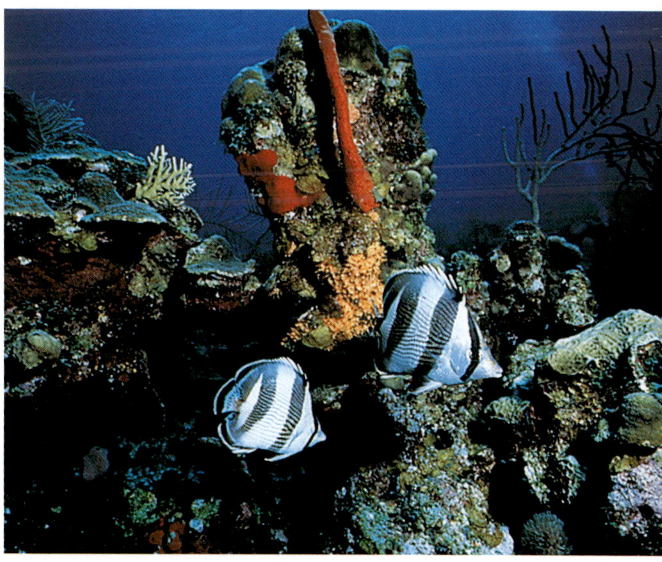

LENSES FOR THE NIKONOS

Sea & Sea has designed four outstanding wide angle lenses for Nikonos cameras. The SWL 12mm Fisheye, WL15, and WL20 are *primary* lenses; the WCL16 is a *conversion* lens. The superior optics of these lenses provide distortion-free, edge-to-edge sharpness, assuring uniformly illuminated images and outstanding color rendition. They are for underwater use only.

Preparation of Primary Lenses

Unlike a conversion lens, a primary lens mounts directly onto the camera body. An O-ring seal protects the internal mechanism from water. This O-ring must be inspected, cleaned, and lubricated as you do the O-rings in your camera and strobe.

1. Before mounting the lens, examine the O-ring carefully for damage and debris. Replace it if you notice any cuts or abrasions.
2. To grease the O-ring, put a dab of silicone grease on your thumb and index finger. Pull the O-ring gently through your fingers till it is evenly coated.
3. Clean the O-ring channel with a cotton swab.
4. Reseat the O-ring.

Lens Check

To check for aperture control knob performance:

1. Hold the lens so that you are looking into the lens from the rear element. Starting at f/22, rotate the aperture control knob down to f/3.5. When rotating the knob, you should hear and feel the click-stops between each f-stop.
2. When turning the aperture knob, the f-stop numbers on the aperture knob should correspond with the correct diameter of the iris.
3. Looking inside the lens, you should observe the aperture blades moving evenly and smoothly.

To test the focusing of the lens:

1. Hold the lens so that you are looking into the lens from the rear element.
2. Turn the focusing knob from infinity to the one foot setting, then back again. The rear element should move in and out approximately 1/8". This movement should be smooth.

12MM SWL FISHEYE FOR NIKONOS

It's the first of its kind and in a class by itself. Never before has it been possible to achieve such extraordinarily wide angle images with an amphibious lens. By definition, fisheye lenses have the shortest focal lengths, 6mm to 15mm for 35mm cameras, and angles of view so wide that they create what is called barrel distortion. A conventional fisheye exaggerates the difference in size between objects close to the lens and those that are far away; it distorts the image by bending straight lines. The image is rounded and the circular effect pronounced. Such curvature results in an image with unnatural perspective. This lens is different. Utilizing advanced optical technology, Sea & Sea has engineered a fisheye lens that produces a flat, rectilinear image free of chromatic aberration and peripheral distortion.

The 12mm Fisheye makes it possible to photograph panoramic reefs, large pelagics, and wrecks from less than a foot away! Imagine full-frame images of sharks and whales and seals. This sterling optic is a coveted tool for the serious amateur and for professionals who are exploring new approaches to underwater photography.

Identification of Parts

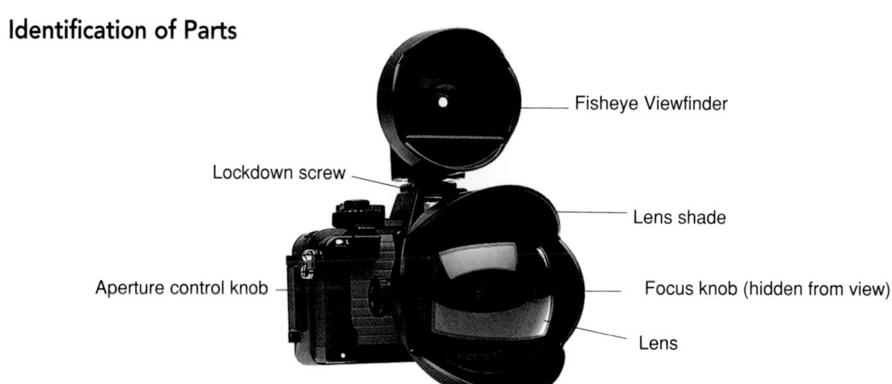

Specifications

Focal length:	12mm	**Dimensions:**	4.3 x 3.7 x 4.3" (D x L x W) (108 x 91 x 107mm)
Coverage:	167°		
Aperture range:	F/3.5 ~ f/22	**Weight:**	20 oz. (570g) land 14.7 ounces (420g) u/w, with Nikonos V
Max. aperture ratio:	1:3.5		
Focusing range:	11.8 in. ~ ∞ (30cm ~ ∞)		
Minimum distance:	4 inches (0.13m)	**Body material:**	Non-corrosive aluminum
Maximum depth:	200 feet (60 meters)	**Included:**	Front and rear lens caps, lens pouch, O-ring set
Construction:	9 elements in 6 groups		

How to Mount

The 12mm Fisheye mounts the same way you do a Nikonos lens:

1. Position focusing and aperture knobs vertical to the camera body.
2. Push the lens into the camera's bayonet mount.
3. Turn the lens clockwise. The lens positioning pins will click and lock into place. Be sure the depth of field decal is on the top of the lens barrel, the aperture control on the right, the focus control on the left.

Note: The lens crops a rectangular image out of the circular field of view. If the lens is mounted incorrectly, there will be a black border at the outer edges of the picture. Therefore, when mounting this lens, be sure to align and lock the two positioning pins on the back of the lens with the index mark on the camera's mount.

To detach: pull it slightly out from the camera body. This will disengage the lens positioning pins. Rotate the lens 90° counterclockwise. When the focusing and aperture knobs are vertical, remove the lens.

Fisheye Viewfinder

The lens angle of coverage is 167°. The fisheye viewfinder covers 90 percent of the viewing area, which equates to 150.3°. When you look through the viewfinder, you are seeing less of the scene than what the lens will record. Always look above the viewfinder at the entire scene to be sure that there is nothing in the field of view that you don't want in your photograph.

The viewfinder is constructed of anondized aluminum with a double-lock thumbscrew that secures the viewfinder to the camera's accessory shoe. When mounting the viewfinder, make sure it is fully engaged; the metal lip on the viewfinder must be over the front edge of the camera mount.

How to Use

The 12mm Fisheye has two large O-ring sealed exterior controls, one on either side of the lens barrel. The aperture control knob has a full range of of seven click-stops: f/3.5, f/4, f/5.6, f/8, f/11, f/16 and f/22. The focus distance scale is calibrated in both *meters* (yellow numerals) and in *feet* (white numerals). On the top of the lens barrel is a reference decal for depth of field at three aperture settings (f/4, f/8, f/16) and three focus settings (0.4 meters, 1 meter, and 2 meters).

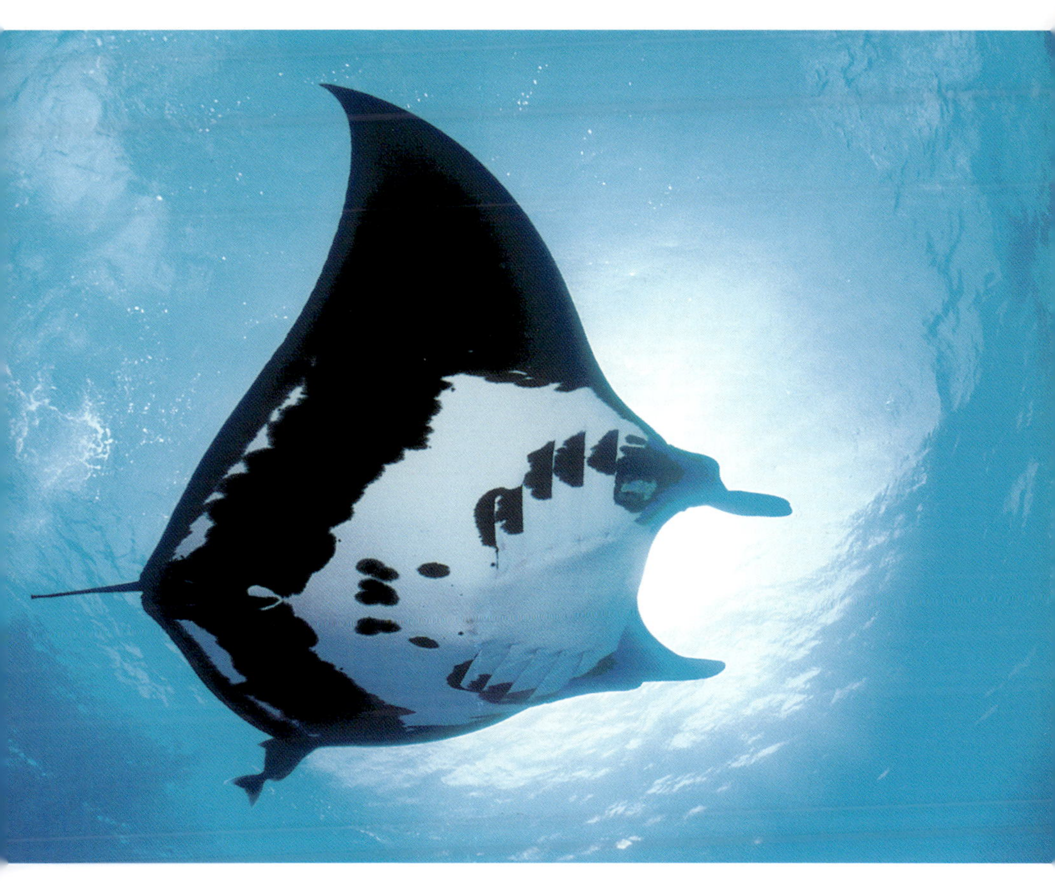

With 167° of coverage, you can photograph a manta with a 15-foot wing span from two feet and still have space in the frame to encircle it with sun-brightened blue water.

Depth of Field

A short focal length lens always provides excellent depth of field. This lens provides *phenomenal* depth of field. Study the following chart. Notice that at f/22, the range of sharp focus is from four inches to infinity! The distances are provided in *feet.*

Focus	F/3.5	F/4	F/5.6	F/8	F/11	F/16	F/22
∞	4.6~∞	4.0~∞	2.8~∞	2.0~∞	1.4~∞	1.0~∞	0.7~∞
7	2.8~∞	2.6~∞	2.1~∞	1.6~∞	1.2~∞	0.9~∞	0.7~∞
3	1.8~8.3	1.7~11.0	1.5~∞	1.2~∞	1.0~∞	0.8~∞	0.6~∞
2	1.4~3.5	1.4~3.9	1.2~6.4	1.0~∞	0.9~∞	0.7~∞	0.5~∞
1.5	1.2~2.2	1.1~2.4	1.0~3.1	0.9~5.6	0.7~∞	0.6~∞	0.5~∞
1	0.8~1.3	0.8~1.3	0.75~1.5	0.7~1.9	0.6~3.2	0.5~∞	0.4~∞

Note: The depth of field decal affixed to the lens is in meters. If you prefer to use calculations in feet, copy the above on a wide strip of surgical adhesive tape and place it on the rear door of your camera.

Taking the Picture

In Manual Mode, ambient light:

1. Set ISO film speed dial.
2. Set the shutter speed dial.
3. While looking through the camera viewfinder, adjust the aperture until a non-blinking shutter speed appears. Aperture and shutter speed are now properly matched for a correct exposure.
4. Estimate camera-to-subject distance, then set the focus control for that distance.
5. Refer to the depth of field chart. Make sure camera-to-subject distance is within the proper range for the f-stop selected.

In Aperture Priority, ambient light:

1. Set ISO film speed dial.
2. Set shutter speed dial at "A" for aperture priority. In aperture priority, you select the f-stop and the camera selects the shutter speed. Or

you can select the shutter speed by adjusting the aperture until the speed you want is displayed in the viewfinder; then set the aperture control knob to the desired f-stop.

3. Estimate camera-to-subject distance, then set the focus control for that distance.
4. Refer to the depth of field chart. Shoot within the zone of focus for the f-stop selected.

Rule-of-Thumb Ambient Light Exposures

Depth	F-stop
10'	f/11
20'	f/8
40'	f/5.6
60'	f/3.5

* Based on a bright sunny day, calm water with 60' visibility or better, ISO 100 film, shutter speed of 1/90.

* * Open up one f-stop if water surface is rough, visibility is 30' or less, the day is overcast, or the sun is low on the horizon.

In Manual Mode with manual strobe:

1. Set ISO film speed dial.
2. Select M90 shutter speed or slower.
3. Select an f-stop. To determine, use the guide number formula on page 209 or the Rule-of-Thumb Exposure Chart on page 223.
4. Estimate camera-to-subject distance, then set the focus control for that distance.
5. Refer to the depth of field chart. Shoot within the zone of focus for the f-stop selected.

In Aperture Priority with TTL strobe:

1. Set ISO film speed dial.
2. Set shutter speed dial at "A", aperture priority. The shutter speed automatically locks in at 1/90 second.
3. Select an f-stop. Use the guide number formula on page 209 or the Rule-of-Thumb Exposure Chart on page 223.
4. Set selected f-stop.
5. Estimate camera-to-subject distance, then set the focus control for that distance.
6. Refer to the depth of field chart. Shoot within the zone of focus for the f-stop selected.

Tip: When shooting close-ups with the 12mm or 15mm wide angle lens, you can measure distance by extending your hand from lens to subject. The distance between thumb and pinkie is approximately eight inches.

Tips

This is the first amphibious fisheye, and creating images with a lens that has nearly twice the angle of view of any other wide angle lens for the Nikonos will be a challenge. There will be a learning curve, so don't hesitate to experiment with your first few rolls. This lens will surprise and impress you.

- ▼ To minimize distortion and curvature, compose on the horizontal plane within the rectangular window inside the viewfinder.
- ▼ Shooting on a horizontal plane in the horizontal format will imply straight lines of direction. Subjects near the center will appear natural. Subjects beyond the 150° of coverage will begin to take on a slight curvature.
- ▼ When shooting on a horizontal plane in the vertical format, subjects near the center will still appear natural, but vertical lines will exhibit slight fisheye curvature.
- ▼ When composing your shot, look over the top of the viewfinder at the scene you're shooting. Remember, the viewfinder shows only 90 percent of the image that will be recorded.
- ▼ Not every picture has to be a literal representation of your subject. Creative photography incorporates special effects. Use the tendency toward curvature to your advantage. Shoot at an upward angle. Lines will gradually converge, yielding an impression of space and dimension. The greater the angle, the more exaggerated the curvature.
- ▼ Strobe placement is critical. Because the angle of view is so wide, strobe must be positioned to the rear and beyond the lens coverage or you will get backscatter in the photo. Even worse, you'll get your strobe.

How to Shoot in Bad Vis

While the 12mm lens lets you get extremely close, thereby dramatically reducing the water column, its angle of view is so wide that more of the particulate-filled water will be in the photograph. The solution?

- ▼ Turn the camera to the vertical position. This will effectively narrow the field of view. Keep the strobe at least six inches behind and parallel to the lens.
- ▼ When shooting in the horizontal format, the worst place to position your strobe is near the deepest cut of the lens hood. Position the strobe above or below, as far as possible from the cut in the lens hood.

Oops!

Too bad about this wreck shot. See that ghostly blemish below and left of the propeller? It's a scratch on the dome. A minor scratch will fill with water and will not impair your image. A deep scratch will.

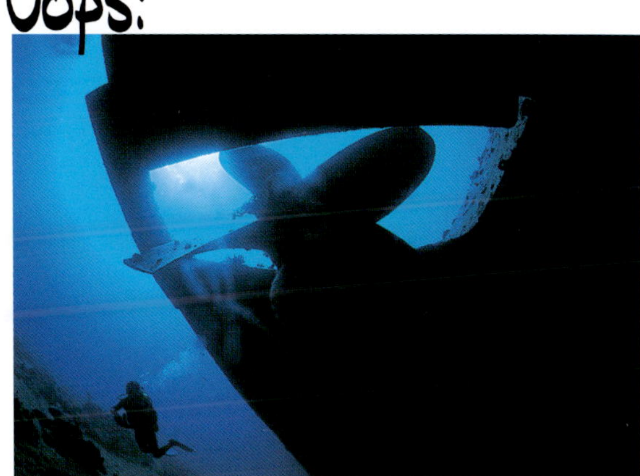

Oops!

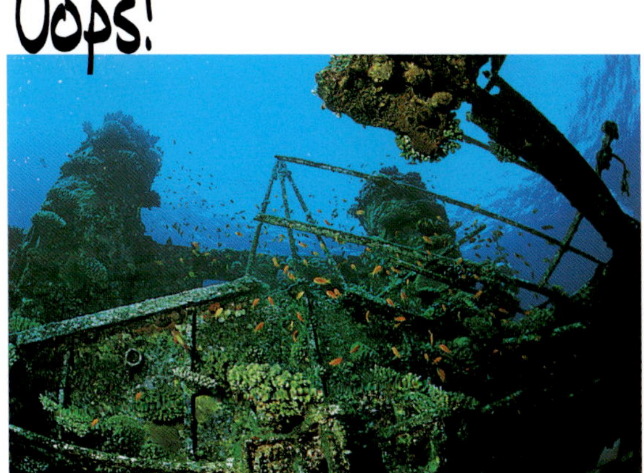

The 12mm lens is a remarkable optic, but it's extreme angle of view makes proper strobe placement more critical than with any other lens.

When you get it right . . . Inches close, infinity and super wide, the 12mm lens embraced them all on this wreck in the Red Sea.

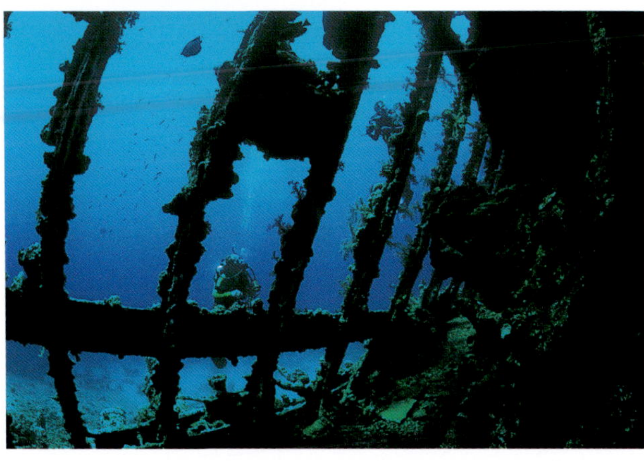

15MM WIDE ANGLE LENS FOR NIKONOS

Sea & Sea's 15mm lens for the Nikonos is a state-of-the-art optical tool for serious underwater photographers. It provides an underwater angle of acceptance of 96° and a minimum critical focus distance of nine inches. You can place your foreground subject as close as nine inches from the film plane and still have an infinity image in sharp focus. The lens consists of a complex assembly of 10 ground glass elements in 8 groups. The rear lens element is designed to be compatible with all Nikonos V TTL auto exposure and TTL auto flash functions. The front lens element is a convex mensicus glass dome which combines with the water to complete the optical formula. It is compatible with Nikonos I through IV cameras in manual mode.

The WL15 is small, lightweight, and as rugged as it is sophisticated. Constructed of hardened aluminum with a black anodized finish, it is impervious to saltwater corrosion and rust.

Identification of Parts

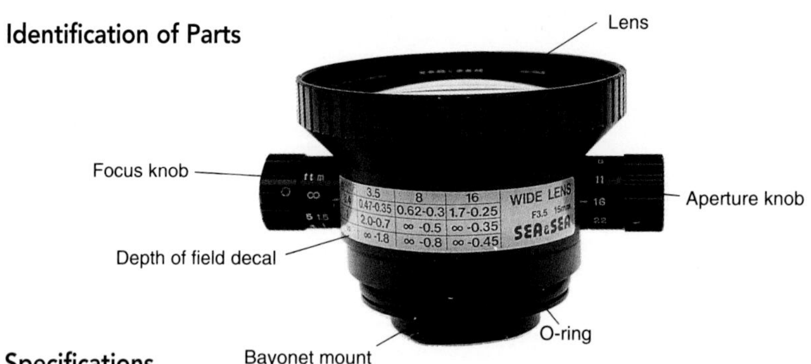

Specifications

Focal length:	15mm
Coverage:	96°
Aperture range:	F/3.5 ~ f/22
Max. aperture ratio	1:3.5
Focusing range:	1 foot ~ ∞ (0.3m ~ ∞)
Minimum distance:	10 inches (0.3 meters)
Maximum depth:	200 feet (60 meters)
Construction:	10 elements in 8 groups

Dimensions:	3.2 x 2.5 x 3.9" (D x L x W) (80 x 64 x 98mm)
Weight:	12 ounces (365g)
Body material:	Non-corrosive aluminum; hard almite treated
Included:	Front and rear lens caps, depth of field decal, O-ring set

How to Mount the Lens

The WL15 is equipped with a standard bayonet mount. It is mounted the same way you would a Nikkor lens:

1. Position focusing and aperture knobs vertical to the camera body.
2. Push the lens into the camera's bayonet mount.
3. Turn the lens clockwise. The lens positioning pins will click and lock into place. Be sure the depth of field decal is on the top of the lens barrel, the aperture control on the right, the focus control on the left.

To detach the lens: pull it slightly out from the camera body. This will disengage the lens positioning pins. Rotate the lens 90° counterclockwise. When the focusing and aperture knobs are vertical, remove the lens.

How to Use

The WL15 has two O-ring sealed exterior control knobs on either side of the lens barrel. The aperture control knob has a range of six click-stop settings: f/3.5, f/5.6, f/8, f/11, f/16, and f/22. The focus control knob offers a focusing range with five calibrated distances in *meters* (yellow numerals), from 0.3 to 1.5 meters and in *feet* (white numerals), from one foot to five feet. The infinity setting is marked in yellow. A depth of field decal provides for three aperture settings (f/3.5, f/8, f/16) and three focus settings (infinity, 1 meter, 0.4 meters).

Depth of Field

The following depth of field table demonstrates the outstanding capabilities of this lens. Study the chart and notice the depth of field range with each change in focus and aperture. All figures are in *feet.*

Focus	F/3.5	F/4	F/5.6	F/8	F/11	F/16	F/22
∞	6.0~∞	5.3~∞	3.9~∞	2.8~∞	2.0~∞	1.5~∞	1.2~∞
5	2.9~25	2.7~∞	2.3~∞	1.9~∞	1.6~∞	1.2~∞	1.0~∞
3	2.1~5.4	2.0~6.1	1.8~11	1.6~∞	1.4~∞	1.1~∞	0.9~∞
2	1.6~2.7	1.6~2.9	1.4~3.6	1.2~5.6	1.2~22.6	1.0~∞	0.9~∞
1.5	1.3~1.8	1.3~1.9	1.9~2.1	1.1~2.7	1.0~3.9	0.9~25	0.8~∞
1.2	1.0~1.4	1.0~1.4	1.0~1.5	0.9~1.7	0.9~2.1	0.8~3.6	0.7~∞
1	0.9~1.1	0.9~1.1	0.9~1.2	0.8~1.3	0.8~1.5	0.7~2	0.7~3.6

See page 126 for auxiliary viewfinder and page 114 for how to take pictures.

20MM WIDE ANGLE LENS FOR NIKONOS

The WL20 fills the gap between the 28mm medium wide lens and the super wide angle 15mm lens, and at an affordable price. It is compatible with the automatic metering systems of the Nikonos V and is capable of automatic TTL function with the Nikonos V. Its spring-loaded bayonet mount adapts to all models of the Nikonos except the RS.

This lens has become the lens of choice for many underwater photographers because of its impressive focusing range, sharp optics, and ability to produce high-contrast high-quality images. While its 80° angle of coverage may not be wide enough to take in a whale, it is an excellent portrait lens for medium-sized fish, schooling fish, and divers.

The WL20 is optically corrected for underwater use only.

Identification of Parts

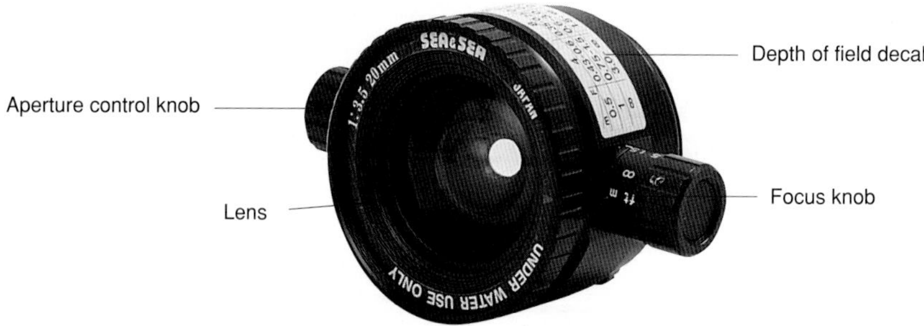

Specifications

Focal length:	20mm	**Dimensions:**	2.5 x 2.4 x 3.9" (D x L x W) (62 x 61 x 98mm)
Coverage:	80°	**Weight:**	9.5 ounces (270g)
Aperture range:	F/3.5 ~ f/22	**Filter diameter:**	58mm
Max. aperture ratio:	1:5.6	**Body material:**	Non-corrosive aluminum, anodized finish
Focusing range:	1.3 feet ~ ∞ (0.4m ~ ∞)	**Included:**	Front and rear lens caps; depth of field decal; O-ring
Minimum distance:	10" ~ ∞ (0.3 ~ ∞)		
Maximum depth:	200 feet (60 meters)		
Construction:	7 elements in 7 groups		

How to Mount

The instructions for mounting and detaching this lens are the same as those for the WL15. Please refer to pages 118-119.

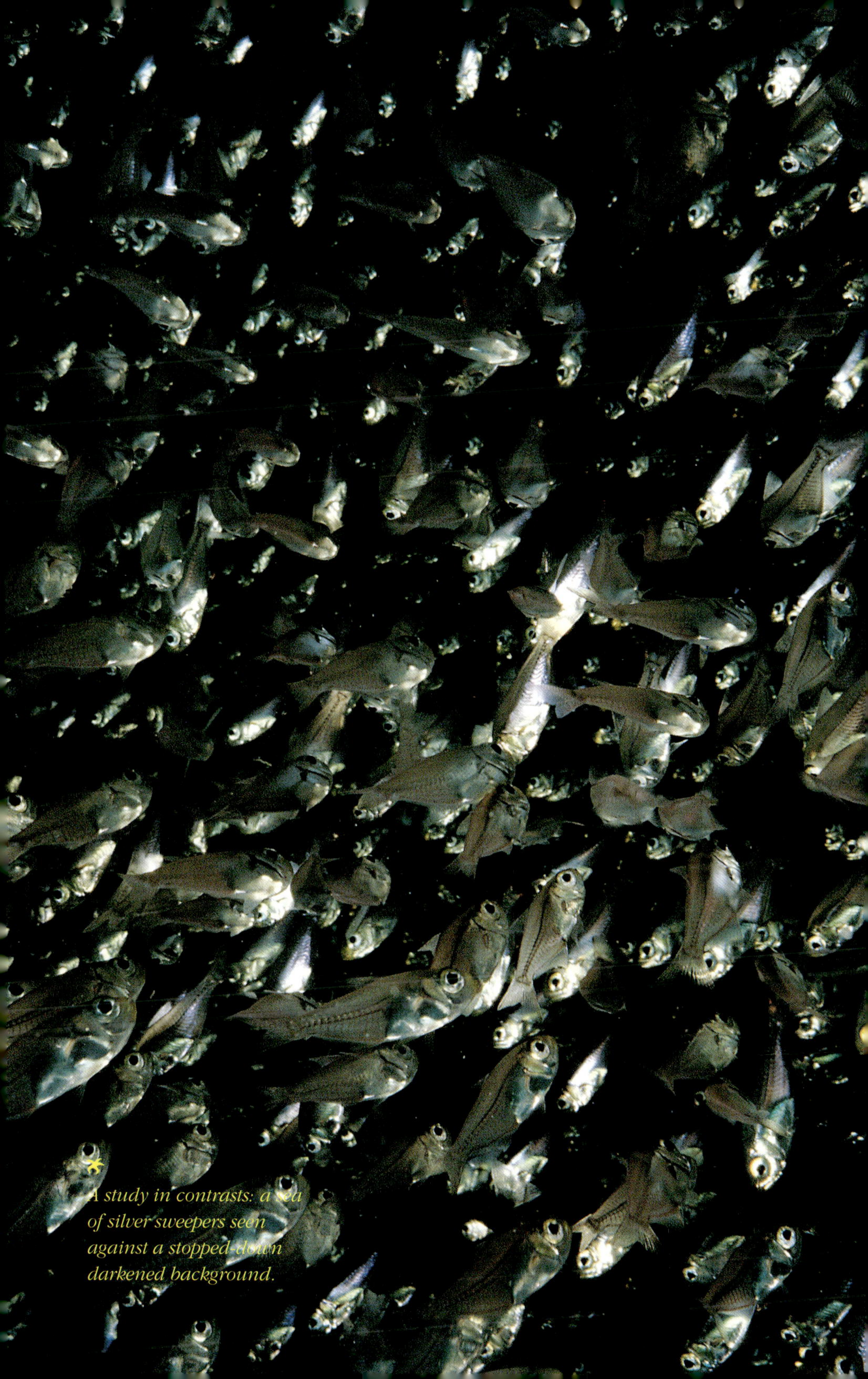

A study in contrasts: a sea of silver sweepers seen against a stopped-down darkened background.

How to Use

This lens has two O-ring sealed rotary-style exterior control knobs. The aperture control has six click-stop settings: f/3.5, f/5.6, f/8, f/11, f/16 and f/22. The focus control knob offers a focusing range with five calibrated distances and one setting for infinity. Yellow numerals designate meters, white numerals designate feet. The infinity setting is delineated in yellow. An accompanying decal, which you affix to the top of the lens, provides the depth of field for three set focal distances: 0.5 meter, one meter, and infinity.

When the 20 over the 15?

The 20 is the better choice when photographing large subjects that won't allow a close approach. The longer focal length of the 20mm lens will enable you to get a full-frame image from a greater shooting distance yet still close enough for good flash coverage and rich color saturation.

Depth of Field

For best results, study the depth of field range of this lens at each focus distance and aperture. The table below demonstrates the capabilities of this lens. The distances are provided in *feet*.

Focus	F/3.5	F/4	F/5.6	F/8	F/11	F/16	F/22
∞	10.0~∞	9.2~∞	6.6~∞	4.6~∞	3.3~∞	2.3~∞	1.7~∞
5	3.4~9.4	3.2~1.0	2.9~19.8	2.4~∞	2.0~∞	1.6~∞	1.3~∞
3	2.4~4.0	2.3~4.4	2.1~5.4	1.8~8.2	1.6~23.2	1.3~∞	1.1~∞
2	1.7~2.4	1.7~2.5	1.6~2.8	1.4~3.4	1.3~4.7	1.1~11.9	0.9~∞
1.5	1.3~1.7	1.3~0.8	1.2~1.9	1.2~2.2	1.0~2.6	0.9~3.9	0.8~9.6
1.3	1.2~1.5	1.2~1.5	1.0~1.6	1.0~1.8	1.0~2.0	0.9~2.8	0.8~4.7

You need an auxiliary viewfinder with this lens. See page 126.

Taking the Picture

See our step-by-step instructions on pages 114-115.

16MM SUPER WIDE CONVERSION LENS FOR NIKONOS

The SWL16 converts the Nikkor 35mm f/2.5 lens to a super wide angle lens. It is identical to the one manufactured for the Motor Marine II-EX *except for the lens mount*. Be sure you buy the one made specifically for your camera.

Identification of Parts

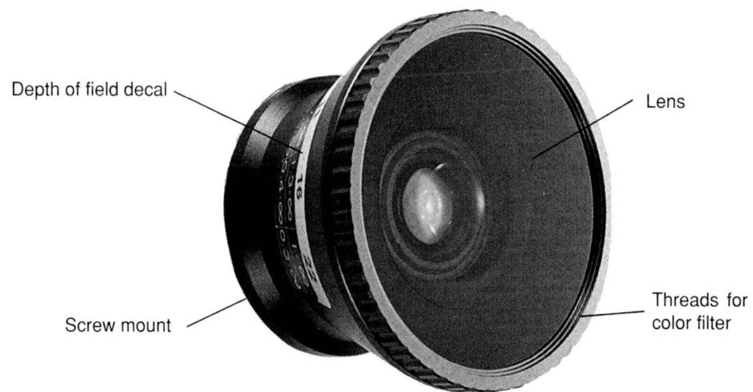

Specifications

Focal length:	16mm	**Weight:**	14 ounces (400g)
Coverage:	91°	**Body material:**	Hardened aluminum, anodized finish
Aperture range:	F/5.6 ~ f/22		
Maximum aperture:	F/5.6	**Included:**	Protective pouch, lens caps, aperture control knob cap, aperture, focus and depth of field decals, lens hood
Focusing range:	1 foot ~ ∞ (1m ~ ∞)		
Maximum depth:	200 feet (60 meters)		
Construction:	4 elements in 4 groups		
Dimensions:	3 x 2"(D x L)(78 x 48mm)		

Preparation for Use

This is the only conversion lens Sea & Sea manufactures for use with Nikonos cameras. Unlike primary lenses, there are no O-rings to service. However, it is still imperative to keep the lens mount and elements clean. The procedure is detailed on page 287.

How to Attach

This lens has a screw mount. The lens screws onto the front of the primary lens in a clockwise direction. Rotate it until it is secure. Be careful not to overtighten or you may damage the threads.

Note: A wide slot at the back of the lens allows water to flood the space between the primary lens and conversion lens. Water is part of the total optical design. Attach underwater. If assembled topside, loosen the lens underwater to allow air to escape. Air in this pocket will adversely affect image quality.

How to Attach the Aperture Cap

After the conversion lens is attached, the aperture and focus settings on the primary lens are hidden from view. You must take your settings from the markings on the aperture cap that fits over the 35mm lens aperture knob.

Clean the decal areas with alcohol, then affix the aperture and focus decals as shown. When the aperture cap is used, the focus knob should be on the right and the aperture knob on the left. ▶

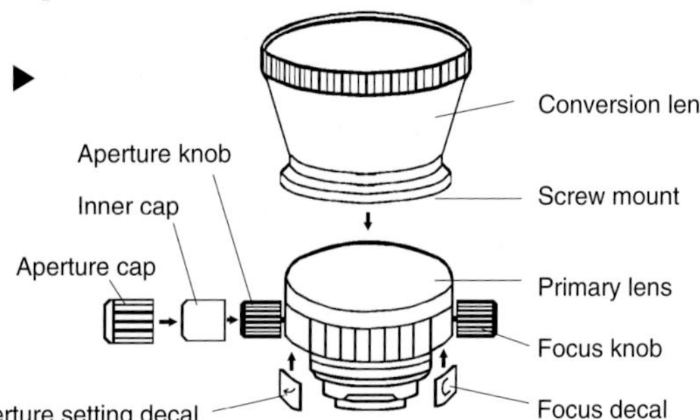

1. Insert the cap into the aperture knob of the primary lens.
2. Set the aperture of the lens at f/5.6. (The inner cap is for use on older models of the Nikonos 35mm lens.)
3. Align f/5.6 on the aperture cap with the arrow on the aperture decal.

To *detach,* unscrew the lens from the primary lens counterclockwise.

Depth of Field

This lens has a maximum aperture of f/5.6. A decal on the lens provides the correct depth of field at each aperture setting.

Preset focus at infinity for all f-stops	**F-stop**	**5.6**	**8**	**11**	**16**	**22**
	Feet	2.7 ~ ∞	2.0 ~ ∞	1.7 ~ ∞	1.3 ~ ∞	1.0 ~ ∞
	Meters	0.8 ~ ∞	0.6 ~ ∞	0.5 ~ ∞	0.4 ~ ∞	0.3 ~ ∞

You need an auxiliary viewfinder with this lens. See page 124.

Taking the Picture

See pages 114-115.

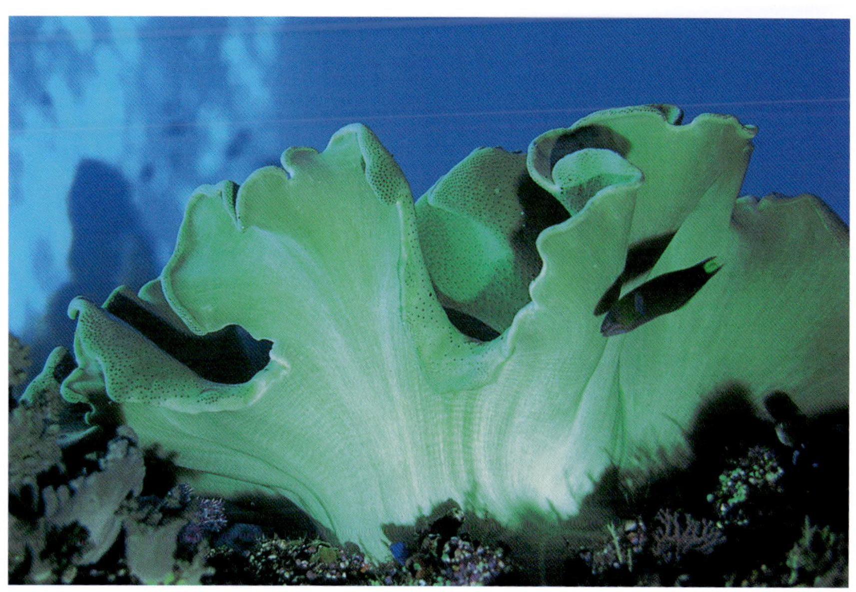

The photographer's perspective and the deep shadows created by dual TTL strobes transformed an ordinary sponge into a powerful image. A personal favorite.

AUXILIARY VIEWFINDERS

An auxiliary viewfinder is an optional accessory. But why buy a viewfinder when the camera has one built in?

The Motor Marine II-EX's built-in viewfinder has 85 percent frame coverage. That means it has a 40° angle of view. The Nikonos V's built-in viewfinder only covers 85 percent of the Nikkor 35mm lens. Obviously, when using a wide angle lens, the built-in viewfinder doesn't afford you a view of the entire scene in front of you. That seriously inhibits your ability to frame your photograph accurately. You can't overcome this problem by looking over the viewfinder. The human eye has an angle of view of 46°; a 16mm lens sees 91°, a 20mm 80°. To compose with the same perspective as the lens, you need a viewfinder with the same perspective as the lens.

The second limitation with the built-in viewfinder has to do with *parallax.*

Parallax is the difference in the position of the subject as you see it through the viewfinder and the position of the subject as seen by the lens. The reason is simple: the viewfinder is mounted several inches above the lens. ▶

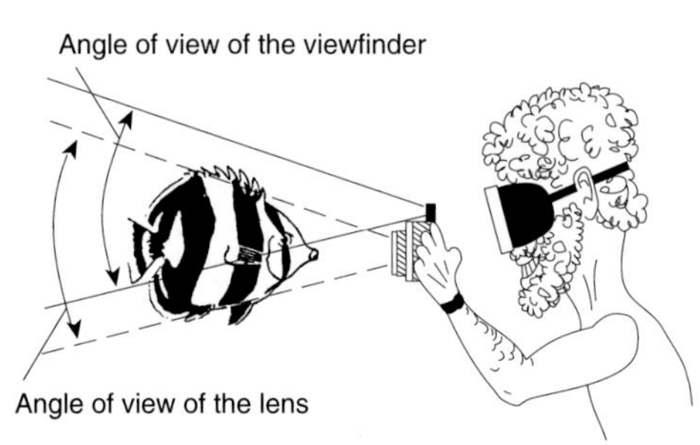

Notice the difference in the angle of view of the viewfinder and that of the lens. What you see through the viewfinder is not what the lens sees. The closer the subject is to the lens, the greater the discrepancy.

The camera's viewfinder includes etched guide marks to help you correct for parallax from three to four feet. For subject-to-camera distances closer than that, you need an auxiliary optical viewfinder.

Sea & Sea offers two auxiliary optical viewfinders.They enable you to see what the lens is seeing so you can compose and frame your photograph precisely.

High EyePoint Optical Viewfinder

The High-Eyepoint Optical Viewfinder is a professional-quality finder that ensures the most accurate framing. It is a dedicated optical viewfinder with a large viewing port and super wide angle coverage of 96°. It features internal etchings with separate parallax correction guidelines for composition and framing for the 15, 20, 35mm and close-up lenses. It has a shoe mount for the top of the camera and a knurled lockdown screw that prevents slippage.

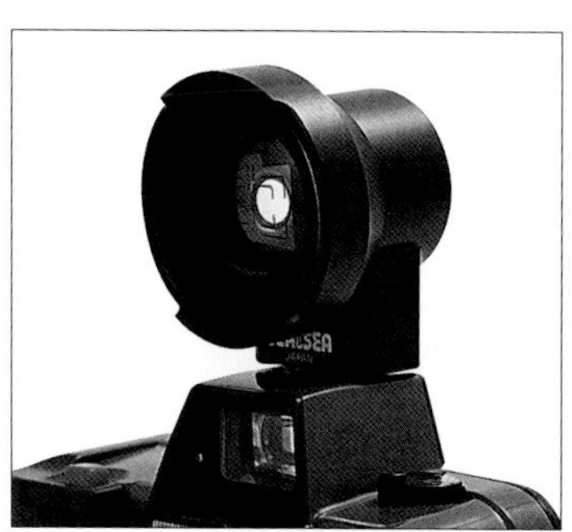

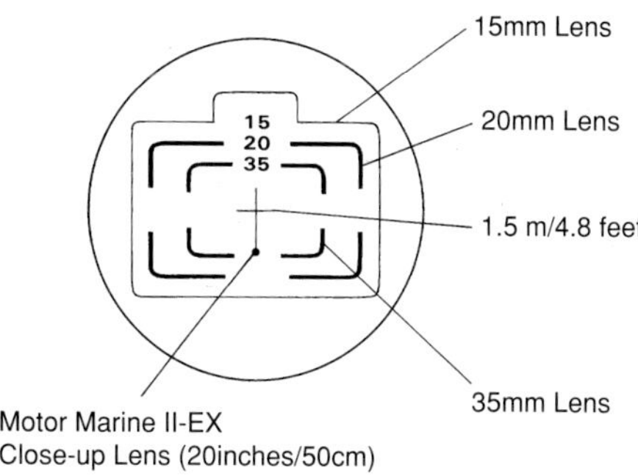

The Optical Viewfinder

This parallax adjustable viewfinder is fitted with a mount that slips into the accessory shoe on the top of the camera. There is a circular distance scale below the eyepiece, calibrated for varying distances. The numbers are in both meters and feet. The distance setting must be the same as that on your camera. As you rotate the scale, the eyepiece will tilt up or down, changing what you view to match what the lens sees.

The viewfinder comes with three different ▶ format masks: 35mm, 28mm, and 20mm. Without any mask, the viewfinder has a field of view of approximately 90°. Thus, when using the 16mm lens, no mask is necessary since the angle of view of the viewfinder is approximately equivalent to that of the 16mm lens.

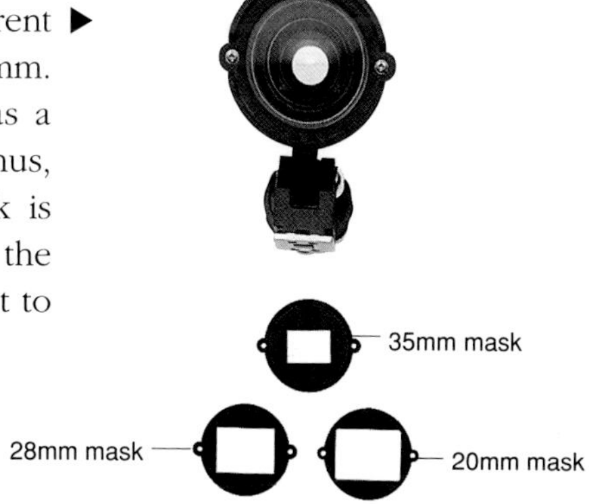

Basic Wide Angle Images

The greater angle of view and expanded depth of field of the wide angle lens offer the photographer the opportunity to create an infinite variety of images. These images fall into six basic categories:

- *Silhouettes.* By now you've mastered silhouettes with your 35mm lens. You know that the sun is behind your subject and you shoot at an extreme upward angle. However, with the 35mm lens you must position yourself pretty far away to get the whole subject in the frame. With a wide angle lens that distance is dramatically shortened. Hence, colors are stronger, contrast is accentuated, the image is sharper.

- *Silhouettes with strobe fill.* By illuminating an area in the foreground, you not only add color to the photograph but you shift the primary area of interest. Focus, aperture, and strobe distance are based on the foreground subject, generally one to two feet away.

- *Ambient light scenics.* These are panoramic photographs using sunlight exposures only. They are usually taken at depths less than 20 feet; the sun is positioned behind you. They capture the scene in hues of blues and green and convey a mood of serenity and peace. Good for taking pictures of large fish and marine mammals.

- *Ambient light scenics with strobe fill.* Even the most powerful strobes are ineffective at distances beyond eight feet. To add color and dimension to wide angle scenics, fill in the foreground area with strobe light and let the background fall to ambient light. These shots are taken at a horizontal or upward angle.

- *Diver portraits.* With a wide angle lens you can get excellent head shots, head-and-shoulder shots, or full figure shots. When photographing a diver, skin tones must be natural, so the shot must be taken at close range, three feet or less. Strobe light is essential to restore color and definition to the diver's features.

- *Marine life portraits.* For remarkable close-ups of sea life, you need a wide angle lens that will focus down to one foot. F-stop will depend on strobe and camera-to-subject distance.

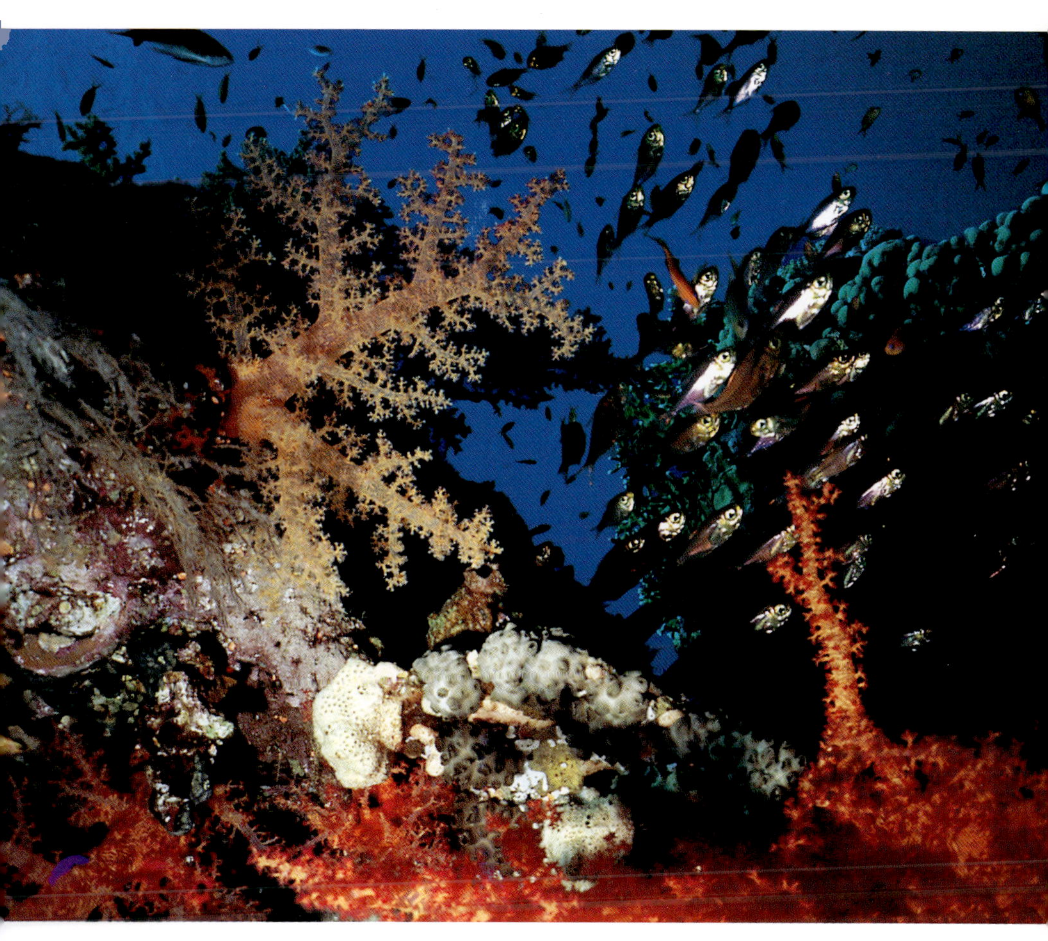

An ambient light scenic with strobe fill of the Red Sea's bountiful life and brilliant colors. Taken with the Motor Marine II-EX and the 20mm Wide Conversion Lens.

Tip for Nikonos Owners
Get into the habit of rewinding the film as soon as possible, even if you don't plan on reloading at that time. It's a safeguard against a mindless mistake. It's easy to get distracted and open the camera before the film is rewound. You went to a lot of trouble to get those pictures—don't lose them!

Advanced Technique: Close Focus Wide Angle Scenic

Many professional underwater photographers have adopted the term *close focus wide angle* for the type of shot we mention on page 128, called an "ambient light scenic with strobe fill."

In this type of photograph, a foreground subject is one to two feet from the lens and is emphasized through composition and strobe illumination. The strobe lights the foreground. It provides "fill light." Since even the most powerful strobe cannot illuminate the seascape, the background exposure is totally controlled by the ambient light.

The strobe is positioned to illuminate and add color to the foreground. The background is a hue of blue or green. To avoid having the background too dark (underexposed) or washed out (overexposed), you must *balance* ambient light with strobe light.

Here's how:

1. Compose your shot. Frame your foreground subject at a horizontal or slightly upward angle.
2. Aim the lens at the water column next to the foreground subject.
3. Take a light meter reading of the water next to or above your foreground subject. Meter the center of the water column. If you take a reading of the top (brightest) part of the column, the bottom part of your photo will be underexposed. If you meter the lower (darkest) portion of the water column, the top part of your photo will be overexposed. Aim at the center for an overall *average* ambient light reading.
5. Determine strobe-to-subject distance for that f-stop. See Chapter 7, *Strobes*.
6. Check positioning of your strobe.
7. Take the picture.
8. Bracket.

Tip: Compose with something colorful in the corner or bottom of the frame. A purple sea fan or a red sea whip will enhance the photograph without detracting from the focus. Pay attention to the foreground. You want only sea *life* in your picture, never anything dead or broken.

Is a Whale Shark Shot Luck?

Yes. And no. Yes, because the photographer happened to be in the right place at the right time. No, because the reason he got the shot was because she was prepared to get it.

The most treasured photos are often taken within moments after the plunge from the boat. So be ready for the unexpected!

▼ Preset all camera controls at average settings. With ISO 100 film, set your f-stop at f/8. For tropical waters, this will be the correct f-stop within one stop.

▼ In turbid water with 25-50' visibility, set aperture at f/5.6.

▼ Preset focus for 3-5 feet. Both the above combinations provide good depth of field.

Another Advanced Technique: Close Focus Portrait

In this type of photograph, the background is intensely dark and serves to frame your subject. The results are dramatic.

1. Pre-set at f/22, 1/60 second.
2. Compose with subject about one foot from the lens.
3. Frame your subject against open water. There should be nothing else in the image area but your subject and water. Use a horizontal or slightly upward camera angle.
4. At such close range, you cannot use the camera's viewfinder. To adjust for parallax, you must use a wide angle viewfinder. If you don't have one, hold the camera slightly in front of you. Extend your index finger like a rod alongside the camera, making sure your finger aligns with the center of the lens and is pointed at the center of the subject. It's simple and it works.
5. Position your strobe approximately 18 inches from the subject.
6. Take the picture, then bracket.

Lighting for Wide Angle Photography

The expanded angle of coverage of a wide angle lens requires that more light be drawn into the lens for a correct exposure. An auxiliary strobe is vital for sharp and vibrant images. See Chapter 7, *Strobes*.

Care after Use

The internal elements on all Sea & Sea lenses are factory sealed in a body of anodized aluminum. There is minimal maintenance required to keep the lenses at optimal performance.

Always rinse well after use to prevent salt deposits from forming; salt crystals can scratch the lens. Apply a few drops of lens cleaning fluid to a lens tissue and wipe with a circular motion. Lightly lubricate the lens fittings with silicone grease.

Read Chapter 9, *Care and Maintenance.*

Storage

Lenses are prone to moisture. Condensation can form and pose a problem with improperly stored lenses. That's why every Sea & Sea lens comes from the factory with a silica gel pack. After cleaning the lens, cover its front and rear elements with their protective lens caps. Store in its lens pouch or in a plastic container with a vacuum sealing lid. Keep the silica gel pack in the case or cabinet where you store your system.

CHAPTER FIVE

Close-up and Macro Photography

Close-up and Macro Photography

The reef is crawling with tiny creatures. Beautiful, colorful creatures you would love to photograph. But what would the photograph look like if you took it with your 35mm lens? If you got close enough to fill the frame with your diminutive subject, your photograph would be out of focus because the minimum focusing distance for a 35mm lens is about three feet. Incontrovertible fact: you cannot get a sharp photograph if you shoot closer than the minimum focus distance. If you keep your distance and shoot from three feet, the little critter will look like an unidentifiable spot amidst the myriad of shapes and colors of the reef.

There's only one way to achieve the image you crave: with a close focusing accessory. Close-up and macro accessories overcome the limitations of your primary lens. They expand the range of its capabilities and enable you to accomplish what would otherwise be impossible: to get very close, to fill the frame and capture your subject with all its stunning color and intricate detail in needle-sharp focus.

Close-up and macro photography offer a new perspective, a view in which tiny subjects usually unnoticed or dwarfed by the larger picture suddenly *become* the picture. We can zero in and make it the focus of attention to the exclusion of all other components of the reef. We can capture even the tiniest inhabitants of the sea with exquisite exactness or in provocative abstract. We can create art.

What is Close-up?

Close-up photography begins where normal photography leaves off. It is a form of photography in which a larger-than-normal image is produced by focusing a lens closer than normal to the subject.

A close-up lens is a single-element supplemental lens mounted to the front of the camera's primary lens. Its purpose is to overcome the minimum focusing limits of the primary lens, to shorten that minimum distance. Close-up lenses magnify objects for the primary lens. Just as reading glasses enlarge the printed page for the human eye, close-up lenses enlarge subjects for the camera's primary lens.

Close-up underwater photography means you can shoot at a distance of less than three feet. You can shoot small subjects or fill the frame with a detail of a subject. At such close range, the image is unaffected by the filtering and scattering effects of water, so images are sharper, more colorful.

What is Macro?

Macro is a form of photography where the lens is positioned very close to the subject and the resultant exposure fills the frame with a very large image. Two types of auxiliary equipment are used for macrophotography: extension tubes and macro lenses.

An *extension tube* is a hollow metal or plastic cylinder that fits between the camera body and primary lens, machined in different lengths to achieve different magnification ratios. It will enlarge an image by physically moving the lens farther away from the film plane. It contains no glass elements. It does not affect image quality. It merely increases the distance between the optical center of the lens and the film, thereby magnifying the image.

An extension tube also extends the focal length of the lens. By increasing the focal length, you decrease the minimum focus distance. This permits the image to spread out and fill the entire frame. A small wire or plastic framing device is attached to the extension tube and positioned out in front of the lens for framing and focus.

Extension tubes allow you to focus the lens at very close distances. For example, the closest focusing distance for the Nikonos 35mm lens is 2.75 feet on your lens scale, which is 3.4 feet measured distance underwater. At this distance the field of view is so wide that a two or three-inch creature will be insignificant in the photo, disappearing into the surrounding colors and patterns of the reef. If you shoot closer than that, your pictures will be fuzzy. But when you add a Sea & Sea extension tube to that lens, the focusing distance can be reduced to *three inches*.

A *macro lens* performs the same function but in a different manner. It is not a tube but a supplemental lens with magnifying elements. Instead of being positioned *between* the camera body and primary lens, it is placed *in front of* the primary lens. It alters the focal length and optical properties of your primary lens, enabling the lens to focus closer. It, too, uses a framer for framing and focus.

Macro Systems vs. Close-Up Lenses: The Difference

Both magnify the subject and allow for closer than normal focusing, so which should you use?

Generally, macro systems (extension tubes and macro lenses) are used for shooting the sea's smallest inhabitants. The rule of thumb is that close-up lenses are appropriate for subjects three to 12 inches tall, and macro systems are best used for subjects smaller than three inches.

Macro systems have greater magnifying power and yield a higher image sharpness than close-up lenses.

Close-up lenses allow focusing closer than the standard lens but not as close as macro. The advantages of close-up lenses over extension tubes: they can be attached and detached underwater, giving you greater flexibility and choice of subject during any single dive, and they afford greater depth of field.

Note: In this chapter we focus on only *one* close-up lens: the MX-10 Close-up Lens. Since the close-up lens for the Motor Marine II-EX is built into the camera, we discuss that in Chapter 3. All other close-focusing accessories manufactured by Sea & Sea are macro accessories: two macro lenses for the Motor Marine II and II-EX cameras and four extension tube systems for Nikonos cameras.

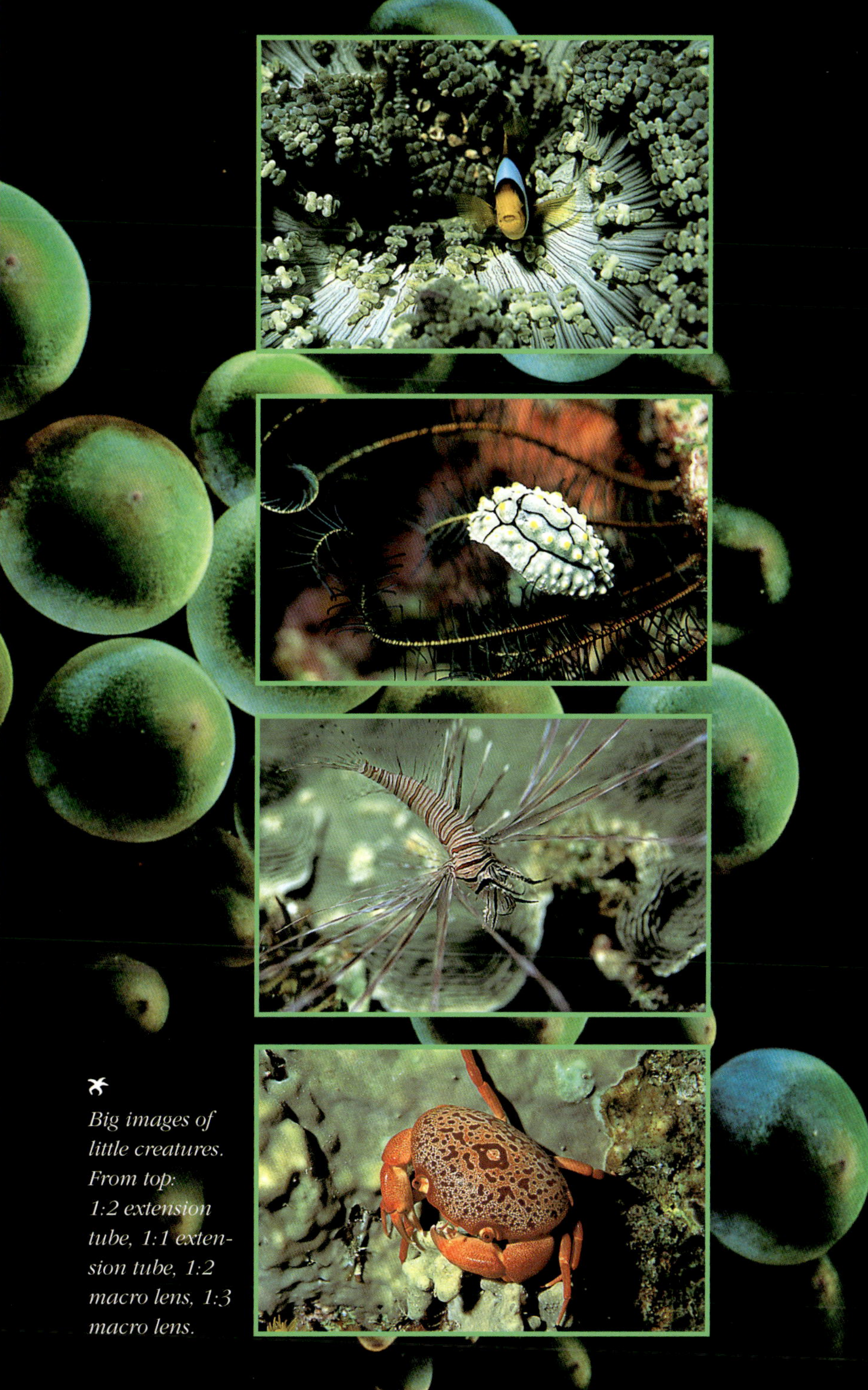

Big images of little creatures. From top: 1:2 extension tube, 1:1 extension tube, 1:2 macro lens, 1:3 macro lens.

MX-10 CLOSE-UP LENS

The MX-10 Close-up Lens is a conversion lens. It converts the camera's built-in lens 32mm lens from a standard lens with a minimum focusing distance of four feet to a close-up lens with a minimum focusing distance of 18 inches. You can achieve larger, sharper, more colorful pictures of small and medium-sized fish, coral, sponges, and head shots of fellow divers. It is ideal for low visibility conditions. The lens is for underwater use only.

Specifications

Construction:	Single lens element, f/4.5	**Depth of field:**	1 ~ 3.6 ft. at f/22
Aperture range:	F/4.5 ~ f/22		0.32 ~ 1.1m at f/22
Minimum focusing distance:	0.5m/1.6 feet	**Dimensions:**	2.5 x 2 x 0.5" (H x W x H) (61.5 x 51 x 12.2mm)

Preparation

Examine the lens for lint, sand, or other debris. If necessary, rinse in clean water; dry thoroughly. Lightly lubricate the lens fitting to facilitate ease of attachment and removal.

How to Assemble

The MX-10 Close-up Lens is fitted with a bayonet mount that attaches onto the face of the built-in lens.

1. Align the white dot on the close-up lens with the white dot on the built-in lens. Make sure that the dot on the close-up lens is at the bottom of the camera and the triangular wedge is at the top of the camera. ▶
2. Turn clockwise till you hear it click into position.

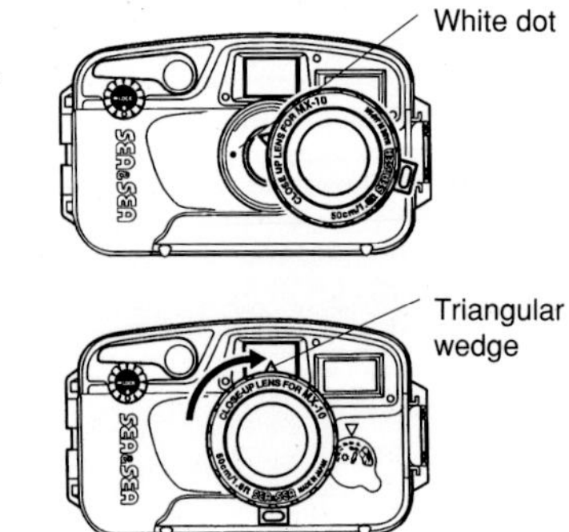

Note: If you mount the lens on land, remove it underwater to allow trapped air bubbles to escape from the space between the lenses. Water must be exchanged for air in this space. Water is part of the optical formula. Air will adversely affect image quality. Be sure to lock the lens back into position.

Note: Forceful impact can knock the lens off the camera. Be especially careful when handing the camera up to a crew member on board a dive boat or climbing the swim step to the dive platform. An accidental jolt against the boat can dislodge the lens and send it careening to the deep. Attach a monofiliment line or tie wrap to the slot on the bottom of the lens and attach the other end to the lanyard holder on the camera.

The right size subjects for your Close-up Lens
Christmas tree worms, anemones, sea stars, sea urchin, octopus, small to medium-sized fish such as damsel, garibaldi, juvenile angelfish

How to Attach the Parallax Correction Mask

When shooting at very close distances, the view of the scene as seen through the camera's viewfinder is different from that seen by the lens. This is called parallax. The companion viewing mask has been designed to adjust for that difference so that what you see through the peep sight is the same as what the lens sees and what the film will record.

With the flat side of the mask ▶ facing toward you, fit the mask into the camera's viewfinder eyepiece. Secure with the mounting screw.

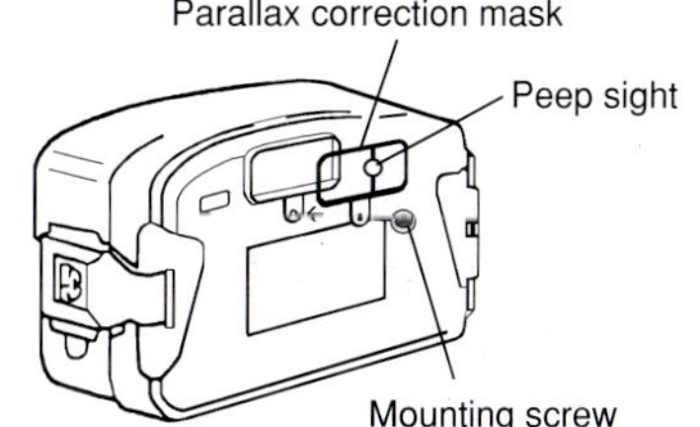

Focusing Range

Minimum focusing distance is always measured at the lens's largest aperture. Therefore, minimum focusing distance for the close-up lens is approximately 18 inches when the aperture is set at f/4.5. *Where is that down there?*

If you aren't proficient at estimating distance, and most novice underwater photographers generally aren't, you should practice on a stationary subject. There are two ways to do this. One, cut a piece of string. Stretch it out from subject to lens (be careful not to touch the subject). Hold your position, put the string away, and take the picture. Do that till you can eyeball the distance.

Or use the "arm's length method." An average adult arm measures approximately 18 inches from fingertip to elbow. Extend your arm so fingertips are just in front of your subject. Memorize the spot. Take the picture.

Master estimating distance before you try photographing fish. They won't cooperate with either the string or the arm's length method.

The right time to use your Close-up Lens

▼ Anytime visibility is poor. It allows you to dramatically reduce the water column between lens and subject for sharper, more colorful pictures.

▼ Night diving. Preset controls, then point and shoot.

Depth of Field

The most difficult aspect of close-up photography is making sure your subject is within the zone of sharp focus.

Depth of field with a close-up lens is quite limited. With limited depth of field, there's little room for error. With your built-in 32mm lens, depth of field is 3 to 5.5 feet at f/4.5. With the close-up lens at f/4.5 it's only inches! To position your subject within the proper camera-to-subject distance, you must accurately estimate distance. F-stop settings determine depth of field. To extend depth of field, use smaller apertures. See the depth of field chart below.

F-stop	F/4.5	F/5.6	F/8	F/11	F/16	F/22
Feet	1.6~1.8	1.4~1.9	1.4~2.0	1.3~2.2	1.2~2.7	1.0~3.6
Meters	0.45~0.56	0.43~0.58	0.42~0.62	0.39~0.81	0.36~0.81	0.32~1.09

Notice how depth of field increases with each successively smaller aperture.

How to Use

1. Set your YS-40A on Auto.
2. Set your f-stop. *With ISO 100 film,* the manufacturer's suggested f-stop with the YS-40A is f/4.5. Depth of field at this f-stop is critical. To extend depth of field and achieve sharper images, set at f/8. *With ISO 400 film,* the manufacturer's suggested f-stop with the YS-40A is f/8. At this f-stop depth of field is extremely limited. To extend depth of field and achieve sharper pictures, set at f/16.
3. Hold the camera about two inches ▶ in front of your face mask and sight your subject through the peep sight. Align with the wedge and take the picture.

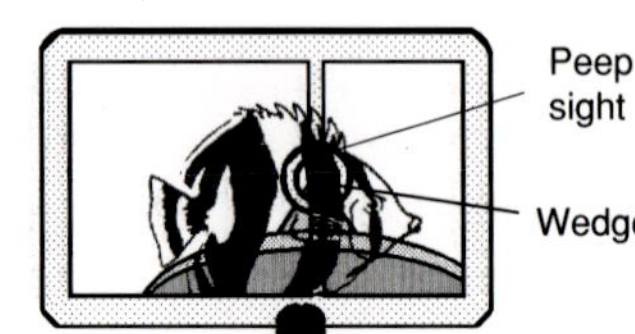

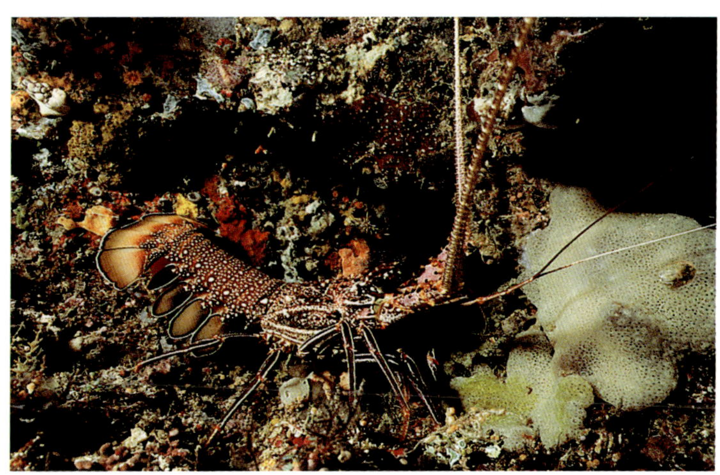

Made for each other: the lobster was the right size subject for the close-up lens, and the close-up lens was the right lens to capture this lobster full-frame. Taken with ISO 400, strobe on Auto, f/16.

MACRO PHOTOGRAPHY

Macro photography is fun and easy. With preset controls and a framing device for foolproof focusing distance, macro is basically a point-and-shoot technique. Even a first-time shooter can get stunning pictures. Suitable subjects are myriad: 95 percent of the sea's inhabitants are invertebrates. And of course, it is indispensable for night diving.

Why Colors Are So Strong

The vibrant colors and impressive image crispness are due to three factors unique to macrophotography:

1. Available light has no effect on macro photographs. The subject is totally illuminated by flash.
2. The distance between the camera lens and your subject ranges from three to seven inches, depending on the macro system used. Thus, the light path through water is too short for there to be any discernible color loss due to absorption.
3. The distance between your strobe and subject is 10 inches or less. The extreme intensity of your flash at this distance enriches color and highlights every nuance of your subject.

Reproduction Ratios

How large a macro system will make the subject appear on film is called the *reproduction ratio.* Reproduction ratio is the size of the image on film as compared to the subject's actual size. The first number represents the subject's *image size on film;* the second number is the subject's *actual life size.*

With a l:l (referred to as *one-to-one*) system, the image on film will be the actual size of the subject. A 1:2 ratio means your subject will appear one-half its actual size. With a l:3 your subject will appear one-third its actual size on film. With a 2:1 the image on film will appear twice its actual size.

Ratio Image	Size on Film	Actual Life Size
1:1	1 inch	1 inch
1:2	1 inch	2 inches
1:3	1 inch	3 inches
2:1	2 inches	1 inches

Sea & Sea offers two macro systems for use with the Motor Marine II and II-EX and four extension tube systems for Nikonos cameras. They are for underwater use only.

Depth of Field

In macrophotography depth of field is extremely narrow because:

- the closer you focus a lens, the shallower its depth of field
- as magnification increases, depth of field decreases.

For example, depth of field with the 1:2 macro lens for the Motor Marine II-EX at f/22 is *one inch*.

Estimating the precise focus distance is critical. And there is no margin for error. Even the most experienced underwater photographer would be hard-pressed to accurately estimate the precise focus distance when the difference between a sharp image and a blurry one is half an inch. That's why macro systems come equipped with framing devices.

Framing Devices

Framing devices consist of two parts: a base plate that protrudes in front of the lens and ends where the camera lens focuses and vertical rods that define the picture area.

Sea & Sea calls the base plate on their macro system a *gauge plate;* indeed it is: it "gauges" the distance. The precise point of sharp focus is delineated by the end of the base plate. You don't have to estimate distance; you simply align the end of the base plate flush with the area of the subject you want in sharp focus.

The guide rods are painted black to prevent reflection and lens glare. Their purpose is to help you frame and focus your subject.

The framer also serves to frame the picture area for you—with one hitch. The actual picture area is smaller than the area outlined by the framer. This prevents the framer from showing in your picture. Therefore, when composing your picture, keep an imaginary 1/8" border within the rods of your framer.

Using a Strobe

No matter how bright and sunny a day it is. No matter how shallow the reef you are diving. When you're taking a picture of a clownfish from five inches, ambient light will not be your source of illumination. In macro the strobe light paints the picture.

In macrophotography your strobe is more than just a functional piece of equipment; it is a creative tool. The final image on film is wholly a result of the beam of light you cast on your subject. And how good, how *interesting* your picture is depends on the angle and distance of your strobe from its subject. You can create wonderful effects with your strobe.

But before you get fancy, begin with your strobe in a fixed, mounted position. Shoot a few rolls of film to familiarize yourself with strobe distancing. Next, experiment with the arm detached. Expose a few rolls of film hand holding the strobe in different positions.

Whether hand holding the strobe or using it mounted in a fixed position, the important thing is to be creative. Unless you're shooting pictures for a marine life textbook, you don't have to strive for a fully-lighted lateral view of every creature. Oftentimes, what you *don't* light makes more of a visual statement than what you *do* light.

Basic Flash Angles

▼ *Top front lighting.* Position the strobe just above the camera and pointed at the front of the subject. The light will cast downward shadows and create dimension and depth.

▼ *Top side lighting.* This is the most realistic and pleasing because it simulates how sunlight illuminates objects on land. Position the strobe above and to the left of the camera. Direct your beam of light at a 45° angle at the top and slightly to the left of your subject. Use this flash angle if there is a lot of sediment in the water; it will reduce backscatter.

▼ *Side lighting.* Hold the strobe off to the left and lowered almost parallel to the camera. The light strikes the side of your subject and casts long shadows on the other side of the subject.

▼ *Overhead lighting.* Sharp, dramatic shadows and bold contours are achieved when the strobe is held directly above the subject and pointed straight downward.

▼ *Back lighting.* Position the strobe above or to the side and slightly forward of the camera and aimed three to four inches behind the subject. This illumination gives some subjects translucence, others a golden halo. Take care that the flash is not pointed directly toward the camera lens or your picture will be overexposed.

Strobe-to-Subject Distance with Macro Lenses

In macrophotography, to compensate for using the smallest aperture, you must position your strobe closer than the manufacturer's recommended strobe-to-subject distance. The following distances are suggested:

1:3 macro lens – 9 - 10 inches
1:2 macro lens – 7 - 9 inches

Note: Adjustments may be necessary depending upon the *reflectivity* of your subject. Bright, light-colored subjects and light backgrounds reflect more light than dark ones. Compensate by pulling the strobe back an inch or two. Likewise, dark subjects and dark backgrounds reflect less light; move the strobe closer an inch or two.

Strobe-to-Subject Distance with Extension Tubes

The longer the extension tube, the more light is lost as it travels down the lens assembly. To create a proper exposure, you must position your strobe closer than your strobe's recommended strobe-to-subject distance. The following distances are recommended:

1:1 extension tube – 4 - 5 inches
1:2 extension tube – 7 - 9 inches
1:3 extension tube – 9 - 10 inches
2:1 extension tube – 3 - 4 inches

Note: Adjustments may be necessary depending upon the power of your flash. If images end up overexposed, move the strobe back. If they are underexposed, move it closer. When shooting a light-colored subject, pull back an inch or two. When shooting a dark subject, move in.

MX-10 MACRO LENS

Specifications

Magnification ratio: 1:4.55
Construction: 2 elements in 2 groups
Aperture range: F/4.5 ~ f/22

Picture area: 4.4 x 6.6" (109 x 164mm)
Depth of field: 10-11" at f/16, 9-11" at f/22 (245~275mm at f/16,239~281mm at f/22)

Preparation

Examine the lens for lint, sand, or other debris. If necessary, rinse in clean water; dry thoroughly. Lightly lubricate the lens mount to facilitate ease of attachment and removal. The base plate and guide rods are made of salt-resistant resin; rinse to remove sand or other debris.

How to Assemble

It is a compact two-part system: the bayonet coupling lens is fitted to the base plate by a hinge, an innovative feature that makes the unit impact-resistant and enables you to fold the lens down out of the way for convenient storage. A detachable guide rod stores on the under side of the base plate in a slotted channel.

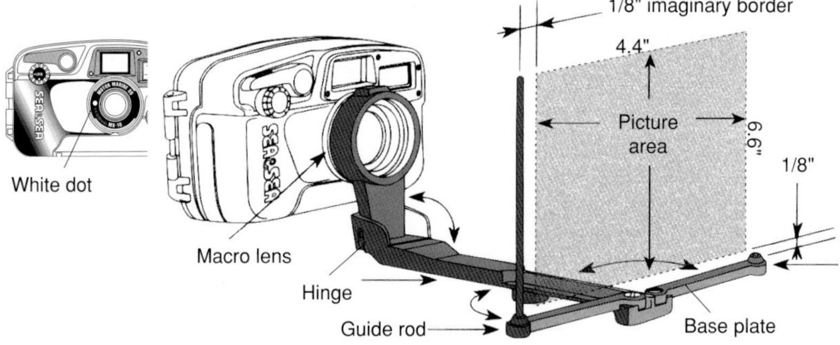

1. Place the lens upright so that the mark on the lens coincides with the mark on the camera body.
2. Turn the lens clockwise until it clicks into place.

Note: This lens should be attached underwater to allow water to flood the space between the camera lens and the macro lens. Water is part of the total optical design. If assembled on land, loosen the lens underwater so that trapped air can escape. Air between the lenses will impair image quality. Be sure to click it back into the locked position.

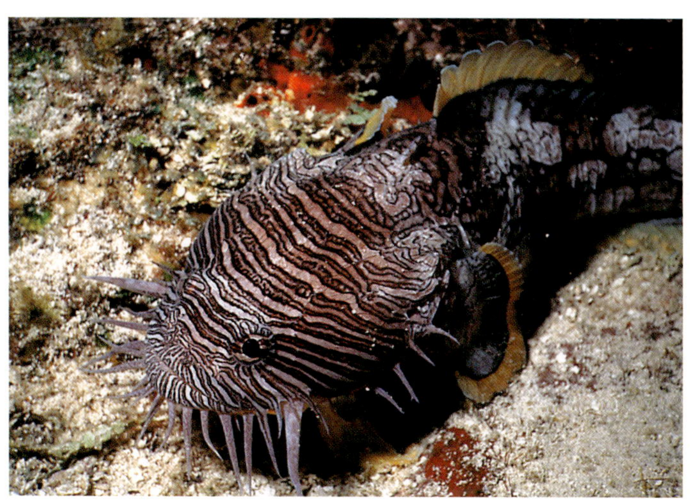

Cozumel's elusive
Splendid Toadfish was
actually quite cooperative.
Posed patiently while
I moved the base plate to
within an inch, and then it
was f/22, point and shoot.

How to Use

1. Extend the base plate to the full extended position. It will lock into place.
2. Open the right and left view bars.
3. Screw the guide rod into the right-hand side of the framer.
4. Check that the gauge plate is set parallel to the bottom of the camera. If not, adjust by loosening the allen screw on the bottom of the lens collar. Align the base plate and tighten the screw. *Caution*: Do not overtighten. The plastic collar can break.
5. Remember, the lens does not see everything that the framer outlines. Indent your subject by about 1/8" all around the framer.
6. Depth of field with macro is critical. Best aperture settings for ISO 100 are f/16 when shooting dark subjects and f/22 when shooting bright or reflective subjects. Gauge distance to the subject is 10.75 inches (260mm).

Taking the Picture

With the YS-40 Strobe or YS-40A in Manual Mode:

1. Turn power to the "On" position.
2. Attach the diffuser to your YS-40 strobe. The diffuser is recommended to disperse light evenly and to minimize backscatter. *Note:* The YS-40A has a built-in diffuser.
3. Set film speed selector to ISO 100.
4. Set aperture to f/16 or f/22 depending upon the reflectivity of your subject.
5. Compose your picture within the framer and guide rod.
6. Hold steady and take the shot.

With the YS-40A in Auto Mode:

1. Turn power to the "Auto" position.
2. Set film speed selector to ISO 100.
3. Set aperture to f/16 or f/22 depending upon the reflectivity of your subject.
4. Compose your picture within the framer and guide rod.
5. Hold steady and take the shot.

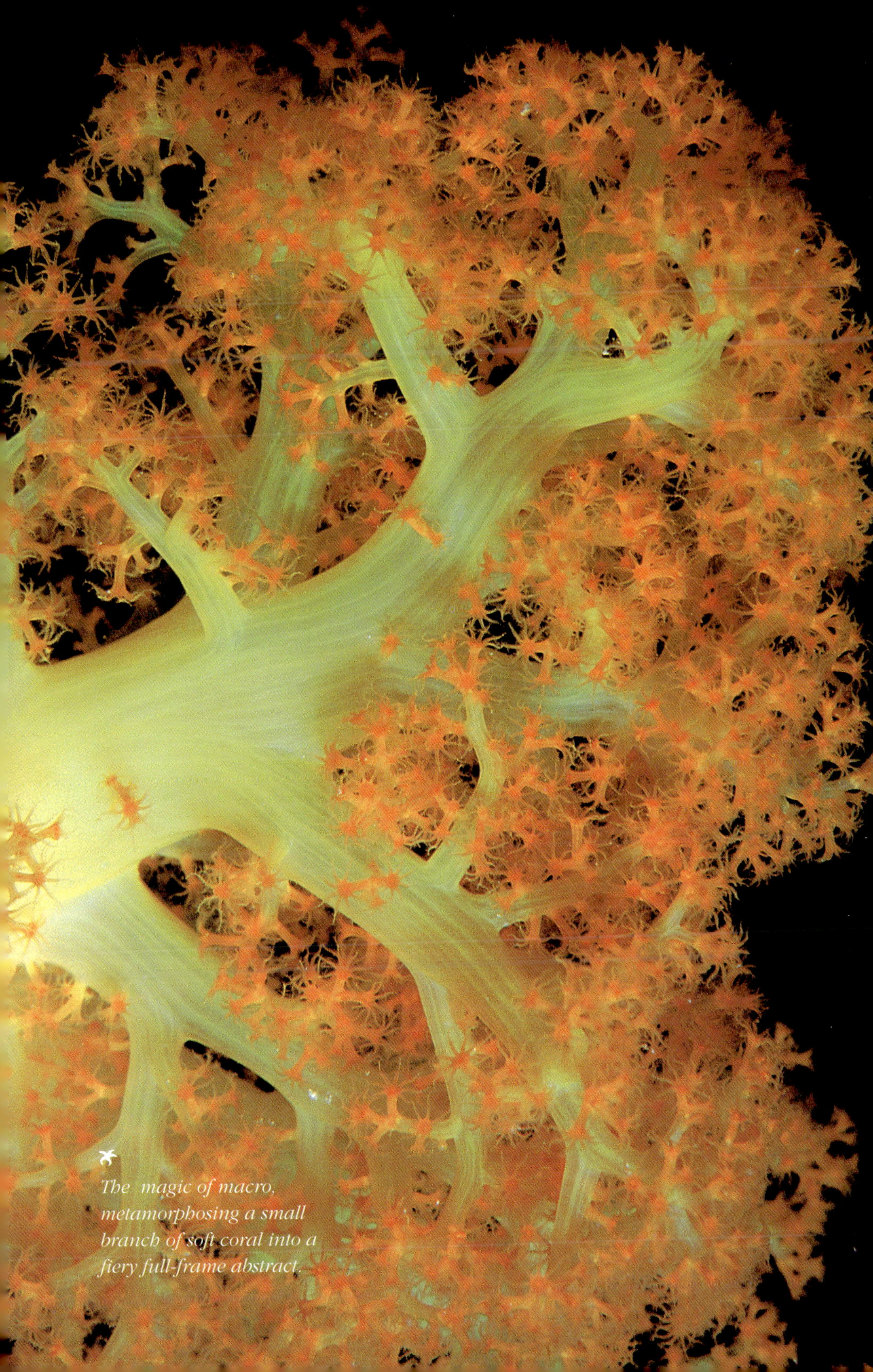

The magic of macro, metamorphosing a small branch of soft coral into a fiery full-frame abstract.

1:2 MACRO LENS ML-II/2T

Specifications

Magnification ratio:	1:2	**Picture area:**	3.2 x 2.1" (79 x 53mm)
Construction:	3 elements in 3 groups	**Depth of field:**	1 inch at f/22 (2.5cm)
Aperture range:	F/5.6 ~ f/22		3/4 inch at f/16 (1.9cm)

Preparation

Examine the lens for lint, sand, or other debris. If necessary, rinse in clean water; dry thoroughly. Lightly lubricate the lens fitting to facilitate ease of attachment and removal. The base plate and guide rods are made of salt-resistant plastic; rinse to remove sand or other debris.

How to Assemble

This system consists of two parts: a macro lens with guide ring permanently attached and a base plate with attached guide rods. The guide rods fold up into position for use or down for storage. This makes them easier to manage, especially underwater, and you can't lose them, either.

1. Insert the macro lens-guide ring into the base plate. Use a coin or screwdriver to tighten the fixing screw. Be sure the base plate is horizontally aligned with the camera.
2. Align the yellow mark on the macro lens with the white dot on the camera. Push the lens into the primary lens. Turn clockwise until secure.

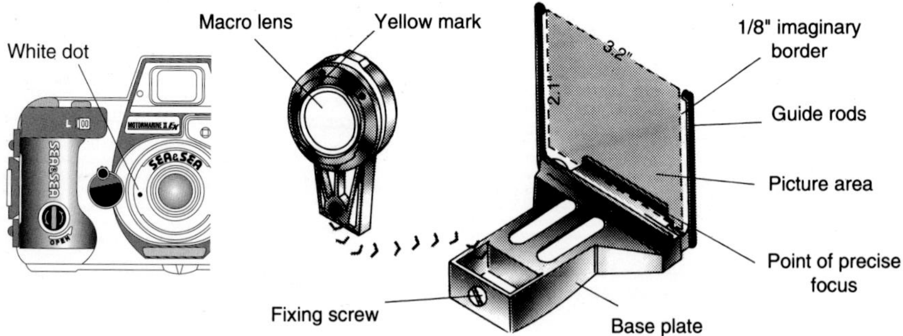

Note: This lens should be attached underwater to allow water to flood the space between the camera lens and the macro lens. Water is part of the total optical design. If assembled on land, shake or loosen the lens underwater so that trapped air can escape. Air between the lenses will affect resolution.

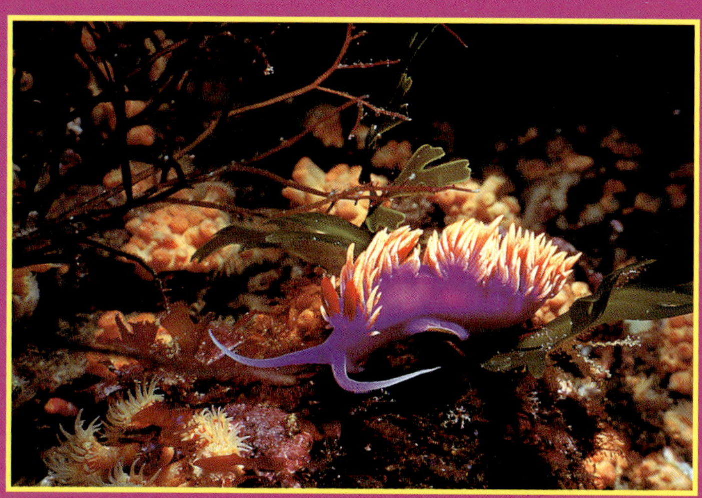

An exquisite Spanish Shawl adorned by Mother Nature's incomparable palette of colors. Recorded by Velvia: ISO 50, super saturated hues, and ultra fine grain.

1:3 MACRO LENS ML-II

Specifications

Magnification ratio:	1:3	**Picture area:**	4.8 x 3.2" (125 x 85 mm)
Construction:	2 elements in 2 groups	**Depth of field:**	1.5 inches at f/22 (3.75cm)
Aperture range:	F/5.6 ~ f/22		1 inch at f/16 (2.5cm)

Preparation

Examine the lens for lint, sand, and other debris. If necessary, rinse in clean water; dry thoroughly. Lightly lubricate the guide rods to facilitate ease of attachment and removal.

How to Assemble

This system comes in four parts: lens, guide ring, base plate, and guide rods. The lens bayonet mount attaches to the camera's built-in lens.

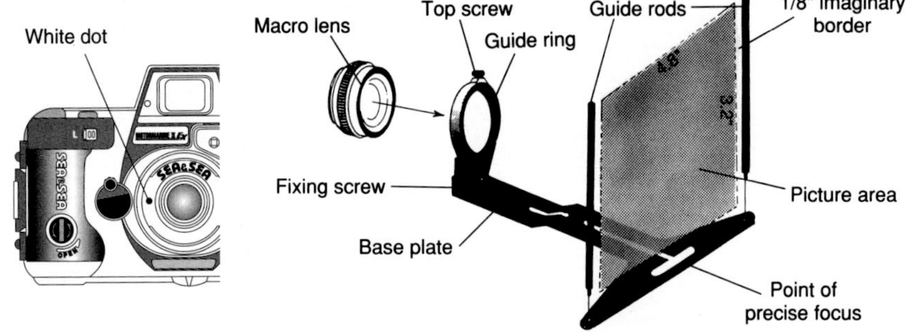

1. Align the yellow mark on the macro lens with the white dot on the camera lens. Push the macro lens into the primary lens and turn clockwise until it snaps securely in place.
2. Attach the guide ring to the base plate. Use a coin or screwdriver to tighten the fixing screw.
3. Attach the guide ring and base plate assembly to the macro lens. The guide ring fits over the macro lens. Tighten the knurled top screw. Be sure the base plate is fixed horizontal to the camera.
4. Screw the guide rods into both ends of the base plate.

Note: Attach underwater to flood the space between the primary and macro lenses. If assembled on land, vent it after descent to release trapped air and allow water to fill the space. Air in this pocket will degrade resolution.

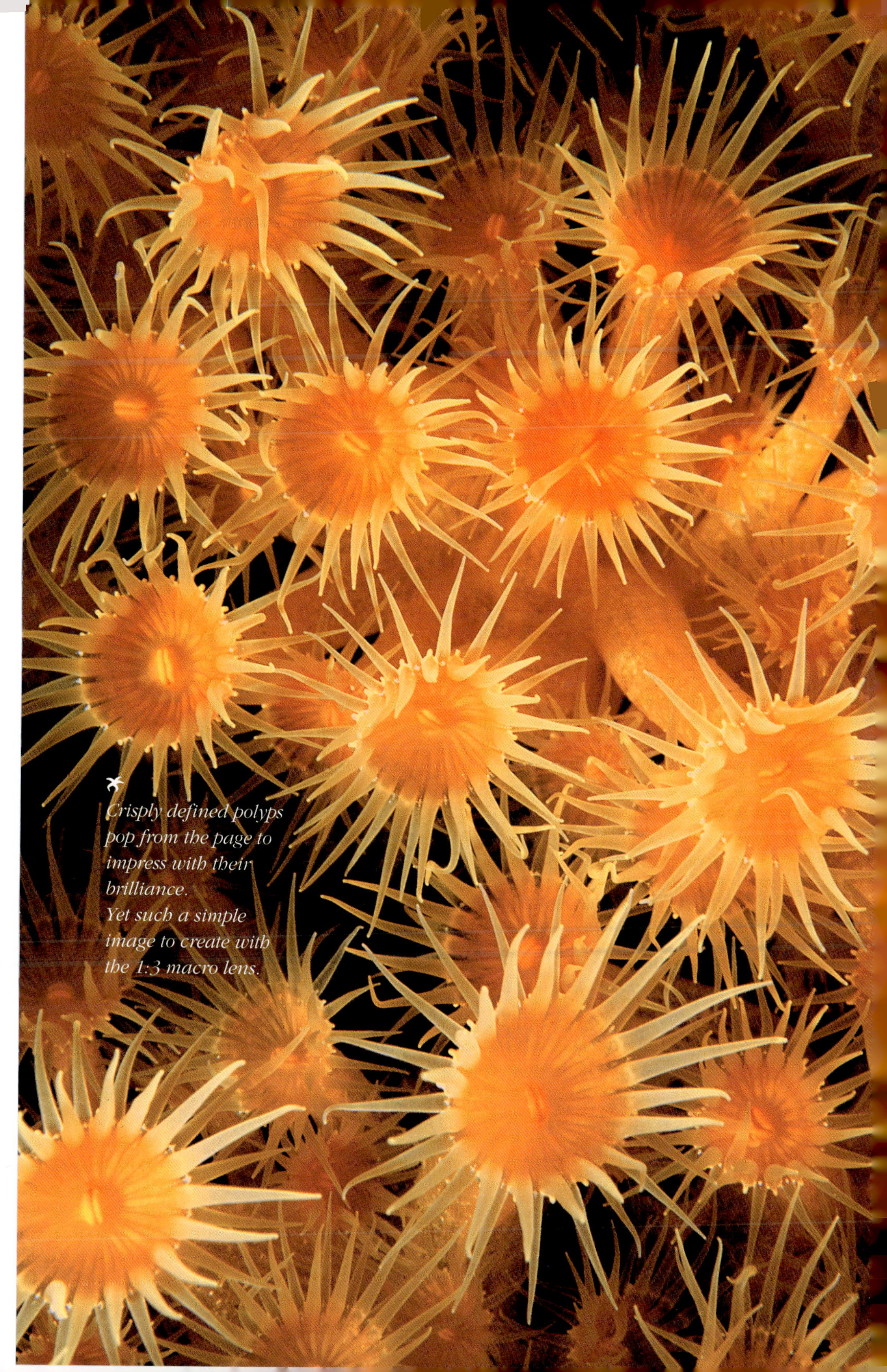

Crisply defined polyps pop from the page to impress with their brilliance. Yet such a simple image to create with the 1:3 macro lens.

1. Set focus dial on the camera:
   1:2 — set at infinity (∞)
   1:3 — set at minimum distance (3 feet/1 meter).
   Note the difference in the settings for the two systems.
2. Set aperture to f/22.
3. Turn strobe power switch to the "TTL" position. Angle strobe head and position for the correct strobe-to-subject distance. See Chapter 7 for strobe-to-subject operating range with your strobe.
4. Compose your picture within the guide rods.
5. Take the picture.
6. Check the strobe's neon light or look into the camera's viewfinder for a TTL confirmation signal of correct exposure. *Note:* It is not necessary to check both lights; it is enough to check just one or the other.
7. Strobe distance may vary between manual and TTL modes. If you did not get a confirmation light, decrease strobe-to-subject distance, and take another picture. A confirmation light confirms a correct exposure. Bracketing is not necessary.

Care After Use

Disassemble after use and rinse in fresh water to ensure that the removable parts do not fuse together by oxidation.

1. 1:2 macro: fold down the guide rods.
   1:3 macro: disassemble the guide rods from the base plate. Soak, dry, and lubricate threads.
2. Unscrew the base plate from the macro lens.
3. Detach the macro lens from the primary lens; turn in a counterclockwise direction and firmly pull out.
4. Soak all parts in fresh water to wash away debris and to prevent salt deposits from forming in the joints of the base plate/guide rod assembly and around the lens/base plate fixing screw.
5. Dry all parts with a clean cloth.
6. Use lens cleaner and lens tissue to clean the lens.
7. Lubricate all threads and fittings with a light coat of silicone grease.
8. Fold down guide rods of the 1:2 before storing. Store the guide rods of the 1:3 in their slotted grooves on the underside of the base plate.

EXTENSION TUBES FOR THE NIKONOS

Sea & Sea manufactures four extension tubes for Nikonos cameras. Each size differs in tube width, base plate length, size of framer rods, and picture area.

Extension Tube	Picture Area	Depth of Field
35mm 1:1	1.4" x .96" (35 x 24mm)	1/8"
35mm 1:2	2.8" x 1.9" (70 x 48mm)	3/8"
35mm 1:3	4 x 2.8" (102 x 70mm)	5/8"
28mm 1:2	2.5 x 1.7" (62 x 42mm)	3/8"

Preparation

Like your primary lens, the extension tube has an O-ring to keep it watertight. This O-ring must be cared for as you do all others in your system.

How to Attach

The extension tube system must be assembled topside.

1. Remove the primary lens from the camera.
2. Attach the extension tube to the camera body in the same manner as you mount Nikonos lenses. Make certain the Sea & Sea label is uppermost.
3. Attach the primary lens to the extension tube.
4. Attach the base plate to the extension tube.
5. Screw the guide rods onto the base plate.
6. Check that the base plate is parallel to the bottom of the camera and that the guide rods are straight.

Taking the Picture

Film speed, shutter speed, f-stop can all be preset. All you need to concentrate on are framing, strobe-to-subject distance, and strobe position.

1. Set your film speed dial. ISO 100 is an excellent all-purpose film, but ISO 50 will produce finer grain images and richer color saturation.
2. Set your aperture at f/22 to achieve the maximum depth of field.
3. Set the focus scale at its minimum focus distance of 2.75 feet for the 35mm lens or two feet for the 28mm lens.

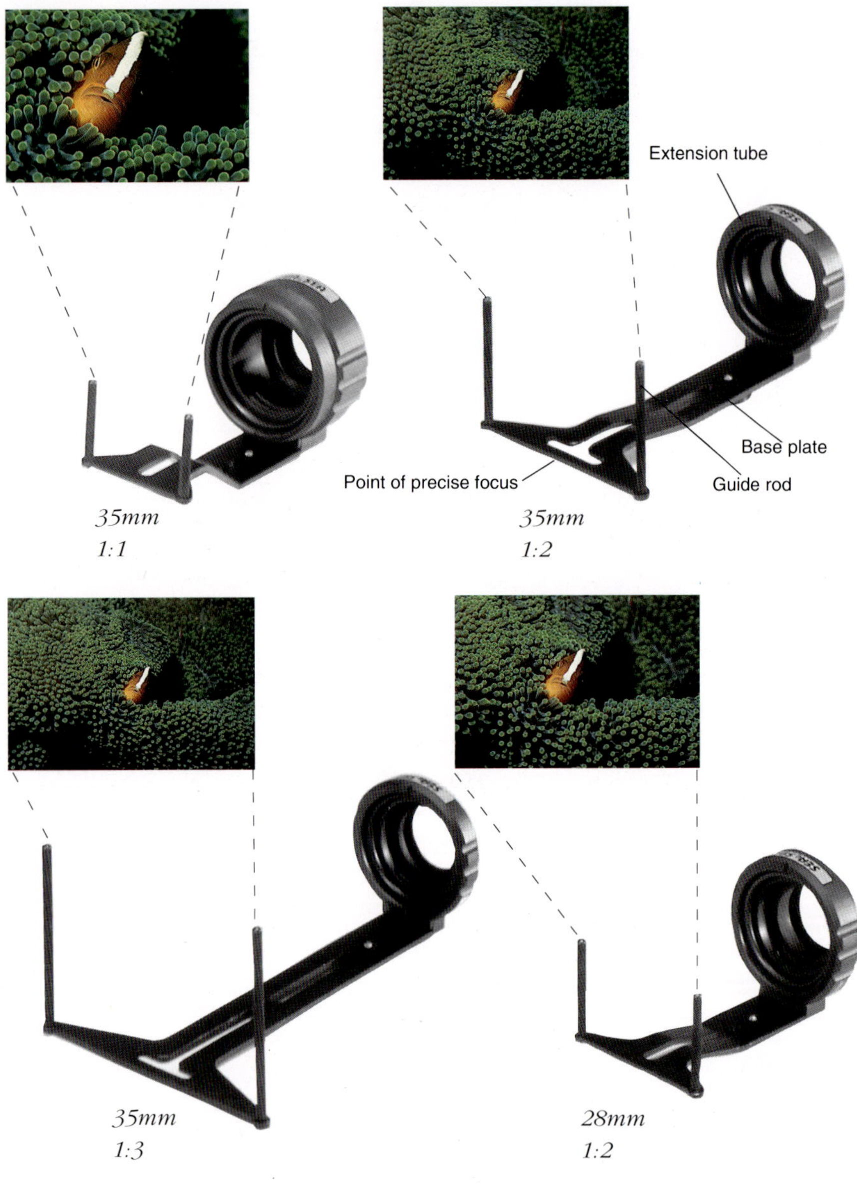

Notice that the 1:1 has the widest tube and the smallest framer. It provides the greatest image magnification. The 1:3 has the narrowest tube and the largest framer. It offers the least image magnification.

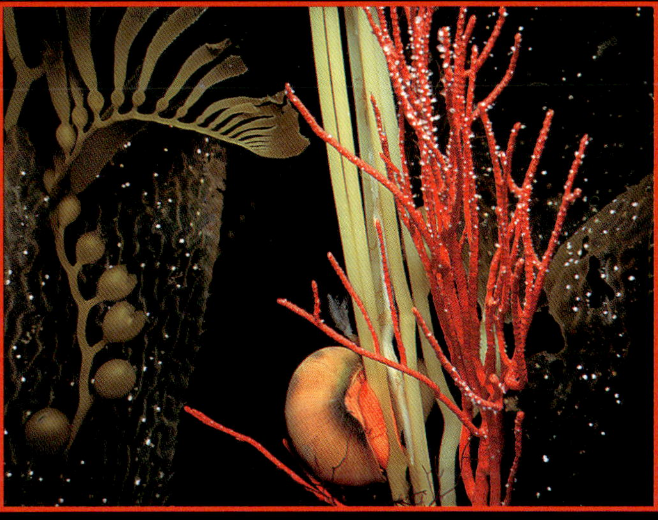

Thanks to macro,
there is never
nothing to photograph.
Ordinary subjects
take on new life
when blown up big
and splashed with light.
Taken with a 1:3 extension tube.

4. If using a TTL strobe, set the camera shutter speed dial to "A" for TTL operation. If shooting in manual mode, set shutter speed at 1/60 (Nikonos III) or M (Nikonos IV) or M90 (Nikonos V).
5. Set power switch on strobe to "TTL" to correlate with the "A" setting on the camera or on "Full" to correlate with manual operation.
6. Position the strobe as desired.
7. Compose your picture within the framer, not through the camera's viewfinder. Use the viewfinder only for TTL flash confirmation. Allow an invisible 1/8" border within the framing area.
8. Hold steady and take your picture.
9. Check camera viewfinder for a confirmation signal. If there is a incorrect exposure signal, move the strobe forward and repeat.
10. Bracket. In manual mode change strobe-to-subject distance. In TTL mode, bracket by changing ISO film speed setting.

Quick Tips for Taking Good Macro Pix

- Subject should face or be lateral to the lens.
- Shoot at a horizontal or slightly upward angle.
- Avoid distracting obstacles in front of your subject.
- Try to isolate your subject against a clear or solid background or against complementary or contrasting colors.

For more on creative picture taking, turn to Chapter 8: *Composition.*

Care After Use

Disassemble after use and rinse in fresh water to ensure that the removable parts do not fuse together by oxidation.

1. Remove guide rods from the base plate.
2. Detach base plate from the extension tube.
3. Detach primary lens from the extension tube.
4. Detach extension tube from camera body.
5. Soak all extension tube parts in fresh water.
6. Dry all parts with a clean cloth.
7. Lubricate threads and fittings with a light coat of silicone grease.
8. Store the guide rods in the slots on the underside of the base plate.

CHAPTER SIX

The NX-90 Pro

The NX-90 Pro

The NX-90 Pro has been designed exclusively for Nikon's highly-acclaimed N90/F90 series AF SLR cameras. Since its introduction in 1997, the NX-90 Pro has become the housing of choice for professionals and serious enthusiasts, heralded for its ease of use, dependability, versatility, and outstanding performance.

If that sounds like a testimonial, that's because it is. Joe has been using housed systems for three decades. His first was custom-made for a Bronica, followed by a Giddings and an Oceanic for Nikon F cameras. He's had Ikelite housings for Nikon's F2 and 8008 and made his own for a Hasselblad 500ELM. He's had Sea & Sea's SX-1000 and NX-50. All good in their way and in their time, but the NX-90 is the first he's called "the ultimate in engineering perfection."

The NX-90 Pro is an ultra-compact, lightweight housing, contoured to conform around the camera like a dive skin. Cast of high-grade marine aluminium with a lustrous baked epoxy veneer, it looks as sleek and sophisticated as it performs. Its hydrodynamic silhouette is complemented by a pragmatic configuration of push buttons, dials, and levers for fast and flawless command of the camera's major functions. Sea & Sea's unique built-in Quick Shoe allows for quick and tool-free camera installation. The bayonet mount enables you to change ports in seconds without the use of tools. It is compatible with an extensive array of Nikon and Sigma lenses and dedicates for TTL automatic flash photography with any strobe with a Nikonos five-pin connector. It is the new standard for discerning photographers.

Why Use a Housed System?

Because you can put an SLR autofocus camera in a housing. Amphibious cameras like the Motor Marine II-EX and Nikonos V are rangefinder cameras and manual focus. While they may be less expensive and more compact, they are actually more difficult to master than a housed system. Today's new land cameras provide state-of-the-art technologies with modes and functions that offer the underwater photographer complete command. For the professional or the dedicated amateur, a housed system is the most flexible and creative tool. For the amateur who wants an exceptional-quality point-and-shoot and doesn't mind if it's pricey, a housed system is that, too.

The advantages of a housed system over an amphibious camera are:

- ▼ Single lens reflex viewing
- ▼ Pinpoint autofocusing
- ▼ The ability to select auto priority, aperture priority, shutter priority and manual exposure modes with TTL or manual flash
- ▼ The ability to select exposure compensation, auto/manual focus, continuous or single servo autofocus
- ▼ High-quality, accurate, and sophisticated metering systems
- ▼ A wider range of lenses to choose from for new creative imaging
- ▼ A wider choice of strobe/camera sync speeds
- ▼ A greater selection of subjects.

With the NX-90 Pro You Can . . .

- ▼ Turn camera on and off underwater
- ▼ Change film without removing camera from housing
- ▼ Install camera without use of tools
- ▼ Change ports without removing camera from housing
- ▼ View frame counter underwater
- ▼ Select ISO film speed manually or automatically
- ▼ Select either matrix, spot or center-weighted averaging metering mode
- ▼ Select motor drive speed
- ▼ Select exposure mode: aperture, shutter, program, manual, auto
- ▼ Select single or continuous autofocus servo
- ▼ Select exposure compensation value
- ▼ Switch from AF or MF with selected lenses
- ▼ Light up LCD panel
- ▼ Choose from 11 lens ports
- ▼ Choose from 10 lenses
- ▼ Shoot TTL or manual flash photography with any strobe with a standard five-pin sync cord connector

What is SLR?

SLR stands for *single lens reflex.* An SLR camera has through-the-lens viewing, also called *reflex viewing*. A mirror reflects the light rays coming through the lens up onto the viewing screen so that when you look through the viewfinder, you are actually looking through the lens. The SLR's pentaprism finder lets you view the image right side and at eye level. The image seen is exactly as it will be recorded on film, regardless of shooting distance or lens focal length.

Amphibious cameras like the Motor Marine II-EX and Nikonos V employ a viewfinding configuration in which you compose your photograph through a window above the lens. The image seen through this window is not the same image seen by the lens. At close range this creates a problem called parallax. The angle of view of the lens and the angle of view of the viewfinder are different because they are fixed at different positions on the camera. The closer you are to your subject, the greater the difference in the angles of view. With through-the-lens viewing and focusing, there is no parallax error. What you see is what you'll get.

What's So Special About Autofocus?

In a word, *speed.* An autofocus camera can focus on a subject far faster than you can manually. If the subject is moving, if you're moving, this is the greatest benefit any underwater photographer can derive from his camera.

When autofocus first became a reality and was incorporated into the design of submersible housings, most professionals scoffed at it. They insisted it would never be viable in the underwater environment. Light levels too low. Ever-present particles. Continually moving subjects. The autofocus mechanism would not be able to react fast enough and accurately enough to function in such conditions.

Autofocus was problematic at the outset. But advanced technology has made today's autofocus systems so sophisticated and reliable that the difficulties inherent in the underwater environment have been dramatically minimized.

Definition of Terms

Your NX-90 is a highly sophisticated instrument. If you already own a land camera, you may be familiar with many of the controls and functions on the NX-90. If this is new to you, you certainly need to know what the terms used in the following pages mean.

Aperture priority mode: an automatic exposure system, designated by the abbreviation AE, in which the photographer selects the f-stop and the camera automatically determines the corresponding shutter speed for a correct exposure. The most effective autofocus mode for controlling depth of field.

Aperture ring: a band on the lens used to control the amount of light reaching the film plane; when turned, it alters the size of the lens diaphragm.

Autobracketing: the automatic consecutive exposure of three frames at varied ambient light exposure levels.

Autofocus: a built-in lens focusing system that focuses the lens when the shutter release button is partially depressed.

Autofocus lock: a control that focuses on whatever you aim the viewfinder at and locks in focus, allowing you to change picture composition without affecting focus. Will hold the focus till you trigger or release the shutter.

Center-weighted light metering system: a metering system that measures light from the whole of the viewfinder but concentrates 75% of its sensitivity within the viewfinder's 12mm circle, because that's where the subject is usually positioned.

Continuous photography: the automatic consecutive exposure of frames, one after another in rapid succession.

Continuous frame shooting: shots are taken continuously with a power driven camera when the shutter release is held down. Some systems, like the N90, offer low and high speed shooting modes.

Continuous servo AF with release-priority: focusing with the shutter release slightly pressed. The AF will continue to focus on the subject until the shutter release is fully pressed. The shutter will release anytime, even when the subject is not in focus.

DX coding: an electronic system in a camera that automatically sets the film speed by "reading" film speed information imprinted on a magnetic strip on the film cassette.

EV: stands for exposure value, which are identification numbers relating to shutter speed, aperture settings, and ISO film speed.

Exposure compensation: also referred to as exposure correction; overriding the exposure set by the camera.

Exposure meter: also called a light meter; it measures the brightness of light available and calculates the correct f-stop and shutter speed combination for a proper exposure on the ISO film speed used.

Exposure mode: refers to exposure control, such as manual, programmed auto, aperture priority, shutter priority, that determines which control you set for an exposure and which ones the camera sets automatically.

Focus control: the focusing mechanism that moves the lens back and forth so that it can project sharp images of both near and far subjects.

Focusing ring: the band on the lens used to focus the image. When turned, it moves the lens in relation to the film plane, focusing the camera for specific distances.

Focusing screen: also called a viewing screen; a matte, ground-glass surface onto which the mirror reflects the image seen by the lens. When the image is sharply focused on the screen, it will be in sharp focus on the film.

Interchangeable lens: a lens that can be removed from the camera and replaced by another lens.

LCD: an acronym for liquid crystal display; generally a panel or screen on the camera which shows camera settings and shooting mode.

LED: an acronym for light emitting diode, a display of colored lights and symbols in a camera's viewfinder which indicates exposure data.

Lens speed: the widest aperture to which the lens can be opened. The wider the aperture possible with a particular lens, the more light is admitted and the *faster* the lens; another characteristic of a lens.

Matrix metering: incorporates a built-in microcomputer which gathers exposure data with several segments and provides the correct exposure for most lighting conditions. The matrix pattern reads the entire image area and takes into account that there may be a bright or dark areas influencing the reading. The microcomputer then compensates for the differences.

Metered manual exposure mode: the photographer selects shutter speed and aperture. The most flexible mode, allowing the photographer total control.

Multiple exposure photography: repeated exposures of the same or different subject on the same frame; a technique used to create unusual images.

Pentaprism: a five-sided optical device in an eye-level viewfinder to correct the image on the focusing screen so that it appears right side up and correct left to right. When the shutter is triggered, it flips up out of the light path.

Program mode: an exposure control system which automatically makes aperture and shutter decisions for a correct exposure.

Shutter priority mode: an exposure control system in which the photographer sets shutter speed and the camera sets aperture for a correct exposure. The best autoexposure mode for controlling visual effects, such as stopping or blurring motion. The advantage is speed: once you set the shutter speed, the camera instantly selects the f-stop.

Single frame shooting: taking one frame at a time with a power drive camera.

Single servo AF with focus-priority: locking the AF with the shutter release. The shutter will not release until the correct focus is achieved. You can lock focus and then recompose the picture and still be in focus.

Spot metering system: a reflected light metering system that reads a very small portion of the scene in the center of the viewfinder, usually 1% of the total image area.

Step: an f-stop. While step and stop mean the same thing, the word step is generally used when referring to increasing or decreasing exposure.

Viewing screen: the surface on which the image in the camera appears for viewing. This image appears upside down and reversed left to right unless the camera contains a pentaprism to correct it.

Identification of Parts

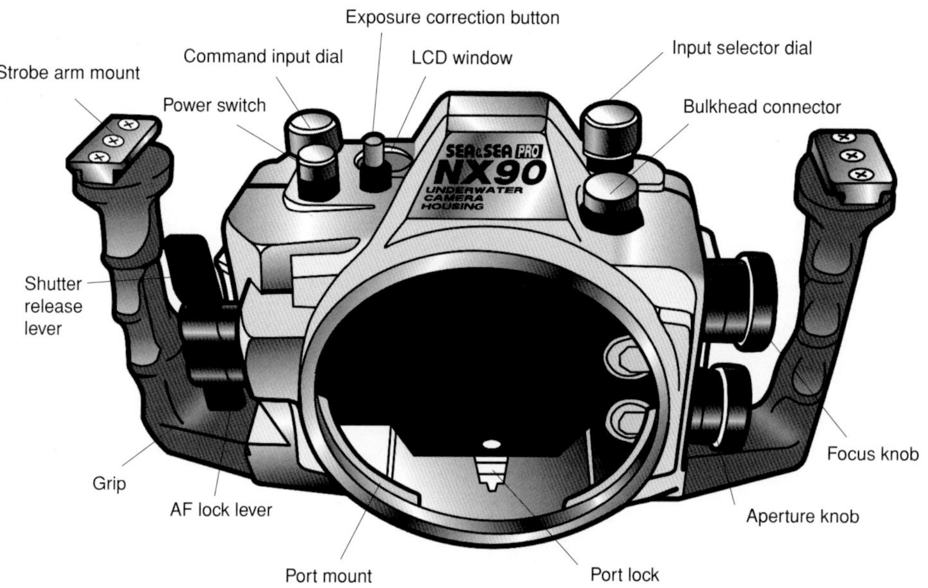

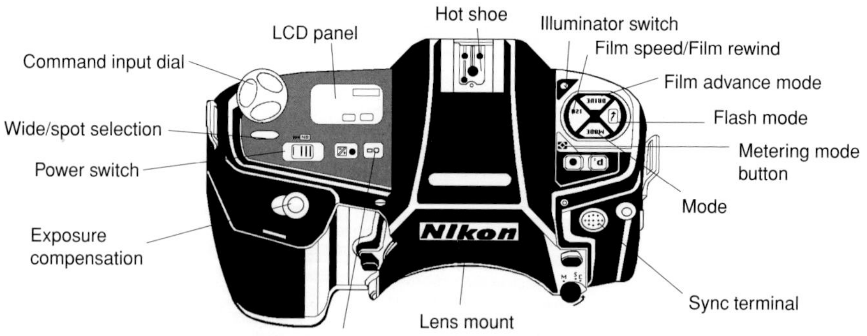

Specifications NX-90 Pro

Construction:	Aluminum alloy, hard-almite galvanized finish
Maximum depth:	200 feet (60m)
Port mount:	Bayonet
Dimensions:	8.6 x 6.2 x 4.3" (W x H x D) (215 x 154 x 107mm)
Weight:	3.9 lbs (1780g) (without hand grip)

Specifications N90 Camera

Type of camera:	35mm AF SLR
Film format:	36mm x 24mm
Type film:	Standard 35mm cartridge
Lens mount:	Nikon F-mount
Power source:	Four AA batteries
Dimensions:	6.1 x 4.2 x 2.7"(W x H x D) (154 x 106 x 69mm)
Weight:	26.7oz. (755g) (body only)

Identification of Parts

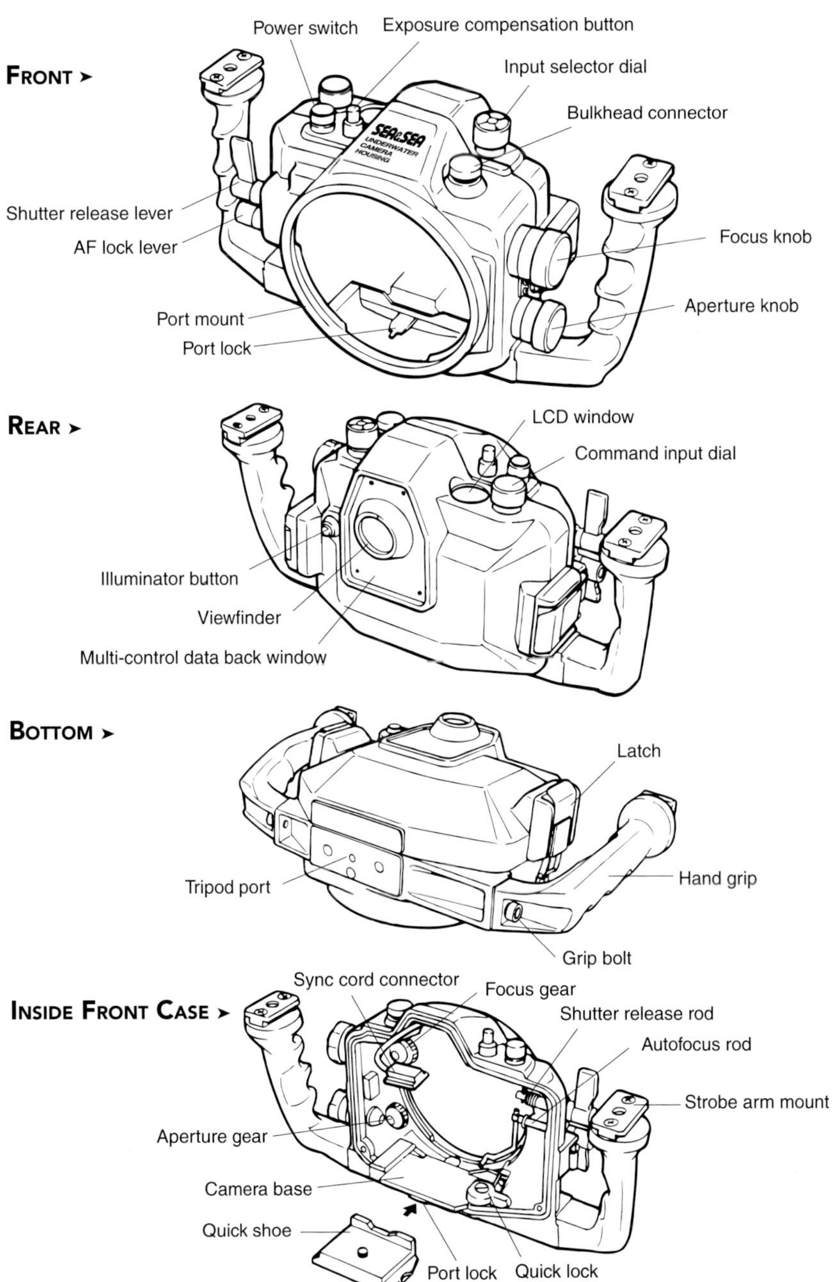

External Controls and Components

The NX-90 is equipped with a strategic configuration of nine multiple-function external controls for fluid operation of the camera's primary functions. All controls needed for immediate change in exposure are conveniently situated on the right. Those controls needed for a change in modes between exposures are positioned on the left.

Power Switch

The power switch activates the camera.

To operate: Make sure the white dot is at the "Off" position. Then press down to make contact with the camera's power switch. When engaged, rotate to align the white dot with "On" to turn the camera on; rotate it to the "Off" position to turn the camera off. Confirm that power is on or off in the LCD window.

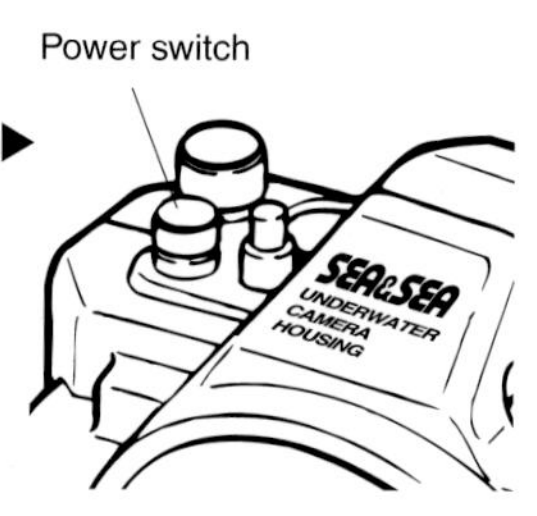

Input Selector Dial

The Input Selector Dial operates the four-segmented control on the N90 camera. That control consists of four triangular-shaped buttons marked MODE, ISO, DRIVE, and FLASH, designated by a lightning bolt.

The name of the control aptly explains its purpose: it is used to select (input) various modes and functions. It is used in conjunction with the Command Input Dial, which then "commands the camera" to activate the selected mode or function. A readout of the mode or function will appear in the topdeck LCD window, confirming your selection.

▾ Mode button

This button is used to select one of the following exposure modes:

P - Auto Multi-Program - Auto selection of shutter speed and aperture

S - Shutter Priority - Photographer selects the shutter speed and the camera selects the appropriate aperture for a correct exposure

A - Aperture Priority - Photographer selects the aperture and the camera selects the shutter speed

M - Manual - Photographer selects shutter speed and aperture.

▼ ISO button

The ISO button is used to select film speed and confirm ISO setting. If the film being used is DX coded, the camera's built-in sensor will read the magnetic data on the cartridge and automatically set that film speed. ISO can also be set manually by pressing down on the button and rotating the Command Input Dial to the desired setting.

▼ Drive mode button

This button is used to select the camera's motor drive film advance rate:

H - continuous high speed film advance at 3.6 frames per second
L - continuous low speed film advance at 2 frames per second
S - single shot film advance at 1 frame per second

▼ Flash sync button

This button is used with the Command Input Dial to select normal flash operation, with the strobe firing at the beginning of the exposure, or rear curtain flash sync, with the strobe firing at the end of the exposure.

To operate:

1. Pull the Input Selector Dial to the ▶ full upward position, then turn to the desired selection. The dial rotates in both directions.

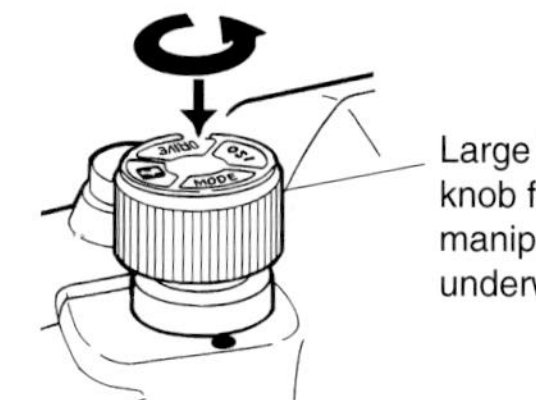

2. Press down to activate the selected function on the camera.
3. While holding the control down, rotate the Command Input Dial to the desired function. *Caution*: Do not rotate the Input Selector Dial while pushing down on it; doing so can damage the camera's Selector Control Buttons.

Command Input Dial

The Command Input Dial is the housing's master control. It is positioned on the right, within easy access while holding the hand grip, and can be operated with eye to the viewfinder. It is used in conjuntion with the Input Selector Dial to set various camera functions. It is also used in conjunction with the exposure compensation button.

To operate: While pressing down on the Input Selector Dial, rotate the Command Input Dial to the desired selection.

Exposure Compensation Control

Located adjacent to the power switch, this control is used in conjunction with the Command Input Dial. It allows you to override the final exposure setting. The exposure compensation control can lighten or darken the exposure in 1/3 step increments to a +5 EV or -5 EV. It is recommended for use with center-weighted metering or spot metering only. *Note:* It can be used with any mode any except Manual.

To operate: While pressing down on the Exposure Control Button, rotate the Command Input Dial for plus (+) or minus (-) selections. Both LCDs will display the numerical value selected. *Note:* After use, be sure to reset to "0" for normal operation.

LCD Window

The LCD window is a small glass-covered port beside the Command Input Dial. This is the window to the camera's LCD panel, providing pertinent readouts of modes and function. *Note:* The data displayed in the LCD panel is not the same as that in the viewfinder display. Read the camera instruction manual to fully understand all the data displayed in the LCD panel.

N90 LCD Panel

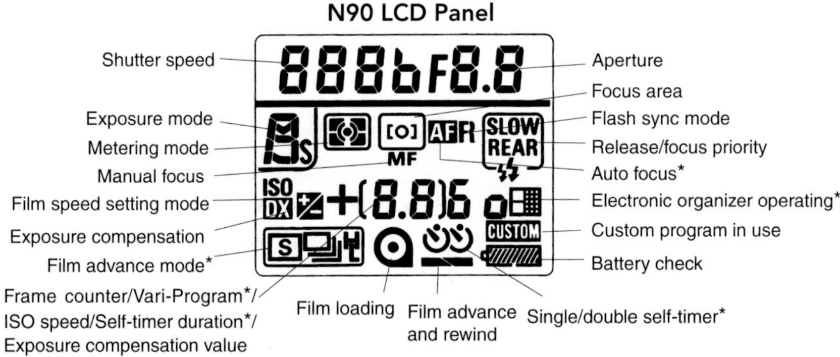

* A mode or function that must be preset; not accessible or cannot be changed through the housing

Viewfinder

The viewing port provides an unimpeded view of the camera's TTL viewfinder and the LCD below it. The lower part of the window allows viewing of the data from the Nikon MF-26 Multi-Control Data Back. The viewfinder is automatically illuminated

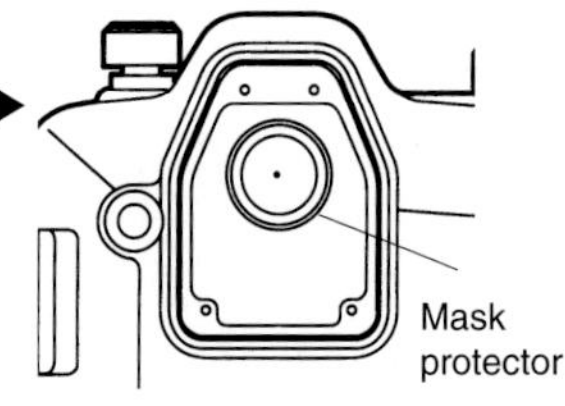

when the shutter release lever is depressed. The standard viewfinder is encased in a rubber protector to cushion your face mask. This viewfinder can be replaced by an optional Optical Viewfinder which affords a full-frame viewing area and brighter view. You can also purchase the housing with this option already installed.

Viewfinder Display

1. Wide area focus brackets
2. 12mm diameter circle for center-weighted metering
3. 3mm diameter circle for spot metering/spot-area focus
4. Clear matte field
5. Focus area
6. Focus indicators
7. Exposure mode
8. Shutter speed
9. Aperture
10. Electronic analog display
11. Frame counter/Vari-program compensation
12. Exposure compensation
13. Flash ready

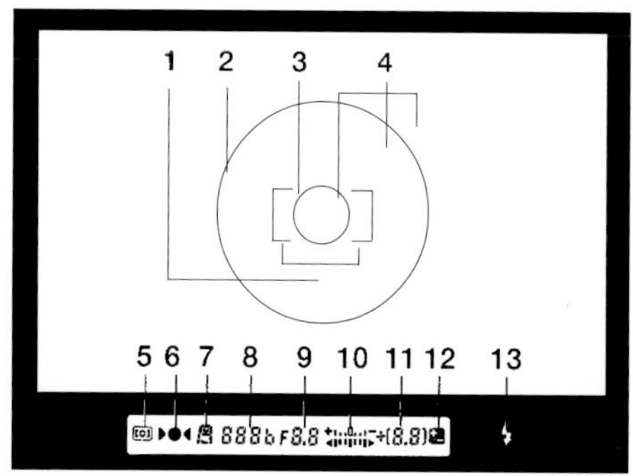

LCD Illumination Button

This control is located on the rear of the housing to the left of the viewfinder. It activates the lights within the LCD panel and viewfinder for night diving and low-light conditions.

To operate:

Press to turn the light on. The light automatically turns off after approximately eight seconds.

Illuminator button

Shutter Release Lever

Conveniently located adjacent to the right-hand grip, this spring-loaded device responds quickly and smoothly to light fingertip pressure to activate the camera's autofocus, turn on the exposure meter, illuminate the viewfinder's LCD panel, and trigger the camera's shutter.

To operate:

1. Pull back lightly to activate. ▶
2. Full pressure will release the shutter to take the picture.

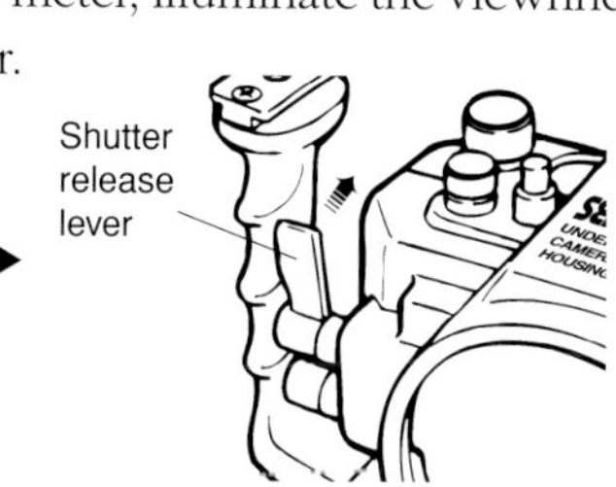

AF Lock Lever

Located just below the shutter release, the AF (AutoFocus) lever is used in conjunction with the shutter release to lock in focus prior to releasing the shutter. It literally "locks in" the autofocus setting, allowing you to change picture composition without affecting focus.

To operate:

Pull back gently on the lever to ▶ engage the auto lock feature. Hold in place. When ready to take the shot, release the shutter.

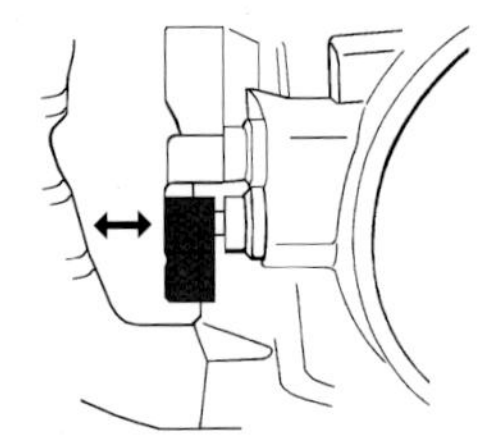

Aperture Control Knob

The aperture, like the focus control, is a large knurled rotary-style knob, positioned close to the housing's left-hand grip. The aperture control knob, with the aid of the aperture gear ring installed onto the lens, allows you to change the f-stop manually.

To operate:

1. Install aperture gear ring on lens.
2. Set camera aperture to minimum aperture setting before installing camera into housing.
3. Set housing aperture knob to correspond with the minimum setting of the camera.
4. F-stop can now be selected with the aperture control on the housing for aperture priority or manual operation.

Zoom /Focus Control Knob

Located above the aperture knob, this control allows operation of both the zoom and focus controls independent of one another when the appropriate gears are installed onto the lens.

To operate:

1. Install appropriate zoom/focus gear ring on lens before installing camera into housing.
2. Check that the gear ring and zoom/focus control mesh properly when camera is locked into position.
3. Rotate control for desired zoom/focus functions.

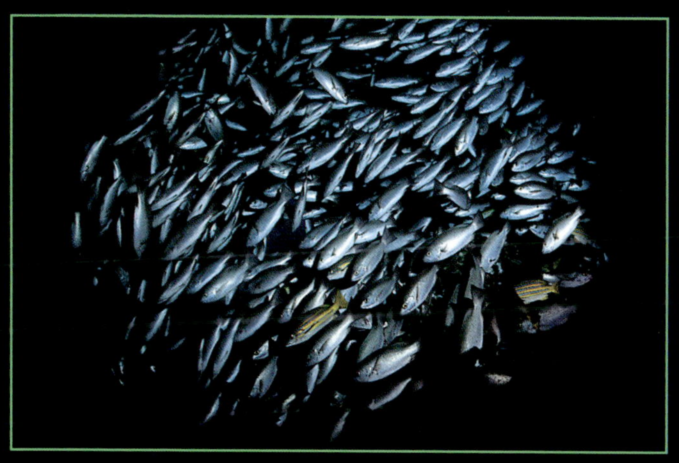

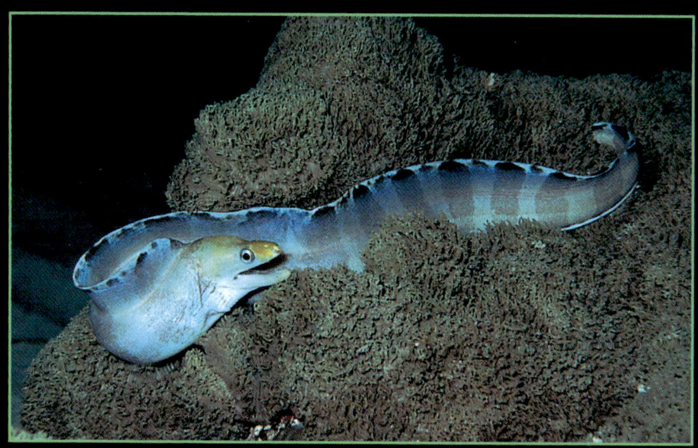

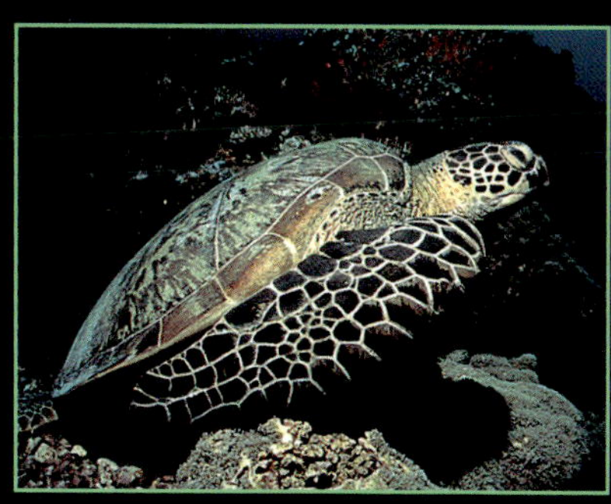

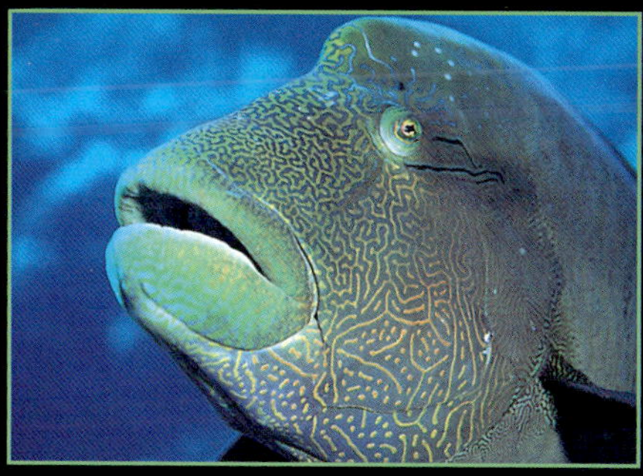

Welcome to underwater imaging with the NX-90 Pro.
Top: 16mm fisheye. Center: 60mm macro. Left: 28-85 zoom. Right: 20mm wide.

15 Steps to Assemble the System

1. Service the O-rings
2. Open housing
3. Mount port
4. Attach quick shoe
5. Mount lens gears to lens
6. Mount lens to camera
7. Set aperture on the housing and camera
8. Select metering system
9. Select exposure mode
10. Mount camera to the camera base
11. Attach housing's sync cord connector to camera
12. Close housing
13. Attach grip spacers
14. Mount base plate and strobe arms
15. Mount strobe and connect sync cord

Preparation for Use: The O-ring

The O-ring on your NX-90 is a distinctive cobalt blue. Its compound contains silicone oil, making it more resilient and pliable. This is the most important component of your system. The O-ring seals it and makes it watertight. If the O-ring is damaged, deformed, or improperly seated in its channel, water can penetrate and flood the camera and lens. An O-ring must be meticulously maintained to ensure its sealing integrity. There are three serviceable O-rings:

- the front case
- the strobe bulkhead connector cap
- the lens port

• Before use, remove the O-ring from its channel and examine it for imperfections. If the O-ring is damaged, replace it.

• Make sure that there are no foreign particles, such as dust, sand or hair, on the O-ring, O-ring channel, or O-ring contact surface. Such contamination will breach the seal and cause flooding. If necessary, wash thoroughly in fresh water and dry with a lint-free cloth. Use a cotton swab to clean the O-ring channel and contact surface.

• Lubricate with the prescribed silicone grease (see sidebar on page 279). Silicone grease protects the O-ring from drying and abrasion. Dab a small amount of grease onto your finger and draw the O-ring through your fingers until evenly coated. Use the silicone grease sparingly. Too much grease attracts debris.

• Do not crimp the O-ring. Hold the O-ring straight and do not bend or twist it when fitting it into the O-ring groove.

See details on O-ring care in Chapter 9, *Care and Maintenance*.

How to Open the Housing

The front and rear sections of the housing are pressure-proof O-ring sealed, secured by two spring-loaded stainless steel latches with a safety lock that prevents accidental opening.

To open:

1. Place fingers on latch as shown. ▶
2. Press down on the lock release with your index finger, then pull the wide part outward with your thumb. The latch will open.

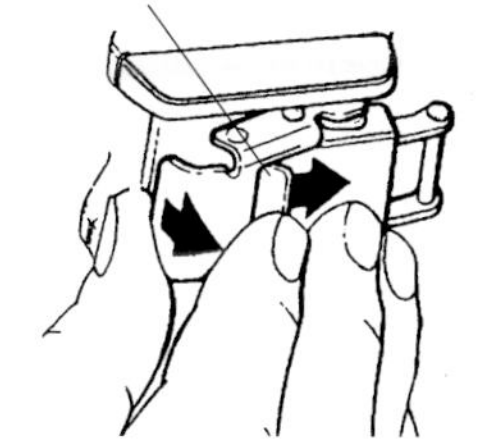

Open both latches simultaneously.

Caution! Do not open the lock while you are holding the grip. When it snaps open, it could pinch your fingers.

How to Attach and Detach the Port

You should mount the port before installing the camera to prevent the camera lens from accidental damage during installation.

1. Switch the port lock on the ▶ camera base to "Open."

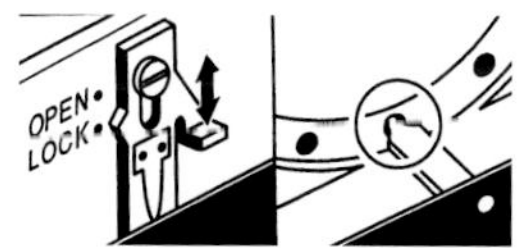

2. Check that the port O-ring is clean, lubricated, and properly seated.
3. Apply a thin coating of silicone grease over the entire surface of the housing mount. This will facilitate attachment and removal.
4. Fit the port onto the front case, aligning the white dots on the port and case. Turn the port one-quarter turn to the "Lock" position.

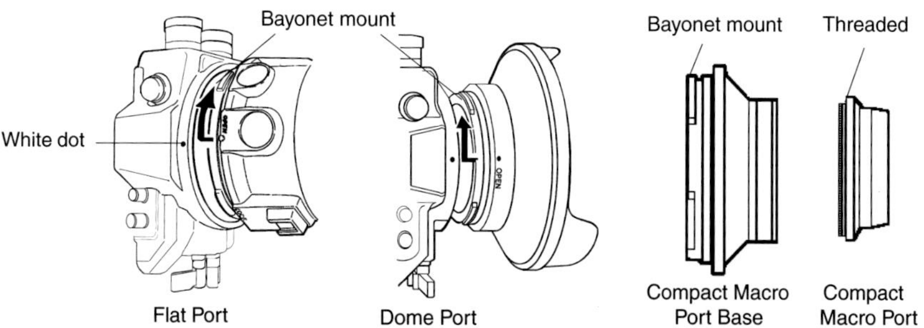

Never let camera or lens get wet!
When opening the housing, make sure that the housing is completely dry, your hands are dry, and the work area is dry. The housing is waterproof. The camera and lenses are not!

4. Confirm that the position guide marks (white dots) on the port and case have been correctly aligned.

5. Switch the port lock to the "Lock" position, making sure the port lock claw is fully engaged within the yellow circled hole in the port.

Important! The port lock claw prevents the port from accidental disengagement.

Note: When using a Compact Macro Port, mount the Compact Macro Port Base to the housing first and then screw on the Compact Macro Port to the base. Turn the port fully to the locked position.

To disassemble:

1. Switch the port lock to the "Open" position.
2. Hold the front case firmly and turn the port counterclockwise to the "Open" position. Pull port out.
3. With the Compact Macro Port: turn counterclockwise to remove from the base. The base is fitted with a bayonet mount and is disengaged from the housing as you would all other ports.

Caution! Do not attempt to disassemble the port with the port in the "Lock" position. That can damage both the port and the camera base.

How to Mount the Quick Shoe

Sea & Sea's innovative Quick Shoe enables one-step installation of the camera into the housing. With this device mounted to the camera, no screws, bolts or tools are required to mount camera to housing.

1. Fit the Quick Shoe to the camera's ▶ tripod socket.

2. Insert the mounting bolt and tighten. Make sure the camera doesn't wobble.

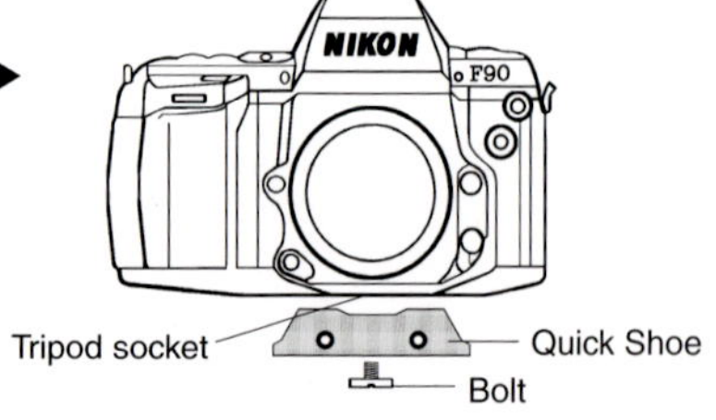

How to Mount the Lens Gears

Sea & Sea manufactures a variety of lens gears for aperture control, switching between autofocus and manual focus, focus control, and zoom control. They are noncorrosive, precision-tooled aluminum, each fitted with a non-slip rubber ring that ensures solid contact. The lens gear design is different for each lens. The following instructions are a sampling of how to attach the assorted gears. For specific instructions, please refer to the instructions packaged with your gear.

Tips

- ▼ All gear components must be installed over the full length of the lens to ensure proper meshing with the gears in the housing.
- ▼ Install gears with camera set at manual mode. If set in autofocus mode and the lens is manually turned during the installation process, the internal AF mechanism could be damaged.
- ▼ If the rubber grip on the barrel becomes displaced while you are sliding the gear down the lens barrel, remove the gear, replace the rubber ring to its channel, and start again.
- ▼ A rubber ring inside the gear holds the gear securely in place. If the gear will not slide smoothly down the lens, if the gear feels too tight, the rubber can be adjusted. Remove the ring, trim off a very small piece, then replace.
- ▼ If the gear is too loose, replace with the thicker rubber ring included with the gear.
- ▼ After installation, check that the gear is parallel to the lens.

▼ *Aperture Gear*

Three different aperture gears are available to work with the lenses and teleconverters. When mounted, the gear enables manual aperture selection. To use, simply turn the aperture knob on the housing to select the aperture.

Slip the aperture gear over the ▶ aperture collar of the lens, making sure that the lug on the lens engages with the notch on the gear.

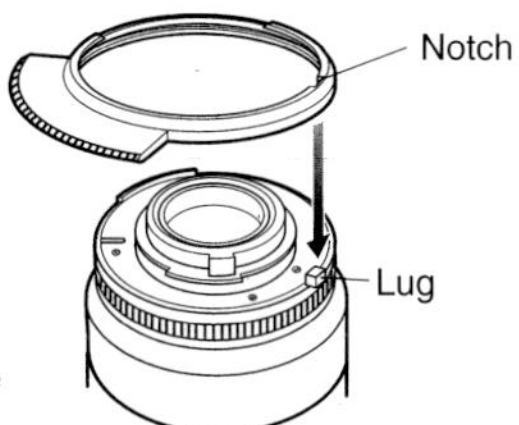

Shown: The aperture gear for the AF Micro-Nikkor 60mm F2.8 lens

▾ *Focus Gear*

The focus gear enables manual focusing. Once the gear has been installed, simply turn the focus/zoom knob on the housing to adjust focus. *Note:* If the lens is to be used in autofocus mode, no focusing gear is necessary.

1. Mount the focus gear over the focus collar on the lens. ▶
2. Slide it down the length of the lens barrel until the space between the focus gear and the camera's viewfinder is approximately 1/16 inch.
3. Check that the gear is properly engaged with the focus control gears inside the housing.

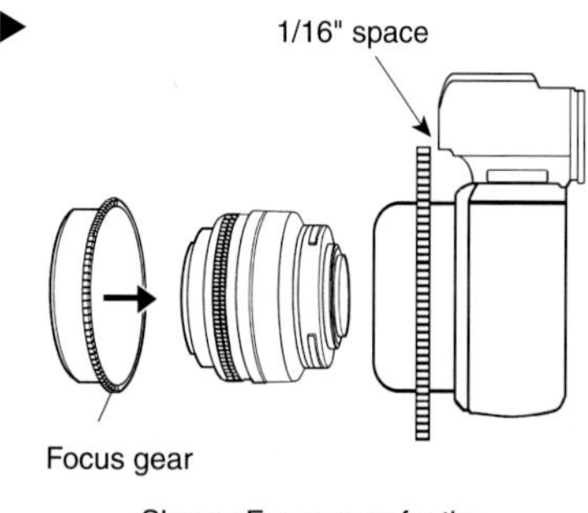

Shown: Focus gear for the AF Nikkor 20mm F2.8D lens

▾ *AF/MF Switching Gear*

This gear is exclusively for use with the Nikkor 60mm and 105mm lenses. It enables you to switch between manual and autofocus modes via the AF/MF Switching/Zoom Knob on the zoom port or custom flat port. To operate manual focus mode, the focus gear must also be installed.

If you have an autofocus lens, why would you want to use it in manual mode? The answer to that is on page 201.

1. Set lens at manual mode.
2. Slip the AF/MF gear over the lens. ▶
3. Align the AF/MF button on the lens with the slotted screw on the gear.
4. While holding down the AF/MF button on the lens, slide the gear over the button.
5. Tighten the screw with a screwdriver. Tightening the screw depresses the AF/MF button, which allows the gear to rotate freely between the "AF" and "MF" positions. *Caution:* Do not overtighten the screw.

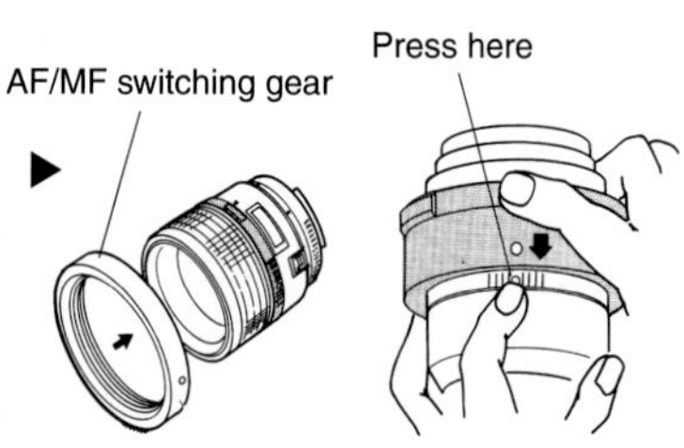

Shown: Switching gear for the AF Nikkor Micro 60mm F2.8D lens

6. Attach the focus gear to the lens by slipping it over the lens barrel as shown. The space between the AF/MF switching gear and the focus gear should be about 1/16" (2mm).

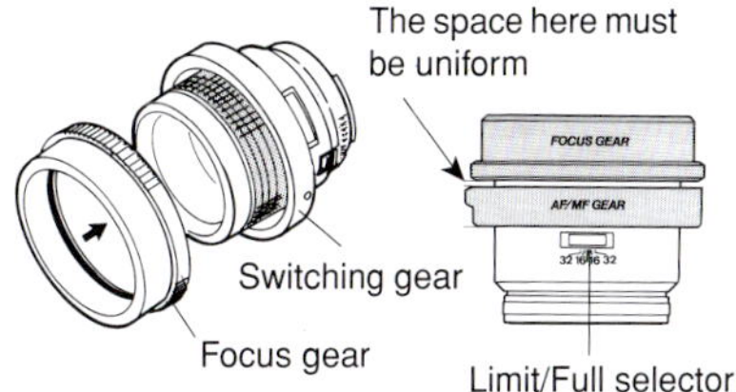

Note: The 60mm and 105mm lenses feature a "Limit/Full" function. Set the "Limit /Full Focus" function on the camera to the "Full" position before mounting the camera in the housing.

▼ *Zoom Gear*

The zoom gear rotates the lens barrel on a zoom lens, enabling the lens to change focal lengths. Once the compatible gear has been installed on your lens, simply turn the focus/zoom knob on the housing or port.

Slide the zoom gear down the length of the lens barrel. Slip the focus gear over the lens and position it with a space about 1/16" inch (2mm) in front of the zoom gear.

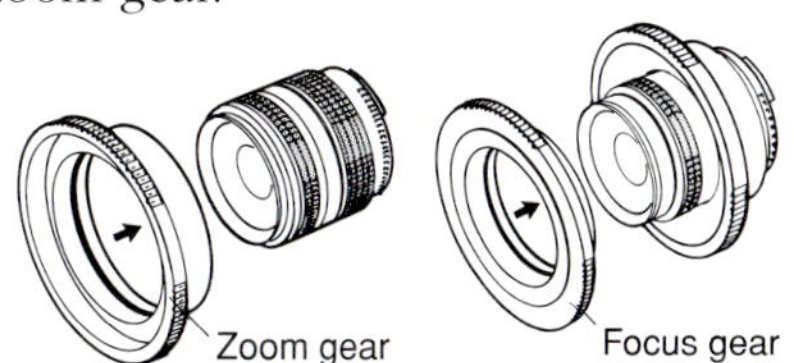

Shown: Zoom gear and focus gear for the AF Nikkor 35-80 F4~5.6D lens

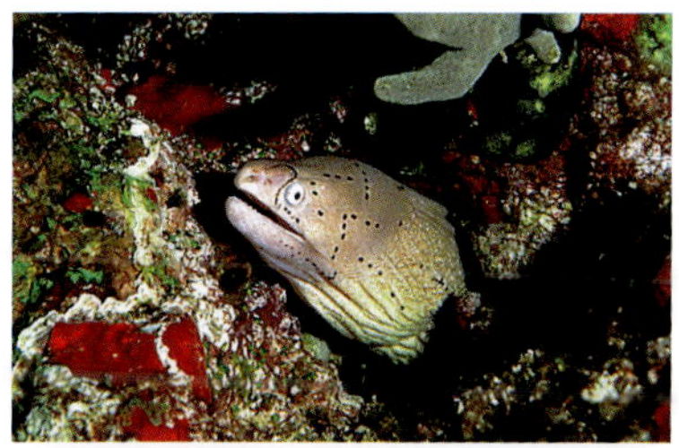

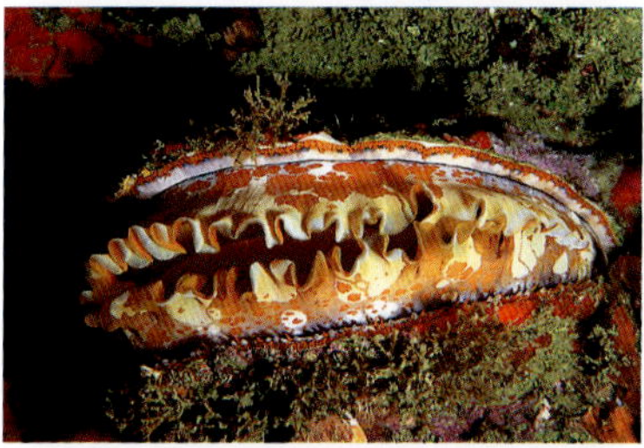

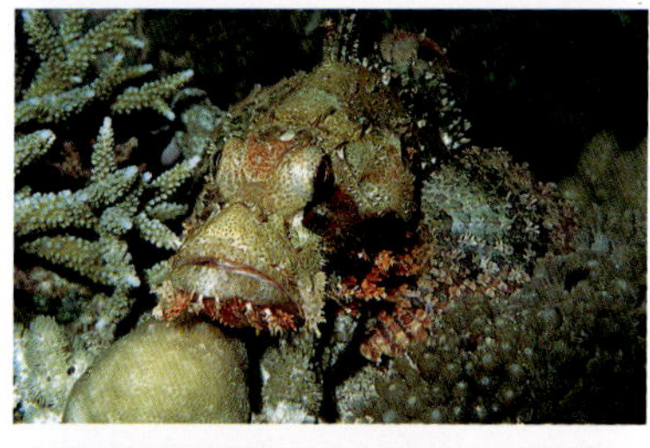

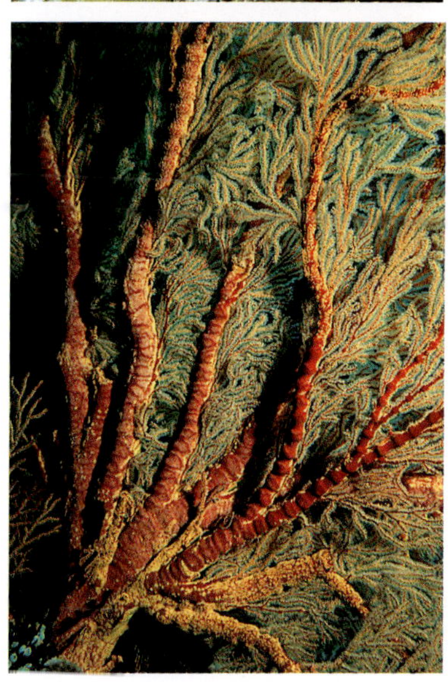

How to Mount the Camera to the Housing

1. Attach aperture gear to the lens, then the lens to the camera.

2. Select focus and metering modes.

3. Switch the Quick Lock lever on the housing to "Open."

4. Pull the AF lock lever outward to allow clearance when inserting the camera into the housing.

5. Set lens to smallest aperture.

6. Set aperture on the housing to correspond with the aperture set on the lens.

7. Make sure that the sync cord connector is extended outside the front case to allow clearance for the camera.

8. Fit the camera onto the Quick Shoe mount and slide forward. If the camera fails to make a smooth entry into the housing, tilt it slightly while adjusting the focus/aperture knobs.

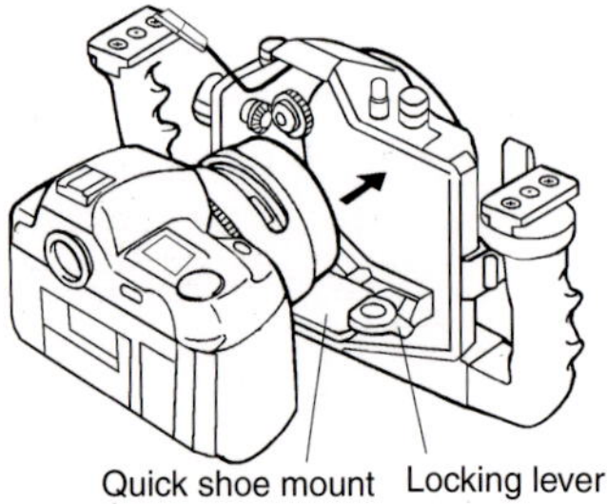

Note: The position of the camera in the housing allows you to change film without removing it from the housing.

What to Do *Before* You Put the Camera in the Housing

1. If it's brand-new, right out of the box, make sure you have all the parts that are supposed to be packaged with the camera.
2. Read the manual to acquaint yourself with basic camera operation.
3. Attach lens to camera. Install battery. Turn the power switch on. Check the LCD. Read-out should be bright and legible and the battery indicator should show full charge.
4. Trip the shutter at various shutter speeds.
5. Set camera on manual; set lens at various f-stops and watch the diaphragm blades as you trigger the shutter. The blades should open and close smoothly.
6. Go through the manual and test each function to confirm that they do, indeed, function.
7. Work each dial, button, and lever to ensure that they operate smoothly.
8. Take pictures. If they come out right, the camera is working and you're working it right.

9. Check that the aperture and focus gears on the lens mesh properly with the pinion gears inside the housing.

10. Check that you've removed the eyepiece from the camera's viewfinder, set the metering system, selected focus mode.

11. Switch the Quick Lock lever to the "Lock" position to secure the camera. *Caution:* If you fail to secure the camera, the camera will move inside the housing and it will not be able to focus.

12. Push the AF lock lever inward to its original position.

13. Attach the housing's sync cord connector to the camera's hot shoe. ▶

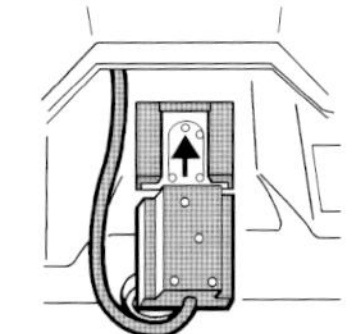

How to Close the Housing

1. Check the housing O-ring. Is it clean, lubricated, properly seated?
2. Fit rear case onto front case. Make sure they are properly aligned.
3. Engage both latches simultaneously.

How to Attach the Grip Spacer

The NX-90 Pro is equipped with twin contoured molded pistol grips. If the grip position is too tight, the grip position can be adjusted.

Remove the grip using the hex wrench included. ▶ Place the spacer or spacers between the grip and housing and secure tightly. *Note:* The grip must be securely re-attached to the housing to prevent accidental injury or loss of or damage to equipment.

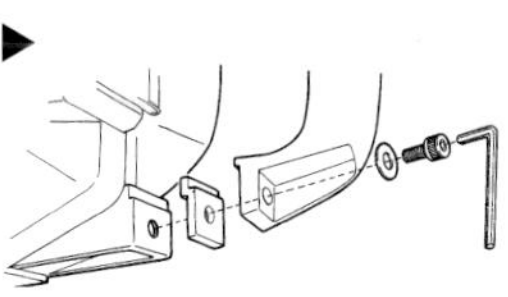

How to Attach the Sync Cord

The NX-90 camera is equipped with a five-pin bulkhead connector that accepts a five-pin sync cord connector for TTL and manual flash photography. ▶ For instructions on how to mate this sync cord connector with this housing, please see page 216.

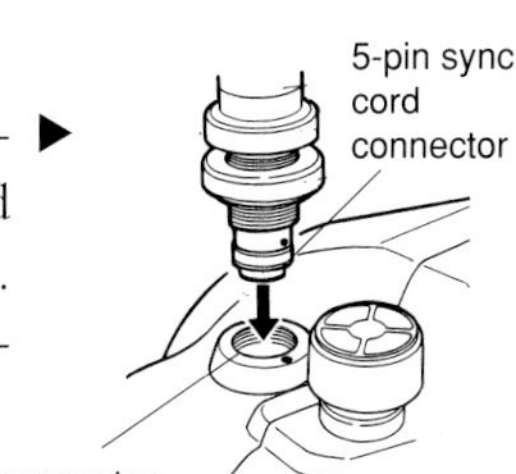

Pre-dive Checklist

You've cleaned it, assembled it, and familiarized yourself with the controls. You're ready to go diving. No, not yet. Don't get it wet till you've performed the following check:

- ❏ Are there fresh batteries in the camera?
- ❏ Have you loaded film in the camera?
- ❏ Is the LCD operational?
- ❏ Have you performed an aperture and focus control lens test?
- ❏ Is the camera secure in the housing Quick Shoe?
- ❏ Are the gears aligned and do they mesh correctly?
- ❏ Is the housing sync cord connected to the camera hot shoe?
- ❏ Is the lens port O-ring clean and lubricated?
- ❏ Is the lens port clean?
- ❏ Is the port lock lever locked?
- ❏ Is the housing O-ring clean and lubricated?
- ❏ Is the housing securely sealed?
- ❏ Are there fresh batteries in the strobe?
- ❏ Is the sync cord connector O-ring clean and lubricated?
- ❏ Is the sync cord connector properly connected to housing bulkhead connector?
- ❏ Is the strobe TTL functioning?
- ❏ Are the strobe arms and base stay securely mounted to the housing?
- ❏ Have you tested the complete system in a bucket of fresh water for signs of leakage?

If you answered *no* to any of the above, you need to check/fix/replace that part or function. If you answered *yes* to all of the above, *let's go diving*!

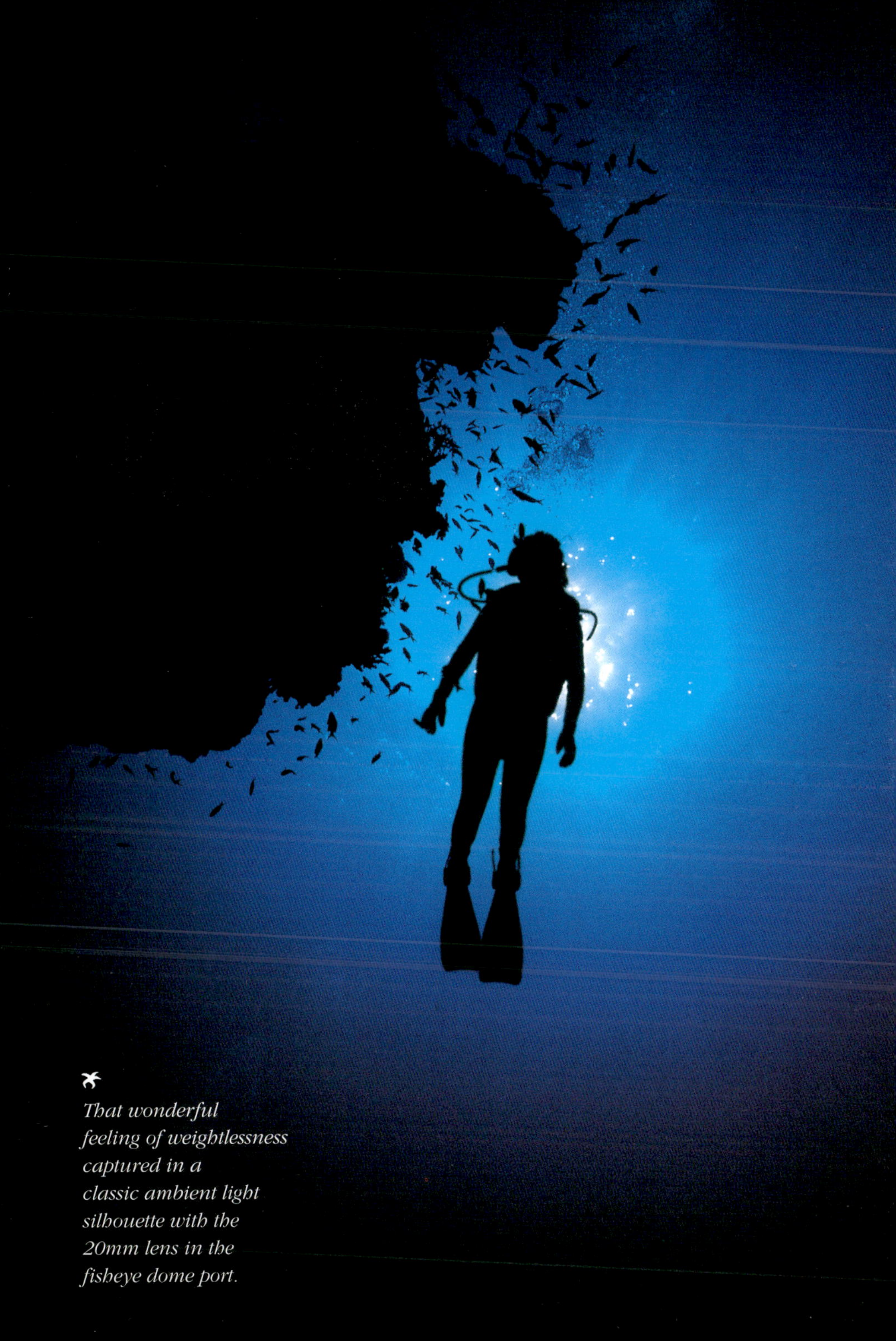

That wonderful feeling of weightlessness captured in a classic ambient light silhouette with the 20mm lens in the fisheye dome port.

PORTS

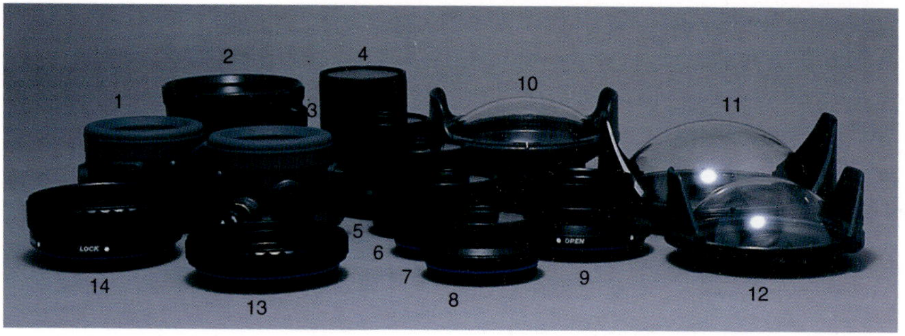

1. Standard Flat Port
2. Zoom Port
3. Custom Flat Port
4. Compact Macro Port 111
5. Compact Macro Port 79
6. Compact Macro Port 67
7. Compact Macro Port 52
8. Compact Macro Port M
9. Compact Macro Port Base
10. Standard Dome Port
11. Fisheye Dome Port
12. Compact Dome Port
13. SX Extension Ring
14. SX Extension Ring 40

Sea & Sea manufactures an integrated system of 11 flat and dome ports that provide a spectrum of lens/port configurations for the NX-90 Pro housing. All ports are specifically designed to accommodate specific lenses and are constructed of lightweight materials to reduce bulk and underwater drag and retain system stability and balance. The flat ports bear an optical grade glass surface, the domes acrylic. They are equipped with standard bayonet coupling mounts that allow for quick and easy attachment and removal. They accommodate 10 interchangeable Nikkor and Sigma lenses.

Flat Ports

The flat ports have been designed specifically for macro and zoom lenses.

Flat ports affect images in the following ways:

- ▼ Because light rays bend as they pass through a flat port, the angle of coverage of any given lens is narrowed. For example, a 28mm lens on land yields 75° coverage; when used with a flat port, the angle of coverage underwater is 56°, 25 percent less than that on land. A flat port enhances lens performance by narrowing the angle of coverage. ▼ Images photographed through this port are magnified and appear larger, the same as when seen through a diver's mask. For this reason, flat ports are best suited for macro and portrait photography.

Note: Lenses wider than 28mm should not be used with a flat port because it will cause blurring, peripheral distortion, and color fading around the outer edges of the photo.

The basic flat port for the NX-90 is the *standard flat port*; it has no exterior controls. The *custom flat port* is equipped with two exterior controls, an AF/MF switching knob which enables you to change between autofocus and manual focus underwater when using the 60mm or 105mm lens, and a zoom knob for zoom operation with zoom lenses.

The *compact macro port* is actually two pieces: an O-ring sealed base, with a bayonet mount that attaches to the housing, and a port with a threaded mount that screws onto the base. There are five different compact macro ports. All assemble to the same compact macro port base. They have been designed to accommodate the AF Micro Nikkor 60 and 105mm lenses in combination with the x1:4 and x2 teleconverters.

The *zoom port* is a flat port that houses zoom lenses. It is equipped with exterior controls that operate the zoom control on the camera lens. The optical properties of the zoom port are the same as those of the standard and custom flat ports.

The two *flat port extension rings* extend the physical length of the flat port. The ring fits between the flat port and the housing body, thus extending the port farther from the housing to accommodate a longer lens.

Dome Port

Dome ports are intended for wide angle lenses. You cannot use a flat port for a wide lens because flat ports reduce the angle of coverage, magnify the image, and increase peripheral distortion. Dome ports are engineered to do the opposite. They are optically corrected to increase angle of coverage, reduce the magnification of water, and limit peripheral disortion. The port's semispherical surface is designed to match the curvature of the lens and reduce refraction.

On land a dome port has no special optical properties and functions like a clear glass window. But underwater it functions like an additional lens element and, like a lens, has unique optical properties.

- It eliminates the bending of light rays as they pass through the dome, thereby correcting for refraction. Angle of coverage of the lens is the same underwater as it is on land.
- As an extension of the lens, it forms an apparent image in front of the dome. This phenomenon is called *the virtual image.*
- The virtual image phenomenon makes the actual image appear just inches from the dome even though the subject may be several feet away. This enables improved focusing and composition. For example, when a lens is focused to infinity, the virtual image is approximately twice the distance of the diameter of the dome. Therefore, the virtual image created by a six-inch dome will be about 12 inches away from the film plane.
- By minimizing refraction, it increases color saturation and image definition.

You can take full-figure diver shots, close focus fish portraits, wrecks, reefs, and large pelagics all on the same dive.

A *fisheye dome port* is the most specialized port. It is distinguished by its large hemispherical shape and has a 180° field of view. It is designed to accommodate ultra-wide lenses. Sea & Sea offers three dome ports for use with Nikkor 16mm fisheye and 20mm lenses and the Sigma 24mm lens.

The dome ports are equipped with a lens hood to keep stray light from striking the front lens element and causing lens flare. The hood won't eliminate flare when the light source actually appears in the picture area but helps when the light source is just outside the frame. By reducing glare, the shade helps increase contrast and minimizes reflection on the dome surface. The hood also provides protection from damage to the dome surface. Small scratches will usually be filled in by water and will not mar the image. Large, deep scratches require replacement of the dome.

LENSES

The ultimate quality of a photograph is determined by the quality of the lens. The Nikon and Sigma lenses compatible with the NX-90 Pro are distinguished by superb optical performance. All project sharp, accurate images. All can be used both on land and underwater.

Why So Many Lenses?

Lenses vary in design with different types engineered to perform certain photographic tasks better than others. One of the most important characteristics of a lens is *focal length*. Focal length, as explained in Chapter 1, is the amount of the scene shown (angle of view) and the size of the objects (magnification) recorded on film. Each of the lenses compatible with the NX-90 has a different focal length, enabling you to select the lens that will produce the precise image you want to create.

Which Lens to Choose

As of this writing, there are 450 different new lenses available from 15 manufacturers. Nikon alone offers 73 different 35mm lenses. It would be an overwhelming task for any underwater photographer to select one or two from such a vast selection.

Sea & Sea has simplified the lens selection process for you. The ports for the NX-90 Pro support a carefully selected assortment of Nikon and Sigma lenses, chosen for their optical excellence and suitability for dynamic underwater photography, as well as for their size and weight. All the compatible lenses are lightweight, the most compact in their class, an important consideration in underwater photography. The lineup of lenses represent a comprehensive selection for photographers of all skill levels, for every shooting situation, in a broad array of price ranges.

Factoid

▼ A specific lens is defined by its maximum aperture: the widest or largest diameter f-stop it can achieve

▼ Fast lenses will allow you to use a fast shutter speed, thus freezing movement and sharpening the image

▼ Picture angle of a lens is measured on a diagonal, from corner to corner in the picture area

▼ A lens is tested for image quality starting at its maximum aperture. An image gets sharper as the aperture is closed, but typically, at f/8 the image is sharpest.

MACRO LENSES

Nikon D lenses
New Nikon D lenses have distance measuring capability. Each D lens has a microcomputer interface engineered into the lens mount to transmit the actual focus distance to the camera's metering system. Exposure readings are analyzed by the camera's computers to determine the best exposure.

Macro lenses essentially do two things: they magnify images and decrease subject-to-lens distance. The result is greater image sharpness and increased color saturation. Macro lenses are multipurpose; they are capable of macro, close-up, and normal focal length images. They will produce crisp high-contrast images from a life-size magnification ratio to infinity.

Sea & Sea offers ports and lens gears for three macro lenses:

AF Micro-Nikkor 60mm F2.8D
AF Micro Nikkor 105m F2.8D
Sigma AF 180mm APO Macro F5.6 UC

Tips

▼ Use aperture priority mode. Select the smallest aperture to maximize depth of field; the camera will select the appropriate shutter speed.

▼ At 1:1 image ratio, depth of field is one-half in front of the focus point and one-half behind. This is actually an advantage. The area behind the subject will be soft, serving to accentuate the subject.

▼ Since depth of field is so limited, focus on a point midway between the central point of interest. When shooting fish, focus on its eye.

▼ Press the shutter release halfway to select a focus point on the subject. Then use the AF lock to hold the focus. Reposition. The focus will remain constant until the shutter is fully released.

▼ With the 60mm and 105mm lenses, set the focus limit switch from Full to Limit. The focusing range limiter will restrict the range of the focusing ring, thus increasing focusing speed.

▼ When shooting autofocus, lack of contrast coupled with dark and bright areas cause the autofocus to seek. Use a focusing light.

▼ In manual mode, preset focus for minimum distance. Move camera toward or away from your subject for precise focusing.

▼ If you intend to switch between program auto and aperture priority, be sure not to lock the lens at the smallest aperture.

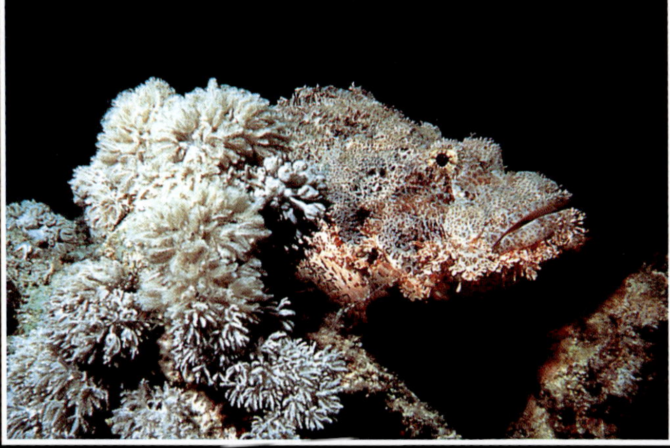

The stonefish, usually seen in camouflage, portrayed here in noble profile. Starkly set apart by the 60mm lens at f/22. A single strobe applied the shadows.

SUPER MACRO WITH TELECONVERTERS

Teleconverters are optical accessories which mount between the camera body and the lens, thereby increasing the effective focal length of the prime lens. They increase the range of magification of the lenses to which they are coupled, magnifying distant subjects so you can achieve a large image without moving in close.

Sea & Sea manufactures four focus gears for use with the Nikon x1.4 and x2 teleconverters for the 60mm and 105mm lenses.

Advantages:

- ▼ Increases the focal length of the lens
- ▼ x1.4 converts a 60mm lens to an 84mm lens
- ▼ x2 converts a 60mm lens to a 120mm lens
- ▼ Extends the range of the lens's macro magification. Small subjects are enlarged to dramatic proportions
- ▼ Lens minimum focusing distance remains the same
- ▼ All camera auto features and functions are retained
- ▼ A macro lens with a teleconverter is smaller, lighter, and costs less than a lens with the same long-range telephoto capabilities.

Some problems and their solutions:

- ▼ Slight loss of image quality and sharpness. Stop down to the smallest aperture possible
- ▼ Vignetting or distortion at the edges of the picture. Use the smallest aperture possible
- ▼ Loss of lens speed. If you attach a x2 teleconverter to a 60mm f/2.8 lens, it becomes a 120mm f/5.6. A 105mm f/2.8 lens with a x2 teleconverter becomes a 210mm f/5. Although there is an effective reduction in lens speed, the TTL meter in your system will automatically adjust for the loss of light
- ▼ Loss in effective aperture, approximately two f-stops. Select manual mode and set a slower shutter speed
- ▼ Lack of contrast causes the autofocus system to hunt. Use manual focus
- ▼ The reduction in light caused by the extension of the lens inhibits autofocus. Use a focus light and dual strobes.

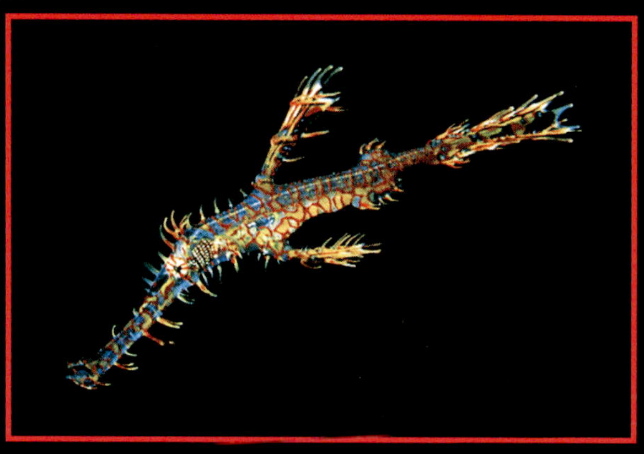

The Ghost Pipefish,
a sliver of a fish.
Full-frame made possible
with the 105mm lens.
From 10 inches.

WIDE ANGLE LENSES

A wide lens is a short focal length lens, by definition providing a wide field of view, extended depth of field, and powerful close focusing capability. Wide lenses have the outstanding ability to approach close to the subject with a minimum focusing distance just inches from the film plane. They assure high-contrast, high-resolution imaging throughout the entire shooting range. They are ideal for panoramic scenics, close focus, full figure divers, schooling fish, large fish portraits, and those novelty above-and-below the surface images.

Sea & Sea dome ports accommodate three wide angle lenses:

AF Fisheye Nikkor 16mm F2.8D
AF Nikkor 20mm F2.8D
AF Sigma 24mm F2.8

Tips

▾ The range of auto modes, autofocus, and TTL work well with the 16mm and 20mm D lenses when used in combination with the camera's matrix metering system. When using Sigma's 24mm lens, autofocus with center-weighted metering and TTL is recommended.

▾ Position strobe six to eight inches behind the housing and at least half an arm's length out to the side. The ultra angle of acceptance allows the dome to capture and reflect stray light. Direct strobe beam parallel to the lens. This will eliminate hot spots and lens flare.

▾ Get close. An ultra wide lens will allow you to capture very large subjects at close range. However, it will distort and alter perspective, making subjects seem very small at normal distances. To compensate, get very close, as close as 12 to 18 inches, and fill the frame.

▾ Center subject in frame. Outer edge distortion is a common characteristic of a fisheye lens. Position the subject in the center of the frame, with open water or sand at the outer edges; this way the subject is not distorted. Any distortion will be be at the periphery and indiscernible in blue water or sand background.

▾ Add extra weight to the housing. A fisheye dome envelops a large bubble of air and tends to make it point up. To regain neutral buoyancy and balance for the housing, add an ankle weight to the system.

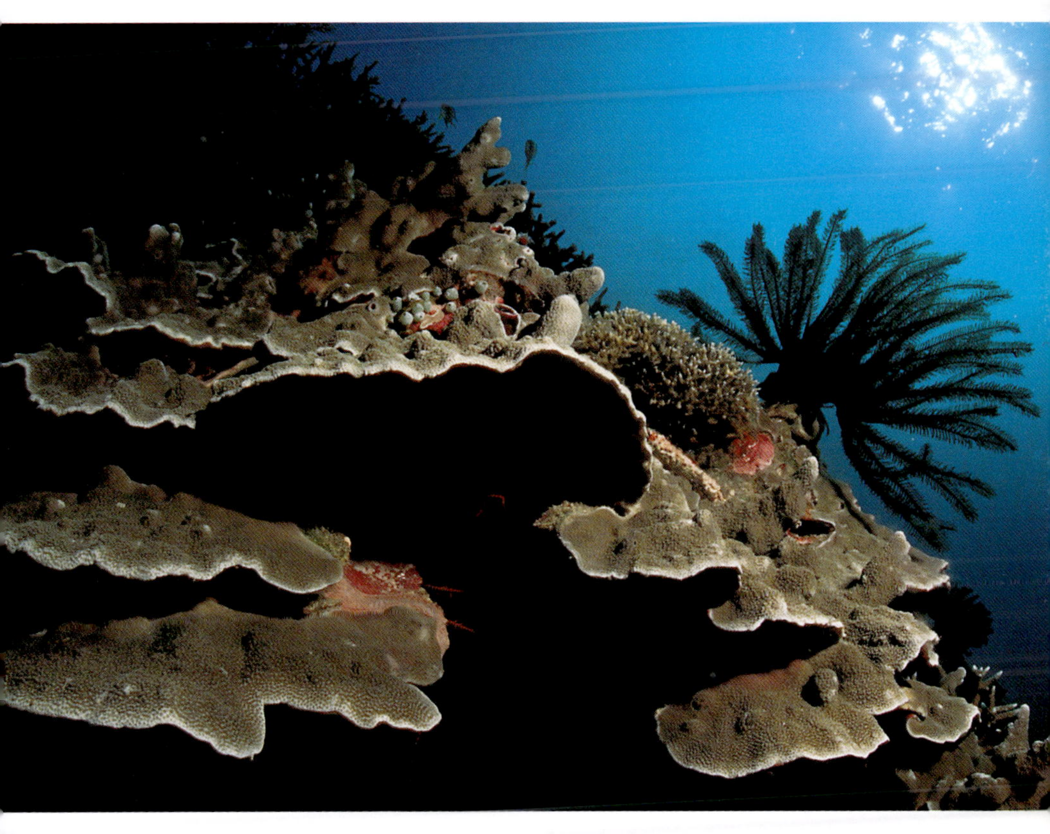

The extreme angle of acceptance of the 20mm wide lens enables close focusing to 18 inches and assures uniform sharpness of subjects from near to far.

ZOOM LENSES

A zoom lens is a lens that combines a range of focal lengths. By turning the zoom ring, the relationships among the lens elements are altered, resulting in a different focal length. As the focal length gets longer, the field of view narrows and the image appears larger. Zooming from 35mm to 70mm, for example, doubles the image size recorded on film.

The name of each zoom has two f-stops after the focal length. For example, the 28-70mm F3.5-4.5: the f3.5 indicates the maximum lens speed at the shortest focal length of 28mm. When zoomed out to 70mm, the lens is altered to a f4.5.

With a zoom lens, you can change focal lengths without changing subject-to-camera distance; you can change image size and position within the frame; you can do all that from a fixed camera position. It's like having a wide angle lens, a normal lens, and a mid-range telephoto lens all in one. It is a good starter lens.

Sea & Sea manufactures ports and gears for four zoom lenses:

AF Zoom Nikkor 28-85mm F3.5-4.5S
AF Zoom-Nikkor 28-70mm F3.5-4.5D
AF Zoom-Nikkor 28-80mm F3.5-5.6D
AF Zoom Nikkor 35-80mm F4.5-5.6D

Tips

▼ It's easier and more accurate to focus a zoom at the maximum focal length. Once the subject is sharply focused, shift to whatever focal length you want. The lens will remain in focus as you zoom. Fine-tune focusing by moving the camera closer or farther from the subject.

▼ To focus manually, rotate the focus knob until the image in the viewfinder is sharp and crisp. To zoom, turn the zoom knob until the desired composition is framed in the viewfinder.

▼ Select programmed auto exposure mode. As you zoom, the camera's TTL metering compensates for the light loss or gain and for proper exposure.

With a zoom lens you can even bracket focal length. Zoom in at 28mm

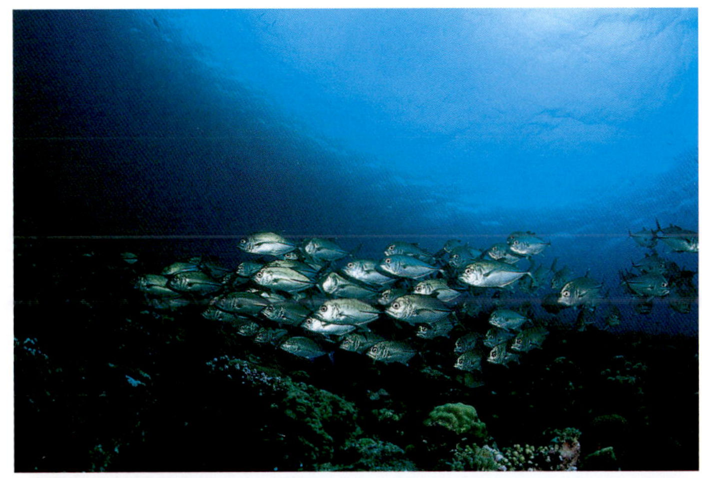

out to 50mm

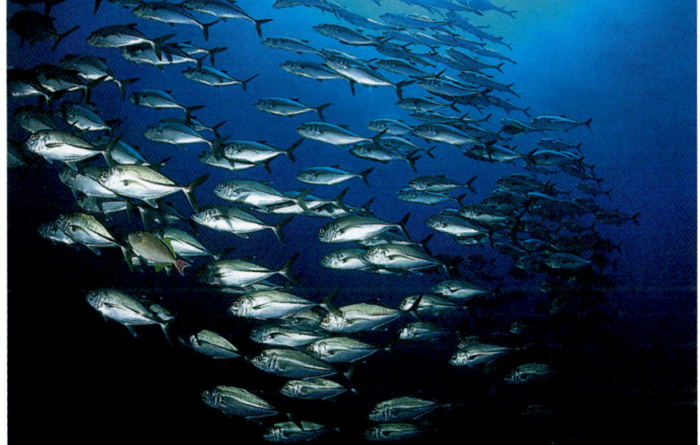

to the max at 85mm. One lens, one school, three views.

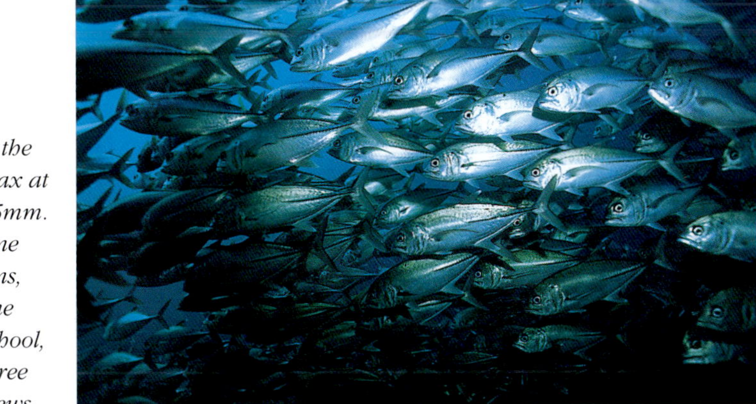

THE 3 MOST-ASKED QUESTIONS ABOUT THE NX-90

Q The system has so many controls and functions, how does a beginner get started?

A The NX-90 Pro is a highly-sophisticated piece of machinery. Yet one of its most impressive features is its user-friendly technology. The best way to get started is to work in auto mode. The camera will determine the correct exposures for you. As you gain experience with the system, you can experiment with other modes. Here's how to start:

1. Use only AF Nikkor D-type/AF-I Nikkor lenses with CPU.
2. Switch to "A" for lenses that feature an A-M switch. Switch to "A" or "M/A" with AF-I lenses.
3. Preset camera to "S" for Single Servo AF with Release-Priority.
4. Preset the metering to Matrix.
5. Preset AF Area: wide focus for large subjects and spot focus for subjects too small for the wide focus to cover.
6. Preset the exposure mode for "Auto Multi-Program Mode (P)".
7. Use only TTL compatible strobes. Set strobe on TTL mode.
8. Compose through the viewfinder and take the picture. The computers within the camera and lens will adjust for shutter speed/ aperture combinations, exposure values and autofocus for nearly 100 percent of all shooting situations.

Q Which metering mode is best?

A The most important element in underwater photography is light. You must make decisions about aperture and shutter speed to get the right amount of light on the subject for the right amount of time. To do that, you ask your camera for an exposure reading. The camera's metering system measures the light that passes through the lens using a metering "pattern." The N-90 offers a choice of three metering patterns:

Matrix metering is a multi-pattern system that analyzes scene brightness and scene contrast, detected by the camera's 8-segment matrix sensor, and focused subject's distance, which is detected and relayed by the D-type Nikkor, to provide an accurate exposure.

Matrix metering is the quickest and easiest way to get near perfect exposure results. It works with Nikkor D, AF and AI-P lenses, but only D lenses can relay distance data. All lenses must be fitted with CPU for all matrix metering options or the system will default to center-weighted metering.

Center-weighted metering is considered the old standby and is the most popular metering system in modern SLRs and compact cameras. It takes approximately 75% of the reading from the 12mm circle within the middle of the viewfinder and 25% from outside the circle. It gives more accurate metering when the exposure is based on a specific area within the scene but can be fooled by backlight, sidelight, spot lighting, or any large light or dark area in the scene.

Spot metering concentrates approximately 100% of the metering pattern on the 3mm circle within the viewfinder; that equates to about 1% of the total image area. It is extremely accurate for metering on a small and selective part of the scene but is tricky and not recommended for novices.

Q What do I do if the autofocus won't?

A The N90 camera has two autofocus systems: wide area focus for wide zone focusing and spot autofocus for small areas. Both are capable of tracking moving subjects quickly. But autofocus systems use contrast and definition for focusing. If the system cannot find that contrast, if the subject is poorly lighted, as in a cave or under a ledge, if there is a lot of particulate in the water, the autofocus system will not perform. The lens will either focus on the wrong subject, continue to "hunt," or the camera will not fire.

Solutions:

- Use a dive light or focusing light to add contrast to the image area
- Get close to your subject. Autofocus works best when the subject fills the frame
- Fill the frame with your subject so there are no "distractions" for the focus sytem. Autofocus will focus on whatever is closest
- Use the AF lock feature
- Use spot metering to isolate your subject from its surroundings
- Turn off AF and switch to manual focus. With the 60mm and 105mm lenses, you can change between AF and MF underwater.

THE NX-90 Pro SYSTEM

MACRO

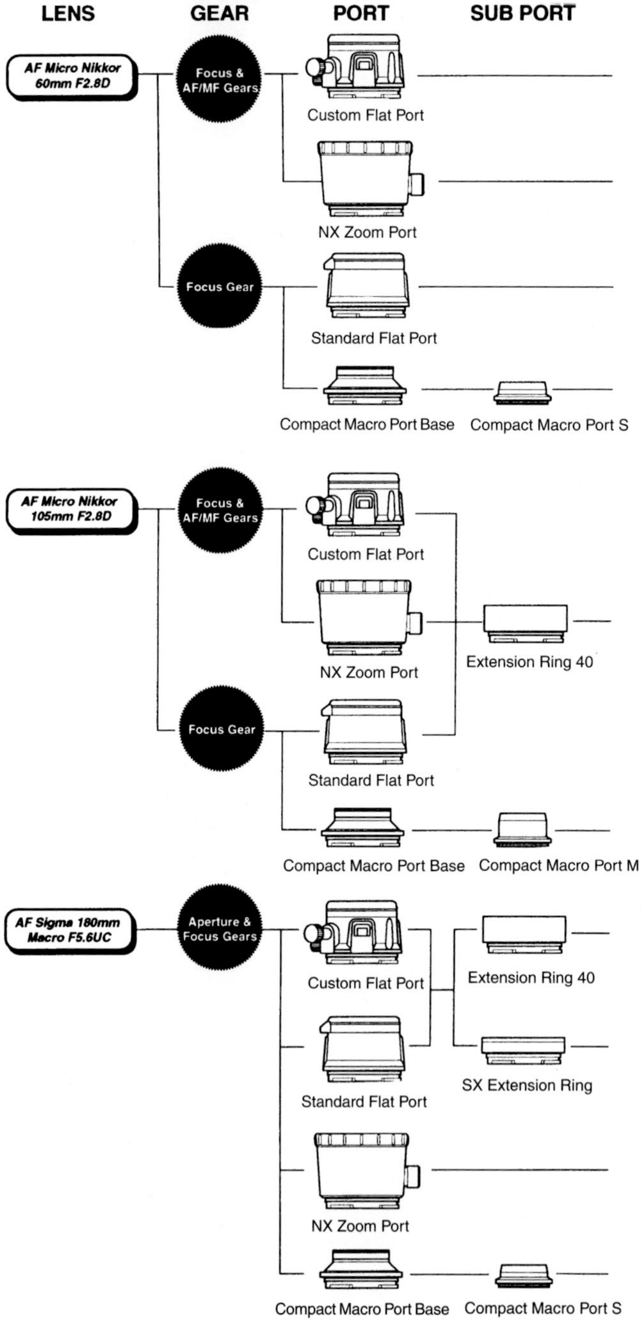

LENS	GEAR	PORT	SUB PORT
AF Micro Nikkor 60mm F2.8D	Focus & AF/MF Gears	Custom Flat Port	
		NX Zoom Port	
	Focus Gear	Standard Flat Port	
		Compact Macro Port Base	Compact Macro Port S
AF Micro Nikkor 105mm F2.8D	Focus & AF/MF Gears	Custom Flat Port	Extension Ring 40
		NX Zoom Port	Extension Ring 40
	Focus Gear	Standard Flat Port	Extension Ring 40
		Compact Macro Port Base	Compact Macro Port M
AF Sigma 180mm Macro F5.6UC	Aperture & Focus Gears	Custom Flat Port	Extension Ring 40
			SX Extension Ring
		Standard Flat Port	Extension Ring 40
			SX Extension Ring
		NX Zoom Port	
		Compact Macro Port Base	Compact Macro Port S

SUPER MACRO

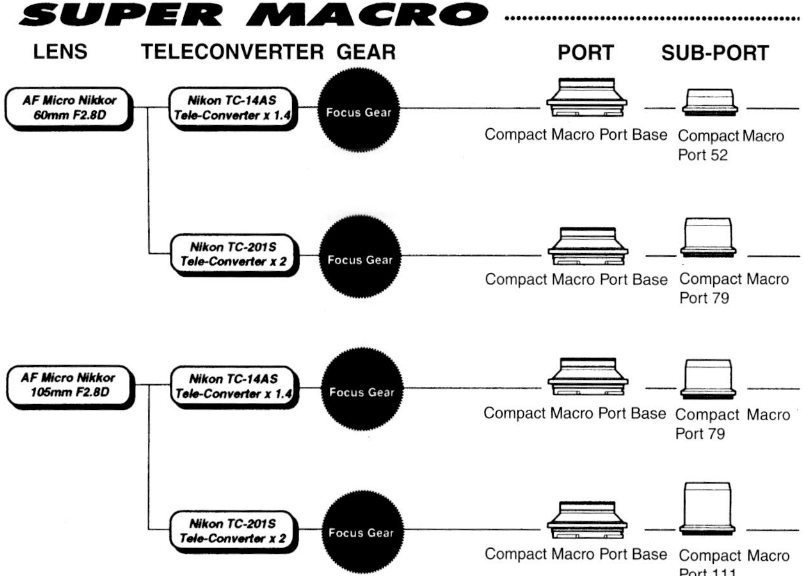

WIDE

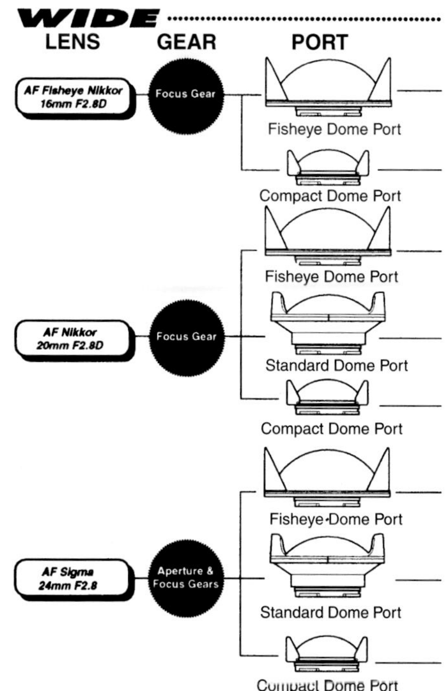

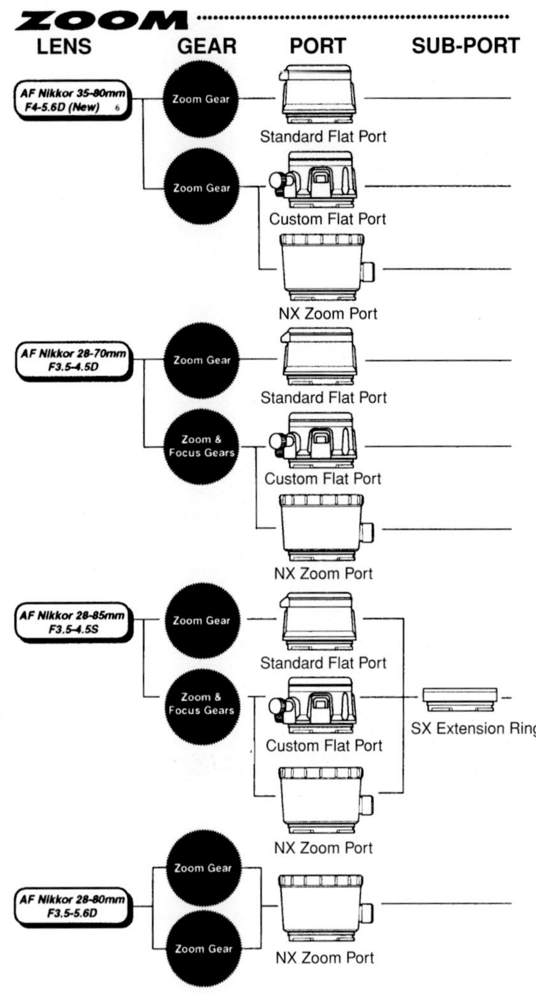

Don't Forget Care and Maintenance

The NX-90 Pro is constructed of rugged, noncorrosive aluminum and requires minimal care and maintenance. But it is a precision electronic instrument and improper handling can adversely affect its performance. Chapter 9 will tell you all about the natural enemies that can hurt your system and what you need do to ensure its efficient performance.

CHAPTER SEVEN

Strobes

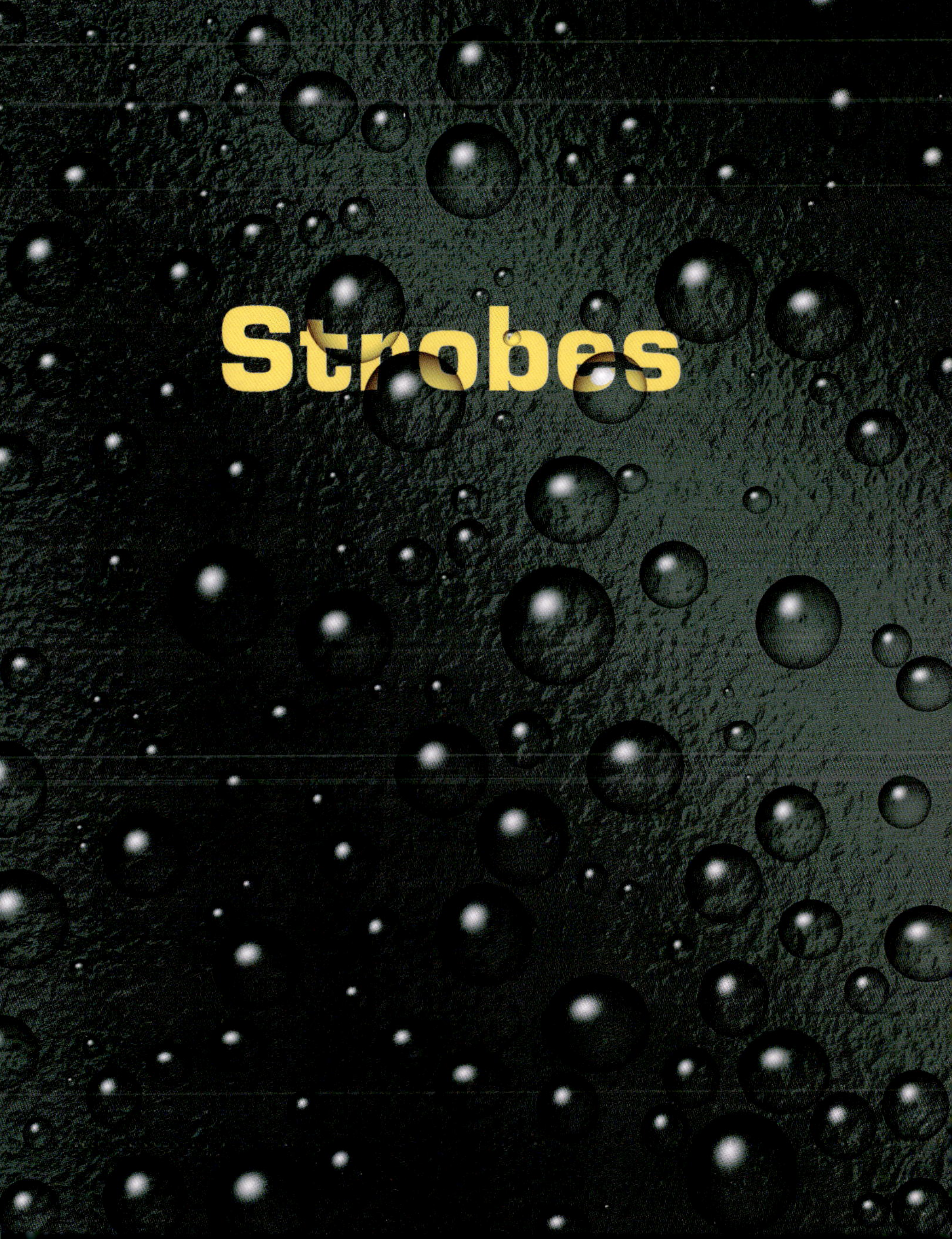

Strobes

Underwater, the deeper you go, the darker it gets, the deeper you go, the less color you see. Those are the facts. If it's a bright, sunny day and the water is very clear and you're diving shallow, then you can use natural light to illuminate your pictures. But even under such optimum conditions, your pictures will have a bluish tint and be mostly void of reds and yellows. If you want sharp, colorful pictures at any depth no matter what the surface or water conditions, you must use artificial light. Thus, the choices are: natural light or artificial light or a combination of the two.

In the beginning there were no choices. There was only natural light.

The first underwater photograph was taken in 1860. William Thompson, an engineer at Weymouth, England, housed his camera in a box clamped to a tripod, which was lowered from a rowboat 18 feet down to the sea bed. He operated the drop shutter from the boat with a piece of string. His exposure time was 10 minutes.

The next known attempts at achieving underwater photographs were made in 1866 by a French photographer named Bazin. He got some fairly clear pictures of sunken ships through a porthole in a diving bell. Electric lights housed inside the bell supplemented the natural lighting.

A French professor of zoology, Louis Boutan, designed the first underwater camera housing. It weighed 400 pounds, and exposure time was 30 minutes. He also invented a "flashgun." This consisted of an alcohol lamp housed in a watertight glass dome. The glass dome was fitted to the top of a 50-gallon wooden barrel that was filled with air and oxygen. A rubber tube attached to a hand pump enabled Boutan to blow magnesium powder into the flame, thus producing a short brilliant flash.

We've come a long way, buddy.

The development of an effective underwater light source became imperative with the introduction of the first amphibious 35mm camera in the early 1950s. For want of anything better, neophyte underwater photographers used the same bare bulbs then commonly used for land photography. These gave one brief burst of light and then had to be replaced. They littered the sea bed, floated on the surface, were costly and difficult to use.

By the 1960s several electronic flash units were being manufactured specifically for underwater photography. These were big, bulky units. Most had circular or coiled flash tubes that caused hot spots. Manufacturers then incorporated lower power settings so photographers could control the light output. In the '70s many strobes had a linear flash tube that provided even better lighting control, but these strobes were still large, heavy and hard to handle. In the 1980s manufacturers introduced smaller, lighter strobes and automatic flash units that synchronized with the camera. These automatic units became known as TTL strobes.

Sea & Sea was born in 1972, born from the need of two university students to light their images. The Yellow Sub was the first submersible strobe manufactured in Japan and was followed in 1974 by the Yellow Sub 35, the world's first submersible strobe constructed of plastic.

Today Sea & Sea is recognized as the industry leader in the manufacture of submersible strobes. There were the YS-20, YS-50, YS-100, YS-150, YS-200. Those models are no longer in production, but thousands are still in service, testament to the enduring quality of Sea & Sea strobes.

In this chapter we focus on the current family of strobes, consisting of the YS-30 Duo, YS-40A, YS-60TTL, YS-120 Duo and YS-300TTL.

Understanding Specs

Strobes are manufactured in a variety of sizes with different features and for different uses. Manufacturers provide a specification chart which defines the individual characteristics of the model you have purchased. To understand how your strobe will perform, you must understand the nomenclature used in these charts. On the following page we define those terms.

Exposure control: how a proper exposure is determined. Basically, strobes are manual or automatic (including TTL). With a manual strobe, the photographer selects the correct f-stop based on film speed and on strobe-to-subject distance. A TTL strobe communicates electronically with a camera that is equipped with a sensor that measures the strobe light reflected off the film plane. An automatic strobe is equipped with a sensor that measures the light reflected from the subject. Both types automatically quench the light output when there is adequate light for a proper exposure.

Beam angle: refers to the angle of the light beam and is expressed in degrees. The wider the beam angle, the greater an area the flash will cover.

Diffuser: an adapter that fits over the flash reflector; it spreads the light and increases coverage area. It also decreases light intensity by about one f-stop.

Guide number: a relative evaluation of a strobe's power output. The higher the GN, the more powerful the strobe. Every manufacturer determines power output based on ideal conditions: fully-charged batteries, clear water, light-colored subjects with high reflectivity.

Color temperature: a rating in degrees Kelvin. Noontime sunlight is about 5500° K. The color of daylight film is set at 5500° K. Most strobes range from 5400-6000°K. The lower temperatures produce warmer (red) light, the higher temperatures produce cooler (blue) light.

Number of flashes: the number of exposures you can make on a set of fresh or fully-charged batteries before having to change or recharge them.

Power source: the type and number of batteries needed to power the flash. Most strobes use either alkaline or nickel-cadmium batteries.

Recycle time: the time it takes for a discharged strobe to recharge.

TTL: an acronym for through-the-lens. A TTL strobe is used with a camera that has a built-in TTL sensor. The system allows for automatic strobe exposures.

Size and weight: the physical dimensions (height, length, width) and weight (usually on land and sometimes called dry weight) of a particular strobe.

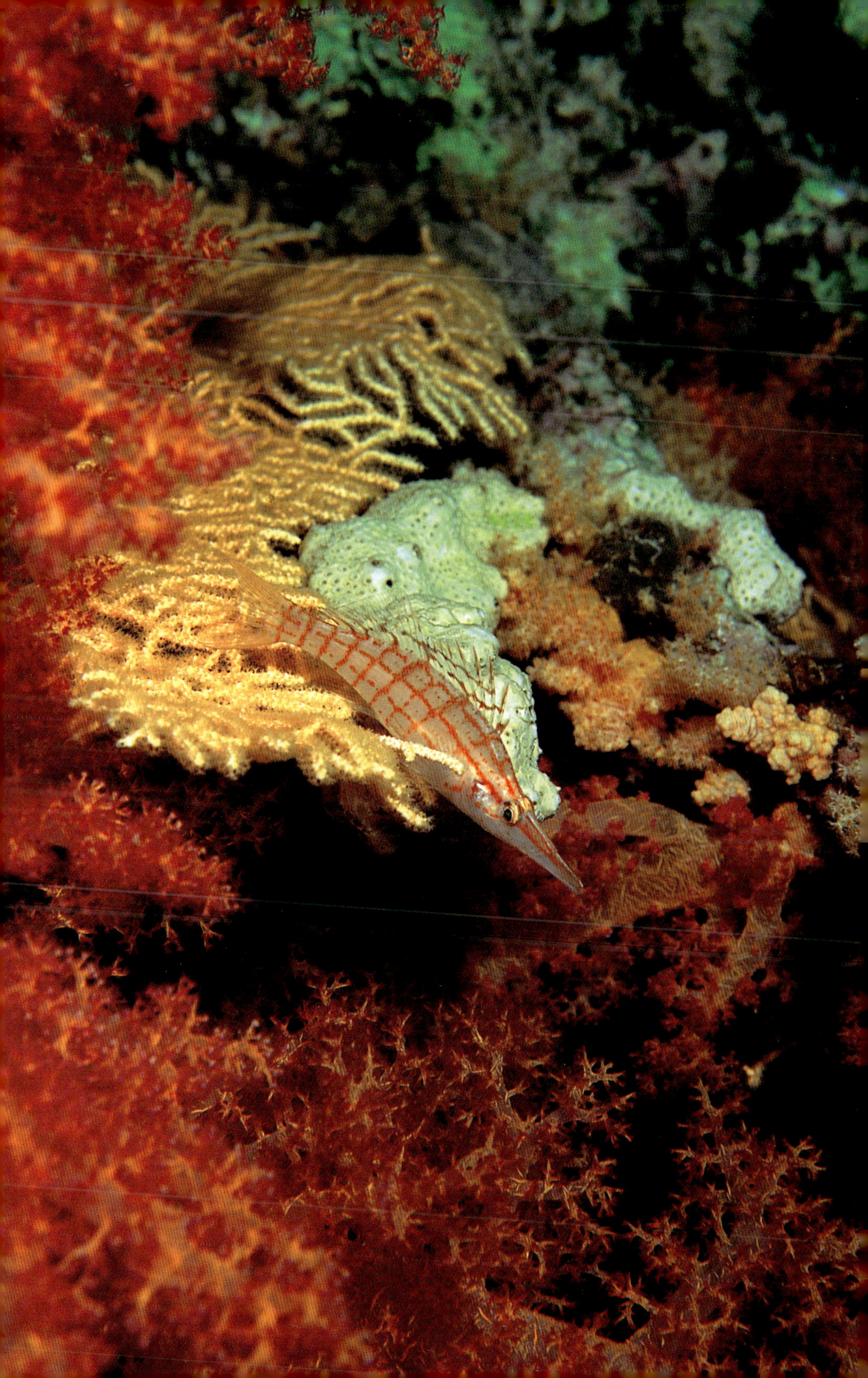

YS-40A

With the YS-40, Sea & Sea broke new ground. It was the world's first underwater accessory flash to synchronize with a camera via an infrared optical triggering system that transmits an electrical impulse between camera and strobe. The possibility of leakage at the strobe and camera connection was thereby eliminated.

With the proverbial pulse on the market, Sea & Sea modified the YS-40 to make photography with the MX-10 easier and better. Introduced in 1997, the YS-40A is an improved version of the YS-40 with three major changes: an automatic exposure mode for guessless f-stop figuring, an elongated strobe arm, which distances the light beam from the subject, and a redesigned reflector to spread the light beam for wider, more even subject coverage. With the new YS-40A strobe, taking perfect pictures is effortless.

Identification of Parts

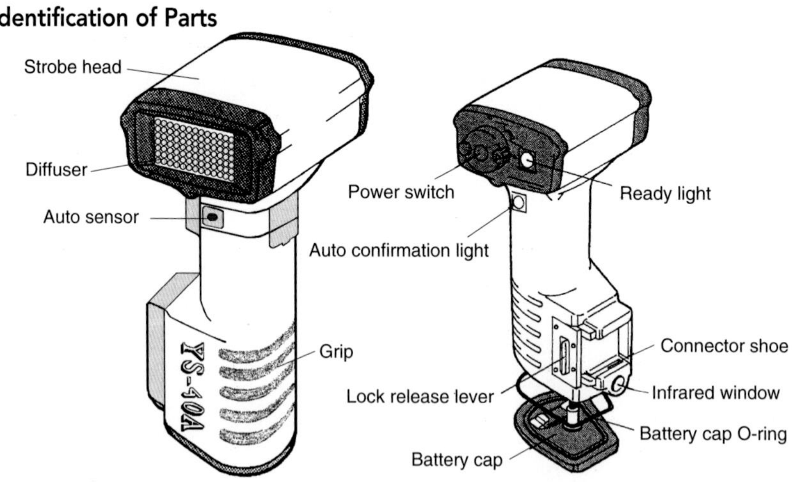

Specifications

Exposure control:	Manual or Auto	**Synchronization:**	Infrared electrical impulse
Beam Angle:	70° x 80°	**Color temperature:**	5500°K
GN (ISO 100):	49 land; 25 u/w (feet)	**Power Source:**	4 1.5 volt alkaline or ni-cads
	15 land; 8 u/w (m)	**Maximum depth:**	150 feet (45 meters)
Recycle time:	5 seconds alkaline*	**Dimensions:**	4 x 3.3 x 7.7"
	3 seconds ni-cad)		100 x 83 x 192mm
No. flashes:	100 alkaline*; 50 ni-cad	**Weight (land):**	17 oz/485g (w/o batteries)
Function indicators:	Ready light, Auto confirmation light	**(u/w):**	0.7 oz/20g (w/o batteries)
		Accessories:	O-ring set, exposure decal

* Varies with manufacturer and freshness of batteries

Installing the Batteries

This unit is powered by four 1.5-volt AA alkaline or ni-cad batteries.

1. Check that the power switch is in the "Off" position.

2. Turn the battery cap knob counterclockwise and lift the battery cap straight up. ▶

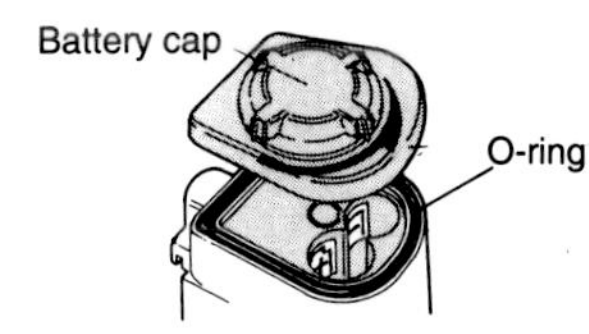

3. Insert the batteries according to the polarity marks inside the battery chamber. ▶

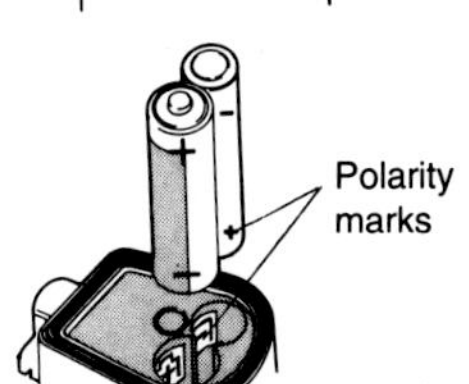

4. Inspect the O-ring. If necessary, clean or replace it. Lightly coat with silicone grease and reseat. Check that it is properly seated.

5. Replace the battery cap, and turn the battery cap knob clockwise until fingertight.

How to Connect Strobe to Camera

The strobe mounts onto a connector shoe on the side of the camera. This shoe is similar to the hot shoe on the top of land cameras. *Note:* Load the film before mating strobe and camera. You cannot open the camera's back door after the strobe has been attached.

1. Hold the strobe in your left hand and the camera in your right. Using your left thumb, move the red lock release lever to the left. The red locking bars will retract. ▶

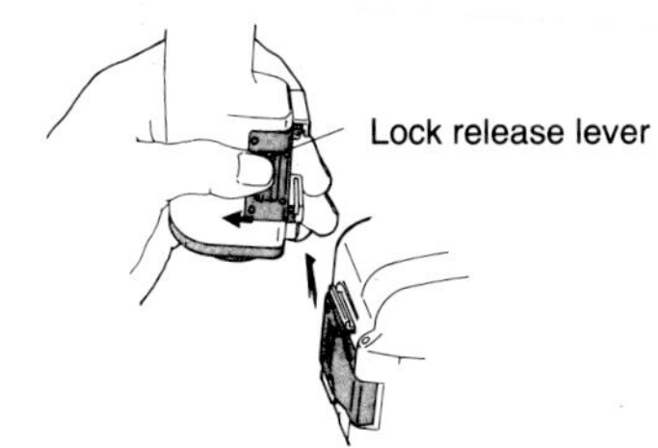

2. Slide the slotted grooves on the strobe onto the metal rails of the camera's connector shoe.

3. Release the lock lever. The lever will move to the right, aligned with the white arrow. The strobe is secured.

Note: The electric impulses are exchanged ▶ through the small clear windows in the camera and strobe. Contamination or damage to these windows will inhibit the exchange of infrared signals. Keep these windows clean to ensure that the infrared impulses can pass through unimpeded.

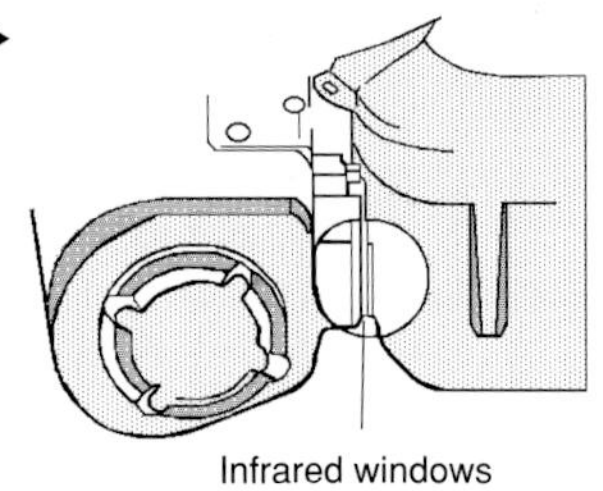

To detach strobe from camera: pull the lock release lever back to disengage the slotted grooves from the metal rails, then pull the strobe away from the camera and slide off the mount.

Power Switch

The power switch has three positions:

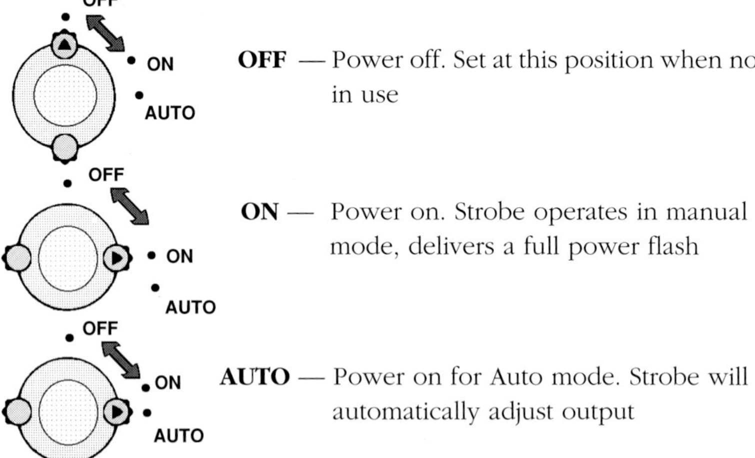

OFF — Power off. Set at this position when not in use

ON — Power on. Strobe operates in manual mode, delivers a full power flash

AUTO — Power on for Auto mode. Strobe will automatically adjust output

What is an Automatic Strobe?

You will see the terms "TTL" and "Auto" and "Automatic" used interchangeably in this book. Do not confuse the automatic capability of the YS-40A will that of a TTL strobe. A TTL strobe measures light that has passed through the lens and reflected off the film plane. With an automatic strobe, the light from the strobe reflects off the subject back into the auto sensor. The auto sensor measures this light and automatically controls strobe output to yield a correct exposure when subject is within the correct range.

How to Use in Manual Mode

1. Turn the power switch clockwise to the "On" position.

2. When the orange light appears in the ready light window, the strobe capacitor is fully charged and the strobe is ready to fire. *Note:* If the shutter is triggered before the ready light appears, the strobe may not fire or will not fire at full capacity. Always wait a few seconds after the ready light comes on.

3. Determine the correct f-stop/strobe-to-subject distance combination. Use the guide number formula on page 209 or use the following exposure table (based on one-half the guide number/ISO 100).

Strobe-to-Subject Distance/Manual Mode						
Feet	**5.5**	**4.4**	**3.0**	**2.2**	**1.5**	**1.1**
Meters	**1.7**	**1.3**	**0.9**	**0.7**	**0.5**	**0.3**
ISO 100	f/4.5	f/5.6	f/8	f/11	f/16	f/22
ISO 400	f/8	f/11	f/16	f/22	-	-

4. With the built-in 32mm lens your subject must be three foot apparent or beyond to ensure proper focus. With the 20mm conversion lens, camera-to-subject distance is 1.4 foot to infinity. Review the depth of field chart for each lens.

5. Compose and shoot.

How to Use in Auto Mode

In Auto mode there is no need for complicated exposure calculations. The strobe will automatically adjust light output. When the subject is within the effective range, the green LED auto confirmation light will illuminate for about two seconds, indicating a correct exposure.

1. Turn the power switch clockwise to the "Auto" position.

2. When the orange light appears in the ready light window, the strobe is ready to fire. *Note:* If the shutter is triggered before the ready light appears, the strobe may not fire or will not fire at full capacity. Wait a few seconds after the ready light comes on.

3. Preset the aperture to f/4.5 for ISO 100 film and f/8 for ISO 400 film.

4. Compose subject within the effective range for the f-stop and shoot.

Strobe-to-Subject Distance/Auto Mode	
Feet	**0.8 ~ 5.5**
Meters	**0.25 ~ 1.7**
ISO 100	f/4.5
ISO 400	f/8

Note: Do not cover the auto sensor with your finger when the strobe is in the auto flashing mode. Covering the auto sensor will disable the automatic function, and the strobe will fire at full power.

Auto isn't Automatically Perfect

The manufacturer recommends using f/4.5 with ISO 100 and f/8 with ISO 400 with the YS-40A in the auto mode. The YS-40A sensor works at all f-stops. You are *not* limited to f/4.5 with ISO 100 and f/8 with ISO 400. These settings are intended for point-and-shoot situations when the subject falls within the appropriate "zone of sharp focus" (depth of field). For example:

- with the 32mm built-in lens at f/4.5 (ISO 100), the zone of focus is 3 to 5.5 feet. At f/8 (ISO 400), zone of focus is 2.6 to 7.9 feet
- with the 20mm lens at f/4.5 (ISO 100), zone of focus is 2.8 to 6.5 feet. At f/8 (ISO 400), zone of focus is 12.6 feet.

If the subject is outside this zone of focus, it will be out of focus. The solution is to use a smaller aperture. Smaller apertures always extend depth of field and produce sharper pictures. The YS-40A in auto mode compensates and delivers the right amount of light.

- With the macro lens, use ISO 100 film at f/16 or f/22.
- With the close-up lens, shoot within the 18 to 36 inch range. Set f-stop at f/8 with ISO 100 and f/16 with ISO 400.
- Stop down one f-stop when shooting highly reflective subjects.
- When using an accessory diffuser, light output is reduced by one f-stop. To compensate, open up by one f-stop.

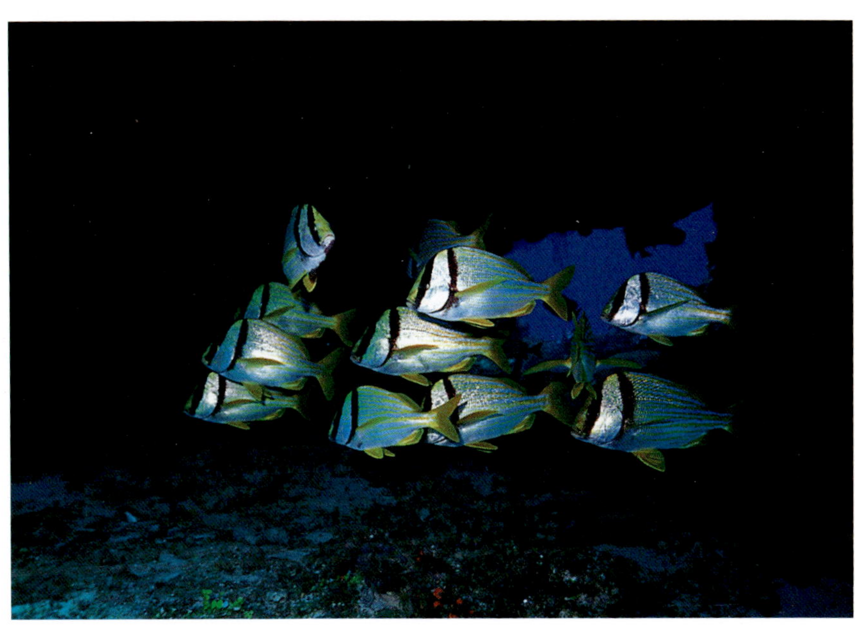

Softly illuminated and nicely separated from its background, a school of porkfish taken by the MX-10 at f/11, the 20mm lens from four feet, the YS-40A on Auto.

YS-60TTL/S AND YS-60TTL/N

The YS-50TTL was manufactured from 1980 to 1997. It was a rugged and reliable mid-sized strobe. There are thousands in service all over the world.

Enough of the old and on with the new! Heeding the call of photographers who wanted more from their strobe, Sea & Sea remodeled the YS-50, keeping its best features intact but making it a more flexible strobe for more creative underwater applications. The YS-60 looks like its predecessor, same size and shape. It's still defined as a mid-size flash, has the same fail-safe battery compartment, but the reflector has been replaced with the new prism diffuser and it now has variable power modes. It also is equipped with Sea & Sea's innovative duo circuitry. The sync cord is permanently fixed, but the cords can be exchanged via factory replacement.

There are two models: the YS-60TTL/S for use with all Sea & Sea cameras or housings with a four-pin bulkhead connector, and the YS-60TTL/N for use with any system with a standard five-pin bulkhead connector.

Identification of Parts

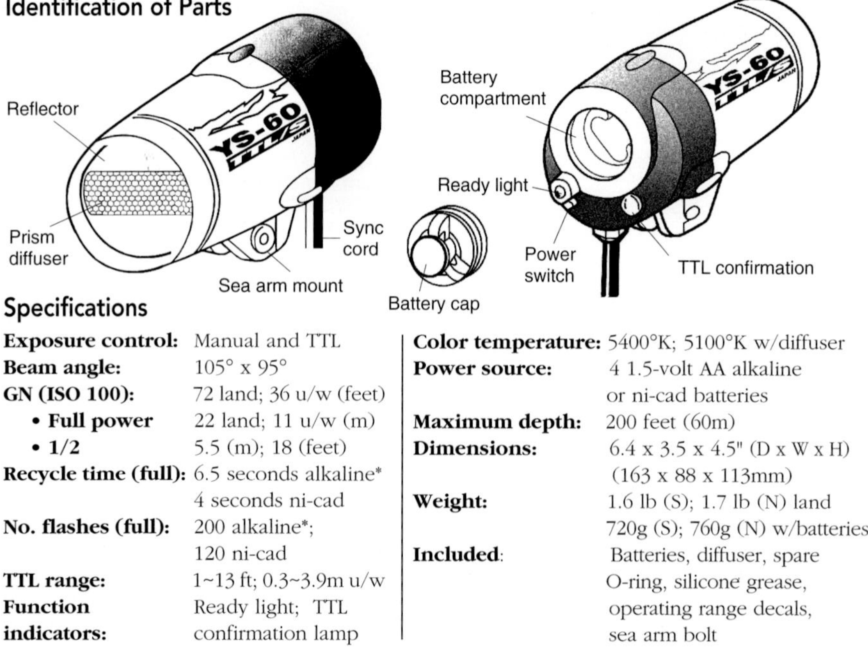

Specifications

Exposure control:	Manual and TTL
Beam angle:	105° x 95°
GN (ISO 100):	72 land; 36 u/w (feet)
• **Full power**	22 land; 11 u/w (m)
• **1/2**	5.5 (m); 18 (feet)
Recycle time (full):	6.5 seconds alkaline* 4 seconds ni-cad
No. flashes (full):	200 alkaline*; 120 ni-cad
TTL range:	1~13 ft; 0.3~3.9m u/w
Function indicators:	Ready light; TTL confirmation lamp
Color temperature:	5400°K; 5100°K w/diffuser
Power source:	4 1.5-volt AA alkaline or ni-cad batteries
Maximum depth:	200 feet (60m)
Dimensions:	6.4 x 3.5 x 4.5" (D x W x H) (163 x 88 x 113mm)
Weight:	1.6 lb (S); 1.7 lb (N) land 720g (S); 760g (N) w/batteries
Included:	Batteries, diffuser, spare O-ring, silicone grease, operating range decals, sea arm bolt

* Varies with manufacturer and freshness of batteries

Installing the Batteries

The YS-60TTL is powered by four 1.5-volt AA alkaline or ni-cad batteries.

1. Before opening the battery chamber, make sure your hands and the strobe are completely dry.

2. Check the power switch. It must be in the "Off" position.

3. Turn the battery cap lever counterclockwise to the "Open" position. (Turn in the direction of the white arrow on the strobe.) ▶

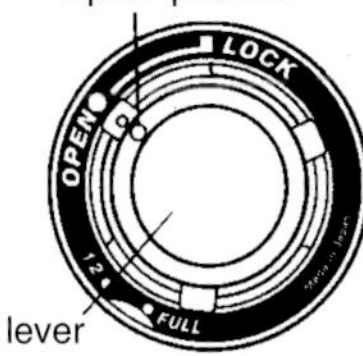

4. Turn the strobe upside down. Though this may be awkward, if there's water trapped beneath the lid, it will flow out and away from the battery compartment instead of into it.

5. Pull the battery cap straight up.

Note: With the strobe in this position, the batteries may fall out of the chamber. Cup your hand over the chamber to catch them.

6. If water is present around the lip of the chamber, wipe it dry.

7. Insert four batteries (*8 for the YS-120*) according to the polarity decals inside the chamber. ▶

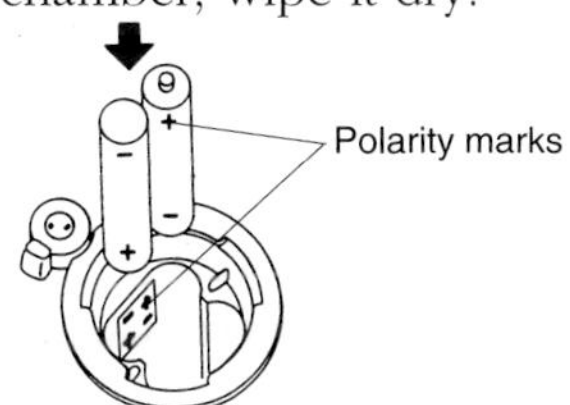

8. Check, clean, and lubricate the battery cap O-ring. To remove it, push forward with thumb and index finger till the O-ring bulges from its groove. Gently lift it out with your other hand. Check it for cuts, debris, or abrasion. Coat it lightly with silicone grease and replace it to its channel.

Note: Low battery power can cause the TTL mechanism to operate erratically and can cause improper synchronization of strobe and shutter. Always use fresh or fully-charged batteries.

How to Install the Battery Cap

The YS-60 has a separate factory-sealed chamber for the electronic circuitry and an O-ring sealed chamber for the batteries. Since the chamber with the electronics is sealed, chances of it flooding are remote. But the battery chamber is subject to user error. If it floods, your strobe will be inoperable. Look at the battery chamber cap. Notice the two raised black dots, one on the stationary part of the cap, the other on the rotating circular dial. These dots are important to the proper installation of the battery cap and protection against flooding.

1. Align the small black dot on the circular dial with the large black dot.

2. Fit the cap into the chamber, aligning the small black dot with the white dot beside the word "Open."

3. Push the cap in. Make sure the O-ring is seated. Turn the lever with the small dot clockwise to "Lock" until it snaps into the sealed position with an audible click.

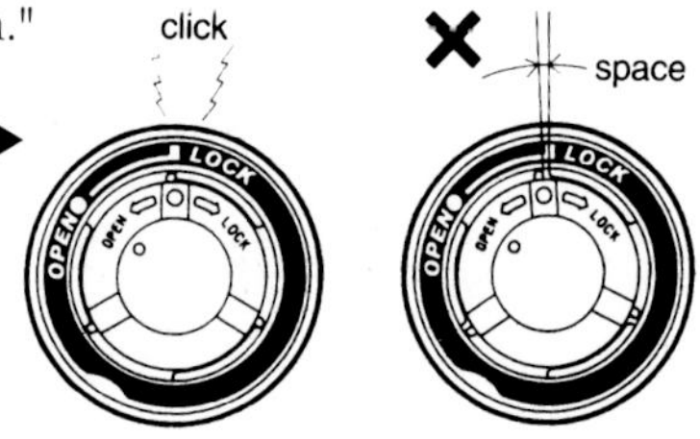

click ✕ space

Right Wrong

Warning: The battery cap should not rotate freely.

How to Connect Strobe to Camera

The YS-60TTL is equipped with an attached and O-ring sealed sync cord. The YS-60TTL/S is compatible with all Sea & Sea camera/housed systems with a four-pin connector. The YS-60TTL/N is compatible with all camera/housed systems with a five-pin connector. The built-in duo circuitry dedicates with both. The sync cord can be changed at a Sea & Sea service facility. A parts and service fee will apply.

For instructions on how to connect four and five-pin cords, see pages 214-215.

Power Switch

The power switch has four positions:

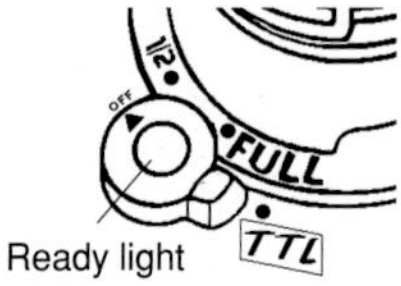

OFF — when not in use
FULL — strobe fires at full power, manual
1/2 — strobe fires at half power, manual
TTL — for TTL operation

Ready light

How to Operate in Manual Mode with a Motor Marine II-EX

In manual mode, the strobe fires at full power.

1. Turn the power switch to the "On" position for full power or "1/2" for a half-power flash. *Note:* At "1/2" the GN is 18.
2. Wait for the red lamp to glow, indicating the unit is ready to fire.
3. Set camera focus control lever for apparent distance.
4. Select f-stop. Determine by using the guide number formula. (See page 209.) Or use the strobe-to-subject distance chart on page 240.
5. Position subject, angle strobe head, and take the picture.

Note: The ready light may come on before the unit has actually reached a full charge. The difference between a full charge and a partial charge is like the difference between a 100-watt light bulb and a 40-watt bulb. Fire too soon and your picture may be underexposed. To ensure a full-powered charge, wait two to three seconds after the ready light comes on before firing.

How to Operate in TTL Mode with a Motor Marine II-EX

1. Connect strobe to the camera's bulkhead connector.
2. Turn the strobe's power switch to the "TTL" position.
3. Wait for the neon lamp to glow, indicating the unit is ready to fire.
4. Set camera focus control dial for apparent distance.
5. Select the strobe-to-subject distance/aperture setting. Refer to the table below for recommended distances.
6. Position subject and take the picture.
7. If the distance/aperture setting is correct, the TTL confirmation lamp will illuminate for about three seconds.
8. If the TTL confirmation light does not come on, you achieved a full power flash and a possible underexposure. Open up one f-stop and shoot again.

Strobe-to-Subject TTL Operating Range							
Feet	**1-2**	**1-2.6**	**1-3.6**	**1-5**	**1-7**	**1-11**	**3-12.8**
Meters	**0.3-0.6**	**0.3-0.8**	**0.3-1.1**	**0.4-1.5**	**0.5-2.1**	**0.6-3.4**	**1-3.9**
ISO 50	f/22	f/16	f/11	f/8	f/5.6	f/3.5	f/2.8
ISO 100	-	f/22	f/16	f/11	f/8	f/5.6	f/3.5
ISO 200	-	-	f/22	f/16	f/11	f/8	f/5.6
ISO 400	-	-	-	f/22	f/16	f/11	f/8

How to Operate in Manual Mode with the Nikonos V

In manual mode, the strobe fires at full power.

1. Set the ISO film index on the camera to match the film speed.
2. Set your camera shutter speed dial on "A" for auto.
3. Set focus control for apparent distance.
4. Turn the strobe power switch to the "On" position for full power or to "1/2" for a half-power flash. *Note:* At "1/2" the GN is 18.
5. Select f-stop based on strobe-to-subject distance and film speed. Use the guide number formula on page 209 or use the strobe-to-subject distance chart on page 240. (The YS-60 has the same guide number as the YS-120. The chart is valid for both strobes.)
6. Check that the strobe ready light is on and take the picture.
7. Bracket.

How to Operate in Manual Mode with a Housed SLR

The following camera settings are made through the controls on the housing.

1. Set film speed on camera.
2. Select exposure mode on camera.
3. Turn the strobe power switch to the "On" position for full power or "1/2" for a half-power flash. *Note:* At "1/2" the GN is 18.
4. In aperture priority, select f-stop. Use the guide number formula on page 209. Or refer to the manual exposure chart on page 240 for the correct strobe-to-subject distance/f-stop combination for the film speed being used. (The YS-60 has the same guide number as the YS-120. The chart is valid for both strobes.) In shutter priority, the camera selects the f-stop.
5. Check that the strobe ready light is on. Compose through the viewfinder and take the picture.
6. Bracket.

How to Operate in TTL Mode with a Nikonos V

1. Set the ISO film speed dial on the camera.
2. Set focus for apparent distance.
3. Set the shutter speed selector dial on "A." The camera will automatically select 1/90 second for flash synchronization.
4. Select an f-stop. Refer to the strobe-to-subject TTL operating range chart on page 235.
5. Set f-stop on your lens.

6. Set the strobe power mode switch to the "TTL" position. With fully-charged ni-cads, the neon light will glow in about four seconds. With a fresh set of alkalines, the light will glow in about six seconds.
7. Compose and frame your image through the viewfinder.
8. Position strobe head and take the picture. If the distance/aperture setting is correct, the TTL confirmation lamp will illuminate for about three seconds to confirm that the TTL has worked properly within the TTL range.
9. If the TTL confirmation light does *not* come on, you achieved a full power flash and a possible underexposure. Open up one f-stop and shoot again.

How to Operate in TTL Mode with a Housed SLR

1. Set film speed.
2. Select exposure mode.
3. Turn the strobe's power switch to the "TTL" position.Wait for the ready lamp to confirm the capacitor is fully charged.
4. In aperture priority, select an f-stop based on the manufacturer's strobe-to-subject TTL operating range chart. Refer to page 235.
5. If aperture and strobe-to-subject distance combination is correct, the TTL confirmation lamp will illuminate for about three seconds. If the TTL lamp does not come on, you achieved a full power flash and possibly an unexposure. Open up to a larger aperture and take another picture.

See *TTL: Exceptions to Perfection* on page 258.

Prism Diffuser

The YS-60 is equipped with a new rectangular bubble-pattern reflector which broadens and softens the light. For a detailed explanation of how this innovation improves the performance of your strobe, please see page 242.

Accessory Diffuser

An accessory diffuser is packaged with your YS-60 strobe. The diffuser fits over the the strobe reflector and will widen the beam angle to 105° x 105°. The color temperature of the light is warmed to 5100°K, and the guide number is half. When using the strobe in manual mode, open up one f-stop.

YS-120 DUO

The YS-120 Duo represents a significant development in flash photography. It is the first submersible strobe to automatically synchronize for TTL photography with both four and five-pin TTL connectors. The cords are independent of the strobe and interchangeable. All you need do is select the appropriate one for your system when you purchase the unit. Clever, convenient, and cost-effective for those with more than one system.

It yields a generous wide beam and emits a warm 5000°K color. It has the power and reach for wrecks, scenics, large pelagics, fast recycling for rapid-firing. It conveys flash readiness and TTL confirmation information via twin sets of neon lamps built into both sides of the strobe head, a true benefit in dual strobe photography. Rugged, sleek and lightweight, the YS-120 is a versatile high-performance flash.

Identification of Parts

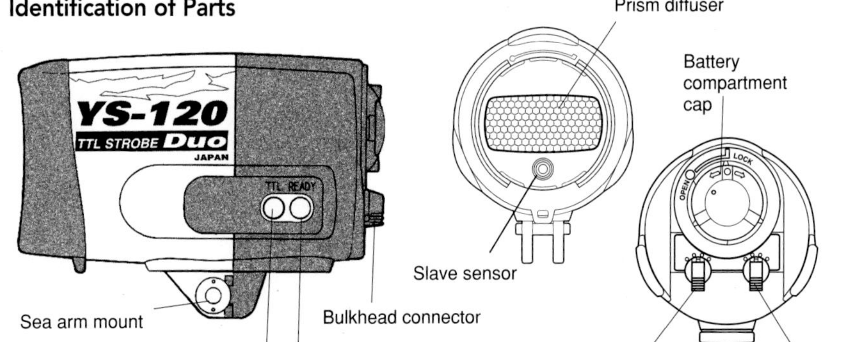

Specifications

Exposure control: Manual and TTL
Beam angle: 105 x 105°
GN (ISO 100): 72/22 (ft./m) land
- **Full** 36 (ft); 11 (m) u/w
- **1/2** 18 (ft) 6 (m) u/w

Recycle time (full): 2~3 seconds ni-cads
3~4 seconds alkalines*
4 seconds lithium
No. flashes (full): 140 ni-cads
280 alkalines*
600 lithium
TTL range (ISO 100):
- **YS-120/S at f/3.5** 2.6~10.3 ft/0.8 ~3.1m
- **YS-120/N at f/2.5** 3.3 ~ 12.8 ft/1 ~ 3.9m

Function indicators: TTL confirmation; ready light
Color temp: 5100°K; 4800°K w/diffuser
Power source: 8 AA alkaline, ni-cad (Sea & Sea brand only) or lithium batteries
Maximum depth: 200 feet (60m)
Dimensions: 7.3 x 4"; 185 x 102mm (L x D)
Weight: 2.9 lb; 1.3 kg (land)
Included: Batteries, diffuser, spare O-ring,silicone grease, operating range decals

* Varies with manufacturer and freshness of batteries

Installing the Batteries

The YS-120 is powered by eight 1.5-volt AA alkaline, lithium or ni-cad batteries. The manufacturer advises use of Sea & Sea brand ni-cads only. The YS-120 has been designed with the same fail-safe battery compartment as the YS-60. Please see pages 233-234 for detailed instructions on how to install the batteries and correctly secure the battery compartment cap.

How to Connect Sync Cords

See pages 214-216 for step-by-step instructions on how to connect four and five-pin connectors to the strobe and to the camera or housing.

Controls

This strobe is equipped with two rotary-style controls.

The Power Switch has four positions:

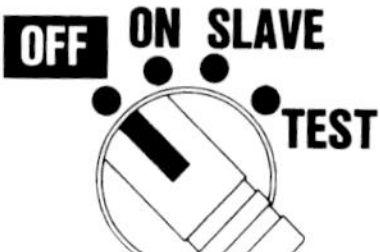

OFF — Power off. Set at this position when not in use
ON — Power on. Strobe fires in manual mode, full power
SLAVE — Slave function is activated
TEST — Used to check that the strobe is firing correctly

The Mode Switch has three positions

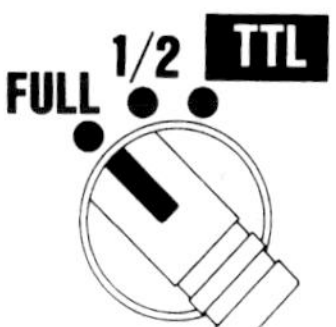

FULL — Strobe delivers a full power flash, manual mode
1/2 — Strobe fires at half-power power, manual mode
TTL — Set at this position for TTL automatic operation

How to Operate in Manual Mode with a Motor Marine II-EX

In manual mode the strobe can be used in full or 1/2 power modes. Changing from full to 1/2 power decreases flash output by one full f-stop. Angle of coverage remains the same.

1. Connect the four-pin cord to the strobe and camera.
2. Turn the power switch to the "On" position.
3. Set desired power setting to "Full" or to "1/2" power.
4. Set camera focus control lever for apparent distance.
5. Wait for the red ready light to glow. The unit is ready to fire.

6. Select desired f-stop. Determine by using the standard guide number formula on page 209 or use the following exposure calculation chart to determine f-stop.
7. Select the appropriate shutter speed to accompany the f-stop.
8. Compose, angle strobe head, and take the picture.

Tip: At 1/2 power the strobe recycles twice as fast, enabling rapid-fire shooting of fast-moving subjects.

Exposure Recommendations in Manual Mode

The following is the recommended f-stop selections when using the Motor Marine II-EX. The calculations are based on 1/2 the land rated GN of 72 (36 underwater) in clear tropical water conditions.

Strobe-to-Subject Distance							
Feet	**1**	**2**	**3**	**4**	**6**	**8**	**10**
Meters	**0.3**	**0.6**	**1**	**1.3**	**1.9**	**2.6**	**3.0**
ISO 50	f/16	f/11	f/8	f/5.6	f/3.5	f/2.8	-
ISO 100	f/22	f/16	f/11	f/8	f/5.6	f/3.5	-
ISO 400	-	-	f/22	f/16	f/11	f/8	f/5.6

Note: When using a diffuser or using 1/2 power mode, open the aperture by one f-stop. In coastal or turbid water conditions, open one f-stop.

How to Use in Manual Mode with Nikonos Cameras

The instructions are the same as those found on page 236 for the YS-60TTL for the Nikonos. Please refer to those instructions.

How to Use in TTL Mode with the Motor Marine II-EX

When using the YS-120 in TTL mode, the light output of the flash is automatically controlled by the electronic light sensor within the camera. The reflected light from the film is measured by the light sensor and determines duration of flash for a correct exposure.

1. Turn the power switch to the "On" position.
2. Turn the mode switch to the "TTL" position.
3. Set camera focus control lever for apparent distance.

4. Wait for the flash ready light to glow. The unit is ready to fire.
5. Select desired f-stop based on the strobe-to-subject TTL operating range chart.
6. Select the appropriate shutter speed to accompany the f-stop.
7. Compose, angle strobe head, and take the picture.
8. The green TTL confirmation light will illuminate and the audible signal will beep for approximately 2-3 seconds when a proper TTL exposure is obtained.
9. If you do not get a TTL confirmation, the strobe has delivered a full flash. Check that your subject was within the correct operating range for the f-stop. If it was, open up one f-stop and shoot again. For an explanation of why you did not achieve a correct TTL exposure, see page 258, *TTL: Exceptions to Perfection*.

Strobe-to-Subject TTL Operating Range

Feet	**1-1.6**	**1-2**	**1-3.3**	**1.3-4.3**	**2-6.3**	**2.6-9**	**3.3-13**
Meters	**0.3-0.5**	**0.3-0.6**	**0.3-1.0**	**0.4-1.3**	**0.6-1.9**	**0.8-2.7**	**1.0-3.9**
ISO 50	f/16	f/11	f/8	f/5.6	f/4~3.5	f/2.8	-
ISO 100	f/22	f/16	f/11	f/8	f/5.6	f/4~3.5	f/2.8
ISO 400	-	f/22	f/16	f/11	f/8	f/5.6	-

Note:

- When shooting macro, distance is measured in inches. At close range TTL is very accurate. Use the smallest aperture to maximize depth of field.
- When using a diffuser, open up one f-stop.

How to Use in TTL Mode with a Nikonos V

Please see instructions on page 236.

How to Use in TTL Mode with a Housed SLR Camera

Please see instructions on page 237.

Tip: Using TTL mode increases strobe battery life two to three times over full power manual.

How to Operate in Slave Mode

The slave mode built into the YS-120 is ideal for multiple strobe operation when using another strobe as a prime unit. See page 261 for multiple strobe operation. When in slave mode, the flash will fire when the slave sensor detects light from another strobe. Maximum effective distance is about 14 feet. The slave fires in full or 1/2 power manual mode only.

1. Turn power switch to "Slave."
2. Set power switch to "Full" or "1/2."
3. Adjust beam angle.
4. Check that the slave sensor is within range of the prime strobe.

Prism Diffuser

Built into the face of the strobe is a rectangular reflector, called by the manufacturer a *prism diffuser*. It has a bubble-type pattern that disperses the emitted light evenly over the image area.

With ordinary strobe reflectors, the light ▶ intensity is greatest at the center of the beam area and diminishes outward. The effective guide number diminishes outward, as well. The prism changes that, spreading the light so the entire picture area is uniformly covered. The strobe specifications now define the beam angle in terms of horizontal and vertical coverage.

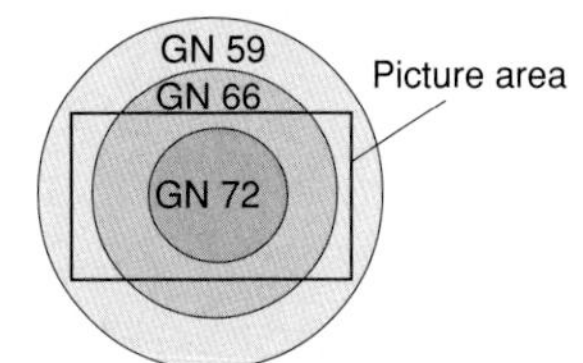

Without prism diffuser

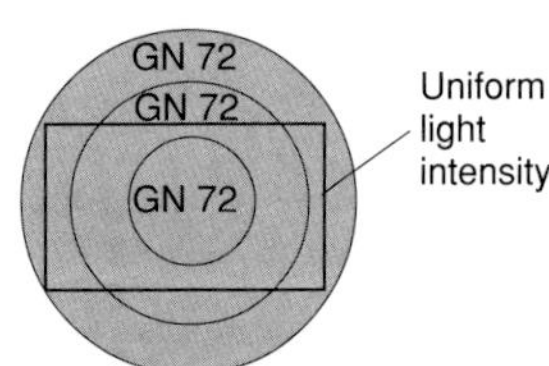

With prism diffuser

Accessory Diffuser

An opaque plastic diffuser is supplied with this strobe to broaden the angle of coverage and soften light. When using the diffuser, light intensity is reduced by approximately one f-stop. Adjust aperture settings accordingly.

Note: When mounting this diffuser, make ▶ sure the hole in the bottom of the diffuser aligns wih the slave sensor on the bottom of the strobe's reflector. Slave mode will not function if sensor is covered.

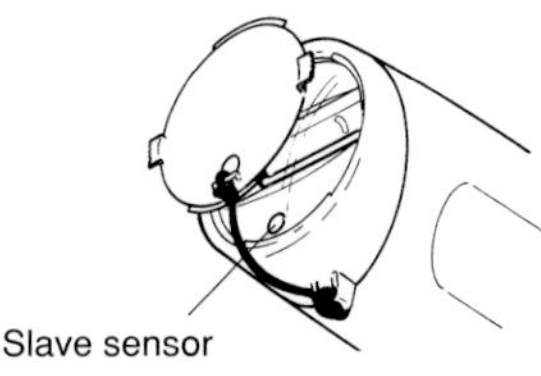

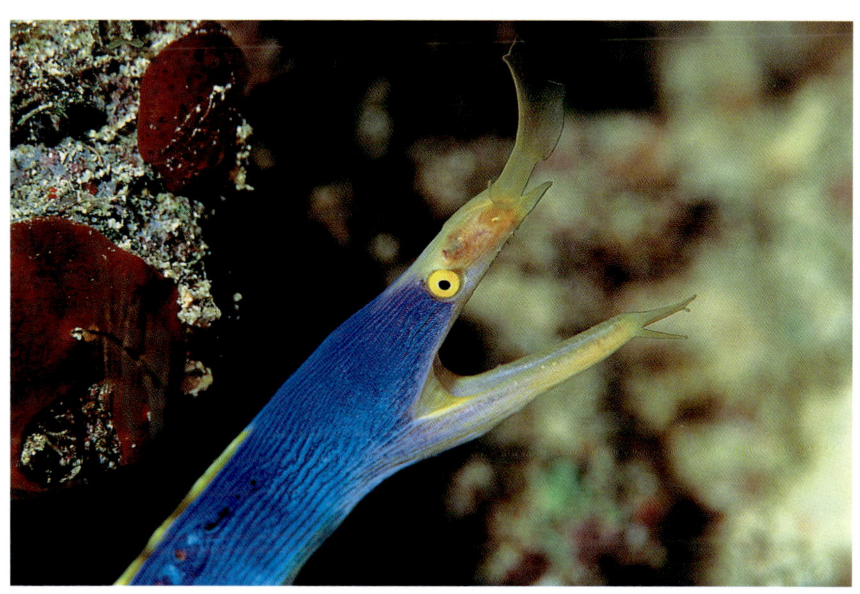

A telephoto lens vividly reveals the details of this Blue Ribbon Eel. The YS-120 paints them fluorescent.

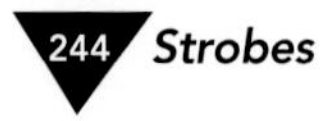

YS-300TTL-S AND YS-300TTL-N

The YS-300TTL is Sea & Sea's top-of-the line strobe, a high-powered, high-intensity unit with a full complement of professional features. It delivers a wide 100° beam to fully cover even a 15mm lens and operates in three manual power modes: full, 1/2, and 1/4 power. A set of visual indicator lights, accompanied by audible signals, convey flash readiness and confirm TTL operation. A built-in separately-powered target light allows for pre-shot viewing. A built-in slave sensor allows for wireless flash triggering. The YS-300TTL-S mates to the MMII, MMII-EX, and SX-1000 via a unique user-replaceable four-pin sync cord. The YS-300TTL-N dedicates with the Nikonos, the RS, NX-90 Pro, and any system with a five-pin bulkhead connector. The S and N models are identical, except for the sync cord. Constructed of high-impact thermopolymers, it is rugged and corrosion-resistant. The YS-300 is a deluxe flash for underwater photographers who want it all.

Identification of Parts

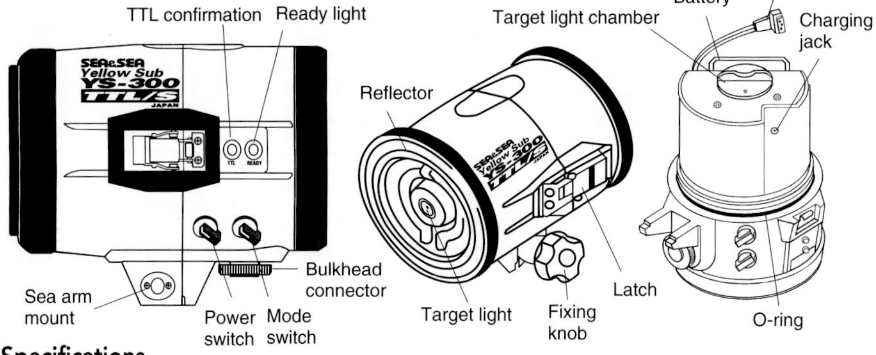

TTL confirmation
Ready light
Sea arm mount
Power switch
Mode switch
Bulkhead connector
Reflector
Target light
Fixing knob
Latch
Target light chamber
Battery
Battery cable
Charging jack
O-ring

Specifications

Exposure control:	Manual and TTL	**Function indicators:**	TTL confirmation; ready light
Beam angle:	100°	**Color temp:**	5500°K; 5000°K w/diffuser
GN (ISO 100)		**Power source:**	7.2-volt ni-cad
• **Full**	98 land; 49 u/w (ft.) 30 land; 15 u/w (m)	**Maximum depth:**	200 feet (60 m)
• **1/2**	49 land; 25 u/w (ft.) 15 land; 8 u/w (m)	**Dimensions:**	5 x 7.6" 124mm x 192mm
• **1/4**	24 land; 12 u/w(ft.) 8 land; 4 u/w (m)	**Weight:**	4.25lbs. 1930g (S); 1950g (N) land incl cord and battery -10.6 oz. (-300g) u/w
Recycle time (full):	4 seconds		
No. flashes (full):	120		
TTL range:	1-22.5 ft; 0.3-6.9m (land) 1-11 ft; 0.3-3.4m (u/w)	**Included:**	Battery, charger, diffuser O-ring set, sync cord

How to Open

Caution: Before opening the strobe, be sure the power switch is in the "Off" position and your hands and the strobe housing are completely dry.

1. Place the strobe on a clean, flat surface with the reflector facing down. In this position the strobe is easy to handle. More importantly, if water is trapped between the upper and lower cases, the water will not penetrate the interior when the strobe is opened.

2. Release the latches. If the strobe ▶ does not open, insert a coin between the two parts of the strobe arm mount. Twist the coin and pry open both halves *gently*.

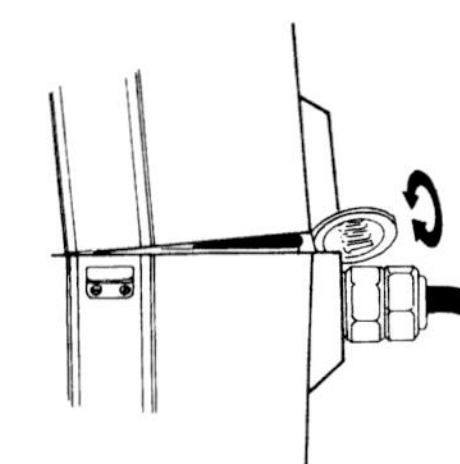

Installing the Batteries

When you unpack your brand-new strobe, you will notice that the manufacturer has packaged the battery pack separate from the strobe; this is to prevent any possible damage during shipping.

1. Remove the battery retaining pin. ▶ Insert the battery pack into the battery compartment.

Battery cable

2. Insert the battery retaining pin to ▶ secure the battery. (A modified model, to be released after this writing, will have a velcro retaining strap in lieu of the pin.)

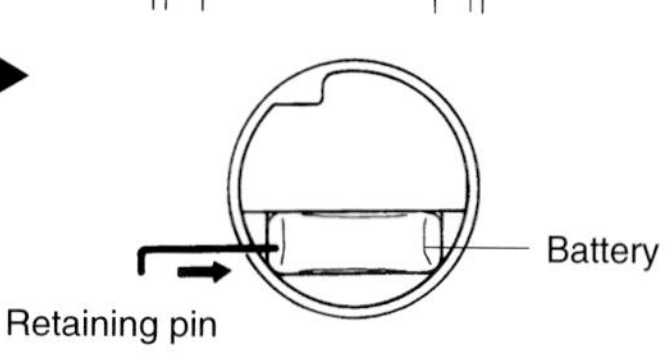

3. Connect the battery cable to the ▶ three-pin socket.

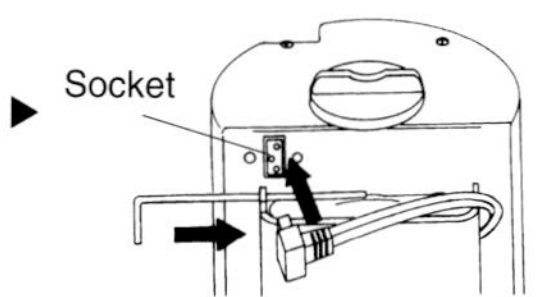

Note: Remove the battery pack from the strobe when the strobe is stored for long periods of time to prevent damage to the electronics should the battery pack leak. Remove the battery pack when traveling to prevent drainage of the battery should the power switch be accidentally moved to the "On" position.

How to Charge the Battery

The battery is charged in-strobe. The charger included operates on either 120v or 240v AC current.The battery can be charged outside the strobe via an accessory cable.

1. Make sure the power switch is in the "Off" position.
2. Be sure the voltage selector on the charger corresponds with the voltage being used.
3. Insert the charger jack into the battery charging socket.
4. Plug charger into electrical outlet. *Note:* Do not plug into electrical outlet first. That can cause an electrical arc. After charging, reverse the order; disconnect from electrical outlet first.
5. Charge for 12 hours. Do not overcharge; this will shorten battery life.

An optional Multi-Volt Charger shortens charge time from 12 hours to six hours. It automatically adapts to the voltage being used (120/240 V).

To extend the life of the ni-cad battery:

▼ Charge it when it is *almost* exhausted: count how long it takes for the ready light to come on. On a full charge, at full power, the ready light will come on in four to six seconds. At half power, it will come on in three to four seconds. If the ready light takes longer than the normal recycling time, it is time to recharge the battery.

▼ Ni-cads are subject to spontaneous discharge. If stored for long periods of time, recharge every few months to prevent full depletion.

▼ Use the AD-1000 battery discharger. It drains the current remaining in the battery to a safe depletion level before recharging or storage.

How to Close the Strobe

Before closing the strobe, examine the O-ring and the O-ring channel. Service the O-ring and channel as necessary.

1. Place the strobe with reflector facing down. Make sure the battery cables are secured, the battery pack is in place and secured with the battery retaining pin.
2. To mate the upper and lower cases, align the strobe arm mount and latches. Press down firmly on the upper part. Engage the latches *simultaneously.* Do not fasten one latch at a time.

How to Connect Strobe to Camera

The YS-300 has a detachable sync cord. The sync cord for the Motor Marine II-EX has a four-pin connector; the five-pin connector mates with the Nikonos V and with housed cameras equipped with a five-pin bulkhead connector. The sync cords are *not* interchangeable. *Note:* Assemble camera and strobe before attaching sync cord. See pages 214-216.

Control Switches

This strobe is equipped with two rotary switches: a *power* switch and a *power mode* switch. The power switch has four positions:

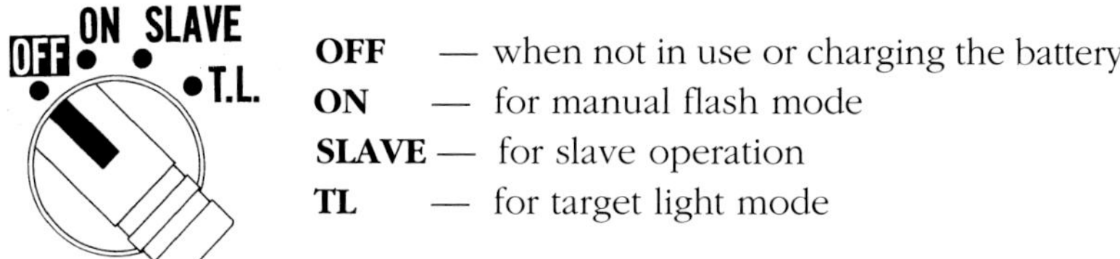

OFF — when not in use or charging the battery
ON — for manual flash mode
SLAVE — for slave operation
TL — for target light mode

The power mode switch has four positions:

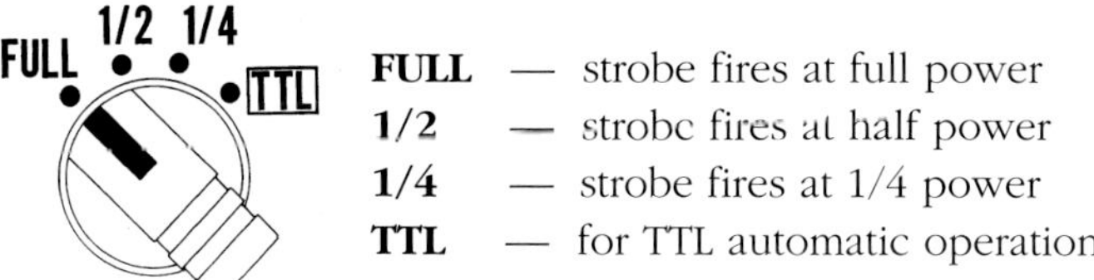

FULL — strobe fires at full power
1/2 — strobe fires at half power
1/4 — strobe fires at 1/4 power
TTL — for TTL automatic operation

How to Operate in Manual Mode with the Motor Marine II-EX

1. Turn the power switch to the "On" position.
2. Select your power mode: Full, 1/2 or 1/4.
3. Wait for the orange ready light to glow. An audible beeping confirms that the capacitor is charged and ready to fire.
4. Set camera focus control for apparent distance.
5. Select f/stop by using the standard guide number formula (see page 209) or use the charts on page 250.
6. Compose in the viewfinder, angle strobe head, and take the picture.

Note: Changing from full power mode to 1/2 or 1/4 decreases flash output. The difference between a full power flash and 1/2 power is one full f-stop. The difference between full power and 1/4 power is two full f-stops. Angle of coverage remains unchanged.

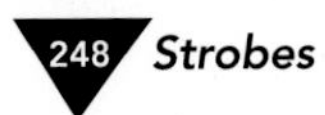

How to Operate in Manual Mode with the Nikonos V

1. Set the ISO film index on the camera to match the film speed.
2. Set your camera shutter speed dial on "A" for auto. The shutter will lock in at 1/90 second.
3. Set camera focus control for apparent distance.
4. Turn the strobe power switch to the "On" position for full power, "1/2" or "1/4." An audible beeping confirms that the capacitor is charged and ready to fire. In full power, the strobe recycles in four seconds. At half power, the recycle time is two seconds or less.
5. Select an f-stop based on strobe-to-subject distance and film speed. Use the guide number formula on page 209 or use the strobe-to-subject distance charts on page 250. *Note:* At "1/2" the GN is 25. At "1/4" the GN is 12.
6. Check that the strobe ready light is on and take the picture.
7. Bracket.

How to Operate in Manual Mode with a Housed SLR

The following camera settings are made through the controls on the housing.

1. Set film speed on camera.
2. Select exposure mode on camera.
3. Turn the strobe power switch to the "On" position for full power, "1/2" or "1/4." A high-pitched beep confirms that the capacitor is charged and ready to fire. In full power, the strobe recycles in four seconds. At half power, the recycle time is two seconds or less.
4. In *aperture priority*, select f-stop. The camera will automatically select the shutter speed. Use the guide number formula on page 209. Or refer to the manual exposure charts on page 250 for the correct strobe-to-subject distance/f-stop combination for the film speed being used. *Note:* At "1/2" the GN is 25. At "1/4" the GN is 12.
   In *shutter priority*, you select the shutter speed and the camera selects the f-stop.
   In *auto program*, the camera selects both the aperture and shutter speed.
5. Check that the strobe ready light is on. Compose through the viewfinder, angle strobe head, and take the picture.
6. Bracket.

Great deepwater gorgonians
delivered in their autumn hues
by the generous beam of a YS-300.

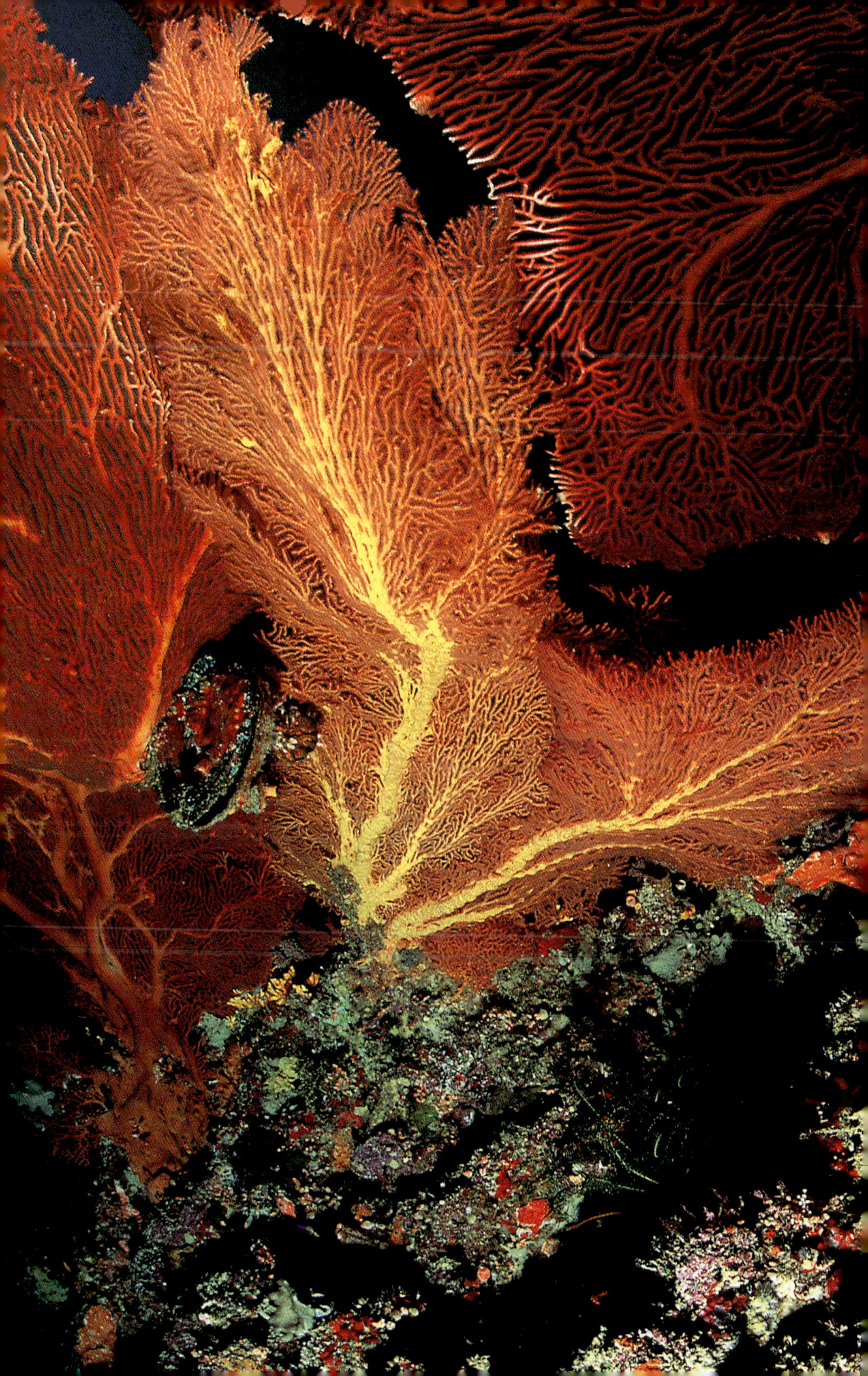

Exposure Recommendations in Manual Mode

The YS-300 has a land GN of 98 (in feet). Chart #1 is based on an underwater GN of 49 at *full power manual mode* in clear tropical water.

Chart #1				**Strobe-to-Subject Distance**				
Feet	**1.7**	**2**	**2.3**	**3**	**4.3**	**6**	**8.6**	**12**
Meters	**0.5**	**0.6**	**0. 7**	**0.9**	**1.3**	**1.8**	**2.6**	**3.7**
ISO 50	f/22*	f/22	f/16	f/11	f/8	f/5.6	f/4	f/2.8
ISO 100	f/22*	f/22*	f/22	f/16	f/11	f/8	f/5.6	f/4
ISO 200	-	-	f/22*	f/22	f/16	f/11	f/8	f/5.6
ISO 400	-	-	-	f/22*	f/22	f/16	f/11	f/8

*Use these f/stops with diffuser to prevent overexposure.

Note: When using a diffuser, open up by one f-stop.

The following is for *1/2 and 1/4 power settings.* These recommendations are for clear tropical conditions.

Chart #2 (ISO 100)			**Strobe-to-Subject Distance**				
Feet	**1**	**2**	**3**	**4**	**5**	**6**	**7**
1/2 GN 24	f/22	f/16	f/11	f/8	f/5.6	f/4	-
1/4 GN 12	f/11	f/5.6	f/4	f/2.8	-	-	-

Note: When using a diffuser, open up by one f-stop.

The following exposures are for *full, 1/2 and 1/4 power settings.* These recommendations are for turbid or coastal waters with limited visibility.

Chart #3 (ISO 100)			**Strobe-to-Subject Distance**				
Feet	**1**	**2**	**3**	**4**	**5**	**6**	**7**
Full GN 32	f/22	f/16	f/11	f/8	f/5.6	f/4	f/2.8
1/2 GN 16	f/16	f/8	f/5.6	f/4	f/2.8	-	-
1/4 GN 8		f/8	f/4	f/2.8	-	-	-

Note: When using a diffuser, open up by one f-stop.

How to Operate in TTL Mode with the Motor Marine II-EX

1. Turn power switch to the "TTL" position.
2. Select the strobe-to-subject distance/aperture setting. Refer to the chart on page 252 for TTL operating range.
3. Position subject and take the picture.
4. If the distance/aperture setting is correct, an audible electronic beep will sound and the TTL confirmation lamp will illuminate for about three seconds. If you do not get these confirmation signals, you did not achieve a correct exposure. Open up to the next f-stop.

How to Operate in TTL Mode with the Nikonos V

1. Set the ISO film speed dial on the camera.
2. Set the strobe power mode switch to the "TTL" position.
3. Select an f-stop based on the TTL operating range on page 252.
4. Set the f-stop on the lens.
5. Set focus for apparent distance.
6. Set the shutter speed selector dial on "A." The camera will automatically select 1/90 second for flash synchronization.
7. With fully-charged ni-cad batteries, the neon light will glow in about four seconds, with a fresh set of alkalines, six seconds.
8. Compose and take the picture. If the distance/aperture setting is correct, the confirmation lamp will illuminate and the TTL beep will sound. If TTL is not confirmed, open up and take another picture.

How to Operate in TTL Mode with a Housed SLR

1. Connect strobe to housing's bulkhead connector.
2. Turn the strobe's power switch to the "TTL" position.
3. Wait for the ready lamp to confirm the capacitor is fully charged.
4. Select an f-stop based on the manufacturer's strobe-to-subject TTL operating range chart. Refer to page 252.
5. For manual focus operation, rotate the focus knob on the housing, composing the image through the viewfinder. For autofocus operation, lens will focus when shutter is depressed halfway.
6. Compose and take the picture. If aperture/strobe-to-subject distance combination is correct, you will get audible and visual TTL confirmations. If you do not, open up and take another picture.

See *TTL: Exceptions to Perfection* on page 258.

Strobe-to-Subject TTL Operating Range							
Feet	**1-2**	**1-3**	**1-4**	**1-6**	**2-9**	**2-12**	**3-17**
Meters	**0.3-0.6**	**0.3-0.9**	**0.3-1.3**	**0.3-1.8**	**0.5-2.7**	**0.7-3.7**	**1.0-5.3**
ISO 50	f/16	f/11	f/8	f/5.6	f/4	f/2.8	-
ISO 100	f/22	f/16	f/11	f/8	f/5.6	f/4	f/2.8
ISO 200	-	f/22	f/16	f/11	f/8	f/5.6	f/4
ISO 400	-		f/22	f/16	f/11	f/8	f/5.6

Slave Mode

The YS-300 has a slave sensor built into the front of the strobe. When you set the mode switch to "Slave," the strobe will be remotely triggered when the sensor detects light from a prime strobe. It can be triggered from any direction. The effective distance is about 10 feet. The slave fires in full power only.

Note: The slave will not fire when the target light is activated.

Diffuser

An opaque diffuser is supplied with this strobe to broaden the angle of coverage to 110° and warm color output for better flesh tones. When using the diffuser, the guide number is 66 (feet)/20(m), based on ISO 100 land. At the lowered guide number, light intensity is reduced by approximately one f-stop. Compensate by opening up one f-stop.

Target Light

The YS-300 has a separate battery-operated modeling light built into the center of the strobe reflector. It is powered by two 1.5 volt AA batteries. It projects a narrow beam for precision aiming, making it an efficient tool for close-ups and macro. It can also be used as a back-up light for night diving should your prime light burn out and as a focusing (aiming) light to aid in autofocus operation with a housed autofocus camera. Approximate burn time with fresh batteries is 90 minutes.

To activate, turn the power switch to the "TL" (Target Light) position. To preview your strobe beam angle, aim the target light at the center of your picture area. Make sure it remains centered on your subject when strobe-to-subject distance increases or decreases.

ACCESSORIES

Sea & Sea manufactures an extensive selection of strobe accessories, far too numerous to detail here. What follows are the newest, most innovative, the time-tested.

Multi Stay System. A complete system of interchangeable components designed to be custom configured to accommodate your particular camera or housing with strobes. The main component is the Multi Stay Base, a universal stay for Motor Marine II-EX and Nikonos cameras and Sea & Sea housings.

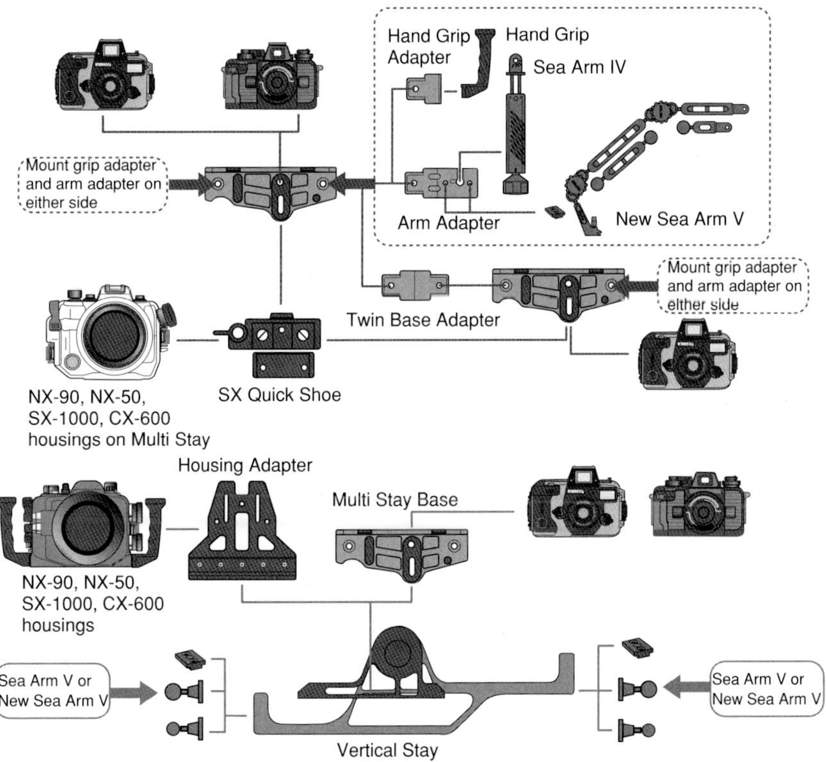

Vertical Stay. A pivoting tray that allows you to change from horizontal to vertical format without turning the whole camera/strobe system. The thumb-controlled button will unlock and release, then rotate and reconfigure. There's no need to reposition the strobes.

Sea Arm IV. Not new but very versatile, this telescopic adjustable arm has been the companion to Motor Marine II systems for years. It measures 9.6" (24cm) when sheathed, 13.6" (33cm) when extended. Easily disengages from the base plate and can be handheld. It's the only Sea Arm that accepts the snap-mounted lens caddy.

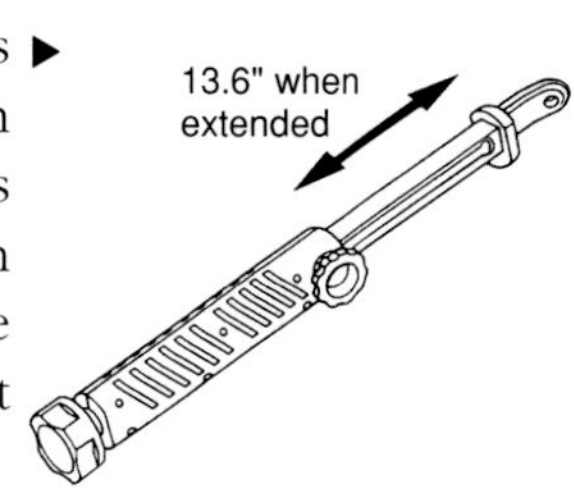

New Sea Arm V. Machined of corrosion-resistant aluminum alloy, the new Sea Arm V is a lightweight robotic strobe arm system capable of multi-directional movement. Enlarged hollow ball joints offer greater flexibility and more varied lighting possibilities than the original Sea Arm V. Features a quick release mechanism for handholding. It is compatible with the Vertical Stay and Multi Stay.

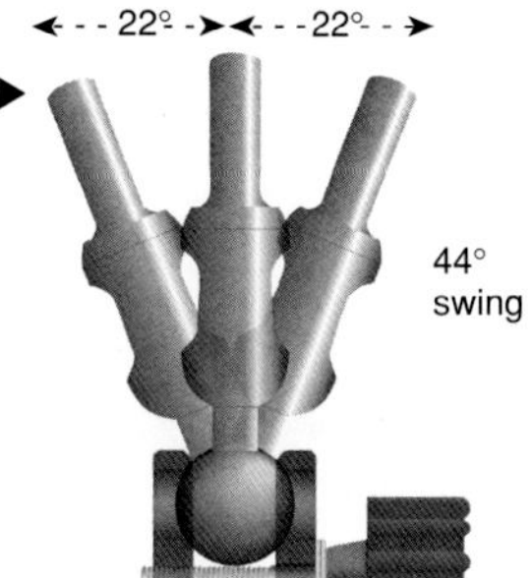

Hot Shoe Arm. A mount that attaches your strobe to the accessory shoe on top of the camera. Specifically designed for macro photography.

Dual Strobe Adapters. The various adapters connect two strobes to a single bulkhead connector on a camera or housing. Dedicates for manual photography with a two-pin connector or TTL photography with four and five-pin connectors. Velcro tape belts mount the adapter quickly and conveniently on your strobe arm or base stay. No screws or tools are required.

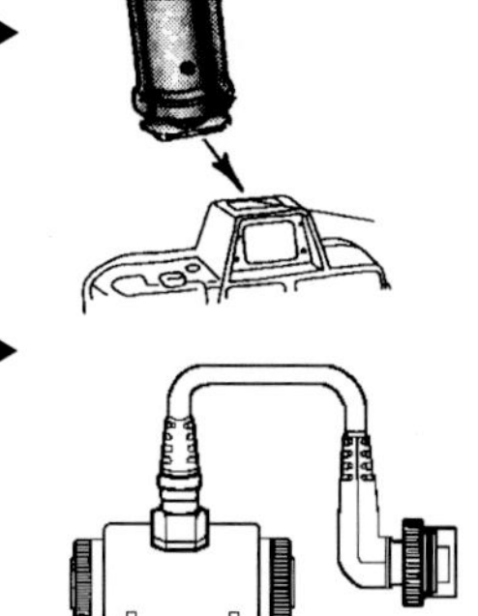
Dual strobe adapter for MMII-EX

Spot Adapter. The adapter for the YS-120 and YS-60 attaches to the front of the strobe to narrow strobe beam angle. It comes with two adapters, a 15° adapter and a 30° adapter so you can choose the angle of coverage. Can be mounted and removed underwater.

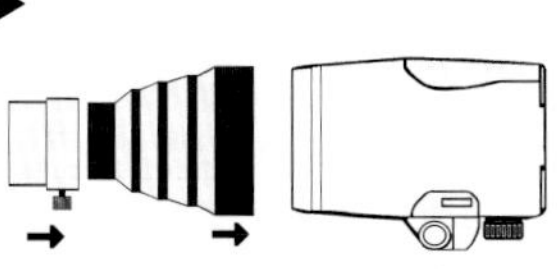
Spot adapter for YS-120 Duo

THE FINE ART OF STROBE PHOTOGRAPHY

Basic Flash Angles

The most important element in flash photography is the *direction* from which the light source strikes the subject. The direction of the light will determine where the highlights and shadows fall, the depth of texture, the mood and drama of the image, and, of course, the brilliance and areas of color.

The dominant light source in the scene is referred to as the *main* or *key* light. The main light determines where the shadows will be. In wide angle scenics that would be the background ambient light, the light from the sun. The second light is call *fill* light; it is used in conjunction with ambient light. Its purpose is to "fill in" the shadows and add color and prominence to a foreground subject. *Balanced* light is when the scene is illuminated by both ambient and strobe light; in this case, strobe light is equal to or less than the ambient light.

How you choose to light a subject is a matter of personal preference. Some photographers are partial to two strobes so as to eliminate shadows and create even color and contrast across the entire frame. Others prefer to use a single strobe because they want to produce shadows. The way in which you light the subject is decided by your vision and your taste. There is only one hard and fast rule about lighting: never point your strobe directly at your subject.

There are five basic flash angles in underwater photography. They are:

- *Front lighting*, when the strobe is positioned in front of and above the camera; shadows fall behind the subject. It is used primarily in macro and close-up photography.

- *Top side lighting* is the usual, most realistic type of lighting because it emulates how sunlight illuminates objects on land. For that reason, it is perhaps the most pleasing angle. As in nature, light does not come from any one direction but rather from several directions. The sun is rarely directly overhead; it is usually at an angle. Position the strobe above and to the left of the camera. Direct your light at a 45° angle at the top of and slightly behind your subject. Use this angle if there is a lot of sediment in the water to reduce backscatter.

- *Side lighting* creates long shadows and accentuates texture and contours. Hold the strobe off to the left and lowered almost parallel to the camera. The light strikes the side of your subject and casts long shadows on the right side of the subject.

- *Overhead lighting,* light coming from above the subject, produces heavy shadows and emphasizes textures. Deep, dramatic shadows and bold contours are achieved when the strobe is held directly above the subject and pointed straight downward.

- *Back lighting* casts shadows toward the camera, produces a bright halo around the subject and makes translucent subjects glow. Position the strobe above or to the side and slightly forward of the camera. Aim behind the subject. This illumination gives some subjects translucence, others a golden halo. Take care that the flash is not pointed directly toward the lens or your picture will be overexposed.

The Apparent Image Problem

Light from your strobe travels measured distance not apparent distance. So while the subject may look three feet away, it is actually four feet away. Most novice photographers tend to aim the strobe at the apparent image. But the subject isn't really there. So what happens? The beam falls short and you end up lighting the area in front of your subject instead of on your subject.

The solution is to compensate by directing your light at the top of and just slightly beyond your subject. *Aim it at the actual position, not the apparent position.*

The second way to correct for apparent image is to use a *target light,* also called a modeling light or focus light. Some strobes, such as the YS-300, are equipped with one. If your strobe does not have one, purchase a small high-intensity light and mount it to the side or top of your strobe. Sea & Sea has an accessory target light holder. The light target will demonstrate where your light beam will fall, so you can direct your strobe light to precisely where you want it. No compensation for apparent distance is necessary when using a target light. Just aim the light at the subject and take the picture.

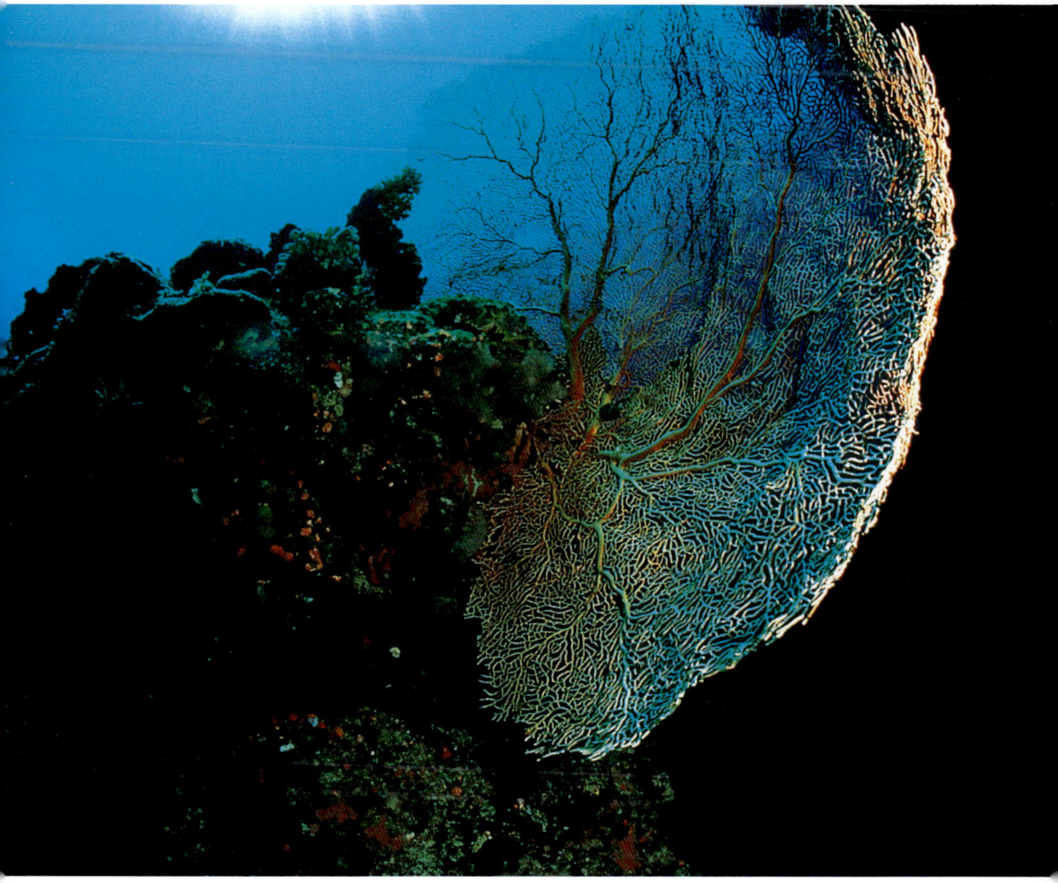

Sidelighting with a twist: instead of a single strobe held off to the left, dual strobes were used. The left was set at 1/4 power, the right on full. The result: dramatic.

TTL: Exceptions to Perfection

Used properly you will get good exposures in the TTL mode. It is accurate because the light is being measured exactly where the film will be exposed. One of its advantages is that the system can yield correct exposures on moving subjects. As the subject moves, the system compensates for the change in distance or background brightness and automatically adjusts the exposure.

But TTL is not foolproof. The TTL sensor can be misled. It is vital that you be aware of those circumstances that can mislead it and compensate accordingly.

When shooting in the TTL mode, remember the following:

▼ TTL works best with subjects of average brightness and reflectivity. If a large portion of your picture area is much lighter or much darker than your subject, the sensor will read that area and flash duration will be based on that area and not on your subject. As a result, that area will be correctly illuminated but your subject will not be. Solution: always study all elements in your field of view to be certain there is nothing that the sensor will read that you don't want it to.

▼ TTL works best with the horizontal camera angle. If you shoot at an extreme upward angle, the TTL sensor will read the sunlight exposure and quench the flash too soon. If you shoot down into a white sandy sea bed, the effect will be the same.

▼ The subject should fill the frame. If the subject is too small, it may not reflect enough light for the sensor to calculate how much light is needed for a proper exposure. The strobe will emit too much light. The result will be an overexposure.

▼ Flash exposure is determined by flash-to-subject distance. If several elements in your field of view are at different distances from the camera, the sensor will measure the light reflecting off the closest one. An example of this is a school of fish. The fish in the foreground will be properly lit since they are the ones metered; the fish behind them will be underexposed. Solutions: one, use manual mode. In manual mode the flash always emits the same amount of light. Two, if your subjects can be arranged, such as a diver holding a starfish, reposition the subjects so that they are both equidistant from the camera.

▼ Strobe-to-subject distance should never exceed eight feet. Even the most powerful strobe cannot effectively illuminate a subject that is more than eight feet away. Remember, the light must travel to the subject and then reflect back into the lens. So the distance the light must travel is double the strobe-to-subject distance.

▼ You can't bracket exposures by changing f-stops as you do with a manual strobe. The TTL system is programmed to adjust light output to effect a proper exposure. Bracketing is possible, though, by intentionally overexposing or underexposing, accomplished by:

- altering strobe-to-subject distance
- changing shutter speed
- changing film speed
- exposure compensation with systems that have this feature.

See page 82, *How to Bracket.*

How to Shoot in Low Vis Conditions

Professional underwater photographers take a lot of pictures. They literally cover all angles, shooting a single subject at different exposures and from various viewpoints to ensure they get the best shot possible. But when conditions are bad, more is not better. Even a pro is going to get more bad pictures.

There are basically two ways to overcome the limitations imposed by poor visibility: one, use a lens that allows you to get close to the subject and two, use light wisely.

When visibility is poor, the first thing to do is reduce the column of water between lens and subject. If using a housed camera system, select a lens that will allow close shooting distances. MX-10 and Motor Marine II-EX users have the advantage of not having to select a lens before the dive. You can take macro, close-up, or wide angle conversion lenses on your lens caddy and change lenses underwater when conditions warrant it.

Best choice:	Shoot macro
2nd choice:	Shoot with a close-up lens
3rd choice:	Shoot close-focus wide angle with any wide angle lens that will reduce the lens-to-subject distance to within one foot. The wider the lens, the closer you can focus.

How do you use light wisely?

Don't use your strobe at all. Sometimes the water is so filled with particulate that all efforts at eliminating backscatter are hopeless. Don't abort the dive. Shoot ambient light.

Break the rules. Don't strive for separation of subject and background. Don't shoot at an upward angle. Shoot at a downward angle and lose some of the backscatter in the clutter and patterns of rocks and reefs. If you have a light sandy seabed, all the better; backscatter will blend with the pale bottom.

Single strobe

- ▼ Use a diffuser. This will spread and soften the light.
- ▼ If your strobe has variable power settings, set it at 1/2 or 1/4 power. By reducing light output, you reduce the amount of reflected light. To compensate for reduced light, open up to a wider aperture. A larger aperture will lighten the background, making backscatter less apparent.
- ▼ Aim your strobe out and away from the camera. Direct the light at the right side and to the highest point of the apparent image. The beam will be directed behind the image, allowing the light to fall on the image at its true distance, which in turn will reduce reflected light on suspended particles and minimize backscatter.

Dual strobe lighting

- ▼ Use diffusers.
- ▼ Use lower power settings.
- ▼ Position the strobe heads so that the edges of the light beams cross over the subject, not in front of it. Aim away and to the sides of the subject. The beams from both strobes will be directed behind the apparent image which in turn will reduce reflected light and minimize backscatter. Do not allow the beams to intersect on the apparent image. You don't want to light the water between lens and subject.

Dual Strobe Photography

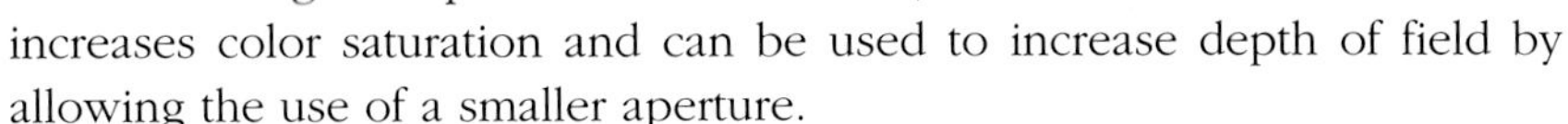

In dual strobe photography two flash units are positioned on either side of the camera. They provide illumination over a greater area. The image can be evenly and fully illuminated in the frame. The increase in light helps eliminate shadows, increases color saturation and can be used to increase depth of field by allowing the use of a smaller aperture.

Double sync cords dedicate both strobes directly with camera. (The YS-30Duo is the only strobe capable of slave function without a sync cord.) When you trip the shutter, both are triggered. If one strobe is a slave, the primary strobe acts as the key light and the slave provides fill light.

Sea & Sea offers a variety of dual base plates, dual strobe adapters, and compatible sea arms, allowing for multiple strobe configurations. See page 253 for some of the most innovative and versatile strobe accessories.

Tips on Using Two Strobes

- If you aim two strobes of equal power and position the strobe heads so that the light beams overlap, approximately twice as much light will fall on the subject. This allows you to use a smaller aperture setting, which results in greater depth of field.
- If you use two strobes of equal power at different distances from the subject, the strobe closer to the subject acts as the key light. The aperture setting is based on this light. The second light is used as a fill light to fill in shadows and brighten color.
- When shooting in TTL, no exposure adjustment is necessary if you are within the TTL operating range.
- If you shoot one strobe in TTL and the other in manual for fill, you must move the manual strobe back one foot to reduce the light output by one f-stop. If you prefer to keep them equidistant from the subject, place a diffuser over the manual strobe to reduce the flash intensity.
- To minimize backscatter, position the heads so the beams are parallel to the lens. The light from both will overlap in the center of the frame, giving minimum illumination to the particles close to the lens.

End Note

What distinguishes underwater photography from land photography, apart from the obvious, is the importance of light and care.

Underwater photography is not point and shoot. It is not "what you see is what you get." It can be, with training and practice, what you want is what you get. In this chapter our intent was to teach you how to manipulate light so that the final image on film is what you wanted it to be. But if you've been reading this book chapter by chapter, you know by now that mastering the controls is only part of the process. The other part is *maintenance.* Keeping your equipment in optimum condition is of paramount importance and can never be underestimated. So on this note, we ask you to please turn to page 271.

CHAPTER EIGHT

Composition

Composition

Once the technical skills are mastered, the difference between a good photograph and a great one is composition. Composition is more than a pleasing arrangement of objects within a frame. It is the art of seeing. It is how you perceive your subject and elect to present it. It is how you want your viewer to see it, what you want the focus of attention to be on. And it is always different from one photographer to another.

Joe and Cara are dive buddies. Joe is a photographer. He sees everything in terms of captured images on film. Like many driven photographers, he has tunnel vision. There could be a school of sharks behind him, but if he has a macro lens on his camera, his nose will be deep into the reef. Cara, when not taking pictures or modeling for Joe, scouts for photogenic subjects for him. On a typical dive, Cara will tap him on the shoulder and indicate that she found something. They'll take a look. He'll nod, *yes, good job.* Joe will mentally crop and light it, arranging it in his mind's eye, creating an image with his own personal style. Cara will at times offer her interpretation of how the shot should be taken. *Take it from this direction, Joe.* Joe will take it her way, too. See the difference on the next page.

Composition is defined as the separate elements that when put together make up a story-telling image. A good photograph communicates. It communicates information, emotion, even mood. It involves the viewer; it portrays beauty, makes one laugh, informs, inspires. A good photograph is not an accident. The skilled photographer consciously assembles or edits the elements in the photograph.

While no one viewpoint is right and the other wrong, in truth, one perspective may be more provocative than another.

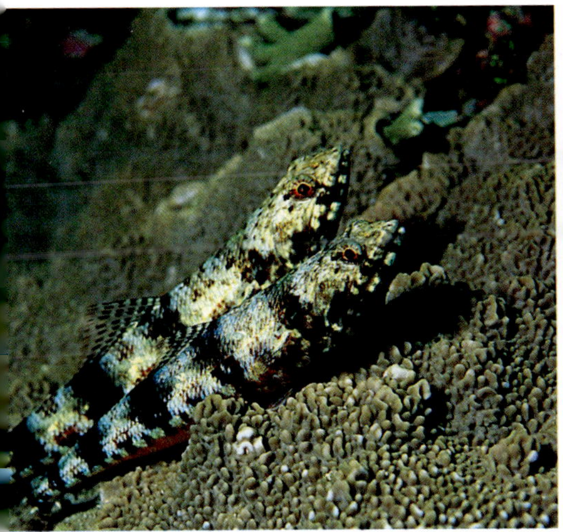

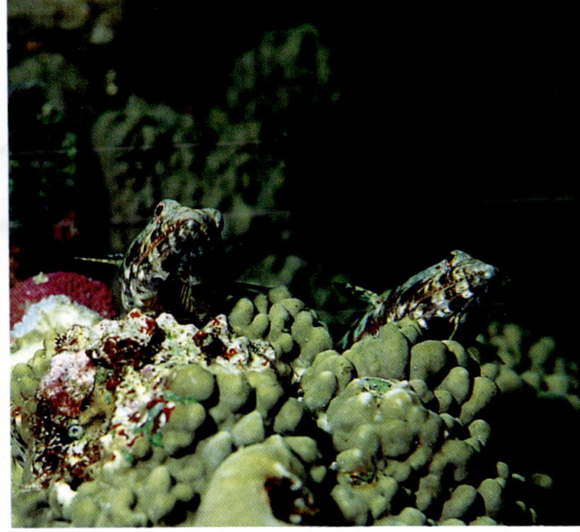

One subject, two views on how it should be shot. One of the above was Joe's perspective, the other Cara's. Can you guess which is which? Hint: Joe's is better.

Our first suggestion, then, is before you start shooting, look at the subject from different angles. Swim around it, if possible, and explore the full range of possibilities. Then decide how you want to present the subject.

Viewpoint is what separates an ordinary snapshot from a dynamic photograph. Amateurs tend to select their viewpoint (shooting position) from familiarity, convenience, and first impressions. They shoot what is familiar, how they have seen the same or similar subjects presented before. The difference between an amateur's photo and a pro's is freshness, the unexpected, unanticipated viewpoint. Look at the ordinary and alter the viewpoint, give it a fresh perspective, try to shoot it in a way you haven't seen before. You are not wasting a shot if it doesn't come out quite right. You are learning. You are being creative.

There will be many dives when you think, there is nothing to shoot here. *There is never nothing to photograph.* The challenge is to approach a seemingly uninteresting or ordinary subject and photograph it in a new and interesting way. That's being creative.

Viewpoint also alters the relationship of one object to another. It is called photographic perspective, meaning the relationship of near to far objects. In this sense, perspective is not just how you see the scene, but it is composing the image so that there is an illusion of depth. It helps separate the various components of the image and lends it a three-dimensional appearance on a one-dimensional medium. As you move closer or farther from your subject, the apparent size of your subjects will change. By changing the size of the subjects, you are deciding which component in your field of view will be the focus of your photograph. This is known as the *principle of dominance* or the *center of interest*. It serves to rivet our attention, focuses eye and thoughts.

Here are some tips for good composition:

- ▼ Look for an unusual perspective but don't compromise the subject just for the sake of being different. You don't want the image to look contrived. But if you can capture it in a fresh, new way, then you'll have an original and interesting photograph.
- ▼ Every picture should have a motif—that's a theme, a main subject, a *focus*. A single motif is stronger and better than numerous ones.
- ▼ The more elements in a photograph, the more confusing and less impact it will have. Looking through the viewfinder, selectively crop the nonessential elements. The best pictures are the simplest.
- ▼ Fill the frame. Moving in closer to your subject not only gives it dominance but almost always improves the picture. Being too far is the mistake beginners make. Learn to move in as tight as the lens allows.
- ▼ Don't take a horizontal picture when a vertical one would be better. Take vertical format shots of vertical subjects. Many novices forget that they can turn the camera around and take vertical shots, too. Look for appropriate subjects and practice taking vertical shots until you are comfortable holding the camera in that position.
- ▼ Odd numbers of objects make more interesting photos than even.
- ▼ Look for patterns. The scales of a fish or the patterns on a flamingo or bivalve shell make unusual and effective abstract photographs. Shoot close and make sure you crop the superfluous from the image. The focus should be on the pattern alone.
- ▼ Add divers to your pictures and you add perspective to the reef, the fish, the school of fish.
- ▼ Bracket composition as you do exposures. Take a few shots of the subject from different angles and with different framing.

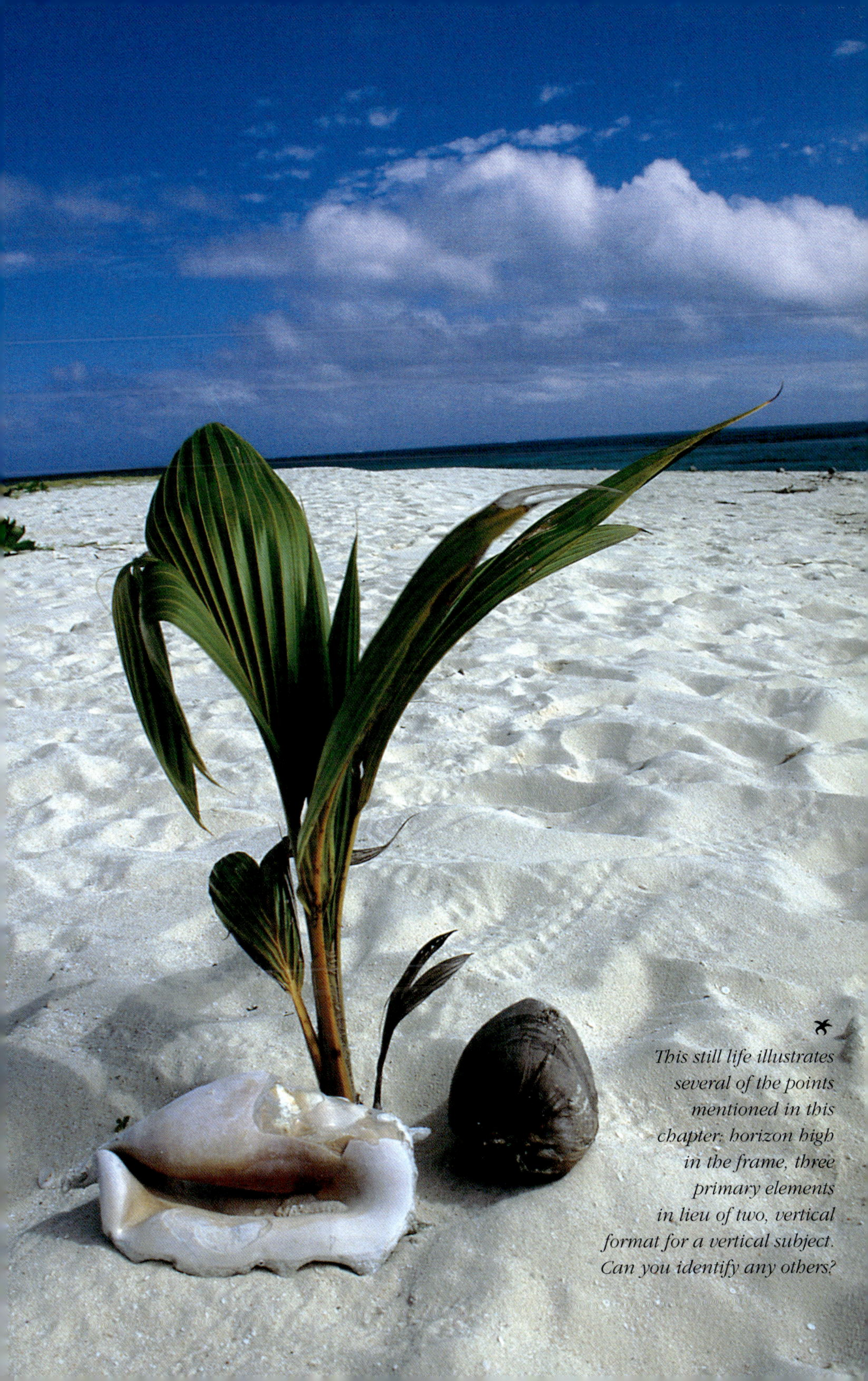

This still life illustrates several of the points mentioned in this chapter: horizon high in the frame, three primary elements in lieu of two, vertical format for a vertical subject. Can you identify any others?

▼ When shooting a scenic, try to add something colorful in the foreground, such as a purple sea fan or a red sea whip or an orange sponge. That will enhance the photo without detracting from the subject. The foreground element will also add depth.

▼ Don't let dead or broken coral sneak into the photo. Check all the corners of the frame in your viewfinder and crop the unappealing.

Placement

Where should you place your subject? As a guide for the beginner, we suggest what is popularly known as the *rule of thirds*. This concept is nothing new. In fact, it was passed down from the ancient Greeks, the same culture that gave us film. You don't have to follow this religiously, but it's an important concept to know, and it will certainly help you get started.

If the picture were divided into thirds, vertically and horizontally, the dominant spots in the overall image are where the points intersect. Points A B C and D will be dominant. ▶

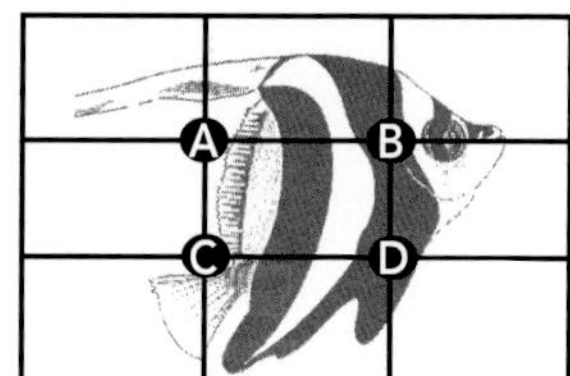

▼ Move your primary subject out of the center of the frame. The center is visually the weakest place.

▼ A viewer's eyes usually enter a picture at the lower left-hand corner then move to center. Using lines that enter from the left permits easy access and therefore compels the viewer to stay within the picture area. When lines exit at the right, so does the viewer. When the lines stop short of the right-hand exit area, the viewer stays within the picture area and the image maintains his/her interest.

Eyes

Focus on eyes. They are the most interesting part of a face, any face, a fish face or a human face.

▼ Eyes should not be looking out of the picture. The viewer will get distracted. Eyes must be directed at the camera (this will engage the attention of the viewer, making it seem like a personal interaction) or at another subject, like a fish, leading the viewer to look at the fish.

▼ People in underwater photographs are too often mere accessories

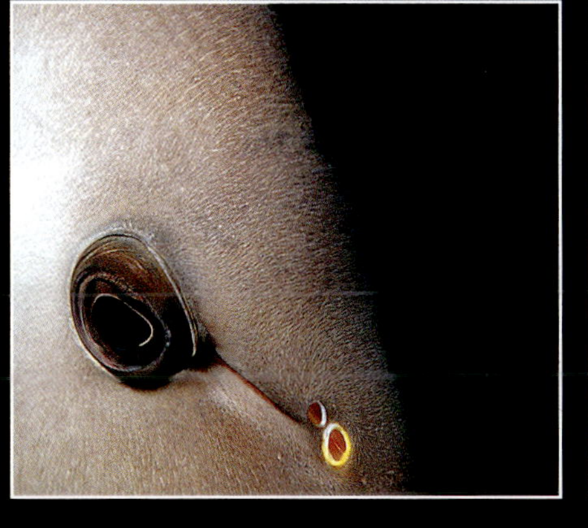

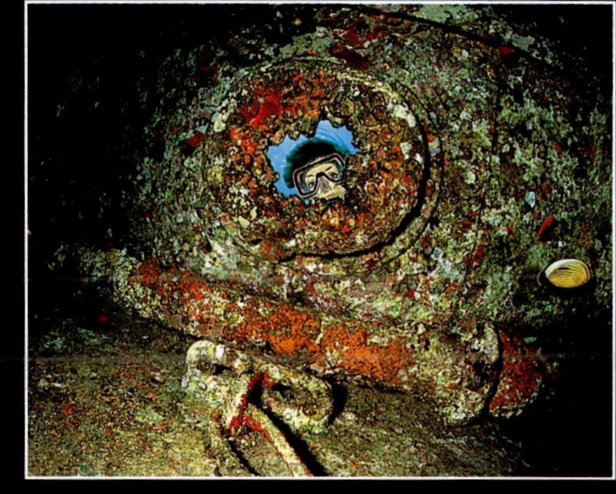

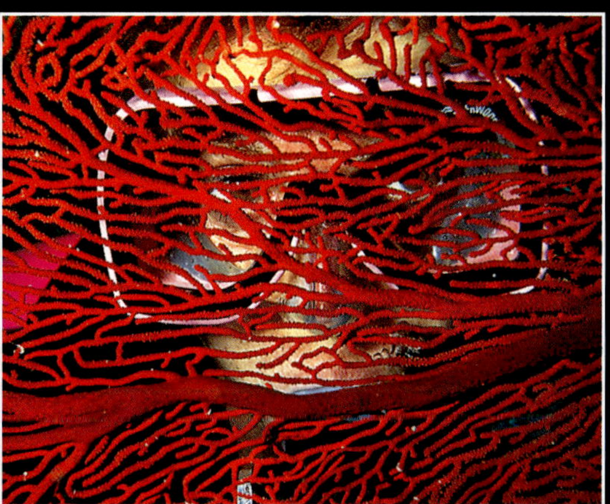

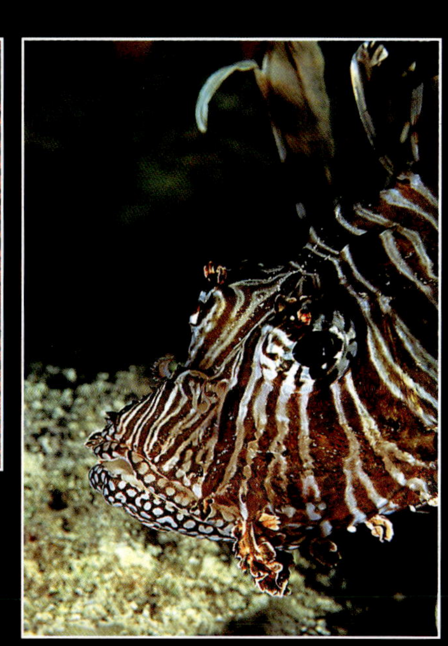

Eyes, the most arresting part of any face, fish or female.

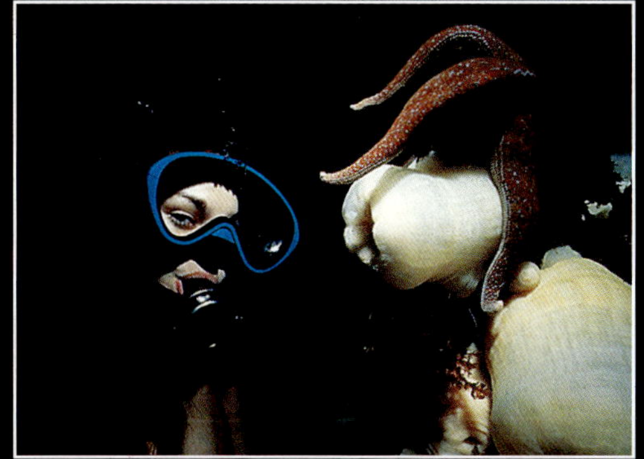

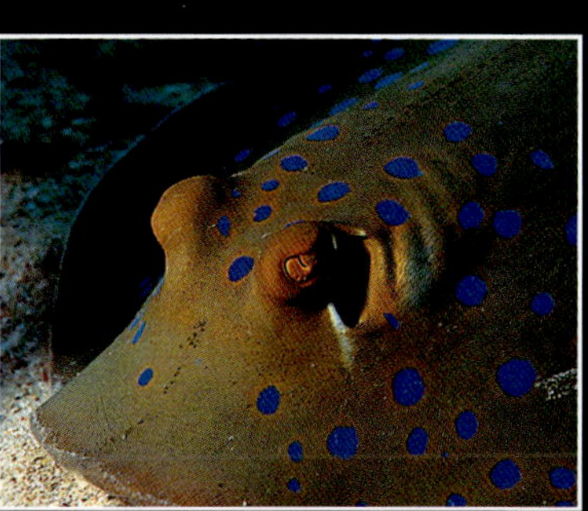

rather than subjects. They serve to add perspective to a reef or to an animal. They decorate a picture. But they also make fascinating subjects. Even in a facemask, eyes can be expressive and tell a story.

Dimension

Photographs are two-dimensional; subjects are three-dimensional. How do you get a three-dimensional feeling in your pictures? The illusion of depth is created by the arrangement and dominance of lines and tones.

- Brighter, warmer tones (reds, oranges, yellows) will command more attention than darker ones. They appear to move the subject forward while darker, cooler tones (blues) appear to recede in the background. Tones are controlled by the use of strobe light.
- Converging lines give a strong feeling of depth and space. Diagonal lines are more interesting than lines square with the edge of the image.

In *wide angle* underwater photography a sense of depth is achieved by focusing the strobe at a foreground subject while the background is illuminated by ambient light. Far objects gradually fade to ambient light. Tilting the camera at a slightly upward angle will separate near and far elements and increase the dimensional effect. In *macro* photography depth is accomplished by positioning the strobe at an angle.

In *topside* photography depth perception is also aided by a subject in the foreground. Framing the subject in an archway or under a tree limb adds a sense of distance and accentuates the perception of near and far. Put the horizon line high in the photo to emphasize foreground and a sense of closeness, low to emphasize the background area and give the impression of distance and space. Avoid placing the horizon smack in the center.

The Unintended Joke

Beware of mergers—that's when extraneous objects appear in the picture accidentally and end up making it comical. You've seen these: a sponge that looks as if it's coming out of the diver's ear. Beware of amputations, too. Don't cut off hands, feet, and tops of heads.

The Ultimate Tip

After you've mastered all the rules, dare to break them.

CHAPTER NINE

Care and Maintenance

Care & Maintenance

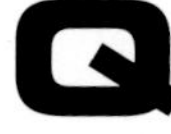

1. O-rings should be checked, cleaned and lubricated:
   a) after every dive
   b) after each day of diving
   c) once a month

2. After a day of diving, underwater photo equipment should be
   a) rinsed in fresh water
   b) soaked in fresh water
   c) washed with soap and water

3. When storing your equipment, you should
   a) remove the batteries
   b) remove the O-rings
   c) both of the above

4. Your camera should be professionally serviced
   a) once a year
   b) once every five years
   c) only when something has broken

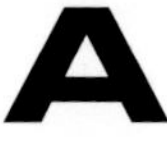

1 a and b, 2 b, 3 c, 4 a. If you got just one wrong, or even guessed at an answer, then *you really need to read this chapter!*

Underwater photographic equipment requires special care and maintenance. Obviously, your equipment has been designed to be submerged. It has been constructed to seal against water; that means it is *watertight*; it is not waterproof. There is a difference. The difference is that the internal electronic mechanisms that drive the system are protected only if you protect the components that keep the water out.

Your system is vulnerable to a host of other natural enemies. Here are the things that can harm your equipment:

- Salt
- Sun
- Dirt
- A bump, bang, drop or jolt
- Improper storage
- Neglect
- Amateur repair

Most avoidable equipment problems are due to oxidation, sediment build up, and lack of lubrication. Oxidation occurs when the materials from which the equipment has been made, such as aluminum and rubber, combine with oxygen in the atmosphere to form new compounds called oxides. Oxidized materials lose their strength and deterioriate. Moving parts may not move properly anymore. Oxidized surfaces allow salt and other foreign particles to invade and adhere to crevices.

The water is filled with salt and suspended particles of sand, clay, and other sedimentary materials which coat the surface of our equipment. Once the water dries, the sediment remains. Sediment build up can trap moisture, thus accelerating oxidation or corrosion.Your job is to keep this from happening.

A preventive maintenance routine is time-consuming. It demands discipline and requires patience; there are no shortcuts. A maintenance regimen is a commitment, but we cannot emphasize strongly enough how essential it is. You've made a considerable investment in your equipment. Treat it properly and it will perform for you for a very long time. Neglect it and it will need costly repairs or, even worse, replacement. Remember, underwater photographic equipment is not forgiving!

Right After a Dive

So, with that dire warning, the first thing you do after a dive is rinse your system in fresh water. Salt is your system's number one enemy. Salt water can dry and form crystals within 10 minutes after you surface. These crystals are hard like cement and just as impossible to dissolve. They have sharp, pointed edges that can split O-rings. Salt water also leaves a residue of mineral deposits in and around your controls, switches, and ports that can oxidize and cause severe damage. Water contaminated with fuel oil can also cause the O-rings to dry and crack.

A Motor Marine II-EX has three user-serviceable O-rings. A Nikonos V has four exterior O-rings. An NX-90 has three. It stands to reason that if salt can damage these O-rings, you would want to make salt removal your first priority.

Most dive boats have a rinsing tank for the photographers on board. Many dive sites have showers or water fountains. Take the time to use them!

If you can't rinse with fresh water, then keep the system wet till you can. Place it in a tank of water. Any kind of water, even sea water. Sea water? Yes, remember, we are not talking about cleaning your system now, we are talking about keeping it wet so that the salt cannot evaporate. Sea water won't hurt it. It is meant to be in sea water.

Fill any type of tub, bucket, or bag. Here are a few ideas:

- Bring your own fresh or distilled water in a plastic jug or thermos.
- Pack plastic resealable storage bags. Disassemble strobe and camera. Remove conversion lenses and viewfinder. Place the sealed components in separate bags; fill with water and seal.
- Tote an ice chest or cooler. They are sturdy, easy to carry, and are available in a wide range of sizes: large enough to place the assembled system in or small enough for just the camera. It will also protect the system from the other natural enemies: vibration, jolts, heat, etc.

If you are able to rinse the system with fresh water, then afterwards you want to dry it with a clean, dry cloth, and disassemble before transport. The following steps apply to the Motor Marine and Nikonos amphibious systems. Heed the steps that apply to your particular system:

1. Remove accessory lenses from the lens caddy.
2. Remove the accessory viewfinder from the hot shoe.
3. Remove the strobe sync cord connector from the camera or housing's bulkhead connector. Wipe away any moisture or debris, then cover the connectors with their protective plastic caps.
4. Remove the strobe from the strobe arm; screw the strobe connecting bolt in place.
5. Remove the strobe arm from the base plate.
6. Remove the camera/housing from the base plate.
7. Pack the system carefully for transport.

Home Care

When you get home, fill your kitchen sink or bathtub with enough water to completely cover the system. (If the water in your area is chemical-laden, use distilled water.) Use lukewarm water. Hot water can melt glues as well as the lubricants in the mechanical parts of the system. If there is still film inside the camera, hot water can damage it. Check that the bulkhead connector cap is securely in place. Check that the back door is properly sealed.

Submerge the system and let it soak for at least 30 minutes, preferably an hour. While the system is soaking, agitate gently and work all the controls at least once. This will help flush out any salt residue. Don't use soap. Soap will dissolve lubricants on internal O-rings and cause friction in operation.

Do not rinse your system with a hose. That is fine for your wetsuit and fins, but it is not okay for photographic equipment. Rinsing with a hose will not dissolve the salt crystals that have penetrated around O-rings and lodged around ports, knobs, and levers. In addition, the high pressure of the water may actually force salt crystals and sand into crevices.

The final step in the washing process is to run a steady stream of fresh water over the system, paying particular attention to the ports and controls.

Lay the system on a clean towel and let it air dry for another half hour; this allows water in inaccessible areas to evaporate. Then, using a clean, dry cloth, wipe excess moisture from the body, ports, levers, connectors, and so on. Do not wipe the lenses. Only lens tissues or photographic lens cloths should be used on lenses.

Prepare a clean, dry work area. You are now ready to service the system.

Essential Supplies

- soft cloth
- cotton swabs
- photographic lens tissues or cloths
- sable or camel's hair brush
- toothbrush
- batteries
- battery tester
- small needle-nose pliers
- Allen wrench set
- electrician's tape
- white vinegar
- resealable plastic bags
- small bowl
- rough cloth
- silicone grease
- lens cleaning fluid
- rubber syringe blower
- pencil with an eraser
- O-rings in assorted sizes
- set of jeweler's screwdrivers
- Phillips screwdriver
- assorted nuts and washers
- assorted stainless steel screws
- hair dryer
- packets of dessicant
- mild liquid detergent

Note: Tools should be chrome, nickel or cadmium plated so they won't rust or corrode.

The Procedure

In preceding chapters we have explained how to open, close, prepare, and operate your Sea & Sea cameras. We talked about how to assemble and care for lenses, strobes, and accessories. In this chapter we will guide you through the all-important maintenance procedure of the system as a whole.

Camera Housing

Sea & Sea amphibious cameras are manufactured from high-impact plastic. The case of the camera is constructed of ultra-violet and corrosion-resistant molded polycarbonate. But it still needs maintenance. This section, then, applies to all Sea & Sea amphibious cameras: the Motor Marine II-EX, the Motor Marine Seamaster Pro, the MX-10, and the older models, the Motor Marine II, Motor Marine 35SE, and the Pocket Marine 110.

To clean the case, use a mild liquid detergent. Do not use alcohol, paint thinner, or other chemical products. Do not use abrasive cleansers, such as Ajax or Comet; these will scratch the plastic.

Inspect the aperture control and focus levers where they meet the body of the camera. Be sure there aren't any sand or salt particles deposited there. Sand will grind down the gears and screw threads so they don't mesh together snugly. Sand can also lock up mechanisms so they don't operate at all. Brush the crevices around the controls. Dab a tiny bit of silicone grease on the area to ensure that the levers move smoothly.

Before opening your camera, make sure it is completely dry. Look for moisture or debris trapped between the back cover O-ring and camera body. When satisfied that none exists, open the camera.

When opening the back door of your camera, or your strobe battery compartment, or any O-ring sealed area, always tilt the unit down and let gravity pull any water droplets or moisture away from the interior. ▶

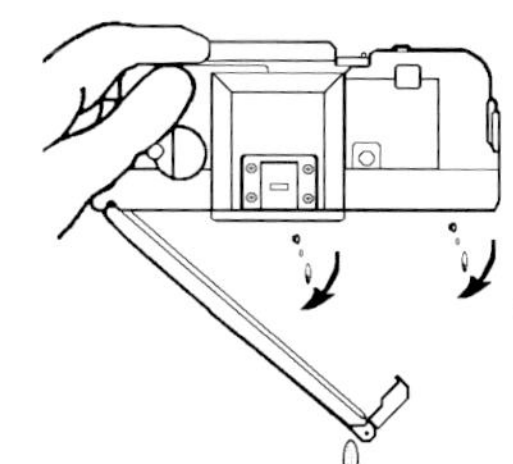

If there is still film in the camera, remove it now. When to unload film is a matter of personal preference. We always unload after each roll is exposed. Be certain the camera is completely dry before you open the back cover.

O-rings

O-rings are the most important components of your underwater camera system.

O-rings are round heavy-duty rubber bands. Under pressure, they flatten in their channels, sealing the openings they are placed around. The deeper you dive, the greater the water pressure, therefore the better the seal.

An O-ring can prohibit water penetration only when it is uniformly compressed in the O-ring channel. When you squeeze rubber in one place, it will stretch and change shape somewhere else. If the O-ring is lubricated, it will be elastic enough to shape itself uniformly around the channel. If it is dry, there will be too much friction to allow it to reshape itself uniformly. It will be unevenly compressed. It will not safeguard against flooding.

The ability of the O-ring to flatten is essential to its sealing capability. It can only change shape (flatten) if it is pliable. Salt residue reduces its pliability by drying it out. If dry and stiff, it will not perform its critical function and the equipment will flood. When salt water dries, it leaves a residue. The residue

> **Make it Your Motto**
>
> When in doubt about the sealing capability of an O-ring, always discard and replace.

dries the O-ring and robs it of its elasticity which prevents it from acting as a seal. Salt crystals can also pierce it. Sand, lint and other debris trapped against the O-ring will create little bumps on its surface, allowing water to seep through. Understandably, O-rings demand the most attention of any component of your system: careful examination, regular and thorough cleaning, and proper lubrication.

When should O-rings be serviced? Some experts say it depends upon the type of diving you've done. After a beach dive, definitely. Normally, after two or three rolls of film. Good judgment prevails here. We suggest that every time you open the camera to change film, examine the O-ring and service if necessary. No matter what, we clean and lubricate ours after every diving day.

O-ring Care

There are three O-rings on the Motor Marine camera that are user serviceable. They are found on the back cover, the battery chamber cover, and the bulkhead connector cap. There is one serviceable O-ring on the MX-10: on the back cover. The Nikonos V has four exterior O-rings: at the lens mount, on the camera back door, on the battery compartment clip, and on the flash socket plug. The NX-90 has three: on the front case, the bulkead connector cap, and the port.

1. To remove the O-ring on the back ▶ cover, press forward on the O-ring with your thumb and forefinger till it forms a loop. Grasp it with your other hand and gently lift it from its groove.

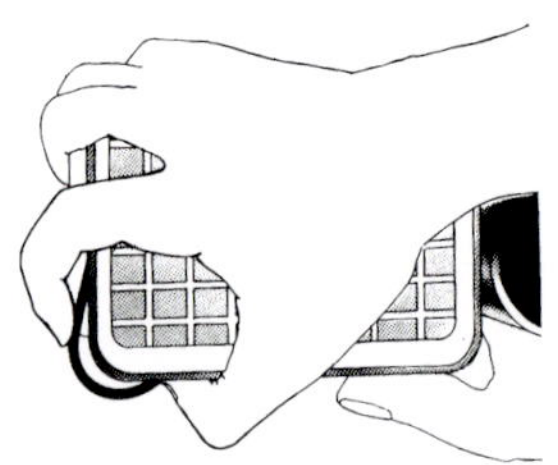

Never use a sharp or pointed object to remove an O-ring! Sea & Sea makes a small plastic O-ring remover. It is available in their accessory maintenance kit. You can also use a credit card or any thin blunt object with a rounded edge. Insert the edge under the O-ring and lift a portion out of the channel. Grasp the O-ring and lift it out entirely. Do not pull or yank the O-ring; rough handling can stretch or tear it.

2. Place the O-ring in a bowl of warm soapy water. The detergent will dissolve the salty encrustation and silicone grease. Let the O-ring soak for at least 30 minutes.

3. While the O-ring is soaking, turn your attention to the pressure seat and the O-ring channel. This is where sand and debris will accumulate. Check for nicks in the channel.

   Apply a dab of silicone grease to the tip of a cotton swab and rotate the tip between thumb and forefinger. This will pack the fibers and prevent fiber residue. Flatten the tip with a pliers so it fits neatly into the groove. Clean the groove.

Use the Grease that Goes with the O-ring

In 1996 Sea & Sea introduced a new blue O-ring that incorporates silicone oil so less lubrication is needed. The blue color allows for easier damage and debris detection. A special silicone grease has been developed for this O-ring.

▼ If your equipment bears a black O-ring, use the Sea & Sea brand lubricant in a yellow tube with BLACK lettering.

▼ If your equipment has a blue O-ring, lubricate only with the Sea & Sea brand in a blue-capped tube with BLUE lettering. *The blue O-ring is not compatible with the black O-ring grease.*

4. Rinse the O-ring in fresh water. Blot dry with a lint-free cloth. Inspect for nicks, cuts, or tears. Use a magnifying glass or a Sea & Sea conversion lens as a magnifying glass. Nikonos owners can use the 35mm or 28mm primary lens: hold the rear elements close to your eye and the front of the lens close to the O-ring. Open the aperture fully and look through the front of the lens. Discard the O-ring and replace with a new one if it is damaged.

5. Now you lubricate the O-ring. The lubricant is non-water soluble silicone grease. Never use any other type of lubricant, such as petroleum jelly, which is water soluble. Do not use silicone sprays; these are manufactured to preserve rubber products from ozone in the atmosphere and are not intended as a lubricant.

   Apply a small amount of silicone grease to the tips of your thumb and forefinger. Rub your fingers together to distribute the grease.

Why such a little tube to do such a big job?
The fact that it's such a little tube should give you a clue. You need very little of it. How long can it last? Quite a long time! The grease is a lubricant. Use just a dab, enough to enable you to pull the O-ring through your fingers smoothly. With practice, O-ring maintenance should take you only 10-15 minutes, not very long to guarantee the watertight integrity of your camera.

Draw the O-ring through your fingers two or three times, making sure you coat the entire surface. A perfectly greased O-ring looks moist and shiny.

Don't overgrease! Too much grease attracts debris that will disrupt the seal and cause flooding. Silicone grease is not a sealant; it only protects the O-ring from abrasion when opening and closing the cover and keeps it supple so it can change shape under pressure. Wipe excess with a lint-free cloth.

6. To reseat the O-ring, insert one side into the channel and, while holding it in position, roll the other side into place. The O-ring must be uniformly compressed in the O-ring channel. When you close the back door of the camera, pressure will squeeze the O-ring from the hinged side to the lock side. If the O-ring is properly lubricated, it will be elastic enough to reshape itself inside the channel. Run your finger along the surface to check that it is not twisted or bulging; it should form a smooth, continuous line in its channel.

Inner Camera Body

Inspect the inner body for moisture, dust, sand, or other debris. Even if you do not detect any foreign matter, as a precaution, clean the interior with a sable or camel's hair brush. Tip the camera so any debris will fall out and won't be pushed further inside the mechanism.You may also use a hair dryer, but be sure to use a low, cool setting. Heat is damaging to delicate circuitry and glues.

A black rubber gasket separates ▶ the internal mechanism from the camera housing. It serves as a buffer against shock from violent impact; it also prevents dirt and dust from penetrating the internal mechanism. *This gasket is not an O-ring seal!*

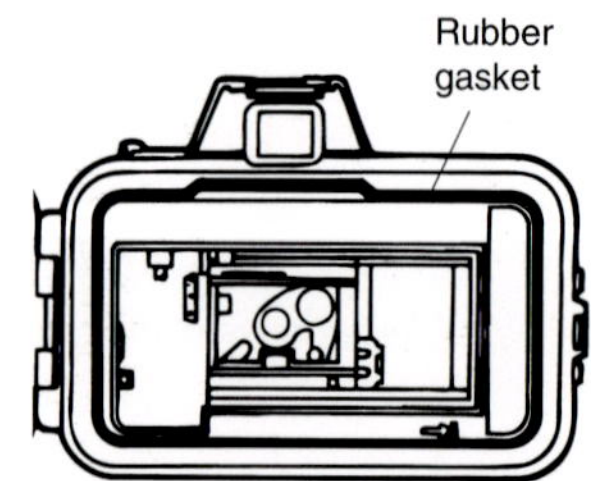

The Film Transport

The film transport system on the Motor Marine II-EX and the MX-10 differ in one important way: the MX-10 has a lightproof film compartment door. The pressure plate is located on the inside of this door. On the MMII-EX, the pressure plate is situated on the inside of the camera back cover.

Check for dust and film chips in and around the film transport. Film chips tend to accumulate around the sprocket drive and the take-up spool. If not removed, they will scratch the film. Use the rubber syringe blower or a hair dryer on a low, cool setting to clean this area.

Check the film pressure plate. Dust or sand or even a hair on the plate will scratch the film. These scratches will show up on your slide or print. Clean with a soft cloth or the rubber syringe.

"WARNING!"
"CAUTION!"
"PRECAUTION!"
About those safety instructions

The safety instructions in your equipment manuals are to be taken very seriously. They are provided to protect you from personal injury and to safeguard your equipment. A few general rules:

- ▼ Read all instructions packaged with the equipment.
- ▼ Heed all warning decals on the equipment.
- ▼ Do not dissasemble, attempt to alter or modify.
- ▼ If the equipment does not operate normally, send it to an authorized repair center.

Close and lock the back cover. Take one more look at the seal. If the O-ring or any foreign matter is protruding, the system is not watertight. Open the cover, remove the O-ring, clean as necessary. Reseat the O-ring, then close the back cover again.

Battery Compartment

Because water can penetrate as far as the O-ring and cause corrosion, it is necessary to inspect the battery compartment of your camera for moisture, salt deposits, and sand.

Turn the camera over and open ▶ the battery compartment as shown to permit any water trapped in the O-ring channel to fall out and away from the inner chamber.

Shown:
Motor Marine II-EX

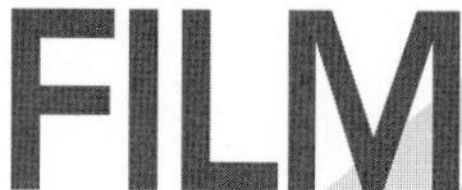

FILM

The film you put in your camera is as important as the camera. Photographic film is perishable. A film's characteristics (speed, contrast, color balance and fog level) gradually change once it leaves the manufacturer. (That's why the expiration date is stamped on the carton.) Rapid change may occur when the film is improperly stored and is exposed to heat and humidity.

Most color films are dated about 18 months from the date of manufacture. Amateur color slide film is released before it has reached its optimum color balance. The manufacturer takes into account the changes that will occur during shipping, retail display, and home storage. Professional slide films are shipped at their optimum color balance; these are stored in refrigerated display cases to retard the aging process.

Film is usually packaged in a snap-cover plastic canister to protect it from contaminants and changes in humidity. So it's best not to open the original package until you're ready to load the film.

One major U.S. processing lab reports that 13% of all ruined rolls of film are caused by improper storage, so . . .

▼ Always note the expiration date on the carton. Don't use if it's expired. Bargain hunters, beware! Expired slide films are on sale because resulting images tend to have a pronounced bluish or purplish cast.

▼ Protect film from heat. Do not leave in the trunk or glove compartment of a car, on a dashboard or car seat, in the sun on a dive boat.

▼ Cold storage is best. Refrigeration retards the aging process and will extend film life up to six months past the expiration date. Freezing is better, extending film life almost indefinitely.

▼ Store in sealed factory cartons (so you can check the expiration date on the package) in airtight plastic bags. Store in plastic canisters. If storing in the factory cardboard carton, in a plastic food storage bag, include a sililca gel pack to keep the cartons from getting soggy.

▼ Before opening, thaw, about an hour, to room temperature. Allow condensation to form on the outer wrapping. If you unwrap it too soon, moisture may form on the emulsion, staining and discoloring your photos.

Remove the batteries. Remove and service the O-ring just as you did the O-ring on the back cover. Clean the O-ring channel with a cotton swab.

Use the rubber syringe to blow away debris inside the chamber. Use the sable brush to clean the battery holder. Examine the battery contacts. Oxides build up and impede the flow of electricity. It is necessary to periodically clean the contacts with a pencil eraser or rough cloth.

Batteries

Batteries are the heart of your system. Since they power both your camera and strobe, it's essential to always use fully-charged batteries. Check the batteries for voltage. A battery tester will tell you if the battery is weak, but it won't tell you how much longer the battery will last. If it tests weak, replace it.

To prevent acid leakage, heed the following five *nevers*:

- ▼ never mix brands of batteries
- ▼ never use batteries with different model numbers
- ▼ never mix old and new batteries
- ▼ never mix alkalines and ni-cads
- ▼ never store or transport your equipment with batteries installed.

If batteries show any evidence of salt water or acid damage, discard them. If there are any signs of battery acid in the battery compartment, clean thoroughly with a cotton swab moistened with white vinegar.

When installing batteries, take care not to reverse positive and negative terminals. This, too, can cause acid leakage. Get into the habit of wiping the ends of the cells with a rough cloth or a pencil eraser before installing them. This will improve the current flow and eliminate unseen oxide build-up.

When using ni-cads in your strobe:

- ▼ Do not allow ni-cad batteries to become fully discharged before recharging. Fully drained ni-cads may refuse to take a charge.
- ▼ Charge ni-cads for the number of hours recommended by the battery manufacturer. Excessive charging can cause battery deterioration.
- ▼ Do not charge ni-cads while they are still hot.
- ▼ Do not use batteries that have been charged for different lengths of time.

Important!
Never use rechargeable batteries in Motor Marine II, Motor Marine II-EX, Seamaster Pro, or MX-10 cameras! Use only alkalines.

Caution!
Your equipment isn't the only thing you must protect. Protect yourself.

- ▼ Never attempt to recharge alkalines that are not specified as rechargeables. They can leak electrolytes and explode.
- ▼ Do not open or mutilate batteries. Released electrolytes are corrosive and injurious to eyes and skin and toxic if swallowed.
- ▼ Don't discard dead batteries in a fire. They can explode.
- ▼ Be careful when handling to avoid shorting out the battery with conducting materials such as keys, rings, and bracelets. The battery can overheat and burn.
- ▼ Don't carry batteries loose. They can short out against each other or against other metal objects and ignite.

Before storing the system, remove the batteries and store them in a cool, dry place. The refrigerator is ideal; the cold slows down the aging process. We keep ours wrapped in an airtight plastic storage bag in the refrigerator. But beware, cold batteries do not perform at peak capacity and can cause faulty equipment operation. Always allow batteries to stabilize to room temperature; they will return to normal power. Dry them before using. Cold batteries exposed to warm air will cause condensation to form and this will cause corrosion of both the battery terminals and contacts inside the battery compartment.

Bulkhead Connector

Inspect and clean the connector's threads. If you notice any salt residue, lint, or sand, use a toothbrush or a cotton swab dipped in a water-vinegar solution and rub all around the threads. Squeeze cotton swab dry before cleaning the threads. *Never* use alcohol, WD-40, or any chemical product on these or any other plastic parts.

Examine the contact pins. They should be bright and shiny. If they look dark or spotted, clean with a pencil eraser or a rough cloth. Dirty contacts will impede the flow of electricity from strobe to camera.

NX-90 Housing

The chassis is constructed of a corrosion-resistant aluminum alloy with a baked epoxy finish. The housing is impervious to corrosion, but the areas in and around the controls can trap water; there are nine external controls on the NX-90 housing. The housing is equipped with locking latches, a viewfinder window, a bulkhead connector, and two hand grips. All of these have joints and fittings which are capable of harboring salt water. To prevent salt residue from forming in and around the crevices, soak and rinse your housing thoroughly after every dive. Dry with a soft, dry cloth. Be sure to wipe dry the viewfinder and LCD windows.

There are two O-rings on the NX-90 housing: on the front case and on the bulkhead connector cap. Both the flat port and the dome port have an O-ring on the mount, and there's one on the flat port extension ring as well. Please see pages 277-280 for detailed instructions on how to care for O-rings.

- ▼ Clean the interior of the housing with canned air or a hair dryer set on a low, cool setting.
- ▼ Handle the internal hot shoe with extreme care. Do not crimp, pull or twist the connector cord. Doing so will damage the wiring.
- ▼ Clean the gears inside the housing with a soft brush.
- ▼ Periodically remove and lubricate the bolts that secure the hand grips to the housing; this will prevent oxidation and "locking up."
- ▼ Never remove the four screws securing the viewfinder port. If sand or other debris accumulates under the lip of the window, send the housing to a Sea & Sea repair center for cleaning.
- ▼ Do not use any chemical agents or cleaners on the outside or inside of this housing!

How to Care for the Lens Port

The front surface of the port must be clean to ensure picture quality. Dome ports need more stringent attention than flat ports as they tend to exaggerate dirt and grease smudges.

- ▼ Never submerge. You do not want to get water inside the port.
- ▼ Wash in a bath with mild liquid detergent *with the port securely mounted to the housing*. Rinse and dry to prevent spotting. If necessary, remove spots with a lens tissue.

▼ Clean the inside of the ports with a soft camel hair brush or blower brush. Debris on the inside will impair image quality.
▼ Do not use abrasive cleansers; they will scratch the port.
▼ Do not use alcohol or commercial window cleaner.
▼ Pat dry with a soft dry cloth or lens tissue; do not use paper towel.
▼ Examine the area where custom and zoom port knobs are attached to the ports. Look for sand, salt residue, or other debris which can inhibit fluid rotation of the controls. When soaking, work these controls to dislodge trapped matter.
▼ Protect the port from damage. Mild scratches will not affect picture image but deep scratches and gouges will.
▼ Store housing and port separately.
▼ Always protect the dome port with its neoprene cover, even when diving. Remove when you start taking pictures. Replace before surfacing.
▼ If storing for long periods of time, remove the port from the housing and store the O-ring in a plastic bag inside the housing.

N90 Camera

One of the advantages of using a land camera in a housing for underwater photography is that the camera is never exposed to the deleterious effects of salt water. Unlike amphibious cameras, it demands little maintenance. Basically, if you treat it kindly, protect it from the elements (sun, sand, and *water*), all you need do is dust it and store it correctly.

1. Use a camel's hair or sable brush to remove dust, hair, sand from the exterior. Pay attention to crevices around knobs and levers, screws, and other areas where debris can lodge.
2. Use a rubber syringe blower to dislodge film chips from the film transport area. When doing this, hold the camera upside down so particles fall out of the camera instead of deeper into it.
3. Ever so carefully and only with a soft brush, dust the shutter curtain.
4. Don't touch the reflex mirror. Use a rubber syringe blower to remove dust.
5. Close camera back and check battery compartment.
6. Clean viewfinder eyepiece with a lens cleaning tissue.
7. Protect interior with body cap.

Never rinse any parts of this camera! Never lubricate any parts of this camera!

Lenses

In this section we will address the four types of lenses: built-in, supplemental, and primary lenses for use with amphibious cameras, and land lenses for use with a housed camera.

The easiest to maintain are the *built-in lenses.* Only the glass surface of the lens need be cleaned. Since you have already soaked and rinsed your Motor Marine II-EX or MX-10, you have already soaked and rinsed the built-in lens.

Use a lens cleaning tissue to dry the lens. If water spots are evident on the glass surface, apply a drop of lens cleaning fluid to a photographic lens tissue and lightly wipe with a circular motion, starting at the center and spiraling outward. As you wipe, the fluid will dry. If lens cleaner isn't available, breathe gently on the lens surface so that moisture fogs it. Wipe quickly with a lens tissue before the moisture evaporates.

Note: The glass surface of the lens is coated with a transparent substance designed to reduce flare and heighten contrast. You can see the coating; it has a rainbow cast. Do not think this is something that needs to be cleaned off. Rather, it is something to *protect.*

The maintenance procedure for *supplemental lenses* is more complex:

1. Detach the accessory lens from the primary lens.
2. Soak the lens in fresh water for at least 30 minutes.
3. Pat the lens body dry with a soft cloth.
4. Clean the lens immediately. Dried water spots can be very difficult to remove. Place a few drops of lens cleaning fluid onto a piece of lens tissue. The lens cleaner is designed to cut away any grease and will not harm the coating of the elements.
5. Hold the lens up to the light; look into the lens at an angle. Check for fingerprints, dirt, or smudges.
6. The rear lens element can be cleaned the same way. Generally, you only clean the rear lens element when it actually needs it—when it has dust, fingerprints, or O-ring grease on it. But because these lenses use water as an additional optical element, they must be washed and cleaned every time you use them.
7. Recheck the elements and replace the lens cap covers.

The maintenance procedure for Sea & Sea *primary lenses* (12mm, 15mm, and 20mm) for Nikonos cameras includes examination and cleaning of the O-ring and O-ring channel.

1. Soak lens and camera *together* for at least 30 minutes, preferably one hour. (Make sure camera is completely sealed before immersing.)
2. While soaking, rotate the aperture and focus control knobs to loosen any trapped particles.
3. Air dry and then completely dry with a soft, dry cloth.
4. Remove lens from camera. Hold the camera with the lens facing down so that any water that may be trapped between the lens and the camera body will not seep into the camera.
5. Remove the O-ring. Hold the lens face down with one hand, put the thumb and forefinger of your other hand on opposite sides of the O-ring, then press forward on the O-ring. The O-ring will bulge out. Slip one finger underneath the O-ring and gently lift it out of its groove. (Sea & Sea's plastic O-ring remover makes this procedure one step, safe and easy.)
6. Soak the O-ring in a bath of warm water and a mild liquid detergent.
7. Inspect the O-ring for nicks, tears, cuts. If questionable, discard and replace with a new one.
8. Replace the front and rear lens caps to protect from silicone grease.
9. Inspect the control knobs, particularly where the shaft joins the lens body. You don't want to overlook salt deposits here. Apply a little silicone grease to this area. Rotate the knobs back and forth several times, allowing the silicone to work into the underlying O-rings. Clean excess with a cotton swab.
10. Grease the O-ring. Put a dab of silicone grease on your thumb and index finger. Pull the O-ring gently through your fingers till it is evenly coated. If silicone grease gets on the lens, use a lens tissue with lens fluid to wipe it clean.
11. Clean the O-ring channel with a cotton swab.
12. To reseat the O-ring, place one side into the groove. While holding it in place with one hand, roll the other side into place. Make sure it forms a smooth, continuous line.
13. Remove lens caps and clean the front and rear elements as described on the preceding page.
14. Store lens in its protective pouch.

Do and Don'ts:

- ▼ *Don't* allow salt water to dry on the lens; salt crystals can scratch the antireflection coating.
- ▼ *Don't* apply cleaning fluid directly onto the lens; it will seep between the elements.
- ▼ *Don't* clean optical glass with a brush; the bristles can scratch the delicate surface.
- ▼ *Don't* use facial tissue. Don't use eyeglass cleaning tissues; these are often impregnated with silicone and may remove the antireflection coating on the lens surface. Don't use man-made materials such as polyester; they are abrasive and may scratch the antireflection coating.
- ▼ *Don't* use a water-vinegar solution. The antireflection coating on lenses are vulnerable to pitting and peeling from the acid in the vinegar.
- ▼ *Don't* get fingerprints on the lens; these can actually etch themselves right into the glass.
- ▼ *Do* protect lenses from dust and accidental damage with lens caps.

While lenses exposed to salt water require a meticulous maintenance regimen, *lenses for a housed camera* need minimal care:

1. Use a soft brush to clean lens barrel and crevices around aperture and focus controls.
2. Use a camel's hair or sable lens brush or a rubber syringe blower to dust particles from the front and rear glass surfaces.
3. Apply a drop of lens cleaning fluid to a lens tissue and, using a circular motion, gently wipe the lens until dry.
4. Hold the lens up to the light and look at it from an angle; check for fingerprints, silicone grease, and other debris. Clean lens surface again, if necessary.
5. Inspect the CPU contacts on the Nikkor D lens. If soiled, gently clean with a soft, dry cloth.
6. Protect with front and rear lens caps.
7. Store in a cool, dry environment.

All the dos and don'ts above apply to these lenses, too. There's just one more thing you must never forget: *don't ever let these lenses get wet!*

Strobes

Assuming you have rinsed, dried, and disassembled the strobe at the dive site, now you want to soak the strobe in fresh water. *Make certain the connectors are covered with their protective waterproof caps.*

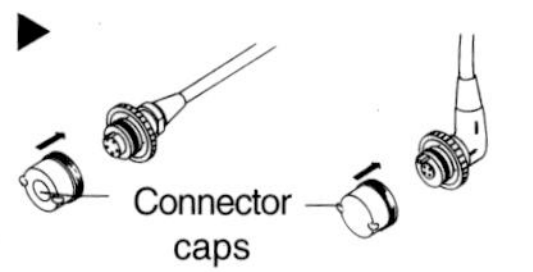
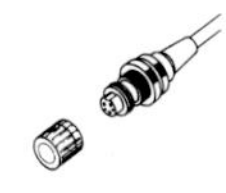

While the unit is soaking, work the power and mode switches a few times to dislodge any salt deposits. Salt deposits at these junctions can damage the internal O-rings. Rinse under fresh running water, then dry with a soft cloth.

Note: If you did not rinse and disassemble the camera and strobe earlier, you may rinse and soak them now as one unit. *Be certain that the sync cord connector is securely attached to the camera's bulkhead connector.* With strobes with a detachable sync cord, you must also check that the connector is securely fitted into the strobe's bulkhead connector.

Strobe Sync Cord

The most overlooked area of the strobe is the sync cord. Sync cords should be inspected for nicks and cuts. Tears in the cord will allow water to penetrate the strobe and cause serious damage. Broken or damaged internal wires can short out the electronic mechanism. A damaged sync cord may test okay on land but will malfunction underwater when compressed by water pressure.

- Do not bend, twist, or pull the sync cord connector from the camera; this will damage the connector.
- Examine the elbow connector on the sync cord. If it becomes separated from the sync cord or damaged, *do not* use the strobe.
- Do not leave sync cord connected to camera for prolonged periods of time. Corrosion and accumulated debris can make separation of these connections extremely difficult.

Inspect the connector for loose terminals, broken contacts, worn threads, a damaged O-ring. Wipe the threads with a soft cloth. Lubricate to facilitate connecting and disconnecting. (Do not get grease on the pins.) Examine the contacts for corrosion .

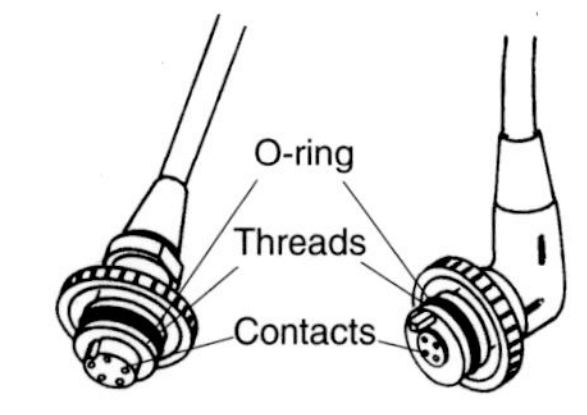

Sync Cord Connector O-ring

The O-ring not only protects the camera's connecting pins, but also protects the strobe's circuitry from water damage. *This O-ring should be serviced after every diving day.*

Follow the same maintenance procedure as outlined for maintenance of the camera O-rings on pages 277-280: soak in soapy water, rinse, dry, inspect, lubricate. When in doubt about the integrity of the O-ring, always discard and replace with a new one.

Strobe Battery Compartment

Hold the strobe with the battery chamber ▶ facing downward position. Unlock the battery chamber cover and remove the batteries. Remove and examine the O-ring on the battery chamber cover. Service this O-ring in the same manner as you serviced the O-rings on your camera.

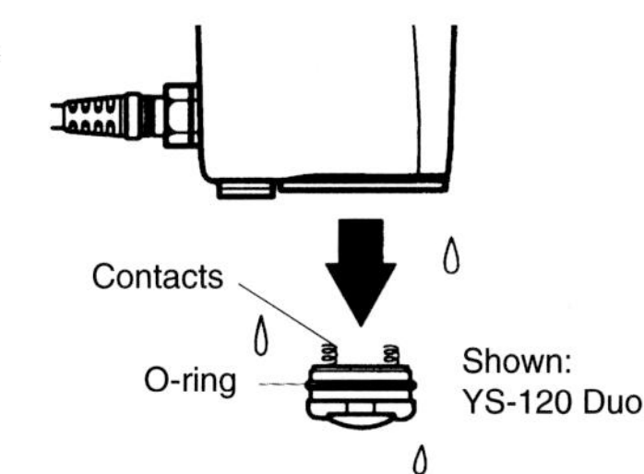

Check inside the battery chamber where the O-ring makes contact for sand, salt deposits, and water droplets. Clean the pressure seat of the battery cover. Check the battery contacts inside the battery chamber for corrosion. Also check the contacts on the battery cap.

Strobe Housing

The electronic assembly of a Sea & Sea strobe is encased in a watertight housing made of high-impact corrosion-resistant plastic. This case should be cleaned with a mild liquid detergent only. Never use paint thinner, alcohol, benzine, abrasives or any other chemical solvents to clean the housing; these can deform, crack, and otherwise damage the plastic casing.

The two cases form a watertight seal by means of an O-ring. *Maintain it as meticulously as you do the O-rings in your camera or housing.*

About the YS-40A.

Obviously, this strobe is different in design from the others in the Sea & Sea line. It is not of two casings, sealed with an O-ring and secured by latches. It does not have a bulkhead connector and does not dedicate via a sync cord.

However, the case is constructed of the same polymers and subject to the same damage if treated with antagonistic chemical agents. The preceding cleaning instructions for the case and O-ring care for the battery compartment apply. Unique to the YS-40A is the infrared optical triggering system. Electric impulses are transmitted via the windows in the strobe and the side of the camera. These windows must be uncontaminated for the impulses to pass. Clean with a lens tissue after every dive. Also inspect the connector. While water cannot penetrate strobe or camera, you want to prevent corrosion, flush out sand and any debris that will inhibit proper engagement of the mount.

Arms, Brackets, and Other Accessories

Several other components should be included in your maintenance. All arms, brackets, trays should be soaked. Even the lens caddy must be bathed. Why must plastic accessories be so laboriously cared for if they can't corrode? Because the nuts, screws, and bolts that assemble them can.

No part is too small to be attended to properly. The lens caddy is plastic; the screws are not. Rinse it. The 1:2 Macro for the Motor Marine II-EX is plastic; it's hinges are not. Rinse it. The lens filter is just a piece of colored glass; it can spot. Rinse it. The Sea Arm IV is a resin compound, but it, too, should be washed in fresh water to prevent the build-up of salt or sediment that will inhabit extension and retraction of the telescopic arm. Get the idea?

Lubricate the threads of the locking knob on the bracket that attaches the strobe to the arm to prevent salt build-up and binding. Use some silicone grease on all screws and threaded components. This will inhibit corrosion and keep all movable parts functioning smoothly.

Special Care in Tropical and Marine Environments

When living in or visiting a tropical environment, you have another natural enemy: *fungus.* Moisture is its breeding ground. It gets inside lenses and destroys lens coatings and elements; it ruins slides, prints, and negatives. To protect your equipment, store everything in a dry environment. Dehumidifiers pull excess moisture from the air. Always use desiccants; this moisture-absorbing substance is available in packets, gel form, tablets, powder, or crystals. Some change colors when they have absorbed their full capacity so you know it's time to replace with a fresh one.

Storage

Just as you need to clean it the right way, you must store it correctly, too. Improper storage is an enemy. Your equipment will function at peak performance if you remember to do the following:

- ▼ Always remove batteries before storing the equipment.
- ▼ Disassemble all equipment with O-rings. Pressure on O-rings for extended periods will flatten them and impair their sealing capability. Store the system with a used set of O-rings in place. The used O-ring will serve as a seal against dust. Put a dab of color (magic marker, nail polish) on the O-ring as a reminder that it's a compromised O-ring and must be replaced with a new one before diving.
- ▼ Store equipment disassembled.
- ▼ Store strobes with housing clasps undone to allow hydrogen gases to escape.
- ▼ Store lenses with their protective dust caps on.
- ▼ Store lenses in lens pouches or in vacuum sealed plastic storage containers.
- ▼ Store with small bags of desiccant; these will absorb moisture and humidity. New equipment usually has these desiccants in the packaging. Don't throw them away. Tuck them into your camera case, on the shelf, and in the closet where you keep your equipment.
- ▼ Store in a cool, dry, dust-free environment.
- ▼ If you use your equipment infrequently and keep it stored for long periods of time, remember to bring it out every few months. Work the controls on your camera. Operate the shutter, the aperture and focus controls to redistribute the lubricants on the internal O-rings. Fire the strobe. Photo equipment needs regular exercise to stay in tip-top shape.

Service

All underwater equipment is subject to corrosion. A camera or lens does not have to flood to become corroded. Just by opening the equipment around or near water, moisture and salt can penetrate the internal mechanisms. Given time, these will accumulate and cause damage.

Therefore, the last but very important step in your maintenance program is annual servicing by an authorized Sea & Sea service facility.

Chapter 10

Troubleshooting

Unlike land cameras, underwater photo equipment needs perpetual maintenance. But even the most vigilant photographer may find something, sometime, not working properly or not working at all. The malfunction may be caused by any of the enemies mentioned in the preceding chapter: salt, sun, dirt, a bump, improper storage, neglect. Or it could be that something broke. A camera system is, after all, a machine, comprised of a myriad of small springs, gears, wires, connections, circuits. And like any machine, one of the components can fail and make a single function or even the entire system inoperable. This chapter, then, is devoted to *what to do if* something goes wrong.

The Warranty

A word to the wise consumer: save your receipts when you purchase photo equipment so you will have a record of the purchase date. Read the warranty card that comes with the equipment. Mail in the warranty card.

Sea & Sea equipment is covered by a one-year warranty. If the equipment is faulty and is still covered by the warranty, do not attempt to disassemble it—this will automatically void the warranty. If the system is not functioning properly and you are unable to locate and solve the problem as advised in this chapter, send the equipment to an authorized Sea & Sea service facility.

First, Don't Overlook the Obvious

Is the camera turned on?

If the answer is yes, then the first thing you must do is check the batteries. Are they the right type? Have they been installed correctly? Are they depleted? Always use a fresh set of batteries when checking out any electrical problem.

Next, check for signs of corrosion. Inspect all electrical contacts and clean with a rough cloth or a pencil eraser. Make sure all mechanical parts are moving freely and are not hampered by corrosion, sand, or debris. If corrosion is evident inside the camera, it is possible that a slight leak exists. As a safety precaution, any equipment with even mild corrosion should be sent to an authorized Sea & Sea service center for an evaluation and pressure test.

Warning: In the course of troubleshooting, do not pry or force any moving parts; mechanical parts should move freely.

WHAT TO DO IF . . .

. . . the shutter won't trigger

Start with the obvious. Is the shutter release lock in the "Open" position? That done, check the batteries, the battery terminals, the battery compartment. Are there salt deposits, sand or other debris around the shutter release obstructing movement? If none of these prove to be the culprit, send the camera in for a professional evaluation.

. . . the film jams

Film jamming is usually due to incorrect loading of the film cartridge. Always make sure that the film is properly inserted into the rewind claw with enough leader extended over the film transport. The tip of the leader must be aligned with the mark on the film transport. The film must be positioned squarely between the guide rails, and the film sprocket holes must be fitted over the sprocket teeth. For the **MX-10**, see illustration on page 40. For the **Motor Marine II-EX**, see illustration on page 64. The film may have jumped the track or is not properly engaged in the sprockets or there's too much slack.

If the film is correctly loaded, and the film is still jammed, check for damage to the rewind claw, the pressure plate, or film rollers.

If the film jams on a **Motor Marine II-EX** while you're diving, hit the rewind lever for a "nano" second. Put your hand over the lens so you don't expose frames already exposed. Press the shutter release twice to advance the film two frames. If slack is the problem, this will often get it wound tightly into the take-up spool.

The second most common problem is a faulty patrone lock plate which is sometimes damaged by incorrect loading. A repair technician would have to diagnose this problem and a new lock plate would have to be installed.

. . . the film won't advance

The film advance system on Sea & Sea cameras is both mechanical and electrical. Malfunction can be due to a range of causes, from weak or dead batteries to broken gears.

1. Check batteries. Check that they have been installed with the correct polarity. Check for corrosion across the contacts. Mild corrosion can be cleaned with a pencil eraser. If there is heavy corrosion, dip a cotton swab into vinegar, press it between your fingers to remove excess vinegar, and gently rub the contacts. Next, check if the batteries are exhausted or not making proper contact, in which case the shutter release *will* depress but the shutter will not function and the film will not advance.
2. Has the film been properly loaded?
3. Remove the film and check for film chips in the transport area.
4. Load a test roll. Press the shutter release. Check that the take-up spool and the film sprockets rotate. If either fails to operate or moves erratically, the problem is with the motor drive system.
5. If the motor drive does not turn on when the shutter release is depressed, the problem may be electrical or the shutter release is not making contact with the release plate. This repair must be performed by an authorized service technician.

Additional check with the **MX-10**: check the wind/rewind switch. The film will not advance if the switch is in the "R" position. Make sure that the lock button is not in the "Lock" position.

. . . the film counter doesn't function

Counter problems are strictly mechanical. No film is needed to check if the counter is operating correctly.

Note: On the **Motor Marine II-EX** the back door must be closed for the film counter to function; on the **MX-10** the film chamber door must be closed for the counter to function.

1. Depress the shutter release. The counter should advance in time with the motor drive system.

2. If the motor drive is operational and the film counter isn't working, check for proper film loading.

3. Check the small tab on the upper right side of the back cover. This tab activates the counter. If this tab is broken, the back cover must be replaced. ▶

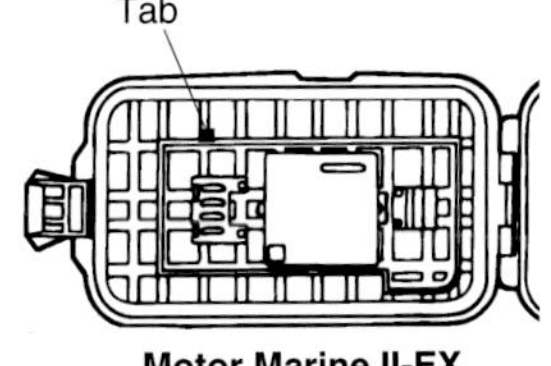

Motor Marine II-EX

On the **MX-10** the tab which activates the film counter is located on the film chamber door. If it is damaged, the door will have to be replaced. ▶

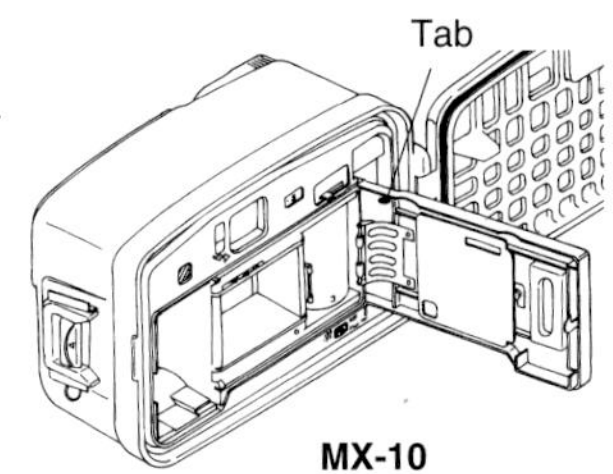

MX-10

. . . the film rewind system doesn't start

The rewind system on the **MX 10** is fully automatic. It is activated when the film reaches the end of the roll. If it doesn't rewind automatically, check for low battery voltage and then check that the rewind claw is not damaged.

If the rewind system of the **Motor Marine II-EX** will not function:

1. Are you sure you have film in the camera?

2. If all other functions are operating normally, inspect the film compartment for film chips that may be lodged around the rewind stop button. Make sure there is free movement of the button. ▶

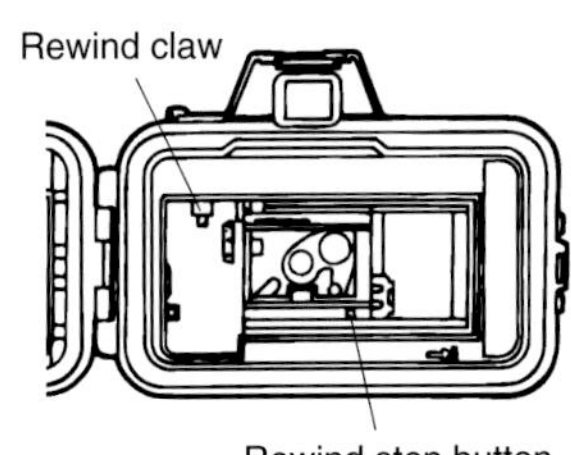

3. Check if the film rewind claw has been damaged. This claw can be dislocated due to improper film loading. When loading film, be sure to engage the film cartridge correctly into the claw. Do not force it; it must engage freely. Undue pressure can break the claw.

4. If there is no visual evidence of damage, check the motor drive system: gently press down on the rewind stop button and at the same time press down on the rewind lever. If the motor drive is functioning but the rewind claw does not rotate, the camera must be sent to an authorized service center.

. . . the rewind stops before the film is rewound

Be sure the batteries are fresh, installed correctly, and that there isn't corrosion on the contacts impeding the flow of electricity. If the battteries aren't the problem, check that the perforations on the film are not broken. If they are, the film will not rewind.

. . . the rewind system starts itself

Oops! You did it. The **Motor Marine II-EX**'s rewind lever can be accidentally activated if the rewind lever is pushed forward, even if all the frames of the film have not been exposed.

. . . the rewind system keeps running after the film is rewound

If the problem is with a **Motor Marine**, check to see if the rewind lever is stuck in the forward position. Check if the rewind stop button is jammed. If it is either of these and they will not disengage, remove the batteries; this will, of course, stop the system. Send the camera to a repair facility.

If this occurs with an **MX-10**, locate the two ▶ rewind buttons in the film transport area. Make sure they move freely, that they aren't jammed due to sand or film chips. Also make sure the pressure plate is not damaged.

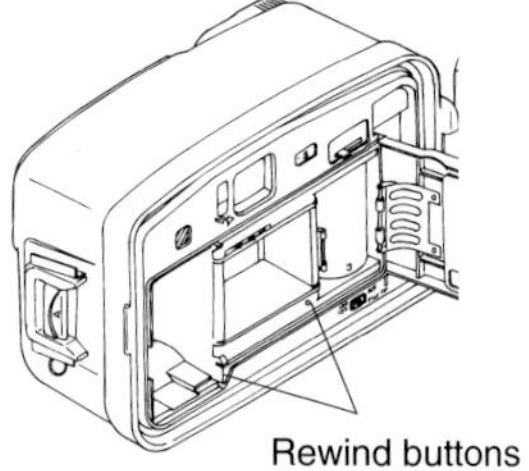

. . . the built-in flash doesn't fire

With low voltage the camera will function but the flash will not fire. Check the batteries. If they are fresh, installed correctly, and the contacts are clean, internal circuit problems exist. Send the camera for repair.

. . . the internal TTL confirmation light doesn't come on

Are you using the built-in flash? If so, please note: the **Motor Marine**'s built-in flash does not operate in TTL mode. Low battery power can cause the TTL mechanism to operate erratically. It can also cause poor synchronization of shutter and strobe. If that should happen, the TTL confirmation light would not come on. Test your batteries.

. . . the low exposure warning light doesn't come on

Check for low battery voltage. If the batteries are fully charged, the problem is electronic and the camera must be sent to a repair facility.

. . . the internal flash ready light does not come on

1. Check for low battery voltage.
2. Clean the battery contacts.
3. Check the obvious: is the aperture control dial on the **MX-10** positioned on the internal flash setting? Is the shutter speed dial on the **Motor Marine II-EX** set on the internal flash position?

. . . the external strobe keeps firing

Repeated firing even when the shutter is not triggered can be caused by broken wires in the sync cord. Inspect the sync cord. Is it bent or twisted? Is the elbow connector damaged? If so, don't use it; send it for repair.

A second reason for continuous flashing is flooding— water shorting out the electrical contacts. A flooded strobe must be sent in for repair.

Note: Sync cord malfunctions cannot apply to the **MX-10.** The YS-40A strobe is triggered by an infrared signal. There is no sync cord mating strobe and camera. If the YS-40A keeps firing, it is an electrical problem or flooding.

. . . the external strobe fails to fire

If the strobe is mated to the **Motor Marine II-EX** camera and the ready light is on but the strobe does not fire, it could be one of several obvious reasons:

- ▼ the sync cord connector isn't properly inserted into the bulkhead connector
- ▼ poor electrical contact; the contact pins need cleaning
- ▼ internal damage to the sync cord wires
- ▼ improper battery installation
- ▼ water inside the camera or strobe shorting out the contacts
- ▼ water inside the bulkhead connector.

If it is none of the above, disconnect the strobe from the camera and perform the following test:

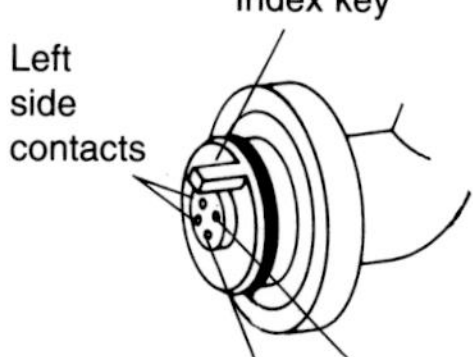

1. Turn the strobe to the "On" position. Hold the index key in the 12 o'clock position. Using a needle-nose pliers, short out the two pin contacts on the right side. The strobe should fire. ▶
2. Turn the power switch to the "TTL" position and short out the upper left and lower right pin contacts. The strobe should fire.

If the strobe passes this test, the problem is not with the strobe but with the camera. Send the camera to an authorized service center for evaluation.

If the strobe is mated to the **NX-90**, check that the sync cord connector inside the housing has been properly mated to the camera's hot shoe.

If the external strobe on the **MX-10** fails to fire, clean the synchronization windows on the camera and on the strobe. If these windows are contaminated by dirt, salt, silicone grease, etc., optical electrical signals cannot be transmitted. Check battery voltage and battery contacts in strobe and camera.

. . . the strobe recycle time is too long

This is usually just a signal that your batteries need to be changed or charged.

. . . the strobe is out of sync when the shutter is released

This is not something that can be fixed by changing batteries. This is caused when the sync contacts are not properly set or by faulty shutter blades. Send the camera to an authorized repair center.

. . . the strobe TTL confirmation light doesn't come on

The TTL system cannot function if the electrical impulses between camera and strobe are impeded. Therefore, a non-functioning TTL may be caused by low battery voltage, dirty battery terminals, dirty battery compartment contacts, contaminated strobe or camera bulkhead connector pins, dirty sync cord connector pins, improper seating of the sync cord to the bulkhead connector. Check all the aforementioned. Clean the contacts. If the TTL still doesn't work, perform the TTL test on page 217. If the strobe fails, send to a repair center.

. . . the Motor Marine's built-in close-up lens is malfunctioning

If there is a circular line in your photographs or if the right-hand side of the photograph is out of focus:

1. Check that the focus indicator is not positioned between "CU" and "1m." Pictures will be blurred if the close-up lens is only partially in the image path. The 35mm lens will also produce unfocused pictures if the close-up lens is partially in its image path.
2. Open the back cover and look ▶ inside the camera. Rotate the focus dial to the "CU" position. Check if the close-up lens frame assembly is loose on the close-up arm assembly. The screw should be tight on the frame assembly.

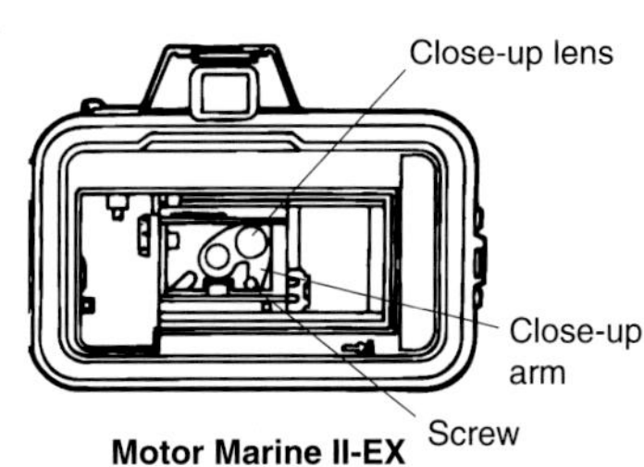

. . . the NX-90 Pro won't trigger

It's not the housing. It's the camera.

1. Check the obvious. Is the shutter locked? Is the camera power switch in the "Off" position? If the camera is off, the LCD panel will not illuminate. Are the batteries depleted? If the batteries are exhausted, the LCD will not illuminate.
2. Check the frame counter. If it reads "E" then the film has been rewound and the shutter release is automatically locked until you unload the film.
3. If it's none of these, remove the lens and mount a different lens; sometimes the problem is with the lens and not the camera. If you can't locate the problem, take the camera to your Nikon dealer.

. . . your pictures are continually out of focus

More than likely, this is neither a mechanical nor an electrical problem. It is a "photographer problem." The **MX-10** is a fixed-focus camera. If your subject is not within the correct camera-to-subject range for the f-stop you are using, your images will be out of focus. Read pages 43, 47, 48 again.

The **Motor Marine II-EX** has a focus dial which must be set for camera-to-subject *apparent* distance and your subject can be no closer than that distance for the f-stop you are using. Read pages 66 and 77 again.

For every camera, whether it's a Motor Marine II-EX, MX-10, Nikonos or N90, images will be out of focus if the film is not advancing properly and is not wound on the take-up spool. Check the film transport system.

With the **NX-90**, if your photographs are out of focus, the problem is often that the autofocus system can't focus. Lack of contrast, the inability to track a moving subject, heavy particulate in the water—these are some of the conditions that exist in the underwater environment that confound the camera's autofocus system.

There are photographer oversights that may cause the problem, too: did you set the exposure mode on manual instead of autofocus? On manual, you would have had to manually focus the lens for the image to be sharp. Did you lock the camera in the Quick Shoe? If the camera isn't stabilized by the Quick Lock, it will take pictures, but the autofocus system will not function. You must lock the camera in its correct position for the aperture gears to mesh.

Note: Please refer to the Nikon N90 owner's manual any time you experience difficulty with your system.

. . . the pictures are always over or underexposed

It could be the obvious: you are using the wrong f-stop or your subject is not within the correct strobe-to- subject distance for the selected f-stop. Or it could be that the light meter is malfunctioning or the LED lamp is faulty. A qualified repair technician should examine the camera.

On the **MX-10** the problem could be as simple as not setting the ISO indicator for the speed of the film you are using or as complex as a faulty ISO switch, which would require professional adjustment.

. . . pictures lack highlight and detail, are washed out and murky

It may be the battery. Or it could be the camera's meter. Or both. An electronic exposure meter will not operate properly if the battery is weak or if you've installed the wrong type of battery. Check the camera's manual to be sure that you have the right battery. Check that the battery has been installed with the + and - terminals correctly oriented.

If it's not the battery, then it could be several other user errors, namely, wrong settings: ISO film speed, shutter speed faster than flash/sync speed, wrong exposure compensation setting, meter not turned on, meter not working. If you suspect your meter is malfunctioning. . .

How to test the meter:

1. You'll need either an 18% gray card (sold in camera shops) or a page from the classified section of the newspaper.
2. Load the camera with fresh batteries and a roll of slide film, definitely not print film. Remember, print film has a five-stop exposure latitude; exposure errors are corrected in processing. Slide films have no exposure latitude.
3. Take the camera out in bright noonday sun.
4. Set to f/16. With an N-90, select aperture priority mode. If the meter is accurate, the shutter speed selected by the camera should be the same as the ISO.
5. Hold the card or paper so it's neither in shadow nor reflecting light back into the lens.
6. Set focus to infinity.
7. Fill the frame.
8. Shoot the roll.

Compare the processed film with the gray card or the newspaper. If the meter is working, the gray tones will be identical.

. . . you see horizontal scratches on your slides or prints

Scratches can occur in the camera, in printing, in the processing lab's developing machine, or the machine that mounts your slide film onto slide mounts. But before you blame the processor, check your camera. Look for dirt, sand, lint, or any type of debris on the film pressure plate. Generally, this is the culprit. A single grain of sand will ruin your film. Clean the film transport area. If you see scratches on your next roll, suspect the photo processing lab. Send the next roll to a new lab and see what happens.

Sometimes, the scratches are caused by scratches on the front of your lens. Minor scratches will fill with water under pressure and won't mar the image. Deep scratches will be discernible. Minor scratches can be buffed out and the optics recoated. If the damage is severe, the front lens element can be replaced.

. . . the focus or aperture control knobs on your primary lens turn with difficulty or with a binding, uneven movement

The control knobs are designed to rotate smoothly and the lens elements to open and close smoothly. If this is not the case, the control shaft may be damaged. Return the lens to a Sea & Sea dealer for evaluation and repair.

. . . you see condensation inside your lens

Warm air contains moisture, which we call *humidity*. Under certain conditions, this warm air changes (condenses) into water. If the humidity is high and the air temperature is warmer than the temperature of the water, trapped air inside the camera condenses to small water droplets, which will cover the inside of the lens. As a result, your pictures will look as though they were taken through a fog.

This problem is more commonly encountered by Nikonos owners. When the primary lens is attached to the Nikonos camera body, the warm humid air becomes trapped between the camera body and the lens.When the camera is submerged in cooler water, the temperature difference is quickly transmitted through the glass elements and the result is condensation inside the lens.

If condensation is forming, try aiming a strobe at the lens and firing it several times. The heat that is generated may help to warm up the lens and camera and often the water droplets will evaporate.

Know What to Leave to the Pros

There are maintenance procedures and minor repairs that fall within the realm of what you *should do* and *can do* and then there are procedures that should be performed only by trained professionals. Proper preparation, cleaning, and storage are your responsibilty. Disassembly, parts replacement, and adjustments require the expertise of professionals.

Resist the urge to perform professional-level service on your Sea & Sea photographic equipment. If something is not working properly, bring it or send it to an authorized Sea & Sea repair facility.

CHAPTER ELEVEN

Traveling

Traveling

You can't take it with you—not all of it anyway. *What* to take and *how* to take it are the two most important considerations when preparing for a trip, be it long-distance for two weeks or just a day at the beach. Air travel, of course, is far more demanding. Airline baggage restrictions require that you be selective in how much equipment you take with you. Rough baggage handling requires that you be very, very careful in the way you pack your equipment. Most of this chapter is devoted to how to prepare and pack for a distant destination. But, please, careful preparation and proper handling are necessary no matter how near nor how far you travel to get to the water.

Off to a Good Start

Read the instruction manuals carefully. *Read this book carefully.* Be sure you are completely familiar with your system before you use it.

Next, conduct a pre-trip system performance check. For step-by-step instructions, refer to the chapters in this book that deal with your particular equipment. If your equipment passes all these tests, take it for a trial run. Test it by exposing a roll of film. Use color slide film. Don't use print film because exposure errors can be corrected in the processing. With slides, what you get is what you've done.

Take a variety of test shots: topside, underwater, with the built-in lens, with accessory lenses, the built-in flash, with the external strobe. This gives you the opportunity to check the camera's controls and circuitry over a wide range of operating conditions.

After processing your test roll, inspect the slides carefully. If something doesn't look right, it could be improper use of the camera, faulty equipment, or poor processing. If you can't decide which, check with your Sea & Sea dealer.

Once satisfied that your equipment is operational, you can pack it.

What to Pack

On international routes, airlines generally limit each traveler to two pieces of luggage, each one weighing no more than 44 pounds. You are also permitted one carry-on, and that must fit under your seat or in the overhead storage compartment. For diver/photographers, this is not a lot of luggage.

You will need one bag or suitcase for your scuba gear, another for clothes. That leaves the carry-on for your photo equipment. Generally the carry-on cannot exceed 21 x 14 x 9 inches. If that size case isn't large enough to hold all your photo gear, you can pack some of it (such as arms, brackets, tool kit, batteries), with your clothes, provided that piece of luggage has a hard shell and a sturdy lock.

Basic Photo Gear

- camera
- lenses
- housing
- ports
- lens gears
- strobe
- sync cord
- strobe arm, bracket, base plate
- tool kit
- film
- batteries
- battery charger
- spare parts

Start with a *detailed* list of every piece of equipment you intend to take with you. Imagine the disappointment of traveling 8,000 miles to a remote island in the South Pacific, unpacking your equipment, and finding that you forgot your sync cord. Or batteries.

Make two photocopies of the Photo Equipment Inventory form on page 311. Fill out one with everything you own. File it in a safe place at home. Fill out the second with the equipment you will be taking and keep it with your passport. This is your record should your luggage be lost or stolen.

Identify Your Property

Mark each piece of equipment with your name.You can buy a small engraving tool in a hardware or arts supply store or hobby shop for under $10. The engraving will, of course, be permanent.You can use waterproof paint or surgical adhesive, which can be removed should you want to sell your equipment in the future. Make sure you have a name and address tag on the outside of each piece of luggage. Put tags on the inside, too, should the case be lost and the outside tag comes off.

How to Pack

In Chapter 9 we said that some of the things that can harm your equipment are: a bump, bang, drop or jolt, improper storage, neglect. That's why packing your equipment properly is so important. A shopping bag that you intend to carry on the plane with you will not do. A canvas tote will not do. A make-up case will not do, either.

Invest in a hard case specifically manufactured for transporting photographic equipment. These are constructed of shock-absorbent materials such as fiberglass, aluminum, or high-impact molded plastic. A good one will have corrosion-proof hinges and latches, an O-ring seal to protect the interior in damp or humid environments, and a pressure vent to equalize internal pressure when flying. Make sure the case is deep enough to accommodate your largest piece of equipment.

The case will come equipped with high-density foam. The foam will protect your equipment from shock, heat, and vibration. These three enemies can attack when traveling by air, boat, or car.

- Vibration can loosen screws and electrical connections and cause focus, diaphragm, and shutter mechanism problems with your camera. Foam absorbs vibrations.
- Heat can melt glues and plastic parts and cause levers and controls to stick. It can impair battery performance and damage film. Foam provides insulation from heat.
- Foam softens the impact of a jolt or bump. For the lens to perform properly, the optical center of each element must be precisely aligned during manufacture. Subjecting the lens to catastrophic shock can cause misalignment and seriously impair its performance. Have you ever seen the way baggage handlers handle baggage? Packing your lenses in foam protects them from the effects of that kind of abuse.

If yours is a housed system, then you have a housing, ports, camera, lenses, lens gears, strobes, connectors. If you prefer to carry your equipment aboard rather than check it through, it's unlikely you will get all this in a case that will fit in an overhead luggage compartment or under your seat. Solution: two bags. A hard case for the housing, ports, strobes and connectors, a soft camera bag for camera and lenses. Best bet: buy a bag specifically designed

Photo Equipment
INVENTORY

Name: ______________________ Date: ______________

Address: ______________________ Destination: ______________

City: ______________________ State: ______________

Country: ______________________ Phone: ______________

	Manufacturer	Model Name	Serial #
Cameras			
Strobes			
Lenses			
Housing			
Ports			
Accessories			
Other			

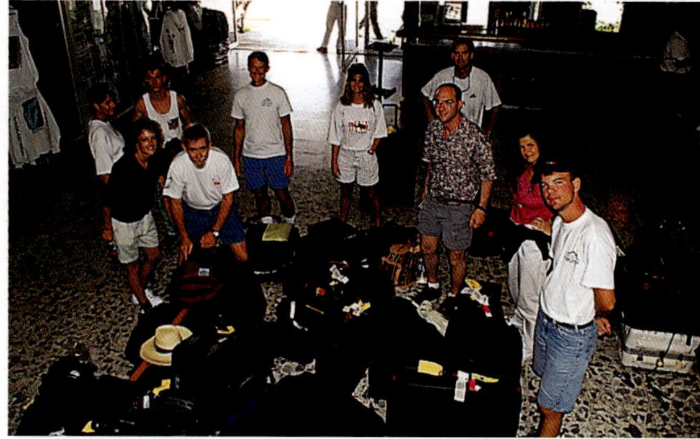

Underwater photographers can't travel light. But you can pack your photo gear so it a) arrives and b) arrives intact.

for photo equipment, compartmentalized with soft partitions. Fragile items go deep within the bag, away from the bag's vulnerable periphery. Hard objects should be cushioned against soft ones or against the padding of the bag. Use bubble wrap. Pack the camera without the lens attached. Use a camera body cap, of course. Distribute weight evenly.

Do not travel with the camera mounted inside the housing. If you do, for the sake of conserving space, remove the lens. Jolts, bumps, any kind of impact can damage the pinion gears inside the housing. Pack the port separately. If, again, you don't have the space, be sure to loosen the port to equalize air pressure inside the housing.

To prevent damage to all O-ring sealed equipment (amphibious cameras, housings, strobes) due to decreased atmospheric pressure, remove O-rings before flying. Cut a tiny nick in an old O-ring and seat it in the O-ring channel. This will serve as a cushion and prevent an air lock within the system. Mark the O-ring with nail polish or paint to identify it as a substitute. Don't forget to replace it with the good one before diving or you'll flood the system.

X-rays at the Airport

Airport security is a necessary inconvenience. But do X-rays fog film? The National Association of Photographic Manufacturers tested 500 rolls of exposed film and concluded that airline passengers need not worry about film being subjected to X-rays at security checkpoints, that it required 100 X-ray inspections to produce any damage. A similar study was conducted by the British Photographic Liaison Committee, and results indicated no visible effects on film subjected to routine X-ray examination. So your film is safe when traveling in Great Britain.

These studies aside, conventional wisdom is that the exposure effect of X-rays is cumulative and that excessive amounts can produce fog and shadowy images. The higher the ISO rating of the film, the more the X-rays may affect it. Most X-ray machines in the United States, and apparently Great Britain, are low dosage and don't pose a serious threat, but overseas machines are another story. These emit high enough doses to ruin your film. On one trip to the Red Sea, we went through five security checks, all with X-ray machines, before we even got to the boat!

Be aware that all of your carry-on luggage and sometimes your checked-through luggage will be scanned. So the best way to protect your film (both exposed and unexposed) from airport X-rays is to avoid having it X-rayed at all.

TRAVEL TOOL KIT

Don't leave home without it!

- cotton swabs
- lint-free cloth
- lens cleaner
- lens tissues
- silicone grease
- batteries
- O-rings
- screwdriver
- phillips screwdriver
- adjustable wrench
- small needle-nose pliers
- recloseable plastic bags
- toothbrush
- pencil eraser
- extension cord
- 24-hour electrical timer
- 220/240v to 120v electrical converter kit

Before the trip, remove the film from their cardboard boxes and replace the black canisters with clear ones, available at photo supply shops. Put the canisters into clear plastic storage bags with a good tight seal. Store in film shield bags.

Shield bags are lead-laminated pouches. These will help you protect your film from low-dose X-ray machines and fluoroscopic inspection devices. Professional camera shops stock super-lead laminated bags which provide even greater protection. They are not unconditionally guaranteed effective against some of the extremely powerful international security devices, so even with these, don't assume your film can tolerate electronic inspection. Don't pass it through. Keep it in your carry-on luggage and request a visual inspection. Security personnel won't have to open anything except the lead bag.

Chapter 12

Flooding

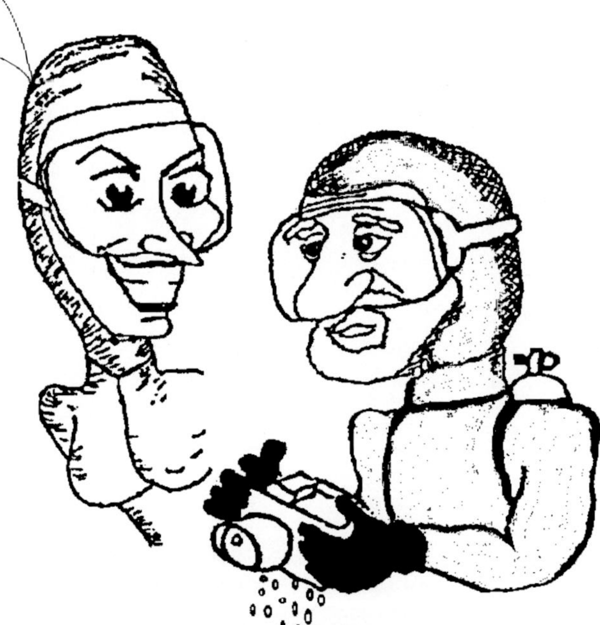

I t's no joke and it's not funny. It could happen. *The unmentionable. . . Water* inside your system. Sometimes it's equipment failure. More times than not, it's your fault. That may sound harsh, but don't feel bad, it happens to the best of us. And if it should ever happen to you, don't just stare at it in despair. React quickly. You *can* salvage your equipment. The important thing is, *do it immediately!*

Warning Signs

A major flooding can be averted if the early signs are detected and you don't dive with the system or continue the dive. Always abort the dive. Surface *safely,* go back to the boat or the beach, and check it out!

▼ With a **Motor Marine II-EX,** if the internal flash fails to fire, there may be water inside the camera.
▼ If the **MX-10**'s motor drive isn't operating and/or the internal flash fails to fire, water may have penetrated the system.
▼ In the case of a **Nikonos**, if the film advance lever jams or operates with difficulty, water may have caused corrosion on the gears or water inside the camera has caused the film emulsion to dissolve.
▼ Also in the case of a **Nikonos**, condensation inside the front port of a primary lens would indicate water inside the camera.
▼ If the external flash fails to fire or fires repeatedly, water may be shorting out the sync cord connector contacts.

First, How Bad is It?

You need to assess the extent of the flooding. Is it a major flooding or a minor one? If you open the camera and water pours out, it's a major flooding. If you notice a few drops of water inside the built-in lens or some moisture in the viewfinder window, it's a minor flooding. Treatment differs. You do not want to subject the interior of a camera to more water than is absolutely necessary.

A Flooded Camera

1. With a totally flooded camera, the first thing you do is remove your film and batteries. These contain chemicals that can contaminate the interior of the camera. The batteries will leak acid; discard them.

2. If the camera is a **Motor Marine II-EX**, remove the internal assembly from the case by removing the four Phillips screws at the corners. Remove the battery case, insert one finger into the battery compartment, and push out the internal assembly. ▶

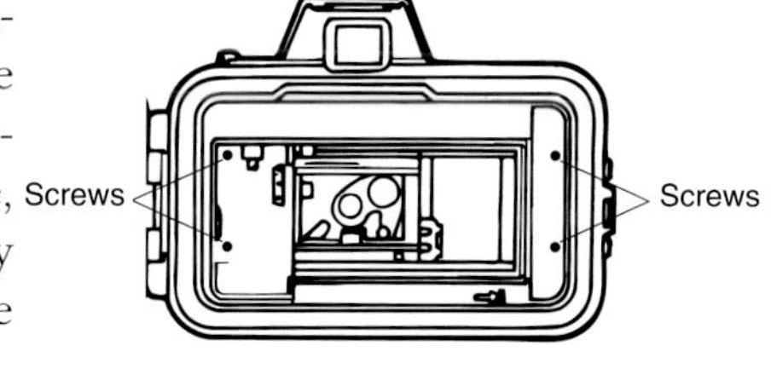

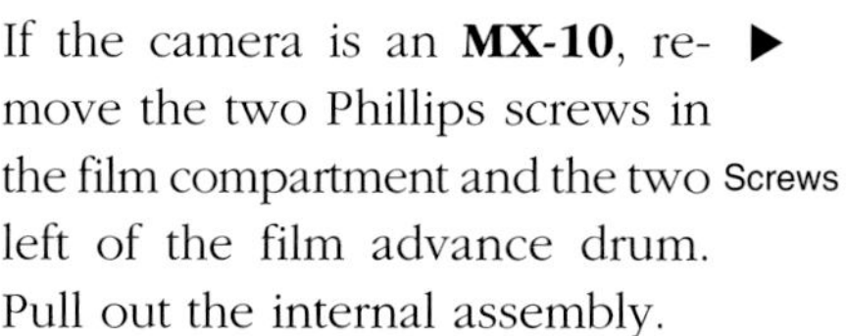

If the camera is an **MX-10**, remove the two Phillips screws in the film compartment and the two left of the film advance drum. Pull out the internal assembly. ▶

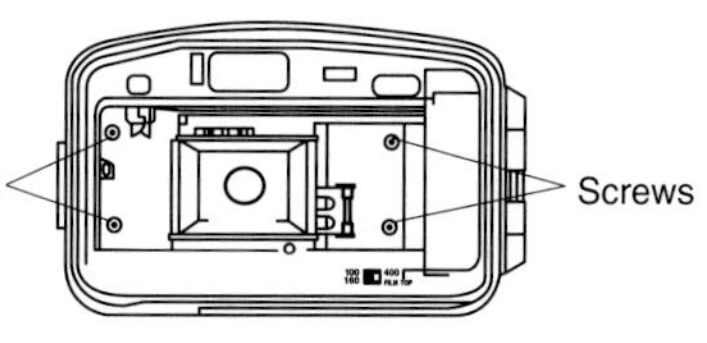

If the camera is a **Nikonos**, separate camera body and primary lens. If the lens is not flooded, put it aside. Do not soak!

3. Fill a basin with fresh water. Do not add any chemicals, such as alcohol, to the bath. Alcohol will damage the plastic housing. Use distilled water if possible. Immerse the camera case and the internal assembly and allow them to soak for at least 30 minutes. Repeatedly operate all the controls on the camera case, particularly the focus and aperture knobs, to wash away any accumulated or trapped salt water from gears, springs, and threads. Salt corrodes quickly. *Do not move any parts on the internal mechanism.*

4. Rinse with fresh water.

5. Again, work the controls to keep them from freezing: shutter release button, aperture control knob, focus control knob.

6. Dry the camera inside and outside with a hair dryer on a low heat setting for 10 to 15 minutes. Be sure to hold the hair dryer at least 12 inches from the camera to prevent damage to the camera's delicate plastic and electrical parts.

7. Place inside an airtight plastic bag and send to an authorized Sea & Sea service facility promptly. Even though you have dried the system carefully, there may be water trapped between springs and gears. If air gets to them and the water evaporates, these parts will corrode. The longer you delay, the more damage will be done.

Note: Leave the O-rings in their channels so the service technician can effectively conduct the appropriate tests to locate the source of the leak.

A Minor Flooding

If a camera has only mild water damage, *do not soak it!* Inspect it to locate the source of the leak or the affected area. Open the camera and check the O-ring. Is it the culprit? Inspect the film compartment. Inspect the battery compartment. Check the bulkhead connector. Clean the affected area with a cotton swab moistened with vinegar. Dry the area thoroughly with a hair dryer on a low setting. While the camera may be operational, it should be sent to a repair facility for evaluation.

A Flooded Strobe

You know your strobe has flooded if there's water inside the front port. If your strobe is a YS-30, YS-40A, YS-60, or YS-120, you know it has flooded if you open the battery chamber and there's water in there. Here's what to do:

1. Make sure the power switch is in the "Off" position.
2. Disconnect strobe sync cord from the camera's bulkhead connector. (Not applicable to the YS-40A.)
3. Drain the water away from the batteries. Remove the batteries. Do so with extreme caution with high-voltage batteries to avoid a shock.
4. Flush the battery chamber with fresh water.
5. Use a soft cloth and hair dryer on low heat to dry the chamber completely. Do not allow heat to build up inside the chamber.
6. Check for corrosion around the battery contacts. Clean with a pencil eraser.
7. Install fresh batteries and a new O-ring on the battery chamber cap. The strobe should be operational. If not, send it to a service center.

Warning: Do not follow the above procedure with a flooded YS-300. It requires cleaning by a professional technician.

What to Do with Wet Film

Hopelessly ruined? No. Sometimes it can be salvaged. Modern films, say Fuji and Kodak technicians, are somewhat resistant to moisture damage. The important thing is to keep it damp. If the film is allowed to dry, the emulsion sticks to itself inside the cassette.

Your camera flooded . . .

▼ Do not roll the film back into the cassette because the felt along the cassette opening could scrape off the emulsion. Take the camera into a dark room and remove the exposed film. Place in a light-tight container.

You dropped the cassette on a wet deck or, worse, overboard. . .

▼ If the film becomes saturated with salt water, soak in fresh water. If subjected to only a little water, just keep it moist in a sealed plastic container or baggie. Refrigerate until you can get the film to a processor.

▼ Get the film processed as soon as possible.

Don't expect perfection. Chemical reactions occur when film gets wet, and the processed film will probably show some discoloration.

Throw away unexposed film. Wet film could damage your camera.

Hotlines: Fuji 800-788-3854
Kodak 800-242-2424

> **Look for Bubbles**
> Upon descent, inspect housing for signs of leakage. If you see moisture or a stream of bubbles, go to the surface. Hold the housing with the lens pointed down so water will pool in the lens port instead of washing over the camera.

A Flooded Housed Camera System

Dry the system with a clean dry cloth to prevent any more contaminants from penetrating the system than already have.

The Camera. A Minor Flooding:

1. Open the housing.
2. Remove camera from housing.
3. Disconnect sync cord from hot shoe.
4. Separate lens from camera.
5. Rewind film, if possible.
6. Open back of camera.
7. Remove film.
8. Remove batteries.
9. Check the rear element of the lens for water.
10. Clean and dry the camera. Salt corrodes quickly. Clean in and around the exterior controls. *Do not touch or move any parts on the internal mechanism.*
11. Place in an airtight plastic bag and send it to an authorized Nikon repair facility promptly.

A Major Flooding:

Modern land cameras that have been totally submerged in salt water are usually beyond repair. However, if you want to try to salvage it, try the following:

1. Remove the film and batteries.
2. Fill a basin with fresh water. Do not add any chemicals, such as alcohol, to the bath. Alcohol will cause further damage. Use distilled water if possible. Soak for at least 30 minutes.
3. Dry the camera inside and outside with a hair dryer on a low heat setting for 10 to 15 minutes. Be sure to hold the hair dryer at least 12 inches from the camera to prevent damage to the camera's delicate plastic and electrical parts.
4. Place inside an airtight plastic bag and send to a Nikon service facility promptly. The longer you delay, the more damage will be done.
5. Cross your fingers. Your camera may be repairable but the cost may be so steep, you may as well buy a new one.

The Housing: A Minor Flooding

1. Remove the camera from the housing and check for water damage. If water has not penetrated the camera, put it aside.
2. Dry the exterior with a clean, dry cloth.You do not want to get more water into the interior.
3. Inspect the interior of the housing for moisture. Use a cotton swab dipped in alcohol or a water/ white vinegar solution to clean the affected metal parts. Do not use on plastic parts.
4. Dry with a hair dryer on a low cool setting.
5. Can you locate the cause of the leak? Was it the O-ring? Change the O-ring, seal the housing, and submerge in a rinse tank. If it leaks, it wasn't the O-ring. Don't use it. Send it to a Sea & Sea repair facility.

An ounce of prevention is worth a pound of cure

Send your camera system to an authorized Sea & Sea service center once a year for a pressure test and to have all internal O-rings changed.

The Housing: A Major Flooding

1. Soak both front and rear cases in fresh water for at least one hour.
2. Work the controls to flush out saltwater and prevent saltwater deposits from freezing the mechanisms.
3. Dry the interior of the housing with a clean dry cloth, then a hair dryer on a low, cool setting. Hold at least 12 inches away.
4. Package and send to an authorized Sea & Sea repair facility.

A Flooded Primary Lens for the Nikonos

If water has not penetrated beyond the lens mount and inner lens barrel, consider it a *minor* flooding and do the following:

1. Remove the four screws on the bayonet mount.
2. Turn the inner lens barrel counterclockwise and remove.
3. Moisten a cotton swab in fresh water and clean infected areas. Dry carefully with a hair dryer on a low setting.
4. Clean the lens with lens cleaner on a lens tissue.
5. Replace the inner lens and secure the bayonet mount.
6. Replace the O-ring with a new one.
7. Check focus and aperture controls. If they are working properly, the lens is ready for use. If not, the lens must be sent for repair.

If water has penetrated to the front elements of the lens, it is a *major* flooding. Place in an airtight bag and send it to a Sea & Sea service center.

A Flooded Auxiliary Lens

1. If you notice seepage inside the elements of an auxiliary lens, detach it from the primary lens.
2. Soak it in fresh water for at least 30 minutes.
3. Dry the lens body with a soft cloth. Wipe elements with a lens tissue. Place in an airtight plastic bag and send to a repair facility.

Precautions

If a camera system floods, it is usually your fault. Yes, we know we said this already, but it's a point that needs repeating. Most floodings are caused by carelessness. You probably assembled the equipment improperly. Or hastily. Or neglected to inspect the O-ring. Or didn't reseat the O-ring properly. Etc.

- ▼ Check your equipment the night before you dive.
- ▼ Check your equipment before you enter the water.
- ▼ Immerse system in a rinse tank to check for leakage.
- ▼ Check that all power switches are in the "Off" position when you enter the water.
- ▼ Never take a giant stride off a boat with your system in hand. Ask someone on board to hand it down to you after you've made your entry.
- ▼ Underwater photo equipment is most vulnerable to flooding in shallow water where the seal is weakest. A jolt can dislodge the O-ring and break the seal. Be gentle and be careful.
- ▼ Be alert! Camera, lens, and strobe should be inspected immediately upon descent. A steady stream of bubbles from the camera or strobe or moisture inside the lens indicates flooding. Make a safe ascent and check your system. If you act fast enough, you can prevent serious and costly damage.
- ▼ Finally, don't wait for a catastrophe to get your system serviced. The old adage, "If it ain't broke, don't fix it" doesn't hold water with photo gear. So learned the sorry photographer who hadn't had his camera serviced in eight years and saw it flood on the very first dive of a seven-day liveaboard trip in Baja. He was very surprised. We were surprised it hadn't happened sooner.

About Products *Not* in this Book

Sea & Sea's line of underwater photographic equipment is so extensive that we could not include all of it in this book. We have elected to focus on the newest and most popular products being manufactured at the time we went to press. But what if you own equipment that is not in this book? Can you use this book? Can you benefit from it?

Absolutely.

More than one-third of this book is devoted to generic information: definitions, explanations, tips and techniques germane to the skillful and artistic use of underwater photographic equipment. These pages speak to anyone with any type of underwater photo system.

Look left. See "Precautions"? There's an example. This book contains practical and important information for everyone. And if yours is a Sea & Sea product, then all the better, because many of the products in this book are modified versions of earlier models. The controls and functions of older models are the prototypes for the newer models, so in most cases you will even be able to follow the step-by-step instructions for assembly and operation. Just remember to bypass those steps or tips that do not, *cannot* apply because of the differences in the model you have and the model described in this book.

The Motor Marine II-EX is a modified **Motor Marine II**. The Motor Marine II has a fixed shutter speed of 1/100 second. The Motor Marine II-EX has variable shutter speeds. The Motor Marine II has DX coding for two film speeds while the Motor Marine II-EX has DX coding for three. Both cameras are identical in body construction, film loading, advance and rewind; they have the same battery compartment, incorporate the same 35mm and close-up lenses, are equipped with the same exterior mount. They are compatible with the same accessory lenses and strobes. If you have a Motor Marine II, you can use this book.

The YS-40A evolved from the **YS-40.** The YS-40A has a different diffuser and operates in auto mode as well as in manual. But both strobes have the same battery compartment and the same infrared triggering system. Both are constructed of the same polymers and mate to the MX-10 the same way. If you have a YS-40, follow all the instructions except for those on auto mode.

The YS-60TTL strobe is a modified **YS-50**. Construction materials, battery compartment, sync cords and connectors are the same. The basic difference is that the YS-60 has 1/2 power mode and a prism diffuser and the YS-50 does not. The chapter on strobes and the section on the YS-60 will aid you in achieving properly illuminated photos.

As of this writing, Sea & Sea manufactures underwater housings for **Nikon's N50**, **N90**, and **NX5** SLR AF cameras, and **Canon's EOS Rebel G.** In this book we focus only on the NX-90 Pro for the N90 camera. Yet all Sea & Sea housings have much in common: the same hard-almite treated aluminum construction, the same Quick Shoe for camera installation, the same locking latches and flash sync connectors, the same ergonomically designed levers, knobs and grips. The port assemblies are bayonet and thread mount, and many of the ports and gears are interchangeable between the housings. All Sea & Sea strobes and connectors are interchangeable as well. So if you have any one of Sea & Sea's housings, the NX-90 chapter can provide you with some of what you need to know to operate your particular system and a lot of what you need to know to take SLR pictures like a pro.

In other words, use this book for the particulars, such as assembly, operation of controls, where those particulars are relevant to your system. Use this book as a photo course. Use Chapter 1 to understand the principles of underwater photography. Use the chapters on composition, strobes, care and maintenance, traveling to improve your photography and protect your equipment.

Whatever equipment you own, whether it's older or newer than those products covered in depth in this book, you *can* use this book.

Glossary

Absorption: The blue filtering effect of water. Sunlight consists of all the colors of the spectrum. Water absorbs light selectively, one by one as depth increases, filtering out the warmer colors first, so that at depths of 60-70 feet, only hues of blue and green remain.

Ambient light: Available sunlight underwater used as a source of illumination. Also referred to as natural light.

Amphibious camera: A specially-designed camera that can operate both underwater and on land. All ports, lids, and controls are sealed with O-rings.

Angle of acceptance: The maximum angle at which light enters a particular lens. Also referred to as angle of coverage and angle of view.

Aperture: An adjustable opening which regulates the precise amount of light passing through the camera lens when the shutter is open. The size of the aperture is referred to as the f-stop.

Aperture priority: An automatic exposure system, usually designated by the abbreviation AE, in which the photographer selects the f-stop and the camera automatically determines the corresponding shutter speed for a correct exposure.

Aperture ring: A band on the lens used to control the amount of light reaching the film plane; when turned, it alters the size of the lens iris.

Apparent distance: The refraction of light underwater creates a magnifying effect which causes objects to appear 25% closer than they actually are. A lens, like the human eye, sees apparent distance.

ASA: An abbreviation for American Standards Association. *See ISO.*

Autobracketing: The automatic exposure of three consecutive frames at varied ambient light exposure levels.

Autofocus: A built-in lens focusing system that focuses the lens when the shutter release button is partially depressed.

Autofocus lock: A control that focuses in whatever you aim the viewfinder at and locks in focus, allowing you to change picture composition without affecting focus.

Automatic exposure: When camera and strobe communicate electronically to create a correct exposure.

Autowind: An electric or spring-driven motor that automatically advances the film after the shutter is triggered.

Backscatter: When suspended particles in the water are illuminated by light from a flash, they reflect the light back at the lens. The particles appear as specks or snow in the photograph.

Beam angle: The angle of a strobe's light beam, expressed in degrees.

Bracketing: The technique of taking several shots of the same image at higher and lower f-stops than the one indicated by the exposure meter.

Built-in meter: An exposure meter in the

camera that measures ambient light and relays exposure data to the electronic controls in an automatic camera or to the photographer if the camera is manually operated.

Capacitor: The unit in the strobe that stores high-voltage electrical energy.

Center-weighted metering: Light measured from the center of the viewfinder, usually a 12mm circle in the middle of the viewfinder. The remaining 25% is read from the outside.

Close-up attachment: A lens that is fitted over the normal camera lens to magnify the image and allow for sharply focused photographs at a closer range.

Color temperature: A rating of the relative blueness or redness of light expressed in degrees Kelvin (K). Noontime sunlight is about 5500°K. Daylight film is set at 5500°K. Most strobe light ranges from 5400-6000°K to emulate sunlight.

Composition: The photographer's arrangement of the separate elements in the image area that are recorded on film.

Connector: A plug that joins the strobe's sync cord directly with the camera.

Continuous photography: The automatic consecutive exposure of frames one after another in rapid succession.

Continuous frame shooting: Shots are taken continuously with a power driven camera when the shutter release is held down.

Continuous servo AF with release-priority: Focusing with the shutter release slightly depressed. The autofocus system will focus on the subject until the shutter release is fully depressed.

Conversion lens: A lens mounted in front of another lens, to change the focal length of the prime lens.

Depth of field: The area in front of and behind the subject that will appear in sharp focus. The range of depth of field is determined by aperture, focal length, and lens-to-subject distance.

Diaphragm: Also called the iris. A mechanism which controls the amount of light that reaches the film. It consists of overlapping leaves inside the lens that form a circular opening of variable sizes. *See Aperture.*

Diffuser: An adapter that spreads the light emitted from a strobe and increases its angle of coverage. It also warms the color temperature and decreases light intensity by approximately one-stop.

Dome port: A semispherical piece of glass or plastic used to eliminate the magnifying distortion caused by refraction.

DX coding: An electronic system that automatically sets the film speed by reading film speed information imprinted on a magnetic strip on the film cassette.

Electronic flash: An electric light source that projects a burst of light. The light is produced from electricity which is stored in a capacitor and is used to energize a small amount of gas in a glass flashtube. *See Strobe.*

Elements: The components of a compound lens, consisting of several pieces of glass precisely ground and polished to different specifications.

EV: An acronym for *exposure value*, which are identification numbers relating to shutter speed and aperture settings on the camera. It specifies the operating range of an exposure metering system.

Exposure: The amount of light regulated by aperture and shutter speed that strikes the film.

Exposure compensation: Also referred to as exposure correction; giving more or less exposure to an image than that considered a correct exposure by the camera's built-in light meter.

Exposure meter: Also referred to as a light meter. It measures the brightness of light available so as to calculate the correct aperture and shutter speed combination for a proper exposure on the film used.

Exposure mode: Camera operation, such as manual, aperture priority, shutter priority, that determines which controls you set for an exposure and which ones the camera sets automatically.

Extension tube: A metal or plastic cylinder fitted between the lens and camera body that magnifies an image and allows for closer-than-normal focusing.

Fill lighting: The use of artificial light to enhance color and brighten shadows when ambient light is the primary source of illumination.

Film: Light sensitive material that records in the form of an image the patterns of light rays that have passed through the lens.

Film format: Dimensions of the image recorded on film by a specific camera.

Film speed: The relative sensitivity of film to light as compared to other films. *See ISO.*

Film transport: The device that enables the film to move smoothly from the cartridge to the take-up spool.

Filter: A piece of transparent glass or plastic or gelatin coating placed over the lens to change the quality of the light.

Fisheye lens: A short focal length lens, generally from 6mm to 16mm, with an extreme wide angle of view.

Fixed focus lens: Also called a focus-free lens. A lens with distance irrevocably set, depending upon depth of field to deliver a subject from several feet away to infinity in acceptably sharp focus.

Flare: Hot spots and loss of contrast and sharpness caused by stray light reflected from the glass elements of the lens.

Flat port: A port designed specifically for macro and zoom lenses. As light rays pass through the port surface, the angle of coverage of any given lens is narrowed and images magnified.

Flooding: Water leakage into camera, lens, or strobe.

F-number: A numerical designation on the aperture scale indicating the size of the lens opening. More commonly referred to as the f-stop.

Focal length: The distance, expressed in millimeters, from the optical center of the lens to the film plane when the lens is focused on infinity. Focal length affects the amount of the scene shown.

Focus: Adjusting the distance setting of the lens to achieve maximum sharpness of the subject. Also refers to a scale on your camera or lens barrel which shows the distance in feet and/or meters.

Focus control: The focusing mechanism that moves the lens back and forth so that it can project sharp images of both near and far subjects.

Focus ring: The band on the lens used to focus the image. When turned, it moves the lens in relation to the film plane, focusing for specific distances.

Focusing screen: Also called a viewing screen; a matte ground-glass surface onto which the mirror reflects the image seen by the lens. When the image is sharply focused on the screen, it will be in sharp focus on the film.

Frame: One single image in a roll of film. Also refers to the edges of an image.

F-stop: A number indicating the diameter of the aperture. The higher the number, the smaller the aperture. The lower the number, the wider the aperture.

Guide number: A relative evaluation of a strobe's power. This number can be used to calculate the correct combination of camera-to-subject distance and f-stop for a particular film speed.

Hot shoe: A mount on the top of the camera to which a flash is attached, providing the electrical connection needed to synchronize camera shutter and flash.

Infinity: The farthest distance indicated on the focusing selector.

Interchangeable lens: A lens that can be removed from the camera and replaced by another lens.

ISO: An abbreviation for International Standards Organization. A number rating system that indicates the speed of a film. Formerly called ASA.

LCD: An acronym for liquid crystal display; generally a panel on the camera which provides information.

LED: Light-emitting diode. A display of lights and symbols in the viewfinder of some cameras that provides exposure data.

Lens: An optically-shaped glass which gathers the light rays and causes them to converge at a specific point.

Lens coating: A thin transparent coating on the lens surface which improves picture quality by reducing reflection.

Lens gear: A lens accessory; a ring, made of high-impact plastic or aluminum, which is fitted onto the lens barrel to control specific functions, such as aperture control, focus control and zoom control.

Lens speed: The widest aperture to which the lens can be opened. The wider the aperture possible with a particular lens, the more light is admitted and the faster the lens; another characteristic of a lens.

Light meter: *See Exposure meter.*

Macro lens: A lens specifically designed for macrophotography, enabling extremely sharp focusing at short distances.

Macrophotography: A type of photography where the camera lens is positioned very close to the subject and the resultant image is magnified.

Manual exposure: Camera operation in which the photographer sets the aperture and shutter speed.

Matrix metering: Light measured from the entire image area. The camera incorporates a microcomputer which gathers exposure data with several segments and provides the correct exposure for most lighting conditions, taking into account bright and dark areas.

Minimum focus distance: The shortest distance at which the focus control can be set. The lens can focus closer if depth of field margin is added to the scale setting.

Motor drive: A camera accessory or a built-in unit that automatically advances the film once it has been exposed.

Multiple exposure photography: Repeated exposures of the same or different subject on the same frame.

Negative: An image of light and dark tones, created when film is exposed, that are the opposite of those in the original subject. Also refers to film that has been processed to create a negative image.

Open up: To make the lens opening larger to allow more light to strike the film.

O-rings: Synthetic rubber gaskets which seal the junctions between parts of all amphibious photographic equipment.

Overexposure: Exposing the film to too much light, resulting in a too-dark negative or a too-light positive.

Parallax: The displacement of an image when photographing at very close range. The image seen through the camera's viewfinder is not what the lens will record because they see the image from different positions in space.

Pentaprism: A five-sided optical device in eye-level viewfinders used to correct the image on the focusing screen so that it appears right side up and correct left to right.

Primary lens: Also called a prime lens. The lens that is either built into the camera or the lens to which supplemental lenses are attached.

Print: A positive image on photographic paper, made from a transparency or a negative.

Program mode: An exposure control system which automatically makes aperture and shutter decisions for a correct exposure.

Proper exposure: A photograph that looks like the scene or subject photographed, with the same balance of highlights and shadows. A photograph that is neither too light (overexposed) nor too dark (underexposed). Also referred to as a correct exposure.

Rangefinder: A type of viewfinder built into the camera, which allows you to view your subject through a window on the back of the camera.

Recycle time: The time it takes for a discharged strobe to recharge.

Refraction: The bending of light rays when they pass through transparent objects of different densities. This property of light underwater causes objects to appear closer and larger than they actually are.

Reflection: When light rays bounce off the water's surface back into the atmosphere. The closer the sun to the horizon, the more light is reflected, affecting the intensity of available light underwater.

Reflector: A device fitted into the face of strobe in front of the flash tube that disperses light.

Reproduction ratio: The size of the image on film compared to the subject's actual size. Commonly used when designating the relative magnification of extension tubes and macro lenses.

Reversal film: Film that produces a positive transparency after it is exposed and developed. Commonly referred to as color slide film.

Shutter: A mechanical device that lets light into the camnera and keeps light out. Functions to control the duration of light that will be allowed to strike the film.

Shutter priority: An exposure control system in which the photographer sets the shutter speed and the camera sets the aperture for a correct exposure.

Shutter speed: A means of controlling the length of time the shutter exposes the film to light. The higher the shutter speed, the less light reaches the film.

Single lens reflex: A viewfinding system which enables you to view the image through the camera's lens. This configuration is typical of land cameras. Commonly called SLR.

Slave sensor: A built-in sensing system that detects light from another strobe and then automatically triggers the slave strobe.

Specifications: The nomenclature used by a manufacturer to describe the individual characteristics of a particular piece of equipment.

Spot metering: Light measured from the center of the viewfinder. Most systems read light from a 3mm circle in the middle of the viewfinder.

Step: An f-stop; used when referring to increasing or decreasing exposure.

Stop down: To make the lens opening smaller, allowing less light to strike the film.

Strobe: An electronic flash. Submersible strobes are specifically designed for underwater photography, and all controls and ports are O-ring sealed.

Sync cord: Synchronization cord. The cord that transmits electrical impulses from strobe to camera. It allows the camera to synchronize the flash with the camera shutter so that the flash fires when the shutter is triggered.

Telephoto lens: A long focal length lens; a lens that magnifies the image on film and make its appear closer.

Transparency: Another word for slide. A positive image mounted in a small cardboard or plastic frame.

TTL: An abbreviation for through-the-lens, as in through-the-lens viewing or metering. Also refers to a type of strobe. *See TTL strobe.*

TTL sensor: A sensor built into the camera which measures the light reflecting off the film plane.

TTL strobe: A type of strobe designed to communicate electronically with a camera that has a TTL sensor, allowing for automatic strobe exposures.

Underexposure: Exposing the film to less light than is required to create an image as the eye sees it; results in a too-light negative or a too-dark positive.

Viewfinder: Window on a camera or an attachment used to see and frame the subject.

Viewfinder camera: A camera with a viewfinding configuration that allows you to view your subject through a window on the camera above the lens.

White light: Light from the sun, composed of all the colors in the visible spectrum.

Wide angle distortion: Changes in appearance or perspective of a subject caused by using a short-focal-length lens very close to the subject.

Wide angle lens: A lens of short focal length, specifically designed to provide a wider angle of view than seen by both human vision and a standard lens.

Zone focusing: Presetting f-stop and camera-to-subject distance.

Zoom lens: A lens that combines a range of focal lengths.

Metric Equivalents & Conversions

How to Convert Metric Length to Customary U.S. Length

Millimeters to Inches: Multiply by .04
Meters to Feet: Multiply by 3.28
Centimeters to Inches: Multiply by .4
Meters to Yards: Multiply by 1.1
Inches to Millimeters: Multiply by 25.4

How to Convert Metric Weights to Customary U.S. Weights

Grams to Ounces: Multiply by .035
Ounces to Grams: Divide by .035
Pounds to Kilograms: Divide by 2.2

Linear Measure

1 inch = 2.54 centimeters
1 foot = 30.48 centimeters
1 yard = 0.91 meter
1 millimeter = .039 inch
1 centimeter = 0.39 inch
1 meter = 3.28 feet
1 meter = 1.1 yards
1 kilometer = 5/8 mile

Weight

1 ounce = 28.35 grams
1 pound = 0.45 kilograms
1 gram = .035 ounce
1 kilogram = 2.2 pounds

Volume

1 ounce = 29.58 milliliters
1 quart = 0.95 liter
1 gallon = 3.79 liters
1 milliliter = 0.035 ounce
1 liter = 1.06 quart
1 liter = 0.26 gallon

How to Convert Centigrade to Fahrenheit

Multiply Centigrade degrees (°C) by 9, divide by 5, add 32

How to Convert Fahrfenheit to Centigrade

Subtract 32 from degrees of Fahrenheit (°F) and multiply by 5, then divide by 9.

How to Convert Distances

Miles to Kilometers: Multiply by 1.6
Kilometers to Miles: Divide by 1.6

Conversion Tables

Feet to Meters		Meters to Feet	
1	0.305	1	3.281
2	0.610	2	6.562
3	0.914	3	9.843
4	1.219	4	13.124
5	1.524	5	16.05
6	1.829	6	19.686
7	2.1344	7	22.967
8	2.438	8	26.248
9	2.743	9	29.529
10	3.048	10	32.810

PSI		Bars
14.3 PSI	=	1 Bar
500	=	35
1000	=	70
1500	=	105
2000	=	140
2500	=	175
3000	=	210
3500	=	245
4000	=	280

ABBREVIATIONS

centimeter = cm
gram = g
inch = in.
kilogram = kg
liter = l
meter = m
millimeter = mm
ounce = oz.
pounds = lbs.

Index

A

B

C

D

E

F

G

H

I

K

L

M

N

THE AUTHORS

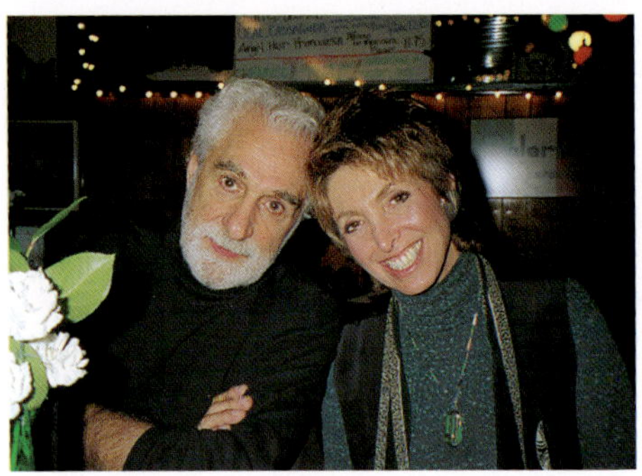

Joe Liburdi learned to dive in Japan in 1952. He was told to "blow and go!" In 1966 he was handed a Calypso and told to "try this." He's been blowing and shooting ever since. The indefatigable Joe is recipient of PADI's Most Distinguished Achievement Award, NAUI's Man in the Sea Award, is an SSI Platinum Pro 5000 Diver, lectures, teaches, and can usually be found at his dive shop in Irvine, California, proselytizing the joys of diving and taking pictures.

Cara Sherman started out writing romance stories and Hollywood gossip. Her career as a writer, editor, and marketing consultant spans 25 years and three coasts. A native of New York City, she discovered Joe, scuba, and underwater photography in the chill of Puget Sound. Today she heads Underwater Exposures, the parent company of Orca Publications and the advertising agency for Sea & Sea Underwater Photography USA.

Joe and Cara put their heads together for this, their fifth book on Sea & Sea.